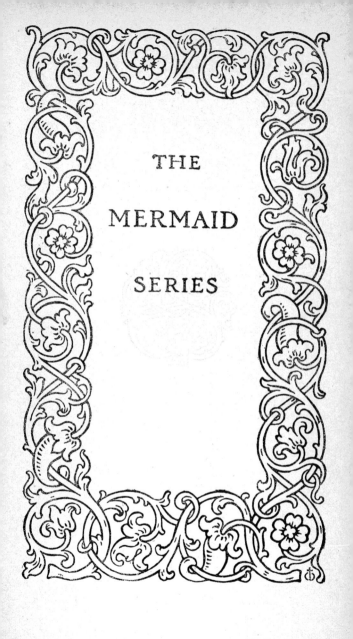

THE

MERMAID

SERIES

BEN JONSON

I

THE MERMAID SERIES.

Literal Reproductions of the Old Text, with etched Frontispieces.

Other Volumes in Preparation.

BEN JONSON.

From the Picture by Gerard Honthorst.

THE MERMAID SERIES

BEN JONSON

EDITED WITH INTRODUCTION AND NOTES

BY

BRINSLEY NICHOLSON AND C. H. HERFORD

I lie and dream of your full Mermaid wine."—*Beaumont.*

IN THREE VOLUMES

I

LONDON

T. FISHER UNWIN

NEW YORK

CHARLES SCRIBNER'S SONS

" What things have we seen
Done at the Mermaid ! heard words that have been
So nimble, and so full of subtle flame,
As if that every one from whence they came
Had meant to put his whole wit in a jest,
And had resolved to live a fool the rest
Of his dull life."

Master Francis Beaumont to Ben Jonson.

" Souls of Poets dead and gone,
What Elysium have ye known,
Happy field or mossy cavern,
Choicer than the Mermaid Tavern ? "

Keats.

CONTENTS

BEN JONSON.

I.

EN JONSON was born in
1573, most probably in the city
in which he lived and died,
and to which more than any
other of its poetic sons, more
even than the author of the
Canterbury Tales, he conse-
crated his art. Like most eminent Londoners, however, he came of a provincial stock, and it would
not be hard to recognise in his close-knitted, in-
effusive intellect the stamp of the North Country,
even if we did not know that his grandfather
had come from Carlisle (" and he thought from
Annandale thither ") to enter the service of
Henry VIII. He was a "gentleman," this
grandfather, as the poet himself, in this point
entirely true to his lineage, told the young laird
of Hawthornden; of some wealth and position

too, since he was able to bequeath to his son
"estate," so far considerable that when the latter
was imprisoned and "forfeited" under Mary, its
loss caused a complete collapse in the fortunes
of the family. Of the grounds of this imprisonment we know nothing, but it is natural to
suspect heresy ; the more so as, when heresy at
length triumphed (without, however, restoring
his "estate") he "at length" took orders, married, and lived as a "minister," we know not
where, until his death in the winter of 1572—3.

A month later his only recorded child was
born, and it may be taken to indicate piety, if
not Puritanism, in the widowed mother, that he
was baptised by the Old Testament name of
Benjamin, familiarly abbreviated, by the subsequent usage of friend and enemy alike, to Ben.

It is clear that the mother was left with few
means of support ; and, though she married
again—a master-bricklayer of London—Jonson
was, as he tells us, "poorly brought up." Fuller,
who was unable to discover his birthplace, traced
him, as a "little child" in "long coats," to a dwell-
ing near Charing Cross, whence he attended
a private school in St. Martin's Lane ; but it is
likely that the "little Latin and less Greek" of
his great brother and comrade in art might have
been his lot also, but for the kindly intervention
of the most laborious and many-sided of Elizabethan scholars, Camden, who, as second master
at Westminster, was in a position to give help

in the most effective and at the same time least ostentatious way. Camden is one of the few antiquaries who may boast of the praise of two great poets. Spenser was to extol "the nourice of antiquity"; and Jonson, in after days, addressed a touching epigram to his old master—

> "Most reverend head, to whom I owe
> All that I am in arts, all that I know."

But this congenial life ended, and Jonson entered the unromantic business of his step-father. It has, indeed, been assumed that his course from the Westminster schoolroom to the bricklayer's yard, near Charing Cross, led him by way of Cambridge; and academic commentators have listened favourably to the theory that the most scholarly of English poets was not quite a stranger to the English Universities. That theory, however, is supported merely by the assertions of Fuller and Wood, and it conflicts not only with Jonson's statement that when at a later time they made him a master, he owed it "to their favour, not to his studie,"[1] but with his own narrative of his life, as reported by Drummond, who, himself of the schools, would hardly have omitted such an incident. Business, however, proved unendurable, and the young

---

[1] At the same time this phrase has been misquoted and misunderstood (Cunningham's note to Gifford's Memoir, p. ix., and thence Ward, I., 516). Jonson's word is *studie* not *studies*, and he surely meant to assert, not that he had not gone through the University course,—though this is on other grounds likely,—but that he had not sought the degree spontaneously offered to him.

poet and scholar, whose relation to his step-
father is probably shadowed in the domestic
circumstances of Edward Kno'well and young
Ovid (*Poetaster*), both ardent students of poetry *in-
vito parente*,—resolved like so many less doughty
spirits, to take his fate into his own hands.
Not, however, in order to throw himself at once
upon literature. He probably found it advisable
for a time to leave London, and the great
struggle in the Netherlands offered a welcome
opening for the sword of a robust adventurer.
As an adventurer he fought; not, indeed, like
the Captain Hungry of his epigram, merely
for pay and rations, but also not with that
passionate devotion to a cause, which nerved the
heroic citizens of Holland to beat down the
Spanish halberds. Passion was never in
Jonson's way, but no man better understood the
stubborn heroism, the arrogance *nescia vinci*,
of the true soldier. One brief but vivid glimpse
we get of a doughty figure advancing before the
English lines to challenge an enemy to single
combat, and after having slain him, stripping
his body of the *spolia opima* in the high Roman
manner, as became the pupil of Camden.

His return to London, not later probably than
1592, is the beginning of a period of several
years during which we almost wholly lose sight
of him. We know, indeed, that he married the
woman whom he afterwards described laconically
as *a shrew yet honest*, and from whom, in the

beginning of the next reign, he found it agreeable to live apart for five years ; and, further, that of the marriage was born, in 1596, a much loved son whose death, seven years later, in the Plague, wrung from him that sad farewell to the—

> ' Child of my right hand and joy." . . .
> My sin was too much hope of thee, loved boy."

"Ben Jonson, his best piece of poetry."

But for the rest we are forced to re-construct the image of Ben Jonson during this momentous but obscure period of slow ripening towards the great first-fruits of his invention, from the brilliant years which immediately followed, with the aid of his own brief hint that he had betaken himself, on his return, to "his studies." Of all the unknown candidates for fame who then walked the streets of London, this young Humanist was certainly the most remarkable. Familiar with every phase of its life, acquainted with all its haunts and all its pleasures, he was already master of that incomparable wealth of observation which stiffens the texture of his writing in the earliest of his dramas as conspicuously as in the last. Fastidious delicacy of taste, sensitive repugnance to the ugly and the foul, imposed even less restriction upon his experience than upon that of most of his fellow dramatists. If he trod the mire it was with open eyes, cool head, and unstained heart. There was no trace of the weakling in him. The discord which arrests us in such unstable compounds of poetry and animalism as Greene and Dekker, born idealists singing fitfully out of the moral squalor of their lives, is wholly absent from the great and massive nature of Jonson. A moral sanity, in which only Shakespeare among contemporary dramatists equalled him, qualified him to drain the cup of experience, not only without intoxication but without at all foregoing or compromising the austere enthusiasm of the scholar. The genial expansive eye and plastic touch of the born artist were combined in him with the lofty aloofness of a didactic mind, proudly conscious of its own integrity and bent on holding the least flattering of mirrors before the world.

If we would learn what the Jonson of these years could do we must turn to *Every Man in his Humour*, but to know what he was, the temper and meaning of his work, we must rather look to its artistically less perfect successors. The vivid and closely studied figures of his earliest comedy contain scarcely a suggestion of the author's profile; but as we advance, the motley crowd of Humours falls back and the figure of the poet gradually emerges into distinctness, assailing them now with sarcasm and invective as Asper, now with serene disdain as Horace, now with sorrowful indignation as Crites. It is difficult not to feel that this last, above all, brings us to the very heart of Jonson's moral nature, and none of his verses ring truer than those of the great and mournful speech of Crites which closes the first act of the *Revels*. They approach as near as the joyous and sanguine Elizabethan age was able to the mood of Wordsworth's "O, friend, I know not which way I shall look for comfort," and of Milton's *Samson*. Only in the great Epode, which also belongs to these years ("Not to know vice at all"), do we catch an echo of the same grave and deep music, elsewhere so rare in Jonson.

Such was the quality of the man who, in 1597, emerges suddenly and finally from the obscurity which surrounds his years of apprenticeship. His son had been born in the previous year, and want may now have been added to the forces which drew him from his study to the theatre, where in July we find him both as a player and as one of the band of playwrights to whom the illiterate old manager of the Fortune Theatre, Philip Henslowe, dispensed his meagre advances for new pieces and "adycions" to old. In the latter process, as well as in ordinary collaboration, the stock method of the hack playwrights, Jonson, like Shakespeare, can never have taken great part. His mind was too strongly individual in its bent and in its methods to catch fire easily from the inspirations of other men, while the ready, random writing of the mere hack would have been checked by one of the sternest intellectual consciences which have ever been applied to literature, if it had not already been made impossible by a certain native want of spontaneity. Of the recorded plays in which he was part author several have perished, like the *Robert the Second King of Scottes* (written in conjunction with Dekker); in *Sejanus*, he himself subsequently eliminated the passages contributed by his unknown coadjutor. After a very brief apprenticeship, in any case, Jonson came forward as a master, and with a work so mature that it is impossible greatly to resent the self-consciousness with which the poet of five-and-twenty ushered it in.

No other play in the whole development of the Elizabethan drama marks so distinctly an epoch as the great comedy with which Jonson opened his career. Its relation to its predecessors was that which marks the work of men who are both original and who, at the same time, comprehend and, as it were, utilise their originality. None of his fellows made their *début* with so much of the air of deliberate innovation. Shakespeare's originality is doubtless greater, but it is less conscious, less sturdily militant, and more sympathetic; it does not obtrude or announce itself, it is rather disguised by his remarkable conservatism of the forms and methods of his immediate predecessors. Shakespeare assimilates and absorbs, where Jonson assails and excludes. Jonson, moreover, comes forward as an innovator in dramatic *art*. Shakespeare, though a great, a far greater, artist, is not primarily a theorist

in art; he does not readily, or often, or very
energetically, take sides upon questions of art.
His probable first piece, *Love's Labour's Lost*, is
a criticism of contemporary life, but, eccentric
and wayward as it is in dramatic construction,
it is not a criticism of the contemporary drama.
The *Every Man in His Humour* is both. Its
famous prologue is, like most of Jonson's, a
manifesto (whether written now or later is of
little real moment), in which the common prac-
tisers of the stage are taken to task in vigorous
terms, and the audience bidden—

> "Be pleased to see
> One such to-day as other plays should be."

The crude romanticism of the popular drama,
the marvels made ridiculous by the slender
resources of an Elizabethan play-house, the
flights over land and sea, over months and years,
rendered plausible by no illusions of scenery, he
will replace by a picture of the familiar London
at their doors, of—

> "Deeds, and language, such as men do use,
> And persons, such as comedy would choose,
> When she would show an image of the times,
> And sport with human follies, not with crimes."

Nothing of the kind had yet been attempted.
The previous history of the Elizabethan drama
could show a profusion of incident and language
more or less comic, and also of futile experiments
in comedy. There was the rough native humour
of the professional clown, with his variant, the

Vice of the Moralities, the humour of practical
jokes and horseplay. There was the more
refined humour of the professional jester, becoming normal in the persistently pointed
dialogue of Lyly. There was the humour of
accident, confusions of identity through disguise
or natural likeness—the offspring chiefly of
Italian novels—which Shakespeare had seized
in the *Two Gentlemen of Verona*, in the *Comedy
of Errors*, and in the *Midsummer Night's
Dream*. There was, lastly, the humour of
mere absurdity and ignorance, that of the clown
by nature, not by profession, of which the
author of the Cade scenes of *The Contention* gave
the first remarkable example; one taken over
with scarcely a change into *Henry VI.* by the
man with a "tiger's heart, wrapt in a player's
hide," who afterwards far outdid his predecessor
in the dramatic venture of the Athenian me-
chanics. Only in *Love's Labour's Lost* is there
something like an attempt to base the comic
effect upon the affectations, not of a single class
only, but of an entire society, and here the
scenery inevitably seems, to critics of Jonson's
mind, hopelessly fantastic and unreal. And the
great comic scenes of *Henry IV.*, which probably
preceded Jonson's comedy, though they represented life in London with unparalleled vividness,
were merely an episode in a serious historical
action. In Jonson, we have the London of
Henry IV., handled in the method of the fantastic

world of *Love's Labour's Lost,* but with more sustained comic power. Every grade of society yields its tribute of "humour" to the robust writer who was himself a gentleman by birth, a citizen by training, a craftsman and a soldier by necessity, and a scholar by nature and choice. Much of the fun is, no doubt, due to mistakes of identity in the Spanish manner; indeed the plot may be said to hang on the various disguises of Brainworm. But it is mainly derived from the "humours," the eccentricities and affectations of social types. Of special excellence is the group of "gentlemen,"—Kno'well and Wellbred, university friends, the town and county gulls, and Captain Bobadill.

The last has established a reputation beside Falstaff, and the two pass for parallel examples of the braggart soldier of the stage. No two characters, however, can be more unlike; and their difference illustrates that of the Shakesperian and Jonsonian types of comedy. Bobadill is, like most of Jonson's "humours," without humour in the modern sense; Falstaff is the soul of humour. Bobadill has not a trace of Falstaff's genial delight in the detection of his romances; he lies without zest, and invents from mere phlegm. His manner of life enforces his natural temperament. He is no glorious reveller familiar with the jests which lie at the bottom of the twentieth cup of sack; but a spare and thin-blooded ascetic (albeit perforce), who closes the orifice of his stomach with a bunch of radishes and "a cup of thy small beer, sweet hostess." He falls naturally into the fashionable melancholy of the day. He is a fop and a pedant, a past master of all the fashions of warfare and of phrase; but he displays his accomplishments with an air of resigned condescension, as of one well aware that his audience is incapable of appreciating him, and that their admiration is likely to be unintelligent. He is to the conventional military braggadocio of the stage what the solemn prig is to the vivacious mountebank. Phlegmatic to the core, he understands his own character sufficiently well, and his boasts are nicely calculated for the particular audience to which they are addressed. He is not easily drawn out, he scrutinises his company narrowly before displaying his vein; he is "no common man," and admits new acquaintances with a hauteur inspired as much by apprehension as by pride.

Bobadill is the most highly finished humourist in the play, as his final discomfiture is the most complete. But none is wholly without this trait. The title may be taken at its word, for in the play at least every man has his humour and every woman hers. No English dramatist had yet attempted comedy on the basis of so severe an interpretation of its scope, as a picture of follies and foibles: none had abstained so rigorously from exciting sympathy as well as laughter. Its relation to classical comedy is indeed unmistakeable. Most of the "humours" have prototypes there. The jealous husband, the timid father, the rakish sons, the boasting soldier, the cunning slave of Plautus and Terence, have helped (*pace* Gifford) to suggest Kitely and Kno'well, Edward Kno'well and Wellbred, Bobadill and Brainworm. But only to suggest them. No more genuine sketches of London character are to be found in the drama. They are drawn, not from books but from observation, and as an observer Jonson had no equal among his contemporaries save Shakespere.

At one point only it would seem that Jonson was in danger of transgressing his own definition of comedy. The character of Edward Kno'well as it appears in the folio is a palpable deviation from the original design. In the opening of the play his father laments his "humour" of "dreaming on nought but idle poetry." We anticipate that young Kno'well's poetry thus emphatically announced will be among the leading humours of the play. Yet, in the final version, almost nothing is made of it. In the quarto, however, which represents at any rate an earlier state of the text, one fragment of the poetic vesture thus torn away from the hero remains,—a veritable purple patch, the heroic enthusiasm of which is still more evidently from the writer's heart than the great speech of Biron, which it strongly recalls.

> "Indeed if you will look on poesy
> As she appears to many, poor and lame,

> Patched up in remnants and old worn-out rags,
> Half starved for want of her peculiar food,
> Sacred invention; then I must confirm
> Both your conceit and censure of her merit;
> But view her in her glorious ornaments
> Attired in the majesty of art,
> Set high in spirit with the precious taste
> Of sweet philosophy; and which is most,
> Crowned with the rich traditions of a soul,
> That hates to have her dignity profaned
> With any relish of an earthly thought,
> Oh then how proud a presence doth she bear!"

It is plain that Jonson who, if any man, honoured his vocation, felt that these glowing lines were not in keeping with their context, that they were, in fact, too absolutely and unmistakeably just to be admitted into a comedy where enthusiasm could only be allowed on condition of being ridiculous.

The triumph of Jonson's first comedy was abruptly followed by an incident which threatened to cut short the career thus brilliantly opened. The trumpery quarrel with the actor, Gabriel Spencer, the "duel" in which Jonson killed his opponent, with a sword, as he boasts, ten inches shorter than his—his arrest and imprisonment, which brought him "almost to the gallows"—form a hardly more glorious or suggestive episode in his life than the miserable brawl which closed that of Marlowe. Recent discoveries tend but little to improve his case. Attempts were made to inveigle him into an admission of the capital charge, but the "two damned villains" thus employed returned un-

successful, and their victim lived to make them
immortal in one of his neatest epigrams. Only
one circumstance gives lasting interest to this
brief imprisonment. It brought him in contact
with a Catholic priest, probably, as Professor
Ward suggests, a fellow inmate, from whom he
received the Roman faith, "on trust," as he
candidly confessed to Drummond. It would be
rash to assert, in the face of this phrase, that
his conviction was very profound, or that it was
reached by a very elaborate process of reasoning.
But it is still more out of the question to treat it
as a mere whim. The heresy which he had
embraced in prison when in the very grasp of
the Queen's Government and danger of his life, he
retained for twelve years among the more subtle
temptations of Court favour : and had recusancy
been a safer and easier game than it was, the
sterling honesty of Jonson is wholly above suspicion. He is entitled to the credit of equal
sincerity when he took his first sacrament in
prison bread, and when, a dozen years later, he
characteristically drained the cup, "in token
of true reconciliation." At the same time the
sturdy heroism involved in recusancy under
Elizabeth may well have had a certain attraction
for this soldier among poets, who, without courting the rôle of Ishmael, played it, when forced
upon him, with a certain grim zest. And it
may be suggested also that the most ancient
of living forms of Christianity appealed power-

fully to the scholar Jonson, whose "humble gleanings in divinity after the Fathers" were long afterwards among the ruined treasures of his study.

Jonson's release was followed at no long interval by the performance of *Every Man out of His Humour*, obviously intended as a companion piece to its predecessor. The two titles would suggest that the later play represents the recovery, as the earlier the disease. In reality, however, it is only a second handling of the same theme, with more elaboration, more system, more airing of critical principles, and more unmeasured self-applause.

The great success of his first comedy produced an unmistakeable effect upon his second. Every restraint formerly imposed by convention upon his headstrong but still unproved genius was now thrown off; he wrote as he had a mind to write, working out to the full the impulses of an intellect stored with curious learning and with sinewy thought, and proudly warning his hearers—

> "Only vouchsafe me your attentions,
> And I will give you music worth your ears—"

while—

> "If we fail
> We must impute it to the only chance,—
> Art hath an enemy called ignorance."

It is in *Every Man out of His Humour*, in fact, that the Jonsonian "humour" itself is first displayed in its full vigour. The first play is a comedy of intrigue, scarcely less than a comedy of character. Brainworm's disguises, for instance, belong to the familiar expedients of that form of comedy. In the second intrigue is not absent, but it is more sternly subordinated to the exposition of humours. In the first the earlier plot was intended to illustrate the humours, in the later only to explode them. In the one they are accordingly inwoven into a texture of continuous action, which provides from the first scene onwards a certain suspense and expectation only to be satisfied in the last. In the other they remain through half the play single threads, the peculiarities of which the author is too much occupied in displaying and expounding one by one to have leisure to set the loom in motion, and it is only towards the close that he succeeds by a *tour de force* in tying them into what is certainly a most ingenious knot. But the cleverness of the climax does not make the play interesting, nor the brilliance of the threads atone for the meagreness of the cloth.

The action itself, too, is far more than before affected by Jonson's predilection, which struck deeper root in every successive drama, for an allusive and symbolic type of incident. The stopping of Buffone's mouth with wax is an anticipation of the forced eructation inflicted on Crispinus in *The Poetaster*, only somewhat nearer to nature, somewhat less redolent of the scholar's

lamp; the palming off of the bourgeois Sogliardo
at Court, resembles a moral apologue on the text,
Nocitura petuntur, rather than a picture of contemporary life; and Puntarvolo's arrival at his
castle is rather an ingenious *reductio ad absurdum*
of his special humour than a good instance of
that *imitatio veri* which Jonson holds up to his
contemporaries as the essence of comedy. It is
plain, indeed, that the scope of the drama is
wider than that of its predecessor. That was a
picture perfectly coherent, if not complete, of the
humours of a specific community. All its figures
bear the stamp of Elizabethan London, all add
something to the vividness of the local colour, to
the flavour of the local atmosphere. But the
second of the pair, though it contains plenty of
London types, has far less of this unity of impression. It ranges over the whole of society,
from the courtier and the court lady to the rustic.
And the Macchiavellian Macilente, who, more
than anyone else, is the mainspring of the
action, is rather an embodiment of the genius of
malignant and astute envy than a portrait of any
local type of it. The contrast between this abstract and bloodless contriver of the harms, and
the unmistakeably English figure of honest
Brainworm, who performs a somewhat similar
office in the earlier play, is a type of the contrast
between the plays themselves.

These qualities, however, make the second
play even more attractive than the first to the

student of Jonson's art. With all his wonderfully keen vision for the follies of the life under his eyes, he was too many-sided a student of human nature at large to be for long the mere satirist of a place or of a day. There remains, nevertheless, abundant material of a kind closely resembling the earlier play. The pictures of gulls who vainly ape the fashions are repeated with only more drastic effect. Fungoso's futile attempts to keep pace with Fastidius Brisk in new suits of clothes are only somewhat more farcical than Master Stephen's mixture of delight and despair at the wonderful oaths of Bobadill.

The brilliant success of Jonson's first two comedies evidently brought his pen into request, and the year 1599 must have been an extraordinarily busy one with him. Henslowe's diary contains the record of payments during the year for three distinct plays, one of them in conjunction with Dekker, a second with Dekker and Chettle; both of which are lost. The same year probably produced a fourth, still extant, in which it seems equally clear that Jonson wrote a part, and that he did not write the whole—*The Case is Altered*. But, as if this were not enough, this "slow" poet whom his enemies taunted with being a year or two about every play, must already have been busy with the comedy which takes the third place in the series of his published dramas, *Cynthia's Revels*.

Cynthia's Revels is as closely connected with

Every Man out of His Humour as this with its
predecessor. It is a third term in the same
series. Where *Every Man out of His Humour* falls
short of *Every Man in His Humour*, *Cynthia's
Revels* falls short still further. As the second
play is less largely and richly human than the
first, so is the third than the second. The genial
laughter of the painter of humours contracts to
the scornful smile of the satirist. The motley
crowd of London types, the varied light and
colour, the picturesque stir and tumult of the
streets, has given place to a collection of
silhouettes, somewhat monotonously reiterating
a single antithesis. This very quality, however,
which detracts from the excellence of *Cynthia's
Revels* as a drama, again, as in the case of its
predecessor, enhances its value for the student
of Jonson's mind and art. At no moment of
his career did he write with a more profound
disdain for any other standard of merit than
that supplied by his own intellect. "By ——,
'tis good, and if you like't you may," the
too famous closing line of the epilogue, was
his characteristic substitute for the classical
"*Plaudite!*" And if the execution had equalled
the conception, even this extravagant claim,
however injudicious, would hardly have been
unjustified. The antithesis between intellect
and the follies of fashion, between the scholar or
poet and the fops and dandies of the Court, is a
theme which is never likely to grow out of date;

and the idea of the Fountain of Self-love, in which the votaries of the Court imbibe their fatal folly, is a device which might have generated superb scenes of Aristophanic humour.

But the execution of this fine conception is from any point of view very imperfect. Nowhere else does he so seriously yield to the habit of describing instead of exhibiting character, induced in him by the analytic and scholarly quality of his mind. From the second act onward, too, the simple severity of the main outline is overlaid with a quantity of rather idle arabesque, culminating in the School of Courtship, the Library to Mercury, and the Masque, which celebrates, as it is supposed to entertain, in a manner less characteristic of Jonson than of his age, the "hoary-headed Cynthia of Whitehall."

Pale and colourless, however, as the figures of *Cynthia's Revels* are, one or two of them were sufficiently recognisable and sufficiently mordant sketches from originals in the London literary world; and this element of personal rancour doubtless contributed to the immediate success of a drama over which posterity, with the best intentions in the world, has never been able to restrain a yawn. The attack was not, however, unprovoked; on the contrary, if we may take literally the subsequent assertion in the Prologue to *The Poetaster*, he had been for a year and a half the victim of certain petulant styles " on every stage," when he produced *Cynthia's Revels*.

That Jonson should be for a while the best-abused man of letters in London, was, in fact, inevitable. His training and his circumstances were unlike those of all his fellows, and Jonson was not the man to overcome natural isolation by conciliatory manners. No man had more of demonic personal fascination among his friends; none, by nature as well as by rugged force of character, was less capable of the outward graces which remove the first obstacles to friendship. His history was a strange blending of contrasted experiences, which prevented him from being the fellow of any rank or class in the literary world. No class sympathy was possible without alloy, for the man of gentle birth who had been a " wright"; for the poet who was also player; for the soldier whose immortal ridicule of certain military types touched the *esprit de corps* of the profession; for the honest praiser of the Queen, who was at the same time the most biting satirist of her Court; for the scholar who, though he had no degree, so immeasurably outweighed the University wits in learning. The moral of his first great comedy had already been marked with blood.

But more redoubtable, if less martial, enemies than the player whose death led him by that strange casual path to Rome, now awaited him. The most important of these was John Marston, an accomplished Oxford scholar of good family, some half-dozen years younger than Jonson, who had made his *début* at the same time in the double field of poetic satire and drama. His talents were undeniable, but they were neutralised by an insatiable thirst for distinction, which made him at once unreal as a writer and untrustworthy as a friend. His style is crowded with pretentious affectations, his invective is more furious than penetrating, his love passages more voluptuous than passionate. His childish vanity, easily irritated and easily soothed, made his quarrels numerous, virulent, and brief. This effeminate figure was in the end caught by the spell of Jonson's personality, and became a devoted disciple; but his first contact with the most masculine of Elizabethans produced only a prolonged explosion of ill-will.

There is no reason to doubt Jonson's boast to Drummond, that he had "beaten" Marston and taken his pistol from him; but whatever his vigour in the field he showed himself long-suffering on the stage. It can hardly be doubted that Hedon, "the light voluptuous reveller," in *Cynthia's Revels* is Marston, but the character, like that of his companion, Anaides, is to our eyes kept studiously within the limits of the abstract and typical satire by which no man's withers are wrung. The portrait was, nevertheless, sufficiently accurate to be fiercely resented, and Marston and his crew prepared an elaborate revenge, calling in the aid of a playwright who for rude and rapid vigour had hardly his living equal, Jonson's recent associate, Thomas Dekker. But instead of awaiting their attack Jonson instantly set to work with wonderful energy to forestall it by a satiric drama, the personal application of which should be unmistakeable. Whatever allured Jonson from his congenial preoccupation with social types to the study of individual character benefited his art; the necessity of working rapidly had the same result; and *The Poetaster* is accordingly more life-like than its predecessor, and falls little short of the first comedy of humours itself.

Its connection with both is, however, palpable enough. The imposing apparatus of Roman scenery and *personnel*, the brilliant company of Augustan poets and courtiers, are only a more elaborate way of conveying the same thought. What was a latent suggestion in *Every Man in His Humour* and a broad hint in *Every Man out of His Humour* becomes the inspiring idea of the *Poetaster*, as of *Cynthia's Revels*. The mass of men have their humours still, and the world is still consumed with ridiculous affectations, but from the mass stands out a little company of privileged censurers, and among them towers more unmistakeably than ever the burly form of our poet, supported by the master spirits of the political and literary world. "Horace," says Jonson in effect, "was assailed as I am by the riff-raff of literature; I, like him, have the friendship of the chosen few who are capable of seeing

merit." Horace is a historical Crites; Virgil
and Mæcenas and Augustus replace Mercury
and Arete and Cynthia, and the shadowy pro-
cession of kindred vices, "sick of self-love,"
Hedon, Anaides, Asotus, Amorphus, &c., are
represented by the group, drawn with the same
drastic pencil which had created Bobadill and
Master Stephen, of Crispinus, Tucca, and Demetrius. Crispinus (Marston) is the effeminate
voluptuary, vain of his writing, vain of his voice,
vain of his rank,—"We are a gentleman besides;
our name is Rufus Laberius Crispinus; we are a
pretty stoic, too,"—now toadying to the great
poet, now conspiring against him, or again in-
triguing with city wives, like Fastidius Brisk, and
displaying his accomplishments with ingenuous
naïveté in their society. Tucca, who, rather
than Demetrius, represents the Anaides of the
Revels, is the most picturesque ruffian of the
Elizabethan stage, a Bobadill in condition, but,
instead of his foppish melancholy, overflowing with the boisterous spirits and the rich
vocabulary of his contemporary, Sir Toby Belch.
The last of the triad is Demetrius (Dekker), the
"dresser of plays," a very simple honest fellow,
though his habit be a little decayed, capable of
whatever virulence of language his employers
may desire, for he has "one of the most overflowing rank wits in Rome, and will slander
any man living if he disgust him."

Like Pope, Jonson is not above twitting his

assailants with their mean condition and con-
descends to remind the well-born Crispinus and
the plebeian Demetrius alike of their defective
doublet and ravelled satin-sleeves. But the satirist was himself acquainted with poverty, and he
not only forestalled a possible *tu quoque* but expressed his own better mind in the fine lines in
which he makes Horace check the emperor for a
casual reference to his narrow means :—

> " As if the filth of poverty sunk as deep
> Into a knowing spirit, as the bane
> Of riches doth into an ignorant soul."

For the rest, the subject of the play is partly a
repetition of comic material already familiar to
Jonson's pen :—the citizen Albius with his ambitious and well-born wife who adores the Court, a
variation of Deliro and Fallace ; partly a rather
gratuitous dramatisation of the *Chronique Scan-
daleuse* of the Augustan Court :—Ovid feeding his
famous passion for the emperor's daughter, in
discourses full of his own frigid ingenuity, or at-
testing his right to the famous " *Quidquid conabar
scribere, versus erat,*" by writing his law cases in
involuntary metre ; Propertius, brooding, savage
and solitary, like Browning's Householder,
over the memory of his lost Cynthia, and then
burying himself in her tomb "from which no
persuasion can allure him." All this and much
more belongs to the superfluous embroidery with
which Jonson encumbered all but the greatest
of his plays. Few richer minds than his ever

created drama ; few so critical in temper, so easily mistook their intellectual abundance for artistic wealth, or pursued the track of the ancient poets with so complete a disregard of the reserve, the austerity of classic art. His talent was in a measure, as has been said of Richter, *ohne Organ ;* it wanted execution. He regretted Shakespeare's faulty but unblotted lines ; yet his own admirably exact and terse expression was often thrown away upon irrelevancies of incident which the elder and greater artist would have "blotted" with very little scruple.

It is difficult, having mentioned Shakespeare, to avoid a reference to the fascinating suggestion that no other than he is intended by the Virgil of *The Poetaster*, the confessedly supreme poet to whom, with fine tact (a superiority which this play possesses over the *Cynthia's Revels*), Horace commits the decision between himself and his assailants (v. 1). No more splendid and no more fitting tribute has in truth ever been paid by one great poet to another than the three great speeches of Horace, Gallus, and Tibullus : and to a modern ear the lines—

> "That which he hath writ
> Is with such judgment laboured, and distilled
> Through all the needful uses of our lives,
> That could a man remember but his lines,
> He should not touch at any serious point,
> But he might breathe his spirit out of him "—

seem incapable of any other application. Nevertheless, the eulogy passed in the preceding

speeches is so exactly contradicted by Jonson's
notorious saying of Shakespeare, that the attri-
bution must be dismissed as untenable.[1] There
can be little doubt that the poet who thus
received the place of honour in the last of Jonson's
first group of comedies, was one with whom his
own subsequent career was to be more closely
linked, and to whom he was intellectually more
cognate than to any other, the *doyen* of Elizabethan dramatists, George Chapman.

It is, at any rate, Chapman who probably
contributed most to the new direction which
Jonson now took. Disdaining to continue the
noisy but unworthy quarrel, he replied to the
Satiromastix of his enemies only by the Apolo-
getic Dialogue affixed to *The Poetaster*, in which
he announced his resolve to abandon comedy for
a form of drama less easily converted into an
arena for vulgar animosities ;—

> "Leave me : There's something come into my thought
>   That must and shall be sung high and aloof,
>   Safe from the wolf's black jaw, and the dull ass' hoof."

For a few months he brooded over his work in
severe and, as the town insinuated, moody, seclu-
sion. "Ben Jonson, the poet," it is said in the
Diary of the law-student Manningham, under the
date February 12th, 1603, "nowe lives upon one
Townshend, and scornes the world." In the

---

[1] Compare especially Gallus' words :—

"And yet so chaste and tender in his ear, &c."

course of the year appeared the result of his labour, the tragedy of *Sejanus*.

Original and independent as Jonson habitually was in his choice of subject, the story of this classic example of the vanity of political greatness nevertheless fell in altogether with a literary fashion of the hour. The years 1600 to 1603, are marked by a group of dramas which turn upon what may be called the tragedy of political adventure. Conspiracies and plots, arrogant usurpations or abuses of authority, are the recurring types of incident. Dekker's Sir Thomas Wyatt and Shakespeare's Brutus and Cassius (to mention small things with great), belong to 1600-2; the close of the following year brought the sombre picture of Angelo. It is of more significance that in 1601 occurred the revolt of Essex, and that in the autumn of 1602[1] was probably written the double drama, in which the most thrilling foreign conspiracy of the day, that of Byron, marshall of France (executed in 1602), was handled by his friend Chapman; while the better-known dramas of the latter on Bussy d'Ambois (whatever their exact date), were still fresh in memory. None of his fellow dramatists stood confessedly so near to Jonson as this one, his only equal in learning; none carried into literature a genius so penetrated with the instincts of the scholar; and in the whole range of Elizabethan

[1] See Henslowe, under dates 25th September and 2nd October, 1602,

drama there is nothing which, in method and in point of view, so nearly resembles Jonson's tragedies as these of Chapman. No others appear to aim so directly at those merits, above all, which Jonson, with great felicity and perfect justice, claims for his own:—*truth of argument, dignity of persons, gravity and height of elocution, fulness and frequency of sentence.* Chapman certainly attempts no such minute reproduction of the historical detail of his subject as Jonson, nor was it in his power; but he does not play fast and loose with his facts or his characters; he treats them as something more than the mere raw material of theatrical effect; he possessed, as has been pointed out by a critic who is himself a historian, that rarest of Elizabethan gifts, a historical sense.

Sejanus, like its companion tragedy, *Catiline*, has always been more admired by scholars than by laymen, and many excellent persons have hinted at the class of intellect for which a profusion of foot-notes atones for all deficiencies of art. No doubt the scholarly student of *Sejanus* has a real advantage, though it does not lie exactly here. For Jonson has written for minds saturated like his own with the life of the ancient world, and capable of supplying for themselves the atmosphere, the scenery, the light and colour, the infinite detail, which his dramatic picture presumes, but does not exactly provide. Jonson has, in fact, taken far less pains to bring home

to the imagination of a common audience the
Rome which they did not know, than the London
which they did; and this parsimonious use of
the brush which Shakespeare dashed with such
magnificent freedom, yet with such essential
truth, upon his canvas, naturally brought its
own revenge. Yet to those who can supply the
mediating atmosphere, *Sejanus* offers an experience not easily found elsewhere.

It is true that the stage is overcrowded with
figures, and that some of them are very slightly
and simply featured. We do not read the hearts
of Jonson's Romans, as we do of Shakespeare's;
we miss the intimate divining eye, the great
illuminating touch which, in a few phrases, lays
bare all the mysteries of personality. But we
move among them, and hear their conversation
and interpret it for ourselves; we jostle them in
the throng of the street and sit beside them in
the senate; we know them as we know the actors
in a political crisis of to-day, no better, no worse.
But from this *turba* of minor figures, there stand
out two characters who are drawn with a profusion of power which Jonson rarely surpassed.
No doubt even here, the pencil is handled with
a haughty disdain for the picturesque, and
neither Sejanus nor Tiberius bite into the
imagination, like Volpone in *The Alchemist*, by
sheer pungency and vivacity of colouring. But
their effect grows. Both were of a type entirely
congenial to Jonson's cast of imagination,—men

who, like Volpone or Subtle, with whatever variety of resource and expedient, whatever depth of duplicity or dissimulation, were at bottom simple and of a piece, driven on by only one motive and wholly innocent of that human clash and confusion of good and evil impulse which lay outside Jonson's artistic sphere, as they lay outside his own great solid, massive nature. They show no trace of the tragic conflict which gives to Shakespeare's Brutus and Coriolanus, to his Antony, or to Claudius in *Hamlet* (his nearest parallel to Jonson's Tiberius) so pathetic a fascination. They are without pathos as they are without passion. To natural and universal sentiment they make little appeal. They are embodiments of the blind, unswerving, passionless egoisms of an age in which principle is too weak to extort more than the homage of hypocrisy.

It is not very strange that such a tragedy failed with an audience which not only lacked qualification to appreciate it, but contained an element pledged to revenge *The Poetaster*. It is more surprising that the Government suspected in it both treason and " popery," and that Jonson was summoned before the Council to explain himself. The judgment of his readers, however, when it was published, differed from that of the audience; and two years later (1605) Jonson appeared with a drama, before which cavil, though not quite silent, was impotent.

II.

The author of *Volpone, or The Fox*, was, in fact, a distinctly more formidable person than even the author of *The Poetaster*. The new King had discovered that no one could so cunningly satisfy his taste for the gorgeous arabesque of Renaissance pageantry as this scholar of thirty, who without high poetic passion and imagination had all the more of the brilliant luxuriance of fancy; and Jonson was becoming the first maker of Court Masques. And his position can hardly have been weakened by a memorable incident of the previous year—his voluntary imprisonment, with his old friend Chapman and his old enemy, newly reconciled, Marston, in order to bear his share of the Scottish displeasure aroused by a casual insult in the comedy of *Eastward Ho*, their common production. For favour in high quarters soon opened their prison doors and revoked the threatened mutilation of their ears and noses; and a joyous company of fellow-poets and fellow-scholars, including Camden and Selden, met at Jonson's house; where his old mother, as her son recounted to Drummond, in words too vivid to be omitted in the briefest account of him, showed the "paper full of strong lustie poison," which she had intended (if the sentence had taken execution) to have mixed in his drink, "and that she was no churle, she told, she minded first to have drunk of it herself." It is plain whence Jonson had his touch of the "antique Roman."

Volpone, performed not many months after this banquet and in the interval between two Royal "Entertainments," is Roman in another sense. Though the scene is laid at Venice, and though some of the characters are wholly English, the suggestion of the plot is rather caught from the lurid pages of Juvenal. No such revolting figures as Volpone and his instrument, Mosca, had yet been drawn with such sustained and merciless vigour, for the English stage. The hideous occupations of the parasite and the "captator," stock subjects of every Roman satirist, are reproduced with incomparable vividness before the relatively innocent English public. Volpone in private life springs plainly from the same fount as Sejanus in public, and the close study of Imperial society, which had been involved in the one, suggested the other. Instead of the old motley company of Humours, loosely strung together in a phantasmagoria of five acts, we have the picture of a single career, about which all the other personages revolve. The turning-point in the fortunes of both is due to their own infatuated confidence. Sejanus is ruined from the moment when he asks for the hand of Livia, and Volpone by his crowning audacity in feigning his own death. And in both, the false step is not immediately fatal, but ruin is postponed by one of those illusory triumphs at the eleventh hour in which Jonson, with his essentially ironical mind, delighted. Sejanus, just before his fall, obtains the coveted tribunitial dignity; Volpone, on the eve of ruin, scores his victory in court.

Volpone is called by its author, with technical accuracy, a "comedy"; but it is such a comedy as Juvenal might have written. The drastic laughter which rings through *Every Man in His Humour* is yet not without gaiety; but the laughter of *Volpone* is the savage scorn of a man burning to make an unanswerable exposure, if not of vice, yet of those who accused the stage of insufficient hostility to it. It is in truth even more obviously enthusiasm for the dignity of poetry than for that of virtue which pervades both the play itself, and the noble Dedication to the sister Universities, composed in the choicest Ciceronian English, with which he ushered it two years later into the world. "My special aim being to put a snaffle in their mouths, that cry out, We never punish vice in our interludes, I took the more liberty"—that is, made the catastrophe more grave than was demanded by "the strict rigour of comic law." But it is not merely the catastrophe which savours of tragedy. The peril which overhangs the innocent wife of Corvino is something more than an outrageous Humour, and the part of Celia is accordingly one of the few pathetic passages in the dramas of this master of Elegy. And of all professedly

comic scenes, surely the most ghastly is that
where Volpone's human playthings, the dwarf,
hermaphrodite and eunuch, entertain their
master with "songs" in which the intentional
"false pace of the verse" parodies their own
imperfect humanity.

This *saeva indignatio* was not, however, an
absorbing mood with Jonson; and the most
sombre of his comedies was followed four years
later by one even more irresistible in its genial
gaiety than his first. He is now visibly less
concerned to "spout ink in the face" and "put
the snaffle in the mouth" of rival or reviler;
but *The Silent Woman* is not unworthy of the
proud hope which he had expressed to the Universities, of the "maturing of some worthier
fruit." The fundamental situation is no doubt
weak; it is one of those fetches of irresponsible
fancy which Jonson imbibed from much study
of Lucian and his school—the last efflorescence
of Attic wit. The idea of Morose, with his
horror of noise, taken from Libanius, had been
already used incidentally in *Volpone* (iii., 2)—
Jonson is extraordinarily fond of resuming his
own former thoughts — and hardly contains
enough stuff to form the basis of a drama.
Jonson's habitual neglect of the psychological
groundwork of character is particularly palpable
in the case of so rare an eccentricity. Morose's
antipathy is introduced simply as a "disease,"
without any attempt to make it credible, and if

the reader speedily surrenders his scepticism, he is rather bribed to assent, by the overplus of splendid fun for which this outrageous hypothesis proves the occasion, than convinced. Jonson's conception of character ended, in fact, where it began, at the "Humour" stage. Men were determined, once for all, by the mode in which their souls were mixed. Development he knew only as the rude buffeting of a man out of his more dangerous idiosyncrasies by the stern shock of experience. Of the more complex forms of character, and of the subtler development, which is only a continuous effort to reconcile its inconsistencies, he had no conception as, in his own massive and four-square nature, he had no experience.

Rarely, however, has so poor a stock burgeoned so luxuriantly with flowers and fruit. The utmost effect is got out of the few but felicitously chosen characters. Sir John Daw, the scholar-fool, and La Foole, the fool of family, are surpassed only by the town and country gull of the first comedy of Humours ; and in the duel scene which Jonson has borrowed from *Twelfth Night*, the most Jonsonian comedy of Shakespeare, he has certainly shown himself worthy of his model, though as usual the one poet is more elaborate and the other more human, for the pathos of Viola's embarrassment is wholly absent.

Both *Volpone* and *Epicœne* failed to entirely

realise the Jonsonian ideal of comedy, as an
"imitation of life;" the one through the archa-
ism, the other through the triviality, of its central
motive.   The following year, however, produced
a drama exempt from both these defects.   In
The Alchemist (1610) Jonson, for the first and also
for the last time, found a subject in which all his
varied faculty could run riot without injury to
the art-quality of his work.   The profession of
alchemy, at once notorious and obscure, with its
mountebank reputations and its mystic preten-
sions, its impenetrable Kabbala of subtleties,
and its Rembrandtesque profusion of sordid and
squalid detail,—the most impudent, venerable,
and picturesque of social plagues—was the fittest
subject then to be found in Europe for such
comedy as his.   Ariosto and Skelton had long
ago in their very different fashions[1] made plays
on it; a year or two later Shakespeare's Prospero,
distantly related, like Subtle, to Dr. John Dee,
attested once more his profound originality.   The
scholar and the observer, the devourer of old folios
and the busy noter of every detail in the life of
contemporary London, found equally pabulum
here.   And the character of the Alchemist admitted, like that of Volpone, of being made the
hinge upon which a whole group of fortunes
turn.   Sir Epicure, gloating over his vision of
endless voluptuousness and endless ostentation,

The assertion is safe, though we do not possess Skelton's *Nigro-
manser*.

the envoys of the Saints of Amsterdam, perplexed between unholy cupidity and pious resignation, the lawyer's clerk and the tobacco man, Dol Common and Dame Pliant,—not one of them can be spared from this wonderful comedy of avarice and lust. The painting is more harmonious if less versatile than in *Volpone*, the pathetic episode of Celia, outlined so sharply against the otherwise scarcely relieved vileness of that picture, is not repeated, and the wonderful group of the impostor and the parasite is not only reproduced with even heightened power in Subtle and Face, but enriched by the addition of the disreputable yet indispensable Dol.

The extraordinary merits of *The Alchemist* were at once recognised. Yet it is probable that Jonson himself was less convinced than most of his critics have been that he had here found his true vein. The very directness of its reference to an abuse of the day, which added to its immediate popularity, seemed a concession of the poet to the satirist, hardly consonant with the heroic aspiration expressed in the Dedication to *Volpone*, that he might one day, "if my muses be true to me, raise the despised head of poetry again, and stripping her out of those base and rotten rags wherewith the times have adulterated her form, restore her to her primitive habit, feature, and majesty, and render her worthy to be embraced and kissed of all the great and master-spirits of the world." In any case *The*

Catiline

Alchemist was followed the next year by a drama which at least fulfilled the negative part of this aspiration, and which, after its failure on the stage, Jonson dedicated, in indignant words recalling those just quoted, to Pembroke, one of the few who "dared in these jig-given times to countenance a legitimate poem." *Catiline* is, in fact, like *Sejanus*, composed in lofty defiance of the "ordinary reader" and his prejudices, as the author with grim humour in effect informed the latter in his unique preface. Far from accepting the disparaging verdict generally passed upon *Sejanus*, he courts a repetition of it by a still more pronounced classicism. And here, as before, his serene scorn for the popular voice was not quite out of place. *Catiline* is not written for laymen, and is not likely to be fully relished by those who do not bring to it something of the historical setting, the atmosphere and background of the ancient world, which the poet has not deigned to provide because he presumes it. If Jonson's weight of learning has injured his work, it is in fact less by suggesting superfluities than by inducing the omission of much vivid illuminating detail. The picture gallery is not in reality overcrowded with learned lumber, but it is placed in an upper story, and the reader is expected to bring his own ladder. The character-drawing is for the most part of the kind which a man may use in describing familiar acquaintances to friends who know them as well as he,—perfectly distinct and faithful so far as it goes, but made up of those slight touches which add finish and delicacy to a portrait, but would have little meaning or force if flung on a bare canvas. In this sense we may still agree with the "great critic" who incurs Gifford's wrath by opining that Jonson was "very learned, as Samson was very strong, to his own hurt." Yet a great poet has a right to impose his own conditions, and those who accept Jonson's will find, not indeed a tragedy of Shakespearian pity and terror, but a dramatic study, worked out with extraordinary skill, of one of the most critical moments in Roman history. It represents a conflict, of a kind which Jonson of all men was qualified to interpret, between the civilian and the soldier, between craft and force, scholarly astuteness and impulsive valour, and each of the two heroes is handled with a certain tenderness which history scarcely justifies. Cicero is allowed the full benefit of his triumph, his portrait is drawn, if with little enthusiasm, yet with no touch of the irony which his too complacent recollection of this exploit makes so obvious; his fussy vanity is not concealed but is also not exposed; his extraordinary discursiveness, while it certainly cannot be said to be ignored in a play in which he speaks some four hundred lines in a single scene, is made to appear for once entirely in place. And Catiline on his part, the rebellious *Junker* with the rabble at his back, the arrogant and outwitted conspirator,—the Essex, as Cicero by a more strained analogy might be called the Bacon, of the hour—is permitted to end his career in a death-scene upon which Jonson has lavished all the rugged sublimity of his poetry, in a passage almost too sharply contrasted with the relatively pedestrian tone of the rest of the play. Of the poetry of passion Jonson knew little, but he had two great qualities which enabled him to achieve higher things in poetry than men far more habitually and easily "poetical" than he;—sublimity, such as we have here —the spontaneous expression of a man of grand habit of mind occupied with a naturally great and moving subject, and the delicate grace which only becomes a first-rate literary quality when it is, as in him, the gentleness of strength. Both qualities meet in the finest of his epitaphs, above all in the incomparable—

> " Underneath this sable hearse
> Lies the subject of all verse. . . ."

Catiline is said, according to a credible tradition, to have been Jonson's favourite play, as we know from his own words that it was his favourite tragedy. He produced no other tragedy, though the few lines of a *Mortimer*, found among his papers, show that he once more thought of doing so ; and three years after the failure of *Catiline*, the audience which had resented its too unrelieved reproduction of a complex and remote political intrigue, were gratified by the most vivid and genial picture ever drawn of their own gross delights. *Bartholomew Fair*, the last of the great comedies of Jonson, may be regarded as a blending of the old scheme of Humour-comedy characteristic of his first period, with the persistent satire upon a single eminent abuse which marks the comedy of his maturity. The *Fair* is a kind of concentrated and heightened reproduction of the "Town" in little. The same humours reappear; but its soil is richer and its air more stimulating, the appliances for growing humours of every kind and for lopping them, are planted at every turn; if the Town in general is a garden, the Fair is a hot-bed. In this heightened and tropical atmosphere every humour comes more rapidly to maturity and to collapse; new kinds of humour, unobserved elsewhere, are developed; every man's weakness finds him out, be it love of pork or of puppet-shows; every gull is confronted with his appropriate knave. Upon this stock, which so far suggests his first attempts, Jonson has grafted a satire upon Puritanism, not less elaborate and finished than his former assault upon Alchemy. The Puritan family-party who, led by the saintly glutton Busy, visit this scene of vain pleasures that the little wife may gratify her opportune longing for Bartholomew pig, is an irresistibly comic invention, and their fate grotesquely appropriate. Hardly less so is the representation of a more respectable phase of Puritanism, the over-zealous magistrate who walks Vanity Fair in a detective's disguise to collect material for justice, and, at length, seated beside Zeal of the Land Busy in the stocks, shares the fate in which a candidly sinning world occasionally unites the inopportunely fanatic and the unskilfully hypocritical. It cannot indeed be said that Jonson has worked out all the splendid possibilities of the subject, as he, if any man, was capable of doing. In the attitude of the true genius of Puritanism towards this carnival of vulgar and riotous pleasures there lay the materials for a contrast as eternal and inexhaustible as that between Don Quixote and Panza. The refinement of Cervantes' satire has left it possible to doubt whether Quixote be not after all his hero. No reader of *Bartholomew Fair* will form any such illusion in regard to Busy or Overdo. The satiric habit of Jonson's mind was too pronounced to admit of that intellectual sympathy, otherwise to be looked for in a man of his reach of thought and knowledge, which presses into the ideal meaning of great historical movements, instead of merely indicating their inevitable train of affectations and absurdities. He has treated Puritanism with far less insight than Alchemy, the abstruse learning of which touched a congenial chord in the scholar, who revolted at the crudity of Puritan culture ; but the neglect has revenged itself, and his Busy has but the effect of a caricature of extraordinary vigour, while Subtle is a type.

Two years after the great success of *Bartholomew Fair* appeared *The Devil is an Ass*. The idea of the plot, happy as it is, suggests that resort to supernatural and allegorical devices for which in his great days he had no need, though he did not always avoid it, but which grew upon him as his genius decayed in sheer plastic power. The "purging" of Crispinus and the Fountain of Self-love on the one hand, the Aristophanic motive of *The Magnetic Lady* on the other, are only less elaborate examples of this quality than the adventures of the "Stupid Devil" in this play. Supernatural motive was rapidly growing old-fashioned on the London stage,[1] where Faustus was nearly a generation old. Jonson's devils are anachronisms, and they know it. The venerable Iniquity and terrible Vice of fifty years ago are become unserviceable against an astuter generation which breeds its own vices as it does its own horses, and the infernal world itself has sunk to the footing of a mere rival state, whose merchandise can be impounded and its citizens carted to Tyburn. Pug is a pretty, petulant boy, more gull than fiend, less removed by many degrees from humanity than the half fairy Puck of Shakespeare, which doubtless

---

[1] Already in the Dedication to *Volpone* he refers indignantly to those who would "rather see fools and *devils* and those antique relics of barbarism retrieved, than" endure a Jonsonian comedy.

helped to suggest him; and the arch-fiend Satan
is a bluff old politician, anxious like a prudent
father to ward off the perils of London from his
young simpleton, who is equally anxious to
plunge into them. We have thus a *rechauffé* of
the familiar theme of the gull, with a new and
piquant dressing, the comic quality of Pug lying
in the contrast between his official status of
mischief maker and his actual insignificance.
He proves, in fact, "too dull a devil to be trusted
forth in these parts." He finds himself surrounded by shrewder contrivers, among whom
he counts for very little. The whole business of
the play,—and this recalls the loose construction of Jonson's early comedies—goes on, with
scarcely an exception, as if he were not present;
he is the fly upon the engine-wheel, fortunate to
escape with a bruising; instead of disconcerting
the plans of men, as he is meant to do, he hangs
helplessly in the background, or awkwardly
intervenes to no one's disadvantage but his own.
And the *dénoûment* of the general intrigue has
no influence upon the *dénoûment* of Pug's fortunes; he comes to grief through none of his
misdeeds in connection with the main plot, but
on account of the preliminary theft of clothes
which enabled him to take part in it.[1]

---

[1] On the relations between *The Devil is an Ass* and earlier
devil-dramas I may be permitted to refer to my own *Studies in the
Literary Relations of England and Germany in the Sixteenth Century*, p. 318 f., from which I have borrowed a few sentences in the
text.

The year of the publication of the *Devil is an Ass*, 1616, which closed the career of Shakespeare, marks a decisive period in Jonson's. Four more plays and the fragment of a fifth were to be produced at intervals during his remaining twenty-one years, and he never wholly ceased to honour a noble wedding with one of the Masques in which, as he and the world allowed, he had no rival. But the summer of his genius was over, and his fame rests upon the almost unbroken series of masterpieces which began with *Every Man in His Humour* and culminated in *The Alchemist.* The folio edition of what, amid the gibes of the literary world, he called his "Works," which appeared in 1616, is therefore, though it ends with *Catiline,* the monument of his career as an artist. But it is also, together with the famous *Conversations* of two years later, the monument of his private life in this period, of his friendships as of his enmities, and no man threw himself with more zest into both. Of his enmities *The Poetaster* remained, so far as we have certain evidence, the last, as it was the first, direct dramatic expression. If he ever again lashed a personal enemy on the stage (putting aside the last comedy of his decline) he, at least, so far disguised the portrait that, as in the case of "Inigo-Lantorn," as Selden calls him, in *Bartholomew Fair*, posterity still disputes whether it be one. But in the *Epigrams* and *The Forest* we have a picture of Jonson's personal relations

as frank as it is on the whole attractive. The
sturdy satirist, in spite of his ungainly person,
could charm refined and graceful women; he
had the impetuous geniality of high spirits, a
teeming mind and a flowing wit, he could be
gracious when he chose, and his grace was the
irresistible grace of the strong.

Nor is it to be forgotton that Jonson was the
grandson of a courtier of position. He was
welcomed by the cultivated nobles whom he
frequented, on terms which wholly excluded the
servility of which he was in any case incapable.
As he wrote later in the *Underwoods*, he had—

> " Eaten with the beauties and the wits
> And braveries of court, and felt their fits
> Of love and hate, and come so nigh to know
> Whether their faces were their own or no."

Or if he anywhere found himself treated with
less than the dignity due to letters he was cable of resenting it, as on the day when, dining
with Lord Salisbury, "who never cared for any
man longer nor he can make use of him," and
finding himself with Inigo Jones placed at the
bottom of the table, he attracted his host's attention by his visible anger, and being questioned
"Why he was not glad?" "My lord," said he, "you
promised I should dine with you, but I do not."
He writes to his correspondents of every rank
with the freedom of an honoured friend, familiar
but never vulgar, delicately playful, easily well-
bred. It was not for nothing that the author of

The Poetaster took the part of Horace for himself. His poetical epistles are among the choicest in the language. Chief among these families were those which inherited the blood of the Sidneys, and with it something of the great Sidneian tradition of " manners, arms, and arts." There is Sir Robert Sidney, the hospitable lord of Penshurst, at whose table every guest may eat—

> " Without his fear, and of my lord's own meat."

There is Sir Robert Wroth, husband of that Lady Mary, Sidney's niece, to whom Jonson dedicated *The Alchemist*,[1] and owner of the still more beloved retreat of Durance, where—

> " If thou list the night in watch to break,
>   A-bed canst hear the loud stag speak."

There is Pembroke, the too-much honoured son of " Sidney's sister," who was accustomed to send him £20 every New Year's Day to buy new books, and whose ungallant assertion that " women were men's shadows," gave occasion to one of the prettiest of Jonson's epigrams. " Pembroke and his lady discoursing," as he told Drummond, " the Earl said, the woemen were men's shadowes, and she maintained (*i.e.* defended) them. Both appealing to Jonson, he affirmed it true; for which my Lady gave a pennance to approve it in verse: hence his epigram." There is Sidney's daughter, the Countess of Rutland, upon whose perfections, if

---

[1] Compare also *Epigrams* 103, 105. In the *Conversations* Jonson hints a reverse to this pleasant picture.

the author of *Arcadia*, Jonson writes to her,
were now to look,—

> "He should those rare and absolute numbers view,
> As he would burn, or better far, his book."

And, outside the Sidneys, there is Lady Rutland,
who consoled herself in a childless marriage by
keeping open table to poets; and that Countess
of Bedford who called forth the exquisite—

> " This morning, timely rapt with holy fire,"—

and who was repaid for a timely present of
venison by another sonorous epigram, with
which its author loved to disturb the echoes
of Hawthornden; and the "loved Aubigny" and
his wife, with whom, probably in the early part
of James's reign, Jonson lived as their guest for
five years.[1]

Of these and kindred intimacies, the most
enduring result was naturally the Masques.
By far the most splendid of the series during
this period are in celebration of marriages.
The ill-omened wedding of the Earl of Essex, in
1606, was adorned by the first and most elaborate
of these pageants, the beautiful *Masque of Hymen*,
with its Catullian marriage hymn severely
abridged in the performance; Jonson printed it
in full, and "I do heartily forgive their ignorance, whom it chanceth not to please."
Two years later, the marriage of Viscount Had-

---

[1] He speaks in the *Conversations* of having been staying there in
1604.

dington, a Scottish favourite of James, with the daughter of the Earl of Sussex, produced the not less beautiful *Hue and Cry after Cupid*. Hardly less splendid than the wedding masques were those prepared for the special entertainment of the Queen and her ladies, particularly at Christmas and Twelfth Night, of which Jonson had been called on to furnish several in the first years of the reign. The most notable of all is the *Masque of Queens*, written when Jonson was busy with *The Silent Woman*, and interesting, both as the first which introduces an antimasque on any scale, and because the antimasque here, a group of admirably drawn witches, is evidently suggested by the example of *Macbeth*, an example of which it falls short only in so far as a masque necessarily falls short of a tragedy.

To his fellow poets his relations were, in some cases, less cordial. Without accepting literally all the peremptory aphorisms of the *Conversations*, it is easy to believe that the friendship of the keenest critic of the time, whose hours of genial toping only quickened the satiric edge of his intellect, and of whom it could be said, however unjustly, that he would rather "lose a friend than a jest," was too strong meat for most men. Not every one could aspire to grasp the hand of the caustic talker who wished to go "into the Church" only that he might have one opportunity of preaching his mind to the king, "and he cared not what after might befal him, for he

would not flatter though he saw death." It was
even questioned, as he tells us, "if I be a friend
at all." Chapman and Fletcher he "loved," and
allowed only to them the glory of being a little
inferior to himself in the making of masques.
Hardly less honoured was Donne, "the first poet
of the world for some things." A little further
stood Beaumont, who was already dead when
Jonson (of all men) noted of him in the *Conversations*, that he "loved too much himself and
his own verses"; and Drayton, that "Michael,"
who "feared him," and whom he "esteemed not
of," but whose friendship with Jonson is sufficiently attested by the after-rumours that they
had ceased to correspond; and Shakespeare, the
man whom Jonson "loved, on this side idolatry, as
much as any," and whose genius he probably
weighed more adequately than any of his contemporaries, who was nevertheless, it is difficult
not to suspect, removed from the inmost circle
of Jonson's intimacy by a profound unlikeness
of intellectual nature. It is no part of the
business of these pages to recur to the acrid
controversies which once composed the staple
of Jonsonian biography. The Jonsonian "sneer"
at Shakespeare is an exploded myth; but the
evidence points rather to a strong mutual admiration, retained in spite of the sharp natural
antithesis of their minds, than to a hearty bosom
friendship. With most of his fellow dramatists,
Jonson can hardly have been on very cordial

terms. Dekker, his old antagonist, was hardly
qualified either as an artist or as a man to win
Jonson's high regard, and still figures with Day
and Middleton, as a "rogue," in the records
of Hawthornden

III.

A few pages will suffice to speak of the
remaining twenty years of Jonson's life, in such
detail as the decline of a genius still robust,
but no longer capable of masterpieces, demands.
Its outward incidents were, some travelling, the
writing of a few masques and comedies, fail-
ing health, growing poverty, and the crowning
calamity which destroyed his library; and, on
the other hand, a steadily rising fame, which
surrounded the ageing poet with young poets
whose glory it was to be sealed of the tribe of Ben,
and which, though it did not prevent his weaker
plays from being damned as they deserved,
made him the unquestioned head of English
letters during the period between the death of
Shakespeare and the decisive *début* of Milton.

Of the travels, one famous journey will be
remembered as long as Jonson himself, the
"unfortunate" (but for posterity most fortunate)
visit to Drummond, the laird of Hawthornden,
between July, 1618, and the following January.
Drummond was not among the young poets who

---

[1] Two of Jonson's lost plays treated Scotch subjects, the *Scotts
tragedy* and *Robert the Second King of Scottes* (both 1599).

aspired to be the "Sons" of Ben, and he played
the part of Boswell without any germ of the
lues Boswelliana to quicken the fidelity of
memory. They were an ill-matched pair, and
the pale, refined, insignificant profile on one
side of the table was not alone physically a contrast to the "mountainous belly and the rocky
face" on the other. A sensitive, temperate and
reserved man, skilled in the elegances of academic
verse, he listened soberly to the often rash but
never random outpourings of the man "whose
element was drink," and Jonson's mind, as
represented in his notes, has suffered double
refraction in the unlike media of his own
vinous ardour and his hearer's unsympathetic
sobriety—heated imagination and dry understanding each contributing their disturbing bias.
The personality of Jonson, however, was too
vivid not to be caught at times even by this
nonchalant painter, and whatever interpretation
his alleged utterances may require, they are, in
essential matter and manner, unmistakeably his.
Boswell himself has not caught the manner of
his hero with more absolute precision than
Drummond has, at moments, caught the manner
of his formidable guest. Nor is it strange that
the bulk of the utterances are critical. Criticism
was the life of Jonson's mind, as of every mind
as keen, as genuine, as fearless, and as amply
stored as his; but it was the criticism of the
scholar, impelled by the conscience of intellect

to define and qualify whatever he sees, not that of the professional fault-finder.

For the rest, Jonson more than once attended (not, as in his journey to Scotland, on foot) the performance of his masques in the provinces. In 1621 he passed with the Court from Burleigh to Belvoir, and from Belvoir to Windsor, at each of which places his *Gipsies Metamorphosed* was given. But the true focus of his life, now as of old, was London, and in London, above other places, the famous taverns of the Devil, the Sun, the Dog, the Triple Tun. Here Jonson reigned, not as of old in the Mermaid, a king among kings, but sole autocrat, drawing up for his company of chosen sons laws conceived and expressed in the very spirit of Attic symposia, and exalting, with his wit's great overplus, those "lyric feasts" where, as the most gifted of those sons afterwards sadly sang—

> "We such clusters had
> As made us nobly wild, not mad,
> And yet each verse of thine
> Outdid the meat, outdid the frolic wine."

The privilege of "sonship" was shared with Herrick, by Cleveland, Randolph, Lucius Cary, afterwards Lord Falkland, Morison (whose fast friendship with Falkland Jonson commemorated in a fine ode), and others. A pleasant tradition also connects the old poet with the literary Duke of Newcastle, who was wont to tell his wife that "he had never heard any man read well but Ben

Jonson"; and whose friendly patronage more
than once appealed to his faint and faltering
hand, during his last years, for a masque. On
the other hand, Jonson's connection with the
Court entertainments ended early in the next
reign, apparently through the influence of Inigo
Jones, and Charles's bounty, though generous
and even lavish when it came, was characteristically uncertain.

In 1625 Jonson took once more to the stage,
with *The Staple of News*, the recently started
news journal of Nathaniel Butter supplying him
with congenial material. It was followed,
four years later, by *The New Inn*,—a disastrous
failure, to which we owe, however, the *Ode to
Himself*; by *The Magnetic Lady*, 1632, and *The
Tale of a Tub*, 1633. In surprising contrast to
the country life which Jonson, deserting his
familiar London, with feeble hand essayed to
portray in this last comedy, is the fragmentary
drama of *The Sad Shepherd*, a picture of country
life, full of a fresh aroma and charm which
Jonson hardly equalled in his palmy days. The
"forty years' feast" of his dramas closed appro-
priately with this dish of delicate fruit and frag-
rant flowers. In spite of poverty and illness
and old age, the poetic heart in him flashed out
unmistakeably at the last, as if to make clear
that this potent manipulator of prosaic detail belonged, after all, by good right to the dells and
glades of Parnassus.

But comedy was only the casual and not wholly congenial occupation of these after years. Neither disease nor poverty, neither the necessity which compelled him sundry times to "devour" (*i.e.* sell) his books, nor the fire which once remorselessly consumed them, checked his patient indefatigable curiosity in every field of learning. Of actual achievement indeed, little remains except the fragmentary *English Grammar*, and the weighty and too brief *Discoveries*; and posterity as well as the poet must "execrate Vulcan" for the loss of the far ampler collections which perished with the library,—the notes to Horace's art of poetry, the history of Henry V. and even the humble gleanings in divinity after the fathers. *The Discoveries* are chiefly devoted to criticism and the theory of criticism, the predominant habit of Jonson's mind; but the critical temper was in him united with a degree of "historical sense," which among his fellow-poets only Chapman could pretend to rival, one of the fruits of his long training under Camden. He strove to get at the oldest sources, in whatever language, and a great collection of grammars attested his keen interest in language as such. Amid the gnawing disappointment of the failure of *The New Inn* he had freedom of mind enough to take up the Celtic studies in which his master Camden had been before him, writing to his friend Howell to aid him in procuring Davies' Welsh grammar, for which he was too ill to seek himself.

In such labours, cheered through growing illness by the sympathy of many friends, Ben Jonson passed the decline of his busy life. The summer of 1637 was to be his last. On the 6th of August he died, and three days after was buried in the Abbey, a few paces from the schoolrooms in which, half a century before, he had laid the foundation of his weight of learning. Public events prevented the execution of the monument for which the literary world of England willingly subscribed; and the famous " O rare Ben Jonson," carved for eighteenpence at the wish of an indignant passer-by upon the undistinguished gravestone which covered him, remained his sole but sufficing memorial.

So passed away the last of the great contemporaries of Shakespere in drama of whom we have certain record, and the one of them who approaches him most nearly in originality, in sheer force and massiveness of genius. Jonson is, in fact, one of the most unique figures in all literature; not that he had any of that subtle complexity of mind which provokes and defies analysis like a rare flavour; his was rather one of those great and single natures which are easy to be understood because they are open to the light and air, but compared with which all mere eccentricity is commonplace. Few great writers make so irresistible an impression of *wholeness* as he. It is his strength as well as his weakness that no tragic conflict, no clash of inner nature disturbs his pedestrian energy with the perplexities and the exaltations of high passion. The lyric intensity of Shakespeare's sonnets, the bitter pessimism of *Timon* and *Measure for Measure* are unknown to the man whose lyric gift was in mere sweetness scarcely surpassed, and who yielded to none in the keenness of his eye for every form of folly. He knows neither the godlike heights nor the abysmal depths of human consciousness. But, with his less eager and ardent sensibility, he unites extraordinary sanity and strength.

Jonson was no ascetic, and plunged with as little concern as any of his contemporaries into the dissipations of London; but no man was ever less defiled by touching pitch. His amours, his deep-drinking, were equally the gratifications of a robust animal nature and were pursued equally as a matter of course; his plays and one or two of his poems shrink from no indelicacy of allusion, and paint filth of precisely its own colour with all the resources of an inexhaustible palette; yet his frankness is without a suggestion of prurience and he could affirm with entire justice, in his noble *Apologia pro arte sua* to the universities, that he had "ever trembled to think towards the least profaneness," and had " loathed the use of such foul and unwashed bawdry as is now made the food of the scene." With all his genial expansiveness in undignified surroundings, Jonson never for a moment relaxed his hold upon the intellectual ideal of the scholar and the artist. He passes with the ease of an ample nature to and fro from the one world to the other, from the study in Blackfriars to the uproarious revels in Fleet Street; from the unsavoury jesting of "A famous voyage" to the delicate grace of "Drink to me only with thine eyes" and the impressive solemnity of the lines "To Heaven." He who had by heart the glorious Bacchic strophes of Spenser's Percie loved equally the stanzas in which Wotton describes the "Happy life" of him—

> "Whose passions not his masters are;
> Whose soul is still prepar'd for death."

Precisely in this double point of view, in the stringency and austerity of the artist, combined with the wide and genial outlook upon every phase of common life, lay the condition of Jonson's splendid achievement in drama. For concentrated intensity of observing faculty he can hardly be matched but by Juvenal and Swift. Set beside his strongest page, the nice distinctions of Pope seem insipid, the trenchant contrasts of Dryden rhetorical. All but unknown out of England, he is instantly recognised as one of the typical Englishmen of all time. English he is, as, in a rarer and higher sense, Shakespeare is English. In Shakespeare the fidelity to facts, the faculty of grappling with brutal realities, of holding up the mirror of art to nature even in her least gracious hours and her least comely moods, is united with a supremely poetical imagination which transmutes and transforms whatever it touches. In Jonson the two faculties are also present, but they are far more loosely combined, and in different proportion. The poet is there, but he is both less relatively eminent and more easily detached from the observer. And, while Shakespeare lives and works the highest embodiment of the serene and joyous temper of the England of Elizabeth, Jonson is already touched by the seriousness and the strenuousness of the dawning age. What chiefly struck him in Shakespeare was his "want of art" and absence of effort. The elder poet is the god, the younger the Titan, labouring to attain the heights where the other serenely sits. Like Fletcher and like Bacon in their different ways, Jonson mediates between the age of Shakespeare and the age of Milton. Fletcher is, at once, an early master of Cavalier poetry, and yet in some sense a disciple of the greatest of his predecessors; Bacon unites the sanguine temper of the Elizabethans with the systematic thought of Hobbes; and Jonson, the equal of Shakespeare in realistic power, recalls less his joyous serenity and instinctive facility of inspiration than the grave and melancholy music, the elaboration, the self-consciousness of Milton.

C. H. HERFORD.

EDITOR'S PREFACE.

THE texts of Jonson's plays contained
in the present and following volumes
of the "Mermaid Series" have been
obtained from three sources; first from
the quartos published shortly after the
production of the plays: secondly from
the 1616 folio, in which each play
produced up to that date was printed from a revised version with additions, except that the then *Every Man in
his Humour* was a new version of the quarto play; and
thirdly from the two-volumed folios of 1631-40, the plays
contained in the first of these two volumes being a reprint
of the first folio of 1616 revised to the extent of an occas-
sional alteration of a word, and of an altered and sometimes increased punctuation, while the second volume,
published by other publishers and after the author's death,
contains versions, revised by the author, of the plays published in quarto after 1613.

In nearly every instance—unless there were some sufficient reason, such as the greater propriety of the original
word or words, the possibility of the change being merely
a printer's error and the like—the latest and most revised
reading has been adopted. So far, therefore, our text is
not that of the date given by Jonson as the first production
of his play. Indeed, he himself put forth his *Sejanus* as
"first acted in 1603," though at that time "a second pen
had good share in it," such share having been replaced
by Jonson's own work when he published it in 1605, two
facts not noted in either of the folios, though both set
forth 1603 as the date of its being first acted. Similarly

he put forth his 1616 published *Every Man in his Humour* as "acted in the year 1598," because the play—though much altered, and the 1616 version written about eight years after 1598—was essentially the same play. All additions, however, made to the quarto editions, save in this play, and save where they are only half a dozen words or less, are marked at either end by an asterisk (*).

From these causes and from various small, supposedly grammatical and metrical amendments and additions by Gifford, the text now given does not agree with his. But except in one most indefensible and every way unwarranted transference of a first folio added *Poetaster* scene (iii. 5) to a sort of postscript at the end, though the real postscript stared Gifford in the face at the end of the folio, and was actually given by him as that postscript—he thus giving both a false and a true postscript scene—with this exception his changes are of less consequence than I had expected after reading those discovered by Cunningham in Gifford's reprint of Jonson's *English Grammar.* And here a word as to Jonson's oaths. He, like most of his day, was apparently a great swearer, and for both reasons naturally gave his characters a superabundance of unseemly oaths. Later in the day he was compelled by the Act of James I. to reduce these—a matter he sometimes accomplished to his own, and seemingly to the censor's satisfaction by printing "god" and "lord" instead of "God" and "Lord"! Some of these alterations of his I have respected, but where oaths were natural to the character, or where their want clearly detracted from the life and naturalness of the scene, they have been restored, that his scenes might represent, as they were meant to do, the persons and the manners of the time. For the same reasons Gifford's alterations in this respect have been re-altered.

As to his verse, our author's arrangement has been followed, rather than the broken music of his editors. His contracted words have also been printed, but where

other syllables have to be apostrophised for the metre's
sake, the original word has generally been retained, as in
the case of amorous for am'rous, such instances being too
common to require such marking. Where, however, the
word intended to be apostrophised might otherwise give
rise in the young student's mind to doubt, the syllable
has been elided, in like manner as apparent hexameters
have been noted as "not hexameters." Similarly all
students of our Elizabethan books know that " I have,"
" do not " and the like were often printed thus, when
intended to be pronounced " I've " and " don't," and
Jonson, though generally precise, was a strange mixture of
preciseness and carelessness.

The orthography has been modernised, but it is right
to say that while I had at first adopted the ——'d, ——ed,
and ——èd rules of the Cambridge editors of Shakespeare,
I now find that the invariable rule of the series for which
the present edition has been prepared, is to print only
——ed and ——èd. I had also inserted in my press
copy Jonson's pasts of verbs in t instead of ed, as in
" toucht," but the rule that I have spoken of forbade this.
I may remark, however, that such pronunciation was not
invariable with Jonson, and was apparently more common
during his later life. As illustrating, however, the at least
later pronunciation of the time, I have retained the frequent 'hem of Jonson for them, as also those of i', o', and
a', for in, of, on and he.

With regard to the punctuation, Jonson's, excessive
though it may appear, has in a great measure been followed.
He evidently after 1600 paid great attention to his
punctuation. He was more than a good reader, had
heard his plays acted, and had evidently given much
thought to marking the way in which his speeches were
to be uttered, so as to produce their intended and their
best effects. Sometimes lesser markings than usual show
the haste of the speaker ; contrariwise an excess of punctuation points, as was intended, to his deliberation or inde-

cision. Every one too, who has attended to the subject, knows how even a comma pause frequently emphasizes the word or words following, as sometimes also those that precede it, and of these things Jonson was aware. So too he, at times, divided his admiratory or interrogatory clauses by two or more ! s or ? s for the sake of tone, expression or emphasis, where a prosaic Lindley Murray would insist on only a final one. He often also uses a ? where Gifford substituted a !. But as the tone required is sometimes between what is indicated by these marks, and as the questioning tone makes the phrase more emphatic or bantering, I, while admitting that Jonson's use of the ? is sometimes redundant, and sometimes out of place, have retained the ? more frequently than did Gifford. More than once also this latter editor by substituting his own punctuation, has dimmed or spoilt the exact force or meaning of his author's words.

Where in the course of a speech, another person has been turned to and addressed, this has been indicated by a ——. Asides—sometimes, but not always, indicated by Jonson by being placed within ( )—when short, and recognisable without the slightest difficulty, have now and then been similarly differentiated. Stage directions have been avoided when mentioned or clearly indicated by the text. Lines marked thus ", and similarly marked " by Jonson and by some of his contemporaries, indicate thoughts which they hold to be worthy of remembrance, worthy of being accepted as axioms or proverbial sayings.

It may be added—the more so that former editors have been led astray through not noticing it—that Jonson, much more than most dramatic writers, makes his personages be recognised, and even be spoken to, before their entry on the stage.

Before concluding, and, while acknowledging generally the courtesy and kindness which I have invariably met with in the prosecution of my work, I would specially mention the obligations I am under to his Grace the Duke of

Devonshire for the loan more than once of some of the original quartos, to S. Colvin, Esq., of the British Museum, and to my friends, P. A. Daniel, Esq., Jas. Gairdner, Esq., of the Record Office, and W. G. Boswell-Stone, Esq., of Shute Haye.

Finally it is right for me to say that these plays have not been selected by me, though I had a voice in the rejection of one. Also that I had on principle adopted Jonson's own divisions into scenes, in nearly each case where another character or characters entered, in accordance with the usage still existent on the Continent, because he had both prided himself on returning to classic usage, and had formed his theory on this point as early as 1600. But though an editor should be an editor and not a maker, Gifford chose to divide the scenes otherwise, and his divisions have been adopted by others as more consonant with our English stage usage. To the general reader, however, this is of little consequence, and as Jonson's divisions are always marked in the notes, the student can if he please refer to them.

Br. Nicholson.

EVERY MAN IN HIS HUMOUR.

AFTER the publication of the quarto edition of *Every Man out of his Humour* in 1601, Jonson took heart of grace and published in 1601—it being entered in the Stationers' Registers on the 14th August, 1600—his *Every Man in his Humour*, his first unaided play, and one which proved a success, though its success, it being a satire on a foible of the day, was mingled with much criticism. It was first produced, as he himself tells us, in 1598 by the Lord Chamberlain's servants at the Globe, that is by Shakespeare's company, the principal comedians according to the folio being, Will. Shakespeare, Aug. Philips, Hen. Condell, Will. Slye, Will. Kempe, Ric. Burbage, Joh. Hemings, Tho. Pope, Chr. Beeston, and Joh. Duke.

This first version of the play, however, was Italian-scened, and Italian-charactered so far as names went. But our present version was first published in the folio of 1616, and as shown by internal evidence was written about or in 1606. Not improbably it was then rewritten that it might be produced before the King of Denmark, who in that year paid a visit to his daughter, Queen Anne, when dramas were among the chief in the entertainments lavishly set before him. Mr. F. G. Fleay indeed has ingeniously argued that this folio version was first produced in 1607, since in that year St. Mark's Day—as stated in Bobadill's speech in III. 1—fell on a Saturday. Unfortunately, however, the same data are found also in the quarto version, and do not allow of its being performed first in 1598, as it undoubtedly was.[1]　In this second version, besides that the scene is changed to England, and the characters are English-named, many of the speeches are altered, some omitted, and some added, the acts and scenes re-arranged, and some of the latter transposed.

Hence, while the quarto version has been read, and as far as possible collated, the originals for our text have—on account of the many variations, and the lateness of the date at which the revision by the author was made—only been the two folios.

Until comparatively recent times, this play was brought on the stage at frequent intervals with considerable success. After the Restoration (in 1675) it was revived by the Duke of York's company, Lord Dorset supplying the prologue. Garrick brought it out at Drury Lane with a very powerful cast of actors.　In the prologue he appealed to the audience to show favour to the work of " immortal Ben," " the rough old bard," and Kitely became one of his most famous parts. In 1800 Cooke appeared as Kitely, which was considered as his best character after Iago ; in 1816 Edmund Kean acted Kitely ; Charles Young rather later : while the elder Charles Mathews frequently took the part of Master Matthew. *Every Man in his Humour* was the first play selected for performance by Charles Dickens and his company of amateur actors.　It was presented at Miss Kelly's Theatre in Dean Street, Soho, in 1845, and on account of its enthusiastic reception it was repeated at St. James's Theatre, and later in the provinces.　Dickens himself took the part of Bobadill, and other characters were assumed by Mark Lemon, Douglas Jerrold, George Cattermole, John Leech and other well-known men.　Forster says that Dickens presented his part " after a richly coloured picture of bombastical extravagance and comic exaltation in the earlier scenes, a contrast in the later of tragical humility and abasement that had a wonderful effect."

[1] For proofs fuller than those given in this volume that the play was first produced in 1598, and that the folio version was written about or in 1606, see a paper by the present editor in *The Antiquary* for July and September, 1882.

To the most learned, and my honoured Friend,

MASTER CAMDEN,
Clarencieux.[2]

Sir,—There are, no doubt, a supercilious race in the world, who will esteem all office, done you in this kind, an injury; so solemn a vice it is with them to use the authority of their ignorance, to the crying down of POETRY, or the professors: but my gratitude must not leave[3] to correct their error; since I am none of those that can suffer the benefits conferred upon my youth to perish with my age. It is a frail memory that remembers but present things: and, had the favour of the times so conspired with my disposition, as it could have brought forth other, or better, you had had the same proportion, and number of the fruits, the first. Now, I pray you, to accept this; such wherein neither the confession of my manners shall make you blush; nor of my studies, repent you to have been the instructor: and for the profession of my thankfulness, I am sure it will, with good men, find either praise, or excuse. Your true lover,

BEN JONSON.

[1] "Yet envy not the poet whom stages feed."
[2] The Dedication and the Prologue first appeared in the folio of 1616.
[3] Omit.

PROLOGUE

Though need make many poets, and some such
As art, and nature have not bettered much;
Yet ours, for want, hath not so loved the stage,
As he dare serve the ill customs of the age,
Or purchase your delight at such a rate,
As, for it, he himself must justly hate.
To make a child, now swaddled, to proceed
Man, and then shoot up, in one beard, and weed,
Past threescore years: or, with three rusty swords,
And help of some few foot-and-half-foot words,
Fight over York, and Lancaster's long jars,
And in the tyring-house brings wounds, to scars.
He rather prays, you will be pleased to see
One such to-day, as other plays should be;
Where neither chorus wafts you o'er the seas;
Nor creaking throne comes down, the boys to please;
Nor nimble squib is seen, to make afeard
The gentlewomen; nor rolled bullet heard
To say, it thunders; nor tempestuous drum
Rumbles, to tell you when the storm doth come;
But deeds, and language, such as men do use:
And persons, such as comedy would choose,
When she would show an image of the times,
And sport with human follies, not with crimes.
Except we make 'hem such, by loving still
Our popular errors, when we know they're ill.
I mean such errors, as you'll all confess,
By laughing at them, they deserve no less:
Which when you heartily do, there's hope left then,
You, that have so graced monsters, may like men.

DRAMATIS PERSONÆ.

KNO'WELL, an old Gentleman.
EDWARD KNO'WELL, his Son.
BRAIN-WORM, the Father's Man.
Master STEPHEN, a Country Gull.
GEORGE DOWN-RIGHT, a plain Squire.
WELL-BRED, his Half-Brother.
KITELY, a Merchant, their Brother-in-law.
THOMAS CASH, his Cashier.
Captain BOBADILL, a Paul's Man.[1]
Master MATTHEW, a Town Gull.
OLIVER COB, a Water-bearer.
Justice CLEMENT, an old merry Magistrate.
ROGER FORMAL, his Clerk.

Dame KITELY, KITELY's Wife.
Mistress BRIDGET, his Sister.
TIB, COB's Wife.

WELL-BRED's Servant.   Other Servants, &c.

SCENE—LONDON.

A frequenter, as such were, of the aisle of St. Paul's.

EVERY MAN IN HIS HUMOUR.

ACT THE FIRST.

SCENE I.—*A Plot before* KNO'WELL'S *House.*

Enter KNO'WELL *from his house.*

KNO'. A goodly day toward! and a fresh
   morning.—Brain-worm,

Enter BRAIN-WORM.

    Call up your young master: bid him
    rise, sir.

    Tell him, I have some business to
    employ him.

Brai. I will, sir, presently.[1]

Kno'.   But hear you, sirrah,
If he be 't his book, disturb him not.

Brai.   Well, sir.   [*Exit.*

Kno'. How happy yet, should I esteem myself,
Could I, by any practice, wean the boy
From one vain course of study he affects.
He is a scholar, if a man may trust
The liberal voice of fame, in her report,
Of good account in both our Universities,[2]

---

[1] Immediately.   [2] Jonson was then, by grace, M.A. of both.

Either of which hath favoured him with graces :
But their indulgence must not spring in me
A fond[1] opinion that he cannot err.
Myself was once a student; and indeed,
Fed with the self-same humour, he is now,
Dreaming on nought but idle poetry,
That fruitless, and unprofitable art,
Good unto none, but least to the professors,
Which then I thought the mistress of all knowledge :
But since, time, and the truth have waked my judgment,
And reason taught me better to distinguish
The vain, from the useful learnings.

Enter STEPHEN.

                Cousin Stephen,
What news with you, that you are here so early?

Step. Nothing, but e'en come to see how you do,
    uncle.

Kno'. That's kindly done; you are welcome, coz.[2]

Step. Ay, I know that, sir; I would not ha' come else.
How does my cousin Edward, uncle?

Kno'. O, well, coz, go in and see; I doubt he be scarce
stirring yet.

Step. Uncle, afore I go in, can you tell me, an he have
e'er a book of the sciences of hawking and hunting? I
would fain borrow it.

Kno'. Why, I hope you will not a hawking now, will
    you?

Step. No, wusse ;[3] but I'll practise against next year,
uncle: I have bought me a hawk, and a hood, and bells,
and all; I lack nothing but a book to keep it by.

Kno'. O, most ridiculous !

Step. Nay, look you now, you are angry, uncle : why
you know, an a man have not skill in the hawking and

---

[1] Foolish.
[2] These two lines are not verse, but rhythmic lea ing to prose.
[3] I wis not, I do not intend.

hunting languages[1] now-a-days, I'll not give a rush for him. They are more studied than the Greek, or the Latin. He is for no gallants' company without 'hem. And by gadslid I scorn it, I, so I do, to be a consort for every humdrum; hang 'hem, scroyles,[2] there's nothing in 'hem i' the world. What do you talk on it? Because I dwell at Hogsden,[3] I shall keep company with none but the archers of Finsbury? or the citizens that come a ducking[4] to Islington ponds? A fine jest, i' faith! 'Slid, a gentleman mun[5] show himself like a gentleman. Uncle, I pray you be not angry, I know what I have to do, I trow, I am no novice.

Kno'. You are a prodigal, absurd coxcomb; go to!
Nay, never look at me, it's I that speak.
Take't as you will sir, I'll not flatter you.
Ha' you not yet found means enow, to waste
That which your friends have left you, but you must
Go cast away your money on a kite,
And know not how to keep it, when you ha' done?
O, it's comely! this will make you a gentleman!
Well, cousin, well! I see you are e'en past hope
Of all reclaim.—Ay, so, now you're told on it,
You look another way.

Step. What would you ha' me do?

Kno'. What would I have you do? I'll tell you, kinsman,
Learn to be wise, and practise how to thrive,
That would I have you do: and not to spend
Your coin on every bauble, that you fancy,
Or every foolish brain, that humours you.
I would not have you to invade each place,
Nor thrust yourself on all societies,
Till men's affections, or your own desert,
Should worthily invite you to your rank.

---

[1] The technical terms, and those of the minutiæ of action, were then insisted on.
[2] Scabs.　[3] Hoxton.　[4] Duck hunting by dogs.　[5] Must.

He, that is so respectless in his courses,
Oft sells his reputation at cheap market.
Nor would I, you should melt away yourself
In flashing bravery,[1] lest, while you affect
To make a blaze of gentry to the world,
A little puff of scorn extinguish it,
And you be left like an unsav'ry snuff,
Whose property is only to offend.
I'ld ha' you sober, and contain yourself,
Not that your sail be bigger than your boat;
But moderate your expenses now, at first,
As you may keep the same proportion still:
Nor stand so much on your gentility,
Which is an airy, and mere borrowed thing,
From dead men's dust and bones; and none of yours,
Except you make, or hold it.——Who comes here?[2]

Enter a Servant.[3]

Serv. Save you, gentlemen!

Step. Nay, we don't stand much on our gentility, friend; yet you are welcome: and I assure you, mine uncle here, is a man of a thousand a year, Middlesex land: he has but one son in all the world, I am his next heir, at the common law, Master Stephen, as simple as I stand here, if my cousin die, as there's hope he will: I have a pretty living o' mine own too, beside, hard by here.

Serv. In good time, sir.

Step. "In good time, sir?" why![4] and in very good time, sir! You do not flout, friend, do you?

Serv. Not I, sir.

Step. Not you, sir? you were not best, sir; an you should, here be them can perceive it, and that quickly too; go to. And they can give it again soundly too, an need be.

---

[1] Gaudy apparel.　　[2] He sees him before he appears on the stage.
[3] Scene ii. in old eds.
[4] He supposes him to imply that his "living" will come to him in good time.

*flashing bravery
save you, such*

Serv. Why, sir, let this satisfy you; good faith, I had no such intent.

Step. Sir, an I thought you had, I would talk[1] with you, and that presently.[2]

Serv. Good Master Stephen, so you may, sir, at your pleasure.

Step. And so I would, sir, good my saucy companion! an you were out o' mine uncle's ground, I can tell you; though I do 'not stand upon my gentility,' neither, in't.

Kno'. Cousin, cousin! will this ne'er be left?

Step. Whoreson-base fellow? a mechanical serving-man! By this cudgel, an 'twere not for shame, I would——

Kno'. What would you do, you peremptory gull?
If you cannot be quiet, get you hence.
You see the honest man demeans himself
Modestly towards you, giving no reply
To your unseasoned, quarrelling, rude fashion :
And still you huff[3] it, with a kind of carriage
As void of wit, as of humanity.
Go, get you in ; 'fore Heaven, I am ashamed
Thou hast a kinsman's interest in me.   [*Exit* STEPHEN.

Serv. I pray you,[4] sir, is this Master Kno'well's house?

Kno'. Yes, marry[5] is it, sir.

Serv. I should inquire for a gentleman here, one Master Edward Kno'well: do you know any such, sir, I pray you?

Kno'. I should forget myself else, sir.

Serv. Are you the gentleman? cry you mercy, sir: I was required by a gentleman i' the city, as I rode out at this end o' the town, to deliver you this letter, sir.

Kno'. To me, sir! What do you mean? pray you remember your court'sy.[6] [*Reads.*] "To his most selected friend, Master Edward Kno'well." What might the

---

[1] He insinuates more than talking.   [2] Immediately.
[3] Quarrellingly swagger.   [4] 2nd F. omits "you."
[5] By Mary (our Lady).   [6] Be covered.

gentleman's name be, sir, that sent it? Nay, pray you be covered.

Serv. One Master Well-bred, sir.

Kno'. Master Well-bred! a young gentleman, is he not?

Serv. The same, sir; Master Kitely married his sister— the rich merchant i' the Old Jewry.

Kno'. You say very true.—Brain-worm!

Re-enter BRAIN-WORM.

Brai. Sir.

Kno'. Make this honest friend drink here:—pray you, go in.   [*Exeunt* BRAINWORM *and* Servant.

This letter is directed to my son:
Yet I am Edward Kno'well too, and may,
With the safe conscience of good manners, use
The fellow's error to my satisfaction.
Well, I will break it ope, (old men are curious)
Be it but for the style's sake, and the phrase;
To see if both do answer my son's praises,
Who is almost grown the idolater
Of this young Well-bred:—what have we here? what's this?

[*Reads.*] Why, Ned, I beseech thee, hast thou forsworn all thy friends i' the Old Jewry? or dost thou think us all Jews that inhabit there, yet? If thou dost, come over and but see our frippery; change an old shirt for a whole smock with us. Do not conceive that antipathy between us, and Hogsden, as was between Jews, and hogs-flesh. Leave thy vigilant father alone, to number over his green apricots, evening, and morning, o' the north-west wall: an I had been his son, I had saved him the labour, long since, if taking in all the young wenches, that pass by at the back-door, and codling[1] every kernel of the fruit for 'hem, would ha' served. But, pr'ythee, come over to me quickly, this morning; I have such a present for thee!— our Turkey company never sent the like to the Grand Signior. One is a rhymer, sir, o' your own batch, you

[1] Taking out

own leaven ; but doth think him himself poet-major o'
the town[1], willing to be shown, and worthy to be seen.
The other, I will not venture his description with you, till
you come, because I would ha' you make hither with an
appetite.   If the worst of 'hem be not worth your journey,
draw your bill of charges, as unconscionable as any
Guildhall verdict will give it you, and you shall be allowed
your viaticum.[2]   From the Windmill.[3]
From the Bordello[4] it might come as well,
The Spittle, or Pict-hatch.[5]   Is this the man
My son hath sung so, for the happiest wit,
The choicest brain, the times hath sent us forth !
I know not what he may be, in the arts,
Nor what in schools ; but, surely, for his manners,
I judge him a profane and dissolute wretch ;
Worse, by possession of such great good gifts,
Being the master of so loose a spirit.
Why, what unhallowed ruffian would have writ
In such a scurrilous manner to a friend !
Why should he think I tell[6] my apricots,
Or play the Hesperian dragon with my fruit,
To watch it ?   Well, my son, I'd thought[7]
Y'd had more judgment t' have made election
Of your companions, than t' have ta'en on trust
Such petulant, jeering gamesters, that can spare
No argument, or subject from their jest.
But I perceive, affection makes a fool
Of any man, too much the father.—Brain-worm !

Re-enter BRAIN-WORM.

Brai. Sir.
Kno'.   Is the fellow gone that brought this letter ?

---

[1] Probably a hit at A. Munday.   [2] Expenses of your journey.
[3] Tavern.   [4] House of ill-fame
[5] The enforced, and the ordinary habitation of disorderly women.
[6] Number.
[7] So Q. and Ff. Gifford reads " had," and takes the " you "
from Y' of next line.

Brai. Yes, sir, a pretty while since.

Kno'. And where's your young master?

Brai. In his chamber, sir.

Kno'. He spake not with the fellow, did he?

Brai. No, sir, he saw him not.

Kno'. Take you this letter, and deliver it my son;
But with no notice that I have opened it, on your life.

Brai. O Lord, sir! that were a jest indeed.[1]   [*Exit.*

Kno'. I am resolved I will not stop his journey;
Nor practise any violent mean to stay
The unbridled course of youth in him; for that,
Restrained, grows more impatient; and in kind,
Like to the eager, but the generous[2] greyhound,
Who ne'er so little from his game withheld,
Turns head, and leaps up at his holder's throat.
There is a way of winning, more by love,
And urging of the modesty, than fear:
Force works on servile natures, not the free.
He that's compelled to goodness, may be good,
But 'tis but for that fit; where others, drawn
By softness, and example, get a habit.
Then, if they stray, but warn 'hem, and the same
They should for virtue've done, they'll do for shame.
    [*Exit.*

SCENE II.[3]—*A Room in* KNO'WELL'S *House.*

Enter E. KNO'WELL, *with a letter in his hand, followed by*
BRAIN-WORM.

E. Kn. Did he open it, say'st thou?

Brai. Yes, o' my word, sir, and read the contents.

---

[1] Another instance of rhythmic prose interposed.   Henceforth
they will not be noted.
[2] Well-bred (Lat. *generosus*).   [3] Scene iii. in old eds.

E. Kn. That scarce contents me.—What countenance, prithee, made he i' the reading of it? was he angry, or pleased?

Brai. Nay sir, I saw him not read it, nor open it, I assure your worship.

E. Kn. No? how know'st thou then, that he did either?

Brai. Marry, sir, because he charged me, on my life, to tell nobody that he opened it; which, unless he had done, he would never fear to have it revealed.

E. Kn. That's true: well, I thank thee, Brain-worm.

                          [*Moves to window to read letter.*

Enter STEPHEN.

Step. O, Brain-worm, didst thou not see a fellow here in a what-sha-call-him doublet? he brought mine uncle a letter e'en now.

Brai. Yes, Master Stephen, what of him?

Step. O, I ha' such a mind to beat him, where is he, canst thou tell?

Brai. Faith, he is not of that mind: he is gone, Master Stephen.

Step. Gone! which way? when went he? how long since?

Brai. He is rid hence; he took horse at the street-door.

Step. And I staid i' the fields! Whoreson Scanderbag rogue! Oh that I had but a horse to fetch him back again!

Brai. Why, you may ha' my master's gelding, to save your longing, sir.

Step. But I ha' no boots, that's the spite on't.

Brai. Why, a fine wisp of hay, rolled hard,[2] Master Stephen.

Step. No, faith, it's no boot to follow him now: let him e'en go and hang. 'Pray thee, help to truss me a little. He does so vex me—

---

[1] G. Castriot, the Albanian patriot. His life was translated in 1596.

[2] An ordinary rustic practice.

Brai. You'll be worse vexed when you are trussed,[1] Master Stephen. Best keep unbraced, and walk yourself till you be cold; your choler may founder you else.

Step. By my faith, and so I will, now thou tell'st me on't:—how dost thou like my leg, Brain-worm?

Brai. A very good leg, Master Stephen! but the woollen stocking does not commend it so well.

Step. Foh! the stockings be good enough, now summer is coming on, for the dust: I'll ha' a pair of silk again winter, that I go to dwell i' the town. I think my leg would show in a silk hose.[2]

Brai. Believe me, Master Stephen, rarely well.

Step. In sadness,[3] I think it would: I have a reasonable good leg.

Brai. You have an excellent good leg, Master Stephen, but I cannot stay to praise it longer now, and I am very sorry for't. [*Exit.*

Step. Another time will serve, Brain-worm. Gramercy[4] for this.

E. Kn. Ha, ha, ha!

Step. 'Slid,[5] I hope he laughs not at me; an he do—

E. Kn. Here was a letter indeed, to be intercepted by a man's father, and do him good with him! He cannot but think most virtuously, both of me, and the sender, sure, that make the careful costermonger of him in our familiar epistles. Well, if he read this with patience, I'll be gelt, and troll ballads for Master John Trundle[6] yonder, the rest of my mortality. It is true, and likely, my father may have as much patience as another man; for he takes much physic, and oft taking physic makes a man very patient. But would your packet, Master Well-bred, had arrived at him in such a minute of his patience! then we had known the end of it, which now is doubtful, and

---

1 To tie the laces that kept up the breeches—also to be beaten.
2 The same conceit is hit at in *Twelfth Night*, i. 3. l. 126-8.
3 Soberness.   4 Fr. *Grande merci* (great thanks).
5 God's lid.   6 A publisher of ballads.

threatens—[*Sees* STEPHEN.] What, my wise cousin! nay then, I'll furnish our feast with one gull more to'ard the mess.[1] He writes to me of a brace, and here's one, that's three: oh, for a fourth, Fortune! if ever thou'lt use thine eyes, I entreat thee——

Step. Oh, now I see who he laughed at: he laughed at somebody in that letter. By this good light, an he had laughed at me——

E. Kn. How now, cousin Stephen, melancholy?

Step. Yes, a little. I thought you had laughed at me, cousin.

E. Kn. Why, what an I had, coz? what would you ha' done?

Step. By this light I would ha' told mine uncle.

E. Kn. Nay, if you would ha' told your uncle, I did laugh at you, coz.

Step. Did you, indeed?

E. Kn. Yes, indeed.

Step. Why, then——

E. Kn. What then?

Step. I am satisfied; it is sufficient.

E. Kn. Why, be so, gentle coz: and, I pray you, let me entreat a courtesy of you. I am sent for, this morning, by a friend i' the Old Jewry, to come to him; it's but crossing over the fields to Moorgate: Will you bear me company? I protest, it is not to draw you into bond, or any plot against the state, coz.

Step. Sir, that's all one an 'twere; you shall command me twice so far as Moorgate, to do you good in such a matter. Do you think I would leave you? I protest—

E. Kn. No, no, you shall not protest, coz.

Step. By my fackins,[2] but I will, by your leave: I'll protest more to my friend, than I'll speak of at this time.

---

[1] Four at dinner made "a mess."

[2] An oath (by my faith?) made innocent by change of form.

E. Kn. You speak very well, coz.

Step. Nay, not so neither, you shall pardon me : but I speak to serve my turn.

E. Kn. Your turn, coz? do you know what you say? A gentleman of your sort,[1] parts, carriage, and estimation, to talk o' your turn[2] i' this company, and to me alone, like a tankard-bearer at a conduit! fie! A wight that, hitherto, his every step hath left the stamp of a great foot behind him, as every word the savour of a strong spirit ; and he ! this man ! so graced, gilded, or, to use a more fit metaphor, so tin-foiled by nature, as not ten housewives' pewter, again a good time,[3] shows more bright to the world than he ! and he ! (as I said last, so I say again, and still shall say it) this man ! to conceal such real ornaments as these, and shadow their glory, as a milliner's wife does her wrought stomacher, with a smoky lawn, or a black cypress![4] Oh, coz ! it cannot be answered ; go not about it : Drake's old ship at Deptford may sooner circle the world again. Come, wrong not the quality of your desert, with looking downward, coz ; but hold up your head, so : and let the idea of what you are, be portrayed i' your face that men may read i' your physnomy, " Here within this place is to be seen the true, rare, and accomplished monster, or miracle of nature," which is all one. What think you of this, coz?

Step. Why, I do think of it; and I will be more proud, and melancholy, and gentlemanlike, than I have been, I'll insure you.

E. Kn. Why, that's resolute, Master Stephen ! [*Aside.*] Now, if I can but hold him up to his height, as it is happily begun, it will do well for a suburb humour : we may hap have a match with the city, and play him for forty pound.—Come, coz.

Step. I'll follow you.

E. Kn. Follow me ! you must go before.

---

[1] Rank.   [2] See Cob's use of it, p. 21.
[3] Time of display.   [4] Linen crape.

Matthew a remembrance of Don Armado.

Step. Nay, an I must, I will. Pray you, show me, good cousin.   [*Exeunt.*

SCENE III.[1]—*The Lane before* COB'S *House.*

Enter MATTHEW.

Mat. I think this be the house :—what, ho ?

COB *opening door.*

Cob. Who's there ? O, Master Matthew ! give your worship good morrow.

Mat. What, Cob ? how dost thou, good Cob ? dost thou inhabit here, Cob ?

Cob. Ay, sir, I and my lineage ha' kept a poor house, here, in our days,

Mat. Thy lineage, Monsieur Cob ! what lineage, what lineage ?

Cob. Why, sir, an ancient lineage, and a princely. Mine ance'try came from a king's belly, no worse man : and yet no man neither—by your worship's leave, I did lie in that—but Herring, the king of fish (from his belly, I proceed), one o' the monarchs o' the world, I assure you. The first red herring that was broiled in Adam and Eve's kitchen, do I fetch my pedigree from, by the harrot's[2] book. His cob[3] was my great-great-mighty-great grandfather.

Mat. Why mighty ? why mighty, I pray thee ?

Cob. O, it was a mighty while ago, sir, and a mighty great cob.

Mat. How know'st thou that ?

Cob. How know I ? why, I smell his ghost, ever and anon.

---

[1] Scene iv. in old eds.
[2] Vulgar for herald's. A hit at their fabricated pedigrees.
[3] His young herring, *i.e.* his son.   *cob*

Mat. Smell a ghost! O unsavoury jest! and the ghost of a herring cob?

Cob. Ay sir: with favour of your worship's nose, Master Matthew, why not the ghost of a herring-cob, as well as the ghost of rasher-bacon?

Mat. Roger Bacon, thou would'st say.

Cob. I say, rasher-bacon. They were both broiled o' the coals; and a man may smell broiled meat, I hope? you are a scholar, upsolve me that, now.

Mat. [*Aside.*] O raw ignorance!—Cob, canst thou show me of a gentlemen, one Captain Bobadill, where his lodging is?

Cob. O, my guest, sir, you mean.

Mat. Thy guest, alas! ha, ha!

Cob. Why do you laugh, sir? Do you not mean Captain Bobadill?

Mat. Cob, 'pray thee advise thyself well: do not wrong the gentleman, and thyself too. I dare be sworn, he scorns thy house; he! He lodge in such a base, obscure place as thy house! Tut, I know his disposition so well, he would not lie in thy bed if thou'dst gi' it him.

Cob. I will not give it him, though, sir. Mass,[1] I thought somewhat was in't, we could not get him to bed, all night! Well, sir; though he lie not o' my bed, he lies o' my bench: an't please you to go up, sir, you shall find him with two cushions under his head, and his cloak wrapt about him, as though he had neither won nor lost, and yet, I warrant, he ne'er cast[2] better in his life, than he has done to-night.

Mat. Why, was he drunk?

Cob. Drunk, sir! you hear not me say so: perhaps he swallowed a tavern-token,[3] or some such device, sir; I have nothing to do withal. I deal with water and not with wine. Gi' me my tankard there, ho! [TIB *brings*

---

[1] Used as an expletive oath.   [2] To throw dice, and to throw up.
[3] A phrase intimating the same.

tankard and exit.]   God b' wi' you, sir.   It's six o'clock :
I should ha' carried two turns by this.   What ho ! my
stopple ! come.

Re-enter TIB *with stopple, and exit.*

Mat. Lie in a water-bearer's house ! a gentleman of
his havings ? Well, I'll tell him my mind. [*Enters house.*
Cob. What, Tib, show this gentleman up to the captain.
O, an my house were the Brazen-head now ! faith it
would e'en speak " Moe fools yet." [1] You should have
some now would take this Master Matthew to be a gentleman, at the least. His father's an honest man, a worshipful [2] fishmonger, and so forth ; and now does he creep and
wriggle into acquaintance with all the brave gallants about
the town, such as my guest is, (O, my guest is a fine
man !) and they flout him invincibly. He useth every
day to a merchant's house where I serve water, one
Master Kitely's, i' the Old Jewry ; and here's the jest, he
is in love with my master's sister, Mistress Bridget, and
calls her " mistress," [3] and there he will sit you a whole
afternoon sometimes, reading o' these same abominable,
vile (a pox on 'hem ! I cannot abide them,) rascally verses,
poyetry, poyetry, and speaking of enterludes, 'twill make
a man burst to hear him. And the wenches, they do so
jeer, and ti-he [4] at him—Well, should they do so much to
me, I'ld forswear them all, " by the foot of Pharaoh !"
There's an oath ! How many water-bearers shall you hear
swear such an oath ? O, I have a guest—he teaches me—
he does swear the legiblest of any man christened : " By
St. George !—the foot of Pharaoh !—the body of me !—
as I am a gentleman and a soldier !" such dainty oaths !
and withal he does take this same filthy roguish tobacco,
the finest, and cleanliest ! it would do a man good to see
the fume come forth at's tonnels. [5]—Well, he owes me
forty shillings—my wife lent him out of her purse, by six-

---

[1] A reference to Friar Bacon and his Head of Brass.
[2] "The Worshipful Company of."   [3] i.e. His lady-love.
[4] Titter, giggle.   [5] Tunnel, funnels, *i.e.* nostrils.

pence at a time—besides his lodging : I would I had it !
I shall ha' it, he says, the next action.[1] Helter skelter,
hang sorrow, care'll kill a cat, up-tails[2] all, and a louse for
the hangman.   [*Exit.*

SCENE IV.[3]—*A Room in* COB'S *House.*

BOBADILL *lying on a bench.*

Bob. Hostess, hostess !

Enter TIB.

Tib. What say you, sir ?

Bob. A cup o' thy small beer, sweet hostess.

Tib. Sir, there's a gentleman below, would speak with
you.

Bob. A gentleman ! 'odso, I am not within.

Tib. My husband told him you were, sir.

Bob. What a plague—what meant he ?

Mat. (*Below.*) Captain Bobadill !

Bob. Who's there ?—Take away the bason, good
hostess ;—Come up, sir.

Tib. [*Goes to the door.*] He would desire you to come
up, sir.—You come into a cleanly house, here !

Enter MATTHEW.

Mat. 'Save you, sir ; 'save you, captain !

Bob. Gentle Master Matthew ! Is it you, sir ? please
you to sit down.

Mat. Thank you, good captain ; you may see, I am
somewhat audacious.

Bob. Not so, sir. I was requested to supper last night
by a sort[4] of gallants, where you were wished for, and
drunk to, I assure you.

---

[1] He understands it "next term time."

[2] Cats pleased turn up their tails : also meaning glasses upside down
and therefore drained.   [3] Scene v. in old eds.   [4] Company, lot.

Mat. Vouchsafe me, by whom, good captain?

Bob. Marry, by young Well-bred, and others:—Why, hostess, a stool here, for this gentleman.

Mat. No haste, sir, 'tis very well.

Bob. Body of me! it was so late ere we parted last night, I can scarce open my eyes yet; I was but new risen, as you came: how passes the day abroad, sir? you can tell.

Mat. Faith, some half hour to seven: now, trust me, you have an exceeding fine lodging here, very neat, and private.

Bob. Ay, sir: sit down, I pray you. Master Matthew, in any case, possess no gentlemen of our acquaintance with notice of my lodging.

Mat. Who? I, sir? no.

Bob. Not that I need to care who know it, for the cabin is convenient! but in regard I would not be too popular, and generally visited, as some are.

Mat. True, captain, I conceive you.

Bob. For, do you see, sir, by the heart of valour in me, except it be to some peculiar, and choice spirits, to whom I am extraordinarily engaged, as yourself, or so, I could not extend thus far.

Mat. O Lord, sir! I resolve so.

Bob. I confess I love a cleanly, and quiet privacy, above all the tumult and roar of fortune. What new book ha' you there? What! "Go by, Hieronymo"? [1]

Mat. Ay: did you ever see it acted? is't not well penned?

Bob. Well penned? I would fain see all the poets of these times pen such another play as that was! they'll prate and swagger, and keep a stir of art and devices, when, as I am a gentleman, read 'hem, they are the most shallow, pitiful, barren fellows, that live upon the face of the earth, again.

[*While* MATTHEW *reads,* BOBADILL *makes himself ready.*

---

[1] *Hieronimo is Mad again*—often the butt of later dramatists. The line is in Act iv.

Mat. Indeed, here are a number of fine speeches in this book. "O eyes, no eyes, but fountains fraught with tears!" there's a conceit! "fountains fraught with tears!" "O life, no life, but lively form of death!" another—"O world, no world, but mass of public wrongs!" a third—"Confused and filled with murder and misdeeds!" a fourth.[1] O, the Muses! Is't not excellent? Is't not simply the best that ever you heard, captain? Ha! how do you like it?

Bob. 'Tis good.

Mat. "To thee, the purest object to my sense,
        The most refinèd essence Heaven covers,
     Send I these lines, wherein I do commence
        The happy state of turtle-billing lovers.
     If they prove rough, unpolished, harsh, and rude,
     Haste made the waste: thus, mildly, I conclude."

Bob. Nay, proceed, proceed. Where's this?

Mat. This, sir! a toy o' mine own, in my nonage; the infancy of my muses. But when will you come and see my study? good faith, I can show you some very good things, I have done of late—That boot becomes your leg passing well, captain, methinks.[2]

Bob. So, so; it's the fashion gentlemen now use.

Mat. Troth, captain, and now you speak o' the fashion, Master Well-bred's elder brother, and I, are fallen out exceedingly: this other day, I happened to enter into some discourse of a hanger,[3] which, I assure you, both for fashion, and workmanship, was most peremptory beautiful and gentlemanlike: yet he condemned, and cried it down, for the most pied and ridiculous that ever he saw.

Bob. Squire Downright, the half-brother, was't not?

Mat. Ay sir, he.

---

[1] All in Act iii. "Enter Hieronimo."

[2] With artificial arrangements, creasings, etc.

[3] Meaning here the side-strap or loop, of a sword belt, which held the dagger, or sometimes a short crooked sword. The word was also applied to the sword itself.

Bob. Hang him, rook![1] he! why he has no more judgment than a malt-horse. By St. George, I wonder you'ld lose a thought upon such an animal; the most peremptory absurd clown of Christendom, this day, he is holden. I protest to you, as I am a gentleman and a soldier, I ne'er changed words with his like. By his discourse, he should eat nothing but hay: he was born for the manger, pannier, or pack-saddle. He has not so much as a good phrase in his belly, but all old iron, and rusty proverbs: a good commodity for some smith to make hob-nails of.

Mat. Ay, and he thinks to carry it away with his manhood still, where he comes: he brags he will gi' me the bastinado, as I hear.

Bob. How! he the bastinado! how came he by that word, trow?

Mat. Nay, indeed, he said cudgel me; I termed it so, for my more grace.

Bob. That may be! for I was sure, it was none of his word: but when, when said he so?

Mat. Faith, yesterday, they say; a young gallant, a friend of mine, told me so.

Bob. By the foot of Pharaoh, an 'twere my case now, I should send him a chartel presently. The bastinado! a most proper and sufficient dependence,[2] warranted by the great Caranza.[3] Come hither, you shall chartel him; I'll show you a trick or two you shall kill him with, at pleasure, the first stoccata, if you will, by this air.

Mat. Indeed, you have absolute knowledge i' the mystery, I have heard, sir.

Bob. Of whom? of whom, ha' you heard it, I beseech you?

Mat. Troth, I have heard it spoken of divers, that you have very rare, and un-in-one-breath-utter-able skill, sir.

Bob. By Heaven, no, not I; no skill i' the earth; some small rudiments i' the science, as to know my time, dis-

---

[1] Simpleton, prater.   [2] The cause on which the duel depended.
[3] A writer on the duel, 1569.

tance, or so. I have professed it more for noblemen and
gentlemen's use, than mine own practice, I assure you.—
Hostess, accommodate us with another bed-staff [1] here
quickly. [*Enter* TIB *with a puzzled air.*] Lend us
another bed-staff—[*Exit* TIB.] the woman does not
understand the words of action.—Look you, sir: exalt
not your point above this state, at any hand, and let your
poniard maintain your defence, thus: [*Re-enter* TIB.]—
give it the gentleman, and leave us. [*Exit* TIB.] So,
sir. Come on: O, twine your body more about, that you
may fall to a more sweet, comely, gentleman-like guard.
So, indifferent. Hollow your body more, sir, thus. Now,
stand fast o' your left leg, note your distance, keep your
due proportion of time—Oh, you disorder your point most
irregularly.

Mat. How is the bearing of it now, sir?

Bob. O, out of measure ill! a well-experienced hand
would pass upon you at pleasure.

Mat. How mean you, sir, pass upon me? [2]

Bob. Why, thus, sir,—make a thrust at me—[MATTHEW
pushes at BOBADILL.] come in upon the answer, control
your point, and make a full career at the body. [3] The best-
practised gallants of the time name it the passada; a most
desperate thrust, believe it.

Mat. Well, come, sir.

Bob. Why, you do not manage your weapon with any
facility, or grace to invite me. I have no spirit to play
with you: your dearth of judgment renders you tedious.

Mat. But one venue, [4] sir.

Bob. Venue! fie; most gross denomination as ever I
heard: O, the "stoccata," while you live, sir; note that.
—Come, put on your cloak, and we'll go to some private
place, where you are acquainted; some tavern, or so—

---

[1] Staff or rod used for beating up the mattress, etc.
[2] He thinks it means, "cheat him."
[3] As he makes his replies to the thrust, he expounds them in these
words.
[4] A bout ending in a thrust; a'so a thrust.

and have a bit. I'll send for one of these fencers, and he shall breathe you, by my direction; and then, I will teach you your trick: you shall kill him with it, at the first, if you please. Why, I will learn you, by the true judgment of the eye, hand, and foot, to control any enemy's point i' the world. Should your adversary confront you with a pistol, 'twere nothing, by this hand; you should, by the same rule, control his bullet, in a line,—except it were hail-shot, and spread. What money ha' you about you, Master Matthew?

Mat. Faith, I ha' not past a two shillings or so.

Bob. 'Tis somewhat with the least; but come. We will have a bunch of radish, and salt, to taste our wine; and a pipe of tobacco to close the orifice of the stomach: and then we'll call upon young Well-bred: perhaps we shall meet the Corydon[1] his brother there, and put him to the question. [*Exeunt.*

---

[1] The country swain, or bumpkin.

ACT THE SECOND.

SCENE I.—*A Hall in* KITELY'S *House*.

Enter KITELY, CASH, *and* DOWNRIGHT.

KIT. Thomas, come hither.
  There lies a note within upon my
    desk,
  Here take my key:—it is no matter
    neither.
  Where is the boy?
      Cash. Within, sir, i'th' warehouse.

Kit. Let him tell over, straight, that Spanish gold,
And weigh it, with th' pieces of eight.[1] Do you
See the delivery of those silver stuffs
To Master Lucar. Tell him, if he will,
He shall ha' the grograns,[2] at the rate I told him,
And I will meet him on the Exchange, anon.

  Cash. Good, sir.   [*Exit.*

  Kit.   Do you see that fellow, brother Downright?

  Dow. Ay, what of him?

  Kit.   He is a jewel, brother.
I took him of a child up at my door,
And christened him, gave him mine own name, Thomas:
Since bred him at the Hospital[3]; where proving
A toward imp, I called him home, and taught him

---

[1] "The peece of eight ryals, value 8s. 6d."
[2] A ribbed and partly silk stuff.   [3] Blue Coat School.

So much, as I have made him my cashier,
And given him, who had none, a surname, Cash:
And find him, in his place, so full of faith,
That I durst trust my life into his hands.

Dow. So would not I, in any bastard's, brother,
As it is like he is, although I knew
Myself his father.   But you said y' had somewhat
To tell me, gentle brother, what is't? what is't?

Kit. Faith, I am very loath to utter it,
As fearing it may hurt your patience:
But, that I know, your judgment is of strength,
Against the nearness of affection——

Dow. What need this circumstance[1]? pray you, be
direct.

Kit. I will not say, how much I do ascribe
Unto your friendship, nor in what regard
I hold your love; but let my past behaviour,
And usage of your sister, but confirm
How well I've been affected to your——

Dow. You are too tedious; come to the matter, the
matter.

Kit. Then, without further ceremony, thus.
My brother Well-bred, sir, I know not how,
Of late is much declined in what he was,
And greatly altered in his disposition.
When he came first to lodge here in my house,
Ne'er trust me, if I were not proud of him:
Methought he bare himself in such a fashion,
So full of man, and sweetness in his carriage,
And—what was chief—it showed not borrowed in him,
But all he did, became him as his own,
And seemed as perfect, proper, and possessed,
As breath with life, or colour with the blood.
But now, his course is so irregular,
So loose, affected, and deprived of grace,
And he himself withal so far fallen off

----
[1] This staying around your matter, this beating about the bush.

From that first place, as scarce no note remains,
To tell men's judgments where he lately stood.
He's grown a stranger to all due respect,
Forgetful of his friends ; and not content
To stale himself in all societies,
He makes my house here, common as a mart,
A theatre, a public receptacle
For giddy humour, and diseasèd riot ;
And here, as in a tavern or a stews,
He and his wild associates spend their hours,
In repetition of lascivious jests,
Swear, leap, drink, dance, and revel night by night,
Control my servants ; and, indeed, what not ?

Dow. 'Sdeins,[1] I know not what I should say to him,
i' the whole world ! He values me at a cracked three-
farthings, for aught I see. It will never out o' the flesh
that's bred i' the bone. I have told him enough, one
would think, if that would serve ; but counsel to him is
as good as a shoulder of mutton to a sick horse. Well !
he knows what to trust to, for[2] George : let him spend,
and spend, and domineer, till his heart ache ; an he think
to be relieved by me, when he is got into one o' your city-
pounds, the Counters,[3] he has the wrong sow by the ear,
i' faith ; and claps his dish[4] at the wrong man's door : I'll
lay my hand o' my halfpenny, ere I part with 't to fetch
him out, I'll assure you.

Kit. Nay, good brother, let it not trouble you thus.

Dow. 'Sdeath ! he mads me, I could eat my very spur-
leathers for anger ! But, why are you so tame ? why do
not you speak to him, and tell him how he disquiets your
house ?

Kit. O, there are divers reasons to dissuade, brother,
But, would yourself vouchsafe to travail in it,
(Though but with plain and easy circumstance,)
It would, both come much better to his sense,

---

[1] God's death, or possibly God's pleasure.
[2] A corruption of "'fore." [3] Two London prisons. [4] Begs.

And savour less of stomach,[1] or of passion.
You are his elder brother, and that title
Both gives and warrants you[2] authority,
Which, by your presence seconded, must breed
A kind of duty in him, and regard :
Whereas, if I should intimate the least,
It would but add contempt, to his neglect,
Heap worse on ill, make up a pile of hatred,
That, in the rearing, would come tottering down,
And in the ruin, bury all our love.
Nay, more than this, brother ; if I should speak,
He would be ready, from his heat of humour,
And overflowing of the vapour in him,
To blow the ears of his familiars.
With the false breath, of telling what disgraces,
And low disparagements, I had put upon him.
Whilst they, sir, to relieve him in the fable,
Make their loose comments, upon every word,
Gesture, or look, I use ; mock me all over,
From my flat cap, unto my shining shoes[3] ;
And, out of their impetuous rioting phant'sies,
Beget some slander, that shall dwell with me.
And what would that be, think you ? marry, this :
They would give out—because my wife is fair,
Myself but lately married, and my sister
Here sojourning a virgin in my house—
That I were jealous !—nay, as sure as death,
That they would say : and, how that I had quarrelled
My brother purposely, thereby to find
An apt pretext to banish them my house.

Dow. Mass, perhaps so ; they're like enough to do it.

Kit. Brother, they would, believe it ; so should I,
Like one of these penurious quack-salvers,
But set the bills up, to mine own disgrace,
And try experiments upon myself ;

---

[1] Ill-humour.   [2] "Your," 2nd F.

[3] Both marks of the citizen-trader as compared with the gallant ;
the shoes were blackened.

Lend scorn and envy, opportunity
To stab my reputation and good name——

[1]*Enter* MATTHEW *struggling with* BOBADILL.

Mat. I will speak to him——

Bob. Speak to him! away! By the foot of Pharaoh,
you shall not! you shall not do him that grace.—The
time of day to you, gentleman o' the house. Is Master
Well-bred stirring?

Dow. How then? what should he do?

Bob. [*To* KITELY.] Gentleman of the house, it is to
you: is he within, sir?

Kit. He came not to his lodging to-night, sir, I assure
you.

Dow. Why, do you hear? you!

Bob. The gentleman-citizen hath satisfied me; I'll talk
to no scavenger.   [*Exeunt* BOBADILL *and* MATTHEW.

Dow. How! scavenger? stay, sir, stay!

Kit. Nay, brother Downright.

Dow. 'Heart! stand you away, an you love me.

Kit. You shall not follow him now, I pray you, brother,
Good faith you shall not; I will overrule you.

Dow. Ha! scavenger? well, go to, I say little; but,
by this good day (God forgive me I should swear), if I put
it up so, say I am the rankest cow that ever pist. 'Sdeins,
an I swallow this, I'll ne'er draw my sword in the sight of
Fleet-street again, while I live; I'll sit in a barn with
madge-howlet, and catch mice, first. Scavenger? 'heart!
—and I'll go near to fill that huge tumbrel-slop[2] of yours
with somewhat, an I have good luck: your Garagantua
breech cannot carry it away.

Kit. Oh, do not fret yourself thus; never think on't.

Dow. These are my brother's consorts, these! these
are his cam'rades, his walking mates! he's a gallant, a

---

[1] Scene ii. in old eds.
[2] Largely puffed breeches were then the fashion, and Bobadill
wore them.

cavaliero too, right hangman cut ! Let me not live, an
I could not find in my heart to swing[1] the whole ging[2] of
'hem, one after another, and begin with him first. I am
grieved it should be said, he is my brother, and take
these courses. Well, as he brews, so shall he drink, for
George, again. Yet, he shall hear on't, and that tightly
too, an I live, i' faith.

Kit. But, brother, let your reprehension, then,
Run in an easy current, not o'er-high
Carried with rashness, or devouring choler ;
But rather use the soft persuading way,
Whose powers will work more gently, and compose
The imperfect thoughts you labour to reclaim ;
More winning, than enforcing the consent.

Dow. Ay, ay, let me alone for that, I warrant you.

[*Bell rings.*

Kit. How now ! Oh,[3] the bell rings to breakfast.
Brother, I pray you go in, and bear my wife
Company till I come ; I'll but give order
For some despatch of business to my servants.

[*Exit* DOWN-RIGHT.

[4] COB *passes by with his tankard.*

Kit. What, Cob ! our maids will have you by the
   back, i' faith,
For coming so late this morning.

Cob. Perhaps so, sir ; take heed somebody have not
them by the belly, for walking so late in the evening.

[*Exit.*

Kit. Well, yet my troubled spirit's somewhat eased,
Though not reposed in that security,
As I could wish : but I must be content,
Howe'er I set a face on't to the world.

---

[1] Editors have adopted "swinge," from the Q. and Ff., but the
reference to the hangman seems to show that "swing" is preferable.
[2] Sometimes less disparaging than gang; not so here.
[3] Seems to be "Oh-h" prolonged into a dissyllable.
[4] Scene iii. in old eds.

Would I had lost this finger at a venture,
So Well-bred had ne'er lodged within my house.'
Why't cannot be, where there is such resort
Of wanton gallants, and young revellers,
That any woman should be honest long.
Is't like, that factious beauty will preserve
The public-weal of chastity, unshaken,
When such strong motives muster, and make head
Against her single peace? No, no: beware.
When mutual appetite doth meet to treat,
And spirits of one kind, and quality
Come once to parley in the pride of blood,
It is no slow conspiracy that follows.
Well, to be plain, if I but thought, the time
Had answered their affections: all the world
Should not persuade me, but I were a cuckold.
Marry, I hope they ha' not got that start;
For opportunity hath balked 'hem yet,
And shall do still, while I have eyes, and ears
To attend the impositions of my heart.
My presence shall be as an iron bar,
'Twixt the conspiring motions of desire:
Yea, every look, or glance mine eye ejects,
Shall check occasion, as one doth his slave,
When he forgets the limits of prescription.

Enter Dame KITELY *and* BRIDGET.

Dame K. Sister Bridget, pray you fetch down the rose-water above in the closet. [*Exit* BRIDGET.] — Sweet-heart, will you come in to breakfast?

Kit. An she have overheard me now!

Dame K. I pray thee, good muss,[1] we stay for you.

Kit. By Heaven, I would not for a thousand angels![2]

Dame K. What ail you, sweet-heart? are you not well? speak, good muss.

---

[1] An endearing form of "mouse."

[2] The coins are here meant. (The angel varied in value from 6s. 8d. to 10s. — *Halliwell.*)

Kit. Troth my head aches extremely on a sudden.

Dame K. [*Putting her hand to his forehead.*] Oh, the Lord !

Kit. How now ? What ?

Dame K. Alas, how it burns ! Muss, keep you warm ; good truth it is this new disease,[1] there's a number are troubled withal. For love's sake, sweet-heart, come in, out of the air.

Kit. How simple, and how subtle are her answers ! A new disease, and many troubled with it ? Why true ; she heard me, all the world to nothing.

Dame K. I pray thee, good sweet-heart, come in ; the air will do you harm, in troth.

Kit. "The air !" she has me i' the wind[2] !—Sweetheart,

I'll come to you presently ; 'twill away, I hope.

Dame K. Pray Heaven it do. [*Exit.*

Kit. A new disease ? I know not, new, or old,
But it may well be called poor mortals' plague ;
For, like a pestilence, it doth infect
The houses of the brain. First, it begins
Solely to work upon the phantasy,
Filling her seat with such pestiferous air,
As soon corrupts the judgment : and from thence,
Sends like contagion to the memory ;
Still each to other giving the infection.
Which, as a subtle vapour, spreads itself
Confusedly through every sensitive part,
Till not a thought, or motion in the mind
Be free from the black poison of suspect.
Ah ! but what misery is it to know this ?
Or, knowing it, to want the mind's erection,
In such extremes ? Well, I will once more strive,
In spite of this black cloud, myself to be,
And shake the fever off, that thus shakes me. [*Exit.*

---

[1] So called for long. Prince Henry died of it.
[2] Scents my thoughts.

SCENE II.[1]—*Moorfields.*

Enter BRAIN-WORM *like a maimed Sub-officer.*

Brain. 'Slid I cannot choose but laugh, to see myself translated thus, from a poor creature to a creator; for now must I create an intolerable sort of lies, or my present profession loses the grace: and yet the lie, to a man of my coat, is as ominous a fruit as the fico.[2] O, sir, it holds for good polity ever, to have that outwardly in vilest estimation, that inwardly is most dear to us: so much for my borrowed shape. Well, the troth is, my old master intends to follow my young master, dry-foot,[3] over Moorfields[4] to London, this morning; now I knowing of this hunting-match, or rather conspiracy, and to insinuate with my young master (for so must we that are blue waiters,[5] and men of hope and service do, or perhaps we may wear motley at the year's end, and who wears motley, you know[6]), have got me afore, in this disguise, determining here to lie in ambuscado, and intercept him in the mid-way. If I can but get his cloak, his purse, his hat, nay, any thing to cut him off, that is, to stay his journey, *Veni, vidi, vici,*[7] I may say with Captain Cæsar, I am made for ever, i' faith. Well, now must I practise to get the true garb of one of these lance-knights,[8] my arm here, and my—young master! and his cousin, Master Stephen, as I am a true counterfeit man of war, and no soldier!   [*Moves away.*

Enter E. KNO'WELL *and* STEPHEN.

E. Kn. So sir, and how then, coz?

Step. 'Sfoot! I have lost my purse, I think.

E. Kn. How! lost your purse? where? when had you it?

---

[1] Scene iv. in old eds.
[2] Our "fig for you," the thumb protruding between the closed fingers. Also the poisoned fig of Spain.
[3] By his scentless foot-prints—by guess.
[4] Then the resort of vagrants, &c.
[5] Servants then wore blue livery.
[6] Meaning, of course, the fool.   [7] I came, I saw, I conquered.
[8] The lowest officer among foot-soldiers, commanding ten men.

Step. I cannot tell ;—stay.

Brai. 'Slid, I am afeard they will know me, would I could get by them !

E. Kn. What ? ha' you it ?

Step. No ; I think I was bewitched, I—— [*Cries.*

E. Kn. Nay, do not weep the loss ; hang it, let it go.

Step. Oh, it's here : No, an it had been lost, I had not cared, but for a jet ring Mistress Mary sent me.

E. Kn. A jet ring ! O the posy, the posy ?

Step. Fine, i' faith.——

> " Though Fancy sleep,
> My love is deep."

Meaning, that though I did not fancy her, yet she loved me dearly.

E. Kn. Most excellent !

Step. And then I sent her another, and my posy was,

> " The deeper the sweeter,
> I'll be judged by St. Peter."

E. Kn. How, by St. Peter ? I do not conceive that.

Step. Marry, St. Peter, to make up the metre.

E. Kn. Well, there the saint was your good patron, he helped you at your need : thank him, thank him.

Brai. [*Aside.*] I cannot take leave on 'hem so ; I will venture, come what will. [*Comes toward them.*] Gentlemen, please you change a few crowns for a very excellent good blade here ? I am a poor gentleman, a soldier ; one that, in the better state of my fortunes, scorned so mean a refuge ; but now it is the humour of necessity, to have it so. You seem to be gentlemen well affected to martial men, else should I rather die with silence, than live with shame : however, vouchsafe to remember, it is my want speaks, not myself ; this condition agrees not with my spirit——

E. Kn. Where hast thou served ?

Brai. May it please you, sir, in all the late wars of Bohemia, Hungaria, Dalmatia, Poland, where not, sir ?

I have been a poor servitor, by sea and land, any time this fourteen years, and followed the fortunes of the best commanders in Christendom. I was twice shot at the taking of Aleppo, once at the relief of Vienna; I have been at Marseilles, Naples, and the Adriatic gulf, a gentleman-slave in the gallies, thrice, where I was most dangerously shot in the head, through both the thighs; and yet, being thus maimed, I am void of maintenance, nothing left me but my scars, the noted marks of my resolution.

Step. How will you sell this rapier, friend?

[*Takes it in his hand.*

Brai. Generous sir, I refer it to your own judgment; you are a gentleman, give me what you please.

Step. True, I am a gentleman, I know that, friend; but what though? I pray you say, what would you ask?

Brai. I assure you, the blade may become the side or thigh of the best prince, in Europe.

E. Kn. Ay, with a velvet scabbard, I think.

Step. Nay, an't be mine, it shall have a velvet scabbard, coz, that's flat; I'd not wear it as 'tis, an you would give me an angel.

Brai. At your worship's pleasure, sir: [STEPHEN *examines the blade.*] nay, 'tis a most pure Toledo.

Step. I had rather it were a Spaniard: but tell me, what shall I give you for it? An it had a silver hilt—

E. Kn. Come, come, you shall not buy it;—hold, there's a shilling, fellow; take thy rapier.

Step. Why, but I will buy it now, because you say so, and there's another shilling, fellow, I scorn to be outbidden. What, shall I walk with a cudgel, like Higginbottom,[1] and may have a rapier for money!

E. Kn. You may buy one in the city.

Step. Tut! I'll buy this i' the field, so I will; I have a mind to't, because 'tis a field rapier.—Tell me your lowest price.

E. Kn. You shall not buy it, I say.

---

[1] Probably the seditious disturber on the Earl of Shrewsbury's estates.

Step. By this money, but I will, though I give more than 'tis worth.

E. Kn. Come away, you are a fool.

Step. Friend, I am a fool, that's granted: but I'll have it, for that word's sake. Follow me, for your money.

Brai. At your service, sir.   [*Exeunt.*

SCENE III.[1]—*Another Part of Moorfields.*

Enter KNO'WELL.

Kno'. I cannot lose the thought, yet, of this letter,
Sent to my son; nor leave t' admire the change
Of manners, and the breeding of our youth
Within the kingdom, since myself was one.
When I was young, he lived not in the stews
Durst have conceived a scorn, and uttered it,
On a gray head; age was authority
Against a buffoon; and a man had then,
A certain reverence paid unto his years,
That had none due unto his life: so much
The sanctity of some prevailed for others.
But now, we all are fallen; youth, from their fear;
And age, from that which bred it, good example.
Nay, would ourselves were not the first, e'en parents,
That did destroy the hopes in our own children;
Or they not learned our vices, in their cradles,
And sucked in our ill customs, with their milk;
Ere all their teeth be born, or they can speak,
We make their palates cunning! the first words
We form their tongues with, are licentious jests!
Can it call, whore? cry, bastard? O, then, kiss it!
A witty child! can't swear? the father's darling!
Give it two plums. Nay, rather than't shall learn

---

[1] Scene v. in old eds.

No bawdy song, the mother herself will teach it!
But this is in the infancy; the days
Of the long coat: when it puts on the breeches,
It will put off all this.   Ay, it is like,
When it is gone into the bone already!
No, no; this dye goes deeper than the coat.
Or shirt, or skin; it stains into the liver,[1]
And heart, in some: and, rather than it should not,
Note, what we fathers do! look, how we live!
What mistresses we keep! at what expense!
In our sons' eyes! where they may handle our gifts,
Hear our lascivious courtships, see our dalliance,
Taste of the same provoking meats with us,
To ruin of our states!   Nay, when our own
Portion is fled, to prey on thei remainder,
We call them into fellowship of vice!
Bait 'hem with the young chamber-maid, to seal!
And teach 'hem all bad ways to buy affliction.
This is one path, but there are millions more,
In which we spoil our own, with leading them.
Well, I thank Heaven, I never yet was he
That travelled with my son, before sixteen,
To show him—the Venetian courtezans;
Nor read the grammar of cheating I had made,
To my sharp boy, at twelve; repeating still
The rule, "Get money; still, get money, boy;
No matter by what means; money will do
More, boy, than my lord's letter."   Neither have I
Dressed snails, or mushrooms curiously before him,
Perfumed my sauces, and taught him to make 'hem;
Preceding still, with my gray gluttony,
At all the ordinaries,[2] and only feared
His palate should degenerate, not his manners.
These are the trade of fathers, now; however,

---

[1] The liver, the supposed seat of fleshly love; the heart, of knowledge.
[2] Eating-houses.

My son, I hope, hath met within my threshold
None of these household precedents, which are strong,
And swift, to rape youth to their precipice.
But, let the house at home be ne'er so clean-
Swept, or kept sweet from filth, nay dust and cobwebs,
If he will live abroad with his companions,
In dung and leystals,[1] it is worth a fear:
Nor is the danger of conversing less
Than all that I have mentioned of example.

Enter BRAIN-WORM, *disguised as before.*

Brai. [*Aside.*] My master! nay, faith, have at you; I
am fleshed now, I have sped so well.—— Worshipful sir,
I beseech you, respect the estate of a poor soldier; I am
ashamed of this base course of life—God's my comfort—
but extremity provokes me to't; what remedy?

Kno'. I have not for you, now.

Brai. By the faith I bear unto truth, gentleman, it is no
ordinary custom in me, but only to preserve manhood.
I protest to you, a man I have been; a man I may be, by
your sweet bounty.

Kno'. 'Pray thee, good friend, be satisfied.

Brai. Good sir, by that hand, you may do the part of
a kind gentleman, in lending a poor soldier the price of
two cans of beer, a matter of small value; the King of
Heaven shall pay you, and I shall rest thankful: sweet
worship.——

Kno'. Nay, an you be so importunate——

Brai. Oh, tender sir! need will have its course: I was
not made to this vile use! Well, the edge of the enemy
could not have abated me so much: it's hard when a man
hath served in his prince's cause, and be thus—[*Weeps.*]
Honourable worship, let me derive a small piece of silver
from you, it shall not be given in the course of time; by
this good ground, I was fain to pawn my rapier last night

---

[1] Filth-heaps.

for a poor supper; I had sucked the hilts long before, I
am a pagan else: Sweet honour——

Kno'. Believe me, I am taken with some wonder,
To think a fellow of thy outward presence,
Should, in the frame and fashion of his mind,
Be so degenerate, and sordid-base!
Art thou a man? and sham'st thou not to beg?
To practise such a servile kind of life?
Why, were thy education ne'er so mean,
Having thy limbs, a thousand fairer courses
Offer themselves to thy election.
Either the wars might still supply thy wants,
Or service of some virtuous gentleman,
Or honest labour: nay, what can I name,
But would become thee better than to beg:
But men of thy condition feed on sloth,
As doth the beetle, on the dung she breeds in;
Not caring how the metal of your minds
Is eaten with the rust of idleness.
Now, afore me, whate'er he be, that should
Relieve a person of thy quality,
While thou insist'st in this loose desperate course,
I would esteem the sin not thine, but his.

Brai. Faith, sir, I would gladly find some other course,
if so——

Kno'. Ay,
You'ld gladly find it, but you will not seek it.

Brai. Alas, sir, where should a man seek? in the wars,
there's no ascent by desert in these days; but——and
for service, would it were as soon purchased,[1] as wished
for! the air's my comfort!—[*Sighs.*]—I know what I would
say——

Kno'. What's thy name?

Brai. Please you, Fitz-Sword, sir.

Kno'.   Fitz-Sword!

---

[1] Obtained.

Say that a man should entertain thee now,
Wouldst thou be honest, humble, just, and true?

Brai. Sir, by the place, and honour of a soldier——

Kno'. Nay, nay, I like not those affected oaths;
Speak plainly, man; what think'st thou of my words?

Brai. Nothing, sir, but wish my fortunes were as
happy, as my service should be honest.

Kno'. Well, follow me; I'll prove thee, if thy deeds
Will carry a proportion to thy words. [*Exit.*

Brai. Yes, sir, straight; I'll but garter my hose. O
that my belly were hooped now, for I am ready to burst
with laughing! never was bottle or bagpipe fuller.
Slid, was there ever seen a fox in years to betray himself
thus! now shall I be possessed of all his counsels; and,
by that conduit, my young master. Well, he is resolved
to prove my honesty; faith, and I'm resolved to prove
his patience: oh, I shall abuse him intolerably. This
small piece of service will bring him clean out of love
with the soldier, for ever. He will never come within
the sign of it, the sight of a cassock,[1] or a musket-rest[2]
again. He will hate the musters at Mile-end[3] for it, to
his dying day. It's no matter, let the world think me
a bad counterfeit, if I cannot give him the slip[4] at an
instant: why, this is better than to have staid his journey!
well, I'll follow him. Oh, how I long to be employed!
[*Exit.*

[1] A loose outer-coat.
[2] A staff that the musket rested on when taking aim.
[3] The training ground of the City-bands.
[4] A slip was a counterfeit coin.

ACT THE THIRD.

SCENE I.—*A Room in the Windmill Tavern.*

Enter MATTHEW, WELL-BRED, *and* BOBADILL.

AT. Yes faith, sir, we were at your lodg
ing to seek you, too.

    Wel. Oh, I came not there to-night

    Bob. Your brother delivered us a
much.

    Wel. Who, my brother Down-right

    Bob. He! Master Well-bred;
know not in what kind you hold me, but let me say t
you this : as sure as honour, I esteem it so much out c
the sunshine of reputation, to throw the least bear
of regard, upon such a——

    Wel. Sir, I must hear no ill words of my brother.

    Bob. I protest to you, as I have a thing to be save
about me, I never saw any gentleman-like part——

    Wel. Good captain, "faces about[1]" to some othe
discourse.

    Bob. With your leave, sir, an there were no more me
living upon the face of the earth, I should not fancy hir
by St. George !

    Mat. Troth, nor I; he is a rustical cut, I know not how
ne doth not carry himself like a gentleman of fashion.

    Wel. Oh, Master Matthew, that's a grace peculiar bu
to a few, *quos æquus amavit Jupiter.*[2]

---

[1] A then military term.
[2] "Whom impartial Jove has loved."—*Virgil.*

Mat. I understand you, sir.

Wel. No question you do, [*Aside.*] or you do not, sir.

Enter E. KNO'WELL *and* STEPHEN.

Ned Kno'well! by my soul, welcome : how dost thou, sweet spirit, my genius? 'Slid, I shall love Apollo and the mad Thespian girls the better, while I live, for this, my dear Fury; now, I see there's some love in thee. [*Lower.*] Sirrah, these be the two I writ to thee of : nay, what a drowsy humour is this now! why dost thou not speak?

E. Kn. Oh, you are a fine gallant, you sent me a rare letter!

Wel. Why, was't not rare?

E. Kn. Yes, I'll be sworn, I was ne'er guilty of reading the like; match it in all Pliny, or Symmachus' epistles, and I'll have my judgment burned in the ear for a rogue : make much of thy vein, for it is inimitable. But I mar'le[1] what camel it was, that had the carriage of it; for doubtless, he was no ordinary beast that brought it!

Wel. Why?

E. Kn. "Why," say'st thou? why, dost thou think that any reasonable creature, especially in the morning, the sober time of the day too, could have mista'en my father for me?

Wel. 'Slid, you jest, I hope?

E. Kn. Indeed, the best use we can turn it to, is to make a jest on't, now; but I'll assure you, my father had the full view o' your flourishing style, some hour before I saw it.

Wel. What a dull slave was this! but, sirrah, what said he to it, i'faith?

E. Kn. Nay, I know not what he said; but I have a shrewd guess what he thought.

Wel. What, what?

E. Kn. Marry, that thou art some strange, dissolute

---

[1] Marvel.

young fellow, and I—a grain or two better—for keeping thee company.

Wel. Tut, that thought is like the moon in her last quarter, 'twill change shortly : but, sirrah, I pray thee be acquainted with my two hang-by's here; thou wilt take exceeding pleasure in 'hem, if thou hear'st 'hem once go ; my wind-instruments; I'll wind 'hem up——But what strange piece of silence is this ? the sign of the Dumb Man ?

E. Kn. Oh, sir, a kinsman of mine, one that may make your music the fuller, an he please ; he has his humour, sir.

Wel. Oh, what is't, what is't ?

E. Kn. Nay, I'll neither do your judgment, nor his folly that wrong, as to prepare your apprehension : I'll leave him to the mercy o' your search ; if you can take him, so !

Wel. Well, Captain Bobadill, Master Matthew, 'pray you know this gentleman here ; he is a friend of mine, and one that will deserve your affection.—[*To* STEPHEN.] I know not your name, sir, but I shall be glad of any occasion to render me more familiar to you.

Step. My name is Master Stephen, sir ; I am this gentleman's own cousin, sir ; his father is mine uncle, sir : I am somewhat melancholy, but you shall command me, sir, in whatsoever is incident to a gentleman.

Bob. Sir, I must tell you this, I am no general man ; but for Master Well-bred's sake, (you may embrace it at what height of favour you please) I do communicate with you, and conceive you to be a gentleman of some parts ; I love few words.

E. Kn. And I fewer, sir ; I have scarce enow to thank you.

Mat. But are you, indeed, sir, so given to it ?

Step. Ay, truly, sir, I am mightily given to melancholy.

Mat. Oh, it's your only fine humour, sir ! your true melancholy breeds your perfect fine wit, sir. I am melancholy myself, divers times, sir, and then do I no more but take pen and paper presently, and overflow you half a score, or a dozen of sonnets at a sitting.

E. Kn. [*Aside.*] Sure he utters them then by the gross.

Step. Truly, sir, and I love such things, out of measure.

E. Kn. I'faith, better than in measure, I'll undertake.

Mat. Why, I pray you, sir, make use of my study, it's at your service.

Step. I thank you, sir, I shall be bold, I warrant you; have you a stool there to be melancholy upon?

Mat. That I have, sir, and some papers there of mine own doing, at idle hours, that you'll say there's some sparks of wit in 'hem, when you see them.

Wel. [*Aside.*] Would the sparks would kindle once, and become a fire amongst 'hem! I might see self-love burnt for her heresy.

Step. Cousin, is it well? am I melancholy enough?

E. Kn. Oh ay, excellent.

Wel. Captain Bobadill; why muse you so?

E. Kn. He is melancholy too.

Bob. Faith, sir, I was thinking of a most honourable piece of service, was performed to-morrow, being St. Mark's day, shall be some ten years now.

E. Kn. In what place, captain.

Bob. Why at the beleaguering of Strigonium,[1] where, in less than two hours, seven hundred resolute gentlemen, as any were in Europe, lost their lives upon the breach. I'll tell you, gentlemen, it was the first, but the best leaguer that ever I beheld with these eyes, except the taking in of—what do you call it,[2] last year, by the Genoways; but that, of all other, was the most fatal and dangerous exploit that ever I was ranged in, since I first bore arms before the face of the enemy, as I am a gentleman and soldier.

---

[1] Graan, retaken from Turks, 1596.
[2] Tortosa in Q., but Jonson, not having a last year's siege in 1606, makes Bobadill ridiculously pretend to forget the name.

Step. 'So[1]! I had as lief as an angel[2] I could swear as well as that gentleman!

E. Kn. Then, you were a servitor at both, it seems; at Strigonium? and "What-do-you-call't"?

Bob. O Lord, sir! by St. George, I was the first man that entered the breach; and had I not effected it with resolution, I had been slain, if I had had a million of lives.

E. Kn. 'Twas pity you had not ten; [*Aside.*] a cat's and your own, i'faith. But, was it possible?

Mat. [*Aside to* STEPHEN.] 'Pray you mark this dis-
Step. [*To him.*] So I do. [course, sir.

Bob. I assure you, upon my reputation, 'tis true, and yourself shall confess.

E. Kn. [*Aside.*] You must bring me to the rack, first.

Bob. Observe me, judicially, sweet sir; they had planted me three demi-culverins[3] just in the mouth of the breach; now, sir, as we were to give on, their master-gunner (a man of no mean skill and mark, you must think) confronts me with his linstock, ready to give fire; I, spying his intendment, discharged my petronel[4] in his bosom, and with these single arms, my poor rapier, ran violently upon the Moors that guarded the ordnance, and put 'hem pell-mell to the sword.

Wel. To the sword! to the rapier, captain.

E. Kn. Oh, it was a good figure observed, sir:—but did you all this, captain, without hurting your blade?

Bob. Without any impeach o' the earth: you shall perceive, sir. [*Shows his rapier.*] It is the most fortunate weapon that ever rid on poor gentleman's thigh. Shall I tell you, sir? You talk of Morglay, Excalibur, Durindana[5] or so; tut! I lend no credit to that is fabled of 'hem: I know the virtue of mine own, and therefore I dare, the boldlier, maintain it.

Step. I mar'le whether it be a Toledo or no.

---

[1] Godso.
[2] The coin. An attempt at a laughably incongruous speech.
[3] Nine-pounder cannon.　　　　[4] A carbine-like gun.
[5] The swords of Bevis, Arthur, and of Orlando.

Bob. A most perfect Toledo, I assure you, sir.

Step. I have a countryman of his, here.

Mat. 'Pray you, let's see, sir ; yes, faith, it is.

Bob. This a Toledo ! Pish !

Step. Why do you pish, captain ?

Bob. A Fleming, by Heaven ! I'll buy them for a guilder[1] apiece, an I would have a thousand of them.

E. Kn. How say you, cousin ? I told you thus much.

Wel. Where bought you it, Master Stephen ?

Step. Of a scurvy rogue soldier—a hundred of lice go with him—he swore it was a Toledo.

Bob. A poor provant[2] rapier, no better.

Mat. Mass, I think it be indeed, now I look on't better.

E. Kn. Nay, the longer you look on't, the worse. Put it up, put it up.

Step. Well, I will put it up ! but by—[*To himself.*] I have forgot the captain's oath, I thought to have sworn by it—an e'er I meet him——

Wel. O, it is past help now, sir ; you must have patience.

Step. Whoreson, coney-catching[3] rascal ! I could eat the very hilts for anger.

E. Kn. A sign of good digestion ! you have an ostrich-stomach, cousin.

Step. A stomach ? would I had him here, you should see, an I had a stomach.[4]

Wel. It's better as 'tis.—Come, gentlemen, shall we go ?

Enter BRAIN-WORM *disguised as before.*

E. Kn. A miracle, cousin ; look here, look here !

Step. Oh—od's lid ! By your leave, do you know me, sir ?

Brai. Ay, sir, I know you by sight.

Step. You sold me a rapier, did you not ?

Brai. Yes, marry did I, sir.

Step. You said it was a Toledo, ha ?

---

[1] The silver coin was worth 3s. 10d., the gold, 5s. 9 d.
[2] A sutler, or commissariat-provided weapon.
[3] Cheating.   [4] A stomach to beat him.

Brai. True, I did so.

Step. But it is none.

Brai. No, sir, I confess it; it is none.

Step. Do you confess it? Gentlemen, bear witness, he has confessed it:—Od's will, an you had not confessed it——

E. Kn. Oh, cousin, forbear, forbear!

Step. Nay, I have done, cousin.

Wel. Why, you have done like a gentleman; he has confessed it, what would you more?

Step. Yet, by his leave, he is a rascal, under his favour, do you see.

E. Kn. [*Aside to* WELL-BRED.] Ay, "by his leave," he is, and "under favour:" a pretty piece of civility! Sirrah, how dost thou like him?

Wel. Oh it's a most precious fool, make much on him: I can compare him to nothing more happily than a drum; for every one may play upon him.

E. Kn. No, no, a child's whistle were far the fitter.

Brai. Sir, shall I intreat a word with you?

[*They move apart.*

E. Kn. With me, sir? you have not another Toledo to sell, ha' you?

Brai. You are conceited,[1] sir: Your name is Master Kno'well, as I take it?

E. Kn. You are i' the right; you mean not to proceed in the catechism, do you?

Brai. No, sir; I am none of that coat.

E. Kn. Of as bare a coat, though: well, say sir.

Brai. Faith, sir, I am but servant to the drum extraordinary, and indeed, this smoky varnish being washed off, and three or four patches removed, I appear—your worship's in reversion, after the decease of your good father, Brain-worm.

E. Kn. Brain-worm! 'Slight, what breath of a conjurer hath blown thee hither in this shape?

Brai. The breath o' your letter, sir, this morning; the

---

[1] Full of pleasant conceits.

same that blew you to the Windmill, and your father after you.

E. Kn. My father?

Brai. Nay, never start, 'tis true; he has followed you over the fields by the foot, as you would do a hare i' the snow.

E. Kn. Sirrah Well-bred, what shall we do, sirrah? my father is come over, after me.

Wel. Thy father! Where is he?

Brai. At Justice Clement's house here, in Coleman-street, where he but stays my return; and then——.

Wel. Who's this? Brain-worm!

Brai. The same, sir.

Wel. Why how, in the name of wit, com'st thou transmuted thus?

Brai. Faith, a device, a device;—nay, for the love of reason, gentleman, and avoiding the danger, stand not here; withdraw, and I'll tell you all.

Wel. But, art thou sure, he will stay thy return?

Brai. Do I live, sir? what a question is that!

Wel. We'll prorogue his expectation, then, a little: Brain-worm, thou shalt go with us.——Come on, gentlemen.——Nay, I pray thee, sweet Ned, droop not; 'heart, an our wits be so wretchedly dull, that one old plodding brain can outstrip us all, would we were e'en pressed[1] to make porters of, and serve out the remnant of our days in Thames-street, or at Custom-house key, in a civil war against the carmen!

Brai. Amen, Amen, Amen, say I.   [*Exeunt.*

SCENE II.[2]—KITELY'S *Warehouse.*

Enter KITELY *and* CASH.

Kit. What says he, Thomas? Did you speak with him? *Cash.* He will expect you, sir, within this half-hour.

---

[1] Impressed.   [2] Scene iii. in old eds.

Kit. Has he the money ready, can you tell?

Cash. Yes, sir, the money was brought in, last night.

Kit. O, that is well; fetch me my cloak, my cloak!—

　　　　　　　　　　　　　　　　　　[*Exit* CASH.

Stay, let me see, an hour, to go and come;

Ay, that will be the least; and then 'twill be

An hour, before I can despatch with him,

Or very near: well, I will say two hours.

Two hours? ha! things never dreamt of yet,

May be contrived, ay, and effected too,

In two hours' absence; well, I will not go.

Two hours! No, fleering Opportunity,

I will not give your subtilty that scope.

Who will not judge him worthy to be robbed,

That sets his doors wide open to a thief,

And shows the felon, where his treasure lies?

Again, what earthy spirit but will attempt

To taste the fruit of beauty's golden tree,

When leaden sleep seals up the dragon's eyes?

I will not go.

　　　　　　Re-enter CASH *with cloak.*

　　　　Business, "go by" for once.

No, beauty, no; you are of too good caract,[1]

To be left so, without a guard, or open!

Your lustre too, 'll inflame, at any distance,

Draw courtship to you, as a Jet doth straws;

Put motion in a stone, strike fire from ice,

Nay, make a porter leap you, with his burden.

You must be then kept up, close, and well watched,

For, give you opportunity, no quick-sand

Devours, or swallows swifter! He that lends

His wife—if she be fair—or time, or place,

Compels her to be false. I will not go.

The dangers are too many.—And then the dressing

Is a most main attractive! Our great heads,

Within the city, never were in safety,

　　　[1] Carat, equivalent to quality, value.

Since our wives wore these little caps : I'll change 'hem ;
I'll change 'hem straight, in mine : mine shall no more
Wear three-piled[1] acorns, to make my horns ache.
Nor will I go. I am resolved for that.
Carry in my cloak again.—Yet stay.—Yet do, too :
I will defer going, on all occasions.

Cash. Sir, Snare, your scrivener, will be there with th'
bonds.

Kit. That's true ! fool on me ! I had clean forgot it ;
I must go. What's a-clock ?

Cash.   Exchange-time, sir.

Kit. 'Heart, then will Well-bred presently be here, too,
With one or other of his loose consorts.
I am a knave, if I know what to say,
What course to take, or which way to resolve.
My brain, methinks, is like an hour-glass,
Wherein my imaginations run like sands,
Filling up time ; but then are turned, and turned :
So that I know not what to stay upon,
And less, to put in act.—It shall be so.
Nay, I dare build upon his secrecy,
He knows not to deceive me.—Thomas !

Cash.   Sir.

Kit. Yet now I have bethought me too, I will not.—
Thomas, is Cob within ?

Cash.   I think he be, sir.

Kit. But he'll prate too, there is no speech of him.
No, there were no man o' the earth to Thomas,
If I durst trust him ; there is all the doubt.
But, should he have a chink in him, I were gone,
Lost i' my fame for ever, talk for th' Exchange !
The manner he hath stood with, till this present,
Doth promise no such change ! what should I fear then ?
Well, come what will, I'll tempt my fortune, once.
Thomas—you may deceive me, but, I hope—
Your love to me is more——

---

[1] Therefore of best quality velvet.

Cash.   Sir, if a servant's
Duty, with faith, may be called love, you are
More than in hope,—you are possessed of it.

Kit. I thank you, heartily, Thomas: gi' me your hand:
With all my heart,[1] good Thomas.   I have, Thomas,
A secret to impart, unto you——but,
When once you have it, I must seal your lips up:——
So far I tell you, Thomas.

Cash.   Sir, for that——

Kit. Nay, hear me out.   Think, I esteem you, Thomas,
When I will let you in, thus, to my private.
It is a thing sits nearer to my crest,
Than thou art 'ware of, Thomas.   If thou should'st
Reveal it, but——

Cash.   How ! I reveal it ?

Kit.   Nay,
I do not think thou would'st; but if thou should'st:
'Twere a great weakness.

Cash.   A great treachery :
Give it no other name.

Kit.   Thou wilt not do't, then ?

Cash. Sir, if I do, mankind disclaim me ever !   [tion,

Kit. [*Aside.*] He will not swear, he has some reserva-
Some concealed purpose, and close meaning, sure ;
Else, being urged so much, how should he choose
But lend an oath to all this protestation ?
He's no precisian, that I am certain of,
Nor rigid Roman Catholic.   He'll play
At fayles, and tick-tack :[2] I have heard him swear.
What should I think of it ? urge him again,
And by some other way ? I will do so.——
Well, Thomas, thou hast sworn not to disclose :—
Yes, you did swear ?

Cash.   Not yet, sir, but I will,
Please you——

---

[1] Said as Kitely gives his own hand.
[2] Varieties of back-gammon.

Kit.   No, Thomas, I dare take thy word,
But; if thou wilt swear, do as thou think'st good;
I am resolved without it;—at thy pleasure.

Cash. By my soul's safety then, sir, I protest,
My tongue shall ne'er take knowledge of a word
Delivered me in nature of your trust.

Kit. It's too much; these ceremonies need not:
I know thy faith to be as firm as rock.
Thomas, come hither, near; we cannot be
Too private in this business. So it is,——
[*Aside.*] Now he has sworn, I dare the safelier venture.—
I have of late, by divers observations—
[*Aside.*] But, whether his oath can bind him, yea, or no,
Being not taken lawfully? ha?—say you?—
[*Aside.*] I will ask counsel, ere I do proceed——
Thomas, it will be now too long to stay,
I'll spy some fitter time soon, or to-morrow.

Cash. Sir, at your pleasure.

Kit.   I will think:—and, Thomas,
I pray you search the books 'gainst my return,
For the receipts 'twixt me, and Traps.

Cash.   I will, sir.

Kit. And hear you, if your mistress' brother, Well-bred,
Chance to bring hither any gentlemen,
Ere I come back; let one straight bring me word.

Cash. Very well, sir.

Kit.   To the Exchange, do you [1] hear?
Or here in Coleman-street, to Justice Clement's.
Forget it not, nor be not out of the way.

Cash. I will not, sir.

Kit.   I pray you have a care on't.
Or, whether he come or no, if any other,
Stranger, or else; fail not to send me word.

Cash. I shall not, sir.

Kit.   Be't your special business
Now to remember it.

---

[1] Should be pronounced, I think, "d'ye."

Cash.   Sir, I warrant you.

Kit. But, Thomas, this is not the secret, Thomas,
I told you of.

Cash.   No, sir; I do suppose it.

Kit. Believe me, it is not.

Cash.   Sir, I do believe you.

Kit. By Heaven it is not, that's enough. But, Thomas,
I would not, you should utter it, do you see,
To any creature living,—yet, I care not.
Well, I must hence. Thomas, conceive thus much;
It was a trial of you, when I meant
So deep a secret to you, I mean not this,
But that I have to tell you; this is nothing, this.
But, Thomas, keep this from my wife, I charge you,
Locked up in silence, midnight, buried here.—
                                   [*Touches his temple.*

[*Aside.*] No greater hell than to be slave to fear. [*Exit.*

Cash. "Locked up in silence, midnight, buried here!"
Whence should this flood of passion, trow, take head? ha?
Best dream no longer of this running humour,
For fear I sink! the violence of the stream
Already hath transported me so far,
That I can feel no ground at all! but soft—
Oh,'tis our water-bearer: somewhat has crossed him now.

[1]*Enter* COB.

Cob. Fasting-days! what tell you me of fasting-days?
'Slid, would they were all on a light fire for me! They
say the whole world shall be consumed with fire one day,
but would I had these Ember-weeks and villanous Fri-
days burnt, in the mean time, and then——

Cash. Why, how now, Cob? what moves thee to this
choler, ha?

Cob. Collar, Master Thomas! I scorn your collar, I,
sir, I am none o' your cart-horse, though I carry and
draw water. An you offer to ride me, with your collar,

---
[1] Scene iv. in old eds.

or halter either, I may hap show you a jade's trick, sir.

Cash. O, you'll slip your head out of the collar? why, goodman Cob, you mistake me.

Cob. Nay, I have my rheum,[1] and I can be angry as well as another, sir.

Cash. Thy rheum, Cob? thy humour, thy humour—thou mistak'st.

Cob. Humour! mack,[2] I think it be so indeed; what is that humour? some rare thing, I warrant.

Cash. Marry, I'll tell thee, Cob: it is a gentleman-like monster, bred in the special gallantry of our time, by affectation; and fed by folly.

Cob. How! must it be fed?

Cash. Oh ay, humour is nothing, if it be not fed. Did'st thou never hear that? it's a common phrase, "Feed my humour."

Cob. I'll none on it: humour, avaunt! I know you not, be gone! Let who will make hungry meals for your monstership, it shall not be I. Feed you, quoth he! 'slid, I ha' much ado to feed myself; especially on these lean rascally days, too; an't had been any other day but a fasting-day—a plague on them all for me—by this light, one might have done the commonwealth good service, and have drowned them all i' the flood, two or three hundred thousand years ago. O, I do stomach[3] them hugely. I have a maw[4] now, an 'twere for Sir Bevis his horse, against 'hem.

Cash. I pray thee, good Cob, what makes thee so out of love with fasting-days?

Cob. Marry, that which will make any man out of love with 'hem, I think: their bad conditions, an you will needs know. First, they are of a Flemish breed, I am sure on't, for they ravin up more butter than all the days of the

---

[1] He was not up in the four humours, but may have heard that "some fleame is salt hot and dry through infection of red choler."

[2] The innocent substitute for "mass."

[3] Am angry with. [4] Stomach, *i.e.* appetite.

week beside: next, they stink of fish, and leek-porridge
miserably: thirdly, they'll keep a man devoutly hungry,
all day, and at night send him supperless to bed.

Cash. Indeed, these are faults, Cob.

Cob. Nay, an this were all, 'twere something, but they
are the only known enemies to my generation. A fasting-day no sooner comes, but my lineage goes to wrack;
poor cobs! they smoke for it, they are made martyrs o'
the gridiron, they melt in passion: and your maids too
know this, and yet would have me turn Hannibal,[1] and
eat my own fish and blood. My princely coz, [*Pulls out
a red herring.*] fear nothing; I have not the heart to devour
you, an I might be made as rich as King Cophetua. Oh,
that I had room for my tears, I could weep salt-water
enough now to preserve the lives of ten thousand of my
kin. But I may curse none but these filthy almanacs;
for an't were not for them, these days of persecution would
ne'er be known. I'll be hanged, an some fishmonger's
son do not make of 'hem, and puts in more fasting-days
than he should do, because he would utter[2] his father's
dried stock-fish and stinking conger.

Cash. 'Slight peace! thou'lt be beaten like a stock-fish[3]
else; here's Master Matthew. [*Aside.*] Now must I look
out for a messenger to my master.   [*Exit with* COB.

[4]*Enter* WELL-BRED, E. KNO'WELL, BRAIN-WORM, MAT-
THEW, BOBADILL, *and* STEPHEN.

Wel. Beshrew me, but it was an absolute good jest,
and exceedingly well carried!

E. Kn. Ay, and our ignorance maintained it as well,
did it not?

Wel. Yes faith; but was 't possible thou shouldst not
know him? I forgive Master Stephen, for he is stupidity
itself.

---

[1] He would say "cannibal."   [2] Send out, sell.
[3] Stock-fish was so hard salted, &c., that it had to be beaten
before being cooked.   [4] Scene v. in old eds.

E. Kn. 'Fore God, not I, an I might have been joined patten[1] with one of the Seven Wise Masters for knowing him. He had so writhen himself into the habit of one of your poor infantry, your decayed, ruinous, worm-eaten gentlemen of the round[2]; such as have vowed to sit on the skirts of the city, let your provost and his half-dozen of halberdiers do what they can; and have translated begging, out of the old hackney pace to a fine easy amble, and made it run as smooth off the tongue as a shove-groat shilling.[3] Into the likeness of one of these reformados[4] had he moulded himself so perfectly, observing every trick of their action, as, varying the accent, swearing with an emphasis, indeed, all, with so special and exquisite a grace, that, hadst thou seen him, thou wouldst have sworn he might have been sergeant-major,[5] if not lieutenant-colonel to the regiment.

Wel. Why, Brain-worm, who would have thought thou hadst been such an artificer?

E. Kn. An artificer? an architect! Except a man had studied begging all his life time, and been a weaver of language from his infancy, for the clothing of it, I never saw his rival.

Wel. Where got'st thou this coat, I mar'le?

Brai. Of a Hounsditch man, sir, one of the devil's near kinsmen, a broker.

Wel. That cannot be, if the proverb hold, for "A crafty knave needs no broker."

Brai. True, sir; but I did "need a broker," ergo—

Wel. Well put off;—"no crafty knave," you'll say.

E. Kn. Tut, he has more of these shifts.

Brai. And yet, where I have one the broker has ten,[6] sir.

---

[1] Joined by a patent.
[2] Sub-officers of the guard inspecting sentinels, &c.
[3] A smooth shilling used at shovel-board.
[4] Disbanded officers.   [5] The then major.
[6] A pun: devices, and shifts of apparel.

Re-enter Cash.

Cash. Francis ! Martin ! ne'er a one to be found, now ? what a spite's this !

Wel. How now, Thomas ? is my brother Kitely within ?

Cash. No sir, my master went forth e'en now ; but Master Down-right is within.—Cob ! what, Cob ! Is he gone too ?

Wel. Whither went your master ? Thomas, canst thou tell ?

Cash. I know not ; to Justice Clement's, I think, sir— Cob !   [*Exit.*

E. Kn. Justice Clement ! what's he ?

Wel. Why, dost thou not know him ? He is a city-magistrate, a justice here, an excellent good lawyer, and a great scholar ; but the only mad, merry old fellow in Europe. I showed him you, the other day.

E. Kn. Oh, is that he ? I remember him now. Good faith, and he has a very strange presence, methinks ; it shows as if he stood out of the rank from other men : I have heard many of his jests i' the University. They say, he will commit a man for taking the wall of his horse.

Wel. Ay, or wearing his cloak of one shoulder, or serving of God ; any thing, indeed, if it come in the way of his humour.

Cash *comes in and out, calling.*

Cash. Gasper !—Martin !—Cob ! 'Heart, where should they be, trow ?

Bob. Master Kitely's man, pray thee vouchsafe us the lighting of this match.

Cash. [*Aside after taking it.*] Fire on your match ! no time but now to "vouchsafe" ?—Francis !—Cob ! [*Exit.*

Bob. Body o' me ! here's the remainder of seven pound, since yesterday was seven-night. 'Tis your right Trini-dado ! did you never take any, Master Stephen ?

Step. No truly, sir ; but I'll learn to take it now, since you commend it so.

Bob. Sir, believe me, upon my relation, for what I tell you, the world shall not reprove. I have been in the Indies, where this herb grows, where neither myself, nor a dozen gentlemen more, of my knowledge, have received the taste of any other nutriment in the world, for the space of one and twenty weeks, but the fume of this simple only: therefore, it cannot be, but 'tis most divine! Further, take it in the nature, in the true kind, so, it makes an antidote, that, had you taken the most deadly poisonous plant in all Italy, it should expel it, and clarify you, with as much ease, as I speak. And for your green wound, your Balsamum and your St. John's wort, are all mere gulleries, and trash to it, especially your Trinidado: your Nicotian is good too. I could say what I know of the virtue of it, for the expulsion of rheums, raw humours, crudities, obstructions, with a thousand of this kind; but I profess myself no quacksalver. Only thus much, by Hercules, I do hold it, and will affirm it, before any prince in Europe, to be the most sovereign, and precious weed, that ever the earth tendered to the use of man.

E. Kn. This speech would ha' done decently in a tobacco-trader's mouth.

Re-enter CASH *with* COB.

Cash. At Justice Clement's he is, in the middle of Coleman Street.

Cob. Oh, oh!

Bob. Where's the match I gave thee, Master Kitely's man?

Cash. [*Aside.*] Would his match, and he, and pipe, and all, were at Sancto Domingo! I had forgot it.   [*Exit.*

Cob. By Gods me, I mar'le what pleasure or felicity they have in taking this roguish tobacco! it's good for nothing but to choke a man, and fill him full of smoke, and embers: there were four died out of one house, last week, with taking of it, and two more the bell went for, yesternight; one of them, they say, will ne'er scape it: he

voided a bushel of soot yesterday, upward, and downward.[1]
By the stocks, an there were no wiser men than I, I'ld
have it present whipping, man, or woman, that should but
deal with a tobacco pipe : why, it will stifle them all in
the end, as many as use it ; it's little better than ratsbane,[2]
or rosaker.[3]   [BOBADILL *cudgels him.*

All. Oh, good captain, hold, hold !

Bob. You base cullion,[4] you !

Re-enter CASH.

Cash. Sir, here's your match.——Come, thou must
needs be talking too, thou'rt well enough served.

Cob. Nay, he will not meddle with his match, I warrant
you : well, it shall be a dear beating, an I live.

Bob. Do you prate ? do you murmur ?

E. Kn. Nay, good captain, will you regard the humour
of a fool ?——Away, knave.

Wel. Thomas, get him away.   [*Exit* CASH *with* COB.

Bob. A whoreson filthy slave, a dung-worm, an excrement ! Body o' Cæsar, but that I scorn to let forth so
mean a spirit, I'ld ha' stabbed him to the earth.

Wel. Marry, the law forbid, sir.

Bob. By Pharaoh's foot, I would have done it.

Step. [*To himself.*] Oh, he swears most admirably ! "By
Pharaoh's foot !"—"Body o' Cæsar !" I shall never do
it, sure. " Upon mine honour, and by St. George !"—No,
I ha' not the right grace.

Mat. Master Stephen, will you any ? By this air, the
most divine tobacco that ever I drunk.[5]

Step. None, I thank you, sir. [*To himself.*] O, this
gentleman does it rarely too : but nothing like the other.
[*Practising to the post.*] " By this air !"—"As I am a
gentleman !" " By——

---

[1] An exaggerated form of King James's statement.
[2] White arsenic.
[3] The proto-sulphuret of the same.
[4] Cowardly stinkard.
[5] The then common phrase.

Brai. [*Pointing to* STEPHEN.] Master, glance, glance!
—Master Well-bred! [*Exeunt* BOBADILL *and* MATTHEW.[1]

Step. "As I have somewhat to be saved, I protest—"

Wel. [*Aside.*] You are a fool; it needs no affidavit.

E. Kn. Cousin, will you any tobacco?

Step. I, sir! Upon my reputation——

E. Kn. How now, cousin!

Step. I protest, as I am a gentlemen, but no soldier, indeed——

Wel. No, Master Stephen? As I remember, your name is entered in the artillery-garden.

Step. Ay, sir, that's true. Cousin, may I swear, "as I am a soldier" by that?

E. Kn. O yes, that you may: it's all you have for your money.

Step. Then, as I am a gentleman, and a soldier, it is "divine tobacco!"

Wel. But soft, where's Master Matthew? Gone?

Brai. No, sir, they went in here.

Wel. O, let's follow them: Master Matthew is gone to salute his mistress in verse. We shall have the happiness to hear some of his poetry now. He never comes unfurnished.—Brain-worm!

Step. Brain-worm? Where? Is this Brain-worm?

E. Kn. Ay, cousin; no words of it, upon your gentility.

Step. Not I, body o' me! By this air! St. George! and the foot of Pharaoh!

Wel. Rare! your cousin's discourse is simply drawn out with oaths.

E. Kn. 'Tis larded with 'hem; a kind of French dressing, if you love it. [*Exeunt.*

Here, or during the next two or three speeches.

SCENE III.[1] — *A Room in* Justice CLEMENT'S *House.*

Enter KITELY *and* COB.

Kit. Ha! how many are there, say'st thou?

Cob. Marry, sir, your brother, Master Well-bred——

Kit. Tut, beside him: what strangers are there, man?

Cob. Strangers? let me see, one, two;—mass, I know not well, there are so many.

Kit. How! so many?

Cob. Ay, there's some five or six of them, at the most.

Kit. [*Aside.*] A swarm, a swarm!
Spite of the devil, how they sting my head
With forkèd stings, thus wide and large!——But, Cob,
How long hast thou been coming hither, Cob?

Cob. A little while, sir.

Kit.   Didst thou come running?

Cob.   No, sir.

Kit. [*Aside.*] Nay, then I am familiar with thy haste!
Bane to my fortunes; what meant I to marry?
I, that before was ranked in such content,
My mind at rest too, in so soft a peace,
Being free master of mine own free thoughts,
And now become a slave? What? never sigh,
Be of good cheer, man; for thou art a cuckold,
'Tis done, 'tis done! nay, when such flowing store,
Plenty itself, falls in my wife's[2] lap,
The cornucopiæ will be mine, I know.——But, Cob,
What entertainment had they? I am sure
My sister, and my wife would bid them welcome: ha?

Cob. Like enough, sir; yet I heard not a word of it.

Kit. No; their lips were sealed with kisses, and the voice—
Drowned in a flood of joy, at their arrival——
Had lost her motion, state, and faculty.——
Cob, which of them was't that first kissed my wife?

---

1 Scene vi. in old eds.
2 " Wives," Q. and Ff., seems to be used as a dissyllable.

My sister, I should say; my wife, alas!
I fear not her: ha? who was it, say'st thou?

Cob. By my troth, sir, will you have the troth of it?

Kit. Oh ay, good Cob, I pray thee, heartily.

Cob. Then I am a vagabond, and fitter for Bridewell
than your worship's company, if I saw any body to be
kissed, unless they would have kissed the post,[1] in the
middle of the warehouse; for there I left them all, at their
tobacco, with a pox!

Kit. How? were they not gone in, then, ere thou cam'st?

Cob. O no, sir.

Kit. Spite of the devil! what do I stay here then? Cob,
follow me.   [*Exit.*

Cob. Nay, soft and fair; I have eggs on the spit[2]; I
cannot go yet, sir. Now am I, for some five and fifty
reasons, hammering, hammering revenge: oh, for three
or four gallons of vinegar, to sharpen my wits! Revenge,
vinegar revenge, vinegar and mustard revenge! Nay, an
he had not lien in my house, 'twould never have grieved
me, but being my guest, one, that I'll be sworn, my wife
has lent him her smock off her back, while his one shirt
has been at washing; pawned her neck-kerchers for
clean bands for him; sold almost all my platters, to buy
him tobacco; and he to turn monster of ingratitude, and
strike his lawful host! well, I hope to raise up an host of
fury for't: here comes Justice Clement.

Enter CLEMENT, KNO'WELL, *and* FORMAL.

Clem. What's Master Kitely gone? Roger?

Form. Ay, sir.

Clem. 'Heart of me! what made him leave us so abruptly?—How now, sirrah? what make you here? what
would you have, ha?

Cob. An't please your worship, I am a poor neighbour
of your worship's——

---

[1] An attempted witticism, for it meant, to be shut out from meals.
[2] Work to do.

Clem. A poor neighbour of mine! why, speak, poor neighbour.

Cob. I dwell, sir, at the sign of the Water-tankard, hard by the Green Lattice: I have paid scot and lot[1] there, any time this eighteen years.

Clem. To the Green Lattice?

Cob. No, sir, to the parish: marry, I have seldom scaped scot-free at the Lattice.

Clem. O, well! what business has my poor neighbour with me?

Cob. An't like your worship, I am come, to crave the peace of your worship.

Clem. Of me, knave? Peace of me, knave! Did I ever hurt thee? or threaten thee? or wrong thee, ha?

Cob. No, sir, but your worship's warrant for one that has wronged me, sir; his arms are at too much liberty, I would fain have them bound to a treaty of peace, an my credit could compass it with your worship.

Clem. Thou goest far enough about for't, I'm sure.

Kno'. Why, dost thou go in danger of thy life for him, friend?

Cob. No, sir; but I go in danger of my death every hour, by his means; an I die within a twelve-month and a day, I may swear, by the law of the land, that he killed me.

Clem. How? how, knave? swear he killed thee? and by the law? What pretence? what colour hast thou for that?

Cob. Marry, an't please your worship, both black, and blue; colour enough, I warrant you. I have it here, to show your worship.   [*Bares his arm.*

Clem. What is he, that gave you this, sirrah?

Cob. A gentleman, and a soldier, he says, he is, o' the city here.

Clem. A soldier o' the city! What call you him?

Cob. Captain Bobadill.

Clem. Bobadill! and why did he bob,[2] and beat you,

---

[1] Portion and charge, *i.e.* rates, taxes, &c.   [2] Strike.

sirrah? How began the quarrel betwixt you, ha? speak truly, knave, I advise you.

Cob. Marry, indeed, an't please your worship, only because I spake against their vagrant tobacco, as I came by 'hem when they were taking on't; for nothing else.

Clem. Ha! you speak against tobacco? Formal, his name.

Form. What's your name, sirrah?

Cob. Oliver, sir, Oliver Cob, sir.

Clem. Tell Oliver Cob, he shall go to the jail, Formal.

Form. Oliver Cob, my master, Justice Clement says, you shall go to the jail.

Cob. O, I beseech your worship, for God's sake, dear Master Justice!

Clem. Nay God's precious! an such drunkards, and tankards as you are, come to dispute of tobacco once, I have done: Away with him!

Cob. O, good Master Justice! [*To* KNO'WELL.] Sweet old gentleman!

Kno'. "Sweet Oliver,"[1] would I could do thee any good!—Justice Clement, let me intreat you, sir.

Clem. What? a thread-bare rascal! a beggar! a slave that never drunk out of better than piss-pot metal[2] in his life! and he to deprave and abuse the virtue of an herb so generally received in the courts of princes, the chambers of nobles, the bowers of sweet ladies, the cabins of soldiers!— Roger, away with him! By God's precious—[COB *would implore.*]—I say, go to.

Cob. Dear Master Justice, let me be beaten again, I have deserved it; but not the prison, I beseech you.

Kno'. Alas, poor Oliver!

Clem. Roger, make him a warrant.—he shall not go, I but fear[3] the knave.

---

[1] A song commenced thus, and the epithet was also applied to the Oliver of the twelve Peers of France

[2] Pewter.

[3] Make him to fear.

Form. Do not stink, sweet Oliver, you shall not go ; my master will give you a warrant.

Cob. O, the Lord maintain his worship, his worthy worship !

Clem. Away, dispatch him. [*Exeunt* FORMAL with COB.] How now, Master Kno'well, in dumps, in dumps ! Come, this becomes not.

Kno'. Sir, would I could not feel my cares——

Clem. Your cares are nothing : they are like my cap, soon put on, and as soon put off. What ! your son is old enough to govern himself ; let him run his course, it's the only way to make him a staid[1] man. If he were an unthrift, a ruffian, a drunkard, or a licentious liver, then you had reason ; you had reason to take care : but being none of these, mirth's my witness, an I had twice so many cares as you have, I'ld drown them all in a cup of sack.[2] Come, come, let's try it [*Takes some.*] : I muse your parcel of a soldier returns not all this while. [*Exeunt.*

---

[1] A pun, stayed.   [2] A white wine, generally sherry.

ACT THE FOURTH.

SCENE I.—*A Room in* KITELY'S *House.*

Enter DOWN-RIGHT *and* Dame KITELY,

OWN. Well, sister, I tell you true; and you'll find it so in the end.

Dame K. Alas, brother, what would you have me to do? I cannot help it; you see my brother brings 'hem in here; they are his friends.

Down. His friends? his fiends. 'Slud! they do nothing but haunt him, up and down like a sort of unlucky sprites, and tempt him to all manner of villany that can be thought of. Well, by this light, a little thing would make me play the devil with some of 'hem: an 'twere not more for your husband's sake than anything else, I'ld make the house too hot for the best on 'hem: they should say and swear, hell were broken loose, ere they went hence. But, by God's will, 'tis nobody's fault but yours; for an you had done, as you might have done, they should have been perboiled,[1] and baked too, every mother's son, ere they should ha' come in, e'er a one of 'hem.

Dame K. God's my life! did you ever hear the like? what a strange man is this! Could I keep out all them, think you? I should put myself against half a dozen men, should I? Good faith, you'ld mad the patient'st

---

[1] Boiled through and through. Not parboiled.

body in the world, to hear you talk so, without any sense
or reason !

[1]*Enter* Mistress BRIDGET, *with* Master MATTHEW, *and*
  BOBADILL ; *followed, at a little distance, by* WELL-BRED,
  E. KNO'WELL, STEPHEN, *and* BRAIN-WORM.

Brid. Servant, in troth, you are too prodigal
Of your wit's treasure, thus to pour it forth
Upon so mean a subject, as my worth !

Mat. You say well, mistress ; and I mean as well.

Down. Hoy-day, here is stuff !

Wel. O, now stand close[2] ; pray Heaven, she can get
him to read ! He should do it, of his own natural impu-
dency.

Brid. Servant, what is this same, I pray you?

Mat. Marry, an elegy, an elegy, an odd toy——

Down. [*Aside.*] "To mock an ape withal !"[3] O, I
could sew up his mouth, now.

Dame K. Sister, I pray you let's hear it.

Down. Are you rhyme-given too?

Mat. Mistress, I'll read it, if you please.

Brid. Pray you do, servant.

Down. [*To himself.*] O, here's no foppery ! Death ! I
can endure the stocks better.   [*Exit.*

E. Kn. What ails thy brother? can he not hold his
water, at reading of a ballad?

Wel. O, no ; a rhyme to him is worse than cheese, or
a bag-pipe. But mark ; you lose the protestation.

Mat. Faith, I did it in a humour ; I know not how it
is ; but—please you come near, sir. This gentleman has
judgment, he knows how to censure of a —— pray you,
sir, you can judge.

Step. Not I, sir ; upon my reputation, and by the foot
of Pharaoh.

Wel. O, chide your cousin for swearing.

---

[1] Scene ii. in old eds.   [2] Secret, quietly apart.
[3] Proverbial saying, meaning to deceive a simpleton with.

E. Kn. Not I, so long as he does not forswear himself.

Bob. Master Matthew, you abuse the expectation of your dear mistress, and her fair sister : fie ! while you live, avoid this prolixity.

Mat. I shall, sir ; well, *incipere dulce.*[1]

E. Kn. How ! *insipere dulce ?*[2] a sweet thing to be a fool, indeed !

Wel. What, do you take *insipere* in that sense ?

E. Kn. You do not ? you ?   This was your villany, to gull him with a *mot.*[3]

Wel. O, the benchers' phrase : "*pauca verba, pauca verba !*"[4]

Mat. [*Reads.*] "Rare creature, let me speak without offence,

Would God my rude words had the influence

To rule thy thoughts, as thy fair looks do mine,

Then shouldst thou be his prisoner, who is thine."

E. Kn. This is in ' Hero and Leander.'[5]

Wel. O, ay ! peace, we shall have more of this.

Mat. " Be not unkind and fair : misshapen stuff

Is of behaviour boisterous and rough."[5]

Wel. How like you that, sir ?

                        [STEPHEN *nods several times.*

E. Kn. 'Slight, he shakes his head like a bottle, to feel an there be any brain in it.

Mat. But observe ' the catastrophe,' now :

" And I in duty will exceed all other,

As you in beauty do excel Love's mother."[5]

E. Kn. Well, I'll have him free of the wit-brokers, for he utters nothing but stolen remnants.

Wel. O, forgive it him.

---

[1] It is sweet to begin.   [2] Explained in next clause.
[3] French for "motto."
[4] "Few words": I take this to be the exclamation of the benchers of the Inns of Court at the disputations held for exercise sake.
[5] Marlowe's poem, book i., ll. 197—202—5, 219—20, with seven verbal alterations.

E. Kn. A filching rogue, hang him!—and from the dead! it's worse than sacrilege.

WELL-BRED, E. KNO'WELL, *and* STEPHEN, *come forward.*

Wel. Sister, what ha' you here?—verses? 'pray you, let's see. Who made these verses? they are excellent good.

Mat. O, Master Well-bred, 'tis your disposition to say so, sir. They were good i' the morning; I made 'hem *extempore* this morning.

Wel. How? *extempore?*

Mat. Ay, would I might be hanged else; ask Captain Bobadill: he saw me write them, at the ——pox on it!— the Star, yonder.

Brai. Can he find in his heart, to curse the stars so?

E. Kn. Faith, his are even with him; they ha' curst him enough already.

Step. Cousin, how do you like this gentleman's verses?

E. Kn. O, admirable! the best that ever I heard, coz.

Step. Body o' Cæsar, they are admirable! The best that ever I heard, as I'm a soldier!

Re-enter DOWN-RIGHT.

Down. I am vext, I can hold ne'er a bone of me still! 'Heart, I think they mean to build and breed here.

Wel. Sister, you have a simple servant here, that crowns your beauty with such encomiums, and devices: you may see what it is, to be the mistress of a wit, that can make your perfections so transparent, that every blear eye may look through them, and see him drowned, over head and ears, in the deep well of desire. Sister Kitely, I marvel you get you not a servant that can rhyme, and do tricks too.

Down. Oh monster! impudence itself! tricks!

Dame K. Tricks, brother? what tricks?

Brid. Nay, speak, I pray you, what tricks?

Dame K. Ay, never spare any body here; but say, what tricks.

Brid. Passion of my heart! do tricks!

Wel. 'Slight, here's a trick vied and revied![1]
Why, you monkeys, you? what a cater-wauling do you
keep! has he not given you rhymes, and verses, and
tricks?

Down. O, the fiend!

Wel. Nay, you lamp of virginity, that take it in snuff[2]
so, come, and cherish this tame poetical fury in your
servant, you'll be begged else shortly for a concealment:[3]
go to, reward his muse. You cannot give him less than
a shilling, in conscience, for the book he had it out of,
cost him a teston[4] at least. How now, gallants? Master
Matthew? Captain? What, all sons of silence? no spirit?

Down. Come, you might practise your ruffian tricks
somewhere else, and not here. I wuss; this is no tavern,
nor drinking-school, to vent your exploits in.

Wel. How now! whose cow has calved?[5]

Down. Marry, that has mine, sir. Nay, boy, never
look askance at me for the matter; I'll tell you of it, I, sir;
you and your companions mend yourselves when I ha' done.

Wel. My companions?

Down. Yes sir, your companions, so I say, I am not
afraid of you, nor them neither; your hangbyes here.
You must have your poets, and your potlings,[6] your
soldados, and foolados to follow you up and down the
city, and here they must come to domineer and swagger.
—Sirrah, you ballad-singer, and slops[7] your fellow there,
get you out, get you home; or, by this steel, I'll cut off
your ears, and that presently,

Wel. 'Slight, stay, let's see what he dare do: cut off his
ears? cut a whetstone! You are an ass, do you see!
touch any man here, and, by this hand, I'll run my rapier
to the hilts in you.

Down. Yea, that would I fain see, boy. [*They all draw.*

---

[1] Seen and re-seen, *i.e.* betted and re-betted on.
[2] In anger.   [3] Monastery lands, &c., unauthorizedly kept.
[4] Sixpence, but it varied in value.   [5] Who is bragging?
[6] Little pots—poetasters whose pot is their muse.
[7] Bobadill. See p. 32.

Dame K. O Jesu! murder! Thomas! Gasper!

Brid. Help, help! Thomas!

Enter CASH *and some of the house to part them. The women
continue their cries.*

E. Kn. Gentlemen, forbear, I pray you.

Bob. Well, sirrah, you Holofernes; by my hand, I
will pink your flesh full of holes with my rapier for this;
I will, by this good Heaven!—Nay, let him come, let him
come, gentlemen; by the body of St. George, I'll not kill
him.   [*They offer to fight again, and are parted.*

Cash. Hold, hold, good gentlemen.

Down. You whoreson, bragging coystril![1]

[2] *Enter* KITELY.

Kit. Why, how now? what's the matter, what's the
      stir here?
Whence springs the quarrel?   Thomas! where is he?
Put up your weapons, and put off this rage:
My wife and sister, they are cause of this.
What, Thomas?—where is this knave?

Cash. Here, Sir.

Wel. Come, let's go: this is one of my brother's
ancient humours, this.

Step. I am glad nobody was hurt by his "ancient
humour."   [*Exeunt all but those of the house.*

Kit. Why, how now, brother, who enforced this brawl?

Down. A sort[3] of lewd rake-hells, that care neither for
God nor the devil.   And they must come here, to read
ballads, and roguery, and trash!   I'll mar the knot of
'hem ere I sleep, perhaps; especially Bob[4] there, he that's
all manner of shapes; and "Songs and Sonnets," his
fellow.

Brid. Brother, indeed you are too violent,
Too sudden, in your humour: and you know
My brother Well-bred's temper will not bear

---

[1] Inferior groom, &c.   [2] Scene iii. in old eds.   [3] Lot.
[4] Ironically short for Bobadill.

Any reproof, chiefly in such a presence,
Where every slight disgrace he should receive
Might wound him in opinion, and respect.

Down. Respect! what talk you of respect 'mong such,
As ha' no spark of manhood, nor good manners?
'Sdeins, I am ashamed to hear you! respect! [*Exit.*

Brid. Yes, there was one a civil gentleman,
And very worthily demeaned himself.

Kit. O, that was some love of yours, sister. [brother!

Brid. A love of mine? I would it were no worse,
You'ld pay my portion, sooner than you think for.

Dame K. Indeed he seemed to be a gentleman of an
exceeding fair disposition, and of very excellent good
parts. [*Exeunt* Dame KITELY *and* BRIDGET.

Kit. Her love, by Heaven! my wife's minion!
" Fair disposition ! " " excellent good parts ! "
Death ! these phrases are intolerable.
" Good parts ! " how should she know his parts?
His parts ! Well, well, well, well, well, well ![1]
It is too plain, too clear:—Thomas, come hither.
What, are they gone?

Cash. Ay, sir, they went in.[2]
My mistress, and your sister——

Kit. Are any of the gallants within?

Cash. No, sir, they are all gone.

Kit. Art thou sure of it?

Cash. I can assure you, sir.

Kit. What gentleman was that they praised so, Thomas?

Cash. One, they call him Master Kno'well, a hand-
some young gentleman, sir.

Kit. Ay, I thought so; my mind gave me as much :
I'll die, but they have hid him i' the house,
Somewhere; I'll go and search :—go with me, Thomas :
Be true to me, and thou shalt find me a master ![3] [*Exeunt.*

[1] The first and second " Well," or the first and last, probably drawn
out disyllabically.
[2] The Ff. gave this in one, the Q. in two lines. " Ay," or " sir,"
should most likely be prolonged.
[3] His tone implies " who will remember thee."

SCENE II.[1]—*The Lane before* COB'S *House.*

Enter COB.

Cob. [*Knocking.*] What, Tib! Tib, I say!

Tib. [*Within.*] How now, what cuckold is that knocks so hard? [*She opens.*] O, husband! is't you? What's the news?

Cob. Nay, you have stunned me, i'faith! you ha' given me a knock o' the forehead will stick by me. Cuckold! 'Slid, cuckold!

Tib. Away, you fool! did I know it was you that knocked?[2] Come, come, you may call me as bad, when you list.

Cob. May I?—Tib, you are a whore.

Tib. You lie in your throat, husband.

Cob. How, the lie? and in my throat too! do you long to be stabbed, ha?

Tib. Why, you are no soldier, I hope.

Cob. O, must you be stabbed by a soldier? Mass, that's true! when was Bobadill here, your captain? that rogue, that foist,[3] that fencing Burgullion?[4] I'll tickle him, i'faith.

Tib. Why, what's the matter, trow?

Cob. O, he has basted me rarely, sumptuously! but I have it here in black and white, [*Touches it in his girdle.*] for his black, and blue, shall pay him. O, the Justice! the honestest old brave Trojan in London! I do honour the very flea of his dog. A plague on him though, he put me once in a villanous filthy fear; marry, it vanished away like the smoke of tobacco; but I was smoked[5] soundly first. I thank the devil, and his good angel, my guest. Well, wife, or Tib, which you will, get you in, and lock the door; I charge you, let nobody in to you, wife, nobody in, to you; those are my words. Not Cap-

---

[1] Scene iv. in old eds.
[2] Being in a more serious flight, these are two quasi-metrical lines.
[3] Pickpocket. [4] Braggadochio. [5] Abused, *i.e.* taken in. *Devon.*

tain Bob himself, nor the fiend, in his likeness; you are a woman, you have flesh and blood enough in you, to be tempted; therefore, keep the door, shut, upon all comers.

Tib. I warrant you, there shall nobody enter here, without my consent.

Cob. Nor with your consent, sweet Tib, and so I leave you.

Tib. It's more than you know, whether you leave me so.

Cob. How?

Tib. Why, "sweet."

Cob. Tut, sweet or sour, thou art a flower. [*Kissing her.* Keep close thy door, I ask no more. [*Exeunt.*

SCENE III.[1]—*A Room in the Windmill Tavern.*

Enter E. KNO'WELL, WELL-BRED, STEPHEN, *and* BRAIN-WORM, *disguised as before.*

E. Kn. Well, Brain-worm, perform this business happily, and thou makest a purchase of my love for ever.

Wel. I'faith, now let thy spirits use their best faculties. But, at any hand, remember the message to my brother; for there's no other means to start him.

Brai. I warrant you, sir, fear nothing: I have a nimble soul has waked all forces of my phant'sie by this time, and put 'hem in true motion. What you have possessed me withal, I'll discharge it amply, sir. Make it no question. [*Exit.*

Wel. Forth, and prosper, Brain-worm.—Faith, Ned, how dost thou approve of my abilities in this device?

E. Kn. Troth, well, howsoever; but it will come excellent, if it take.

Wel. Take, man? why it cannot choose but take, if the circumstances miscarry not: but tell me, ingenu-

---

[1] Scene v. in old eds.

ously, dost thou affect my sister Bridget, as thou
pretend'st?[1]

E. Kn. Friend, am I worth belief?

Wel. Come, do not protest. In faith, she is a maid of
good ornament, and much modesty: and, except I conceived very worthily of her, thou shouldest not have her.

E. Kn. Nay, that, I am afraid, will be a question yet,
whether I shall have her, or no?

Wel. 'Slid, thou shalt have her; by this light thou shalt.

E. Kn. Nay, do not swear.

Wel. By this hand, thou shalt have her; I'll go fetch
her presently. 'Point but where to meet, and as I am an
honest man, I'll bring her.

E. Kn. Hold, hold, be temperate.

Wel. Why, by ——what shall I swear by? thou shalt
have her, as I am——

E. Kn. 'Pray thee, be at peace, I am satisfied; and do
believe, thou wilt omit no offered occasion, to make my
desires complete.

Wel. Thou shalt see, and know, I will not.   [*Exeunt.*

SCENE IV.[2]—*The Old Jewry.*

Enter FORMAL *and* KNO'WELL.

Form. Was your man a soldier, sir?

Kno'. Ay, a knave, I took him begging o' the way,
This morning, as I came over Moorfields.

Enter BRAIN-WORM, *disguised as before.*

O, here he is!—You've made fair speed, believe me:
Where, i' the name of sloth, could you be thus?

Brai. Marry, peace be my comfort, where I thought I
should have had little comfort of your worship's service.

Kno'. How so?

---

[1] Settest forth.   [2] Scene vi. in old eds.

Brai. O, sir! your coming to the city, your entertainment of me, and your sending me to watch——indeed all the circumstances either of your charge, or my employment, are as open to your son, as to yourself!

Kno'. How should that be! unless that villain, Brain-Have told him of the letter, and discovered [worm, All that I strictly charged him to conceal? 'Tis so.

Brai. I am, partly, o' the faith 'tis so, indeed.

Kno'. But, how should he know thee to be my man?

Brai. Nay, sir, I cannot tell; unless it be by the black art! is not your son a scholar, sir?

Kno'. Yes, but I hope his soul is not allied Unto such hellish practice: if it were, I had just cause to weep my part in him, And curse the time of his creation. But, where did'st thou find them, Fitz-Sword?

Brai. You should rather ask, where they found me, sir; for I'll be sworn, I was going along in the street, thinking nothing, when, of a sudden, a voice calls, "Master Kno'well's man!" another cries "Soldier!" and thus half a dozen of 'h:m, till they had called me within a house, where I no sooner came, but they seemed men,[1] and out flew all their rapiers at my bosom, with some three or fourscore oaths to accompany 'hem; and all to tell me, I was but a dead man, if I did not confess where you were, and how I was employed, and about what; which when they could not get out of me, (as, I protest, they must ha' dissected, and made an anatomy o' me first, and so I told 'hem,) they locked me up into a room i' the top of a high house, whence, by great miracle (having a light heart) I slid down by a bottom[2] of packthread into the street, and so 'scaped. But, sir, thus much I can assure you, for I heard it while I was locked up, there was a great many rich merchants and brave[3] citizens' wives with 'hem at a feast, and your

---

[1] Possibly a pun, men, mad or angry, Greek μηνυη, &c.
[2] Ball or skein.
[3] Richly dressed.

son, Master Edward, withdrew with one of 'hem, and has 'pointed to meet her anon, at one Cob's house, a water-bearer, that dwells by the Wall. Now, there your worship shall be sure to take him, for there he preys, and fail he will not.

Kno'. Nor, will I fail to break his match, I doubt not.
Go thou, along with Justice Clement's man,
And stay there for me. At one Cob's house, say'st thou?

Brai. Ay, sir, there you shall have him. [*Exit* KNO'-WELL.] Yes!—invisible? Much wench, or much son! 'Slight, when he has staid there, three or four hours, travailing with the expectation of wonders, and at length be delivered of air! Oh, the sport that I should then take, to look on him, if I durst! But now, I mean to appear no more afore him, in this shape: I have another trick, to act yet. O, that I were so happy, as to light on a nupson,[1] now, of this justice's novice!——Sir, I make you stay somewhat long.

Form. Not a whit, sir. 'Pray you what do you mean, sir?

Brai. I was putting up some papers——

Form. You ha' been lately in the wars, sir, it seems.

Brai. Marry have I, sir, to my loss; and expense of all, almost——

Form. Troth, sir, I would be glad to bestow a pottle[2] of wine o' you, if it please you to accept it——

Brai. O, sir——

Form. But, to hear the manner of your services, and your devices in the wars, they say they be very strange, and not like those a man reads in the Roman histories, or sees at Mile-end.[3]

Brai. No, I assure you, sir; why, at any time when it please you, I shall be ready to discourse to you all I know: [*Aside.*] and more too somewhat.

Form. No better time than now, sir; we'll go to the Windmill: there we shall have a cup of neat grist, we

---

[1] Simpleton.   [2] Two quarts.
[3] Exercise ground of the City bands.

call it. I pray you, sir, let me request you, to the Wind-mill.

Brai. I'll follow you, sir ; [*Aside.*] and make grist o' you, if I have good luck.   [*Exeunt.*

SCENE V.[1]—*Moorfields.*

Enter MATTHEW, E. KNO'WELL, BOBADILL, *and* STEPHEN.

Mat. Sir, did your eyes ever taste the like clown of him, where we were to-day, Master Well-bred's half brother ? I think the whole earth cannot show his parallel, by this daylight.

E. Kn. We were now speaking of him : Captain Bobadill tells me, he is fallen foul o' you too.

Mat. O, ay, sir, he threatened me with the bastinado.

Bob. Ay, but I think, I taught you prevention, this morning, for that :—You shall kill him, beyond question ; if you be so generously minded.

Mat. Indeed, it is a most excellent trick.   [*Fences.*

Bob. O, you do not give spirit enough to your motion, you are too tardy, too heavy ! O, it must be done like lightning, hay !   [*Practises at a post.*

Mat. Rare captain !

Bob. Tut ! 'tis nothing, an't be not done in a—*punto.* [2]

E. Kn. Captain, did you ever prove yourself, upon any of our masters of defence here ?

Mat. O, good sir ! yes, I hope, he has.

Bob. I will tell you, sir.   Upon my first coming to the city, after my long travail[3] for knowledge (in that mystery only) there came three or four of 'hem to me, at a gentle-man's house, where it was my chance to be resident at that time, to intreat my presence at their schools, and withal so much importuned me, that—I protest to you, as I am a gentleman—I was ashamed of their rude

[1] Scene vii. in old eds.   [2] Instant.   [3] Used in sense also of travel.

Jon. I.

G

demeanour, out of all measure : well, I told 'hem, that to
come to a public school, they should pardon me, it was
opposite (in diameter) to my humour ; but, if so be they
would give their attendance at my lodging, I protested
to do them what right or favour I could, as I was a
gentleman, and so forth.

E. Kn. So, sir, then you tried their skill ?

Bob. Alas, soon tried ! you shall hear, sir. Within two
or three days after, they came ; and, by honesty, fair sir,
believe me, I graced them exceedingly, showed them
some two or three tricks of prevention, have purchased
'hem since, a credit to admiration ! they cannot deny this :
and yet now, they hate me, and why ? because I am
excellent ! and for no other vile reason on the earth.

E. Kn. This is strange, and barbarous ! as ever I
heard !

Bob. Nay, for a more instance of their preposterous
natures, but note, sir. They have assaulted me some
three, four, five, six of them together, as I have walked
alone, in divers skirts i' the town, as Turnbull, White-
chapel, Shoreditch,[1] which were then my quarters ; and
since, upon the Exchange, at my lodging, and at my
Ordinary[2] : where I have driven them afore me, the whole
length of a street, in the open view of all our gallants,
pitying to hurt them, believe me. Yet all this lenity will
not o'ercome their spleen ; they will be doing with the
pismire, raising a hill, a man may spurn abroad with his
foot, at pleasure. By myself, I could have slain them all,
but I delight not in murder. I am loth to bear any other
than this bastinado for 'hem : yet I hold it good polity
not to go disarmed, for though I be skilful, I may be
oppressed with multitudes.

E. Kn. Ay, believe me, may you, sir : and, in my
conceit, our whole nation should sustain the loss by it, if
it were so.   [seen.

Bob. Alas, no ! what's a peculiar man to a nation ? not

---

[1] Suburbs of ill repute.   [2] Public dining-room.

E. Kn. O, but your skill, sir.

Bob. Indeed, that might be some loss; but who respects it? I will tell you, sir, by the way of private, and under seal; I am a gentleman, and live here obscure, and to myself. But, were I known to her Majesty and the Lords, —observe me,—I would undertake—upon this poor head, and life—for the public benefit of the state, not only to spare the entire lives of her subjects in general, but to save the one half, nay, three parts of her yearly charge in holding war, and against what enemy soever. And how would I do it, think you?

E. Kn. Nay, I know not, nor can I conceive.

Bob. Why thus, sir. I would select nineteen more, to myself, throughout the land; gentlemen they should be, of good spirit, strong, and able constitution; I would choose them by an instinct, a character that I have: and I would teach these nineteen, the special rules, as your punto, your reverso, your stoccata, your imbroccata, your passada, your montanto[1]; till they could all play very near, or altogether as well as myself. This done, say the enemy were forty thousand strong, we twenty would come into the field, the tenth of March, or thereabouts; and we would challenge twenty of the enemy; they could not, in their honour, refuse us, well, we would kill them; challenge twenty more, kill them; twenty more, kill them; twenty more, kill them too; and thus, would we kill, every man, his twenty a day, that's twenty score; twenty score, that's two hundred; two hundred a day, five days a thousand; forty thousand; forty times five, five times forty, two hundred days kills them all up, by computation And this, will I venture my poor gentleman-like carcase to perform (provided there be no treason practised upon us) by fair, and discreet manhood, that is, civilly by the sword

E. Kn. Why, are you so sure of your hand, captain, at all times?

---

[1] Rapier play then included cuts as well as thrusts, and, as shown by "imbroccata," the parrying use of the dagger.

Bob. Tut ! never miss thrust, upon my reputation with you.

E. Kn. I would not stand in Down-right's state then, an you meet him, for the wealth of any one street in London.

Bob. Why, sir, you mistake me ! if he were here now, by this welkin, I would not draw my weapon on him ! let this gentleman do his mind ; but, I will bastinado him, by the bright sun, where-ever I meet him.

Mat. Faith, and I'll have a fling at him, at my distance.

E. Kn. Gods so, look where he is ! yonder he goes.

[DOWN-RIGHT *walks over the stage.*

Down. What peevish luck have I, I cannot meet with these bragging rascals ?

Bob. It's not he, is it ?

E. Kn.   Yes faith, it is he.[1]

Mat. I'll be hanged then, if that were he.

E. Kn. Sir, keep your hanging good for some greater matter, for I assure you that was he.

Step. Upon my reputation, it was he.

Bob. Had I thought it had been he, he must not have gone so : but I can hardly be induced to believe it was he, yet.

E. Kn. That I think, sir.   [*Re-enter* DOWN-RIGHT.

But see, he is come again.

Down. O, " Pharaoh's foot," have I found you ? Come, draw, to your tools[2] : draw, gipsy, or I'll thrash you.

Bob. Gentleman of valour, I do believe in thee, hear me—

Down. Draw your weapon then.

Bob. Tall man, I never thought on it, till now, body of me, I had a warrant of the peace served on me, even now, as I came along, by a water-bearer ; this gentleman saw it, Master Matthew.

Down. 'Sdeath ! you will not draw then ?

[*Cudgels him, disarms him, and throws him down.*

MATTHEW *runs away.*

---

[1] One line, F.2.   [2] His rapier and dagger.

Bob. Hold, hold, under thy favour, forbear !

Down. Prate again, as you like this, you whoreson foist[1]
you ! You'll "control the point," you ! [*Looking about.*]
Your consort is gone ? had he stayed he had shared with
you, sir.   [*Exit.*

Bob. Well, gentlemen, bear witness, I was bound to
the peace, by this good day.

E. Kn. No faith, it's an ill day, captain, never reckon it
other : but, say you were bound to the peace, the law allows
you to defend yourself : that'll prove but a poor excuse.

Bob. I cannot tell, sir. I desire good construction, in
fair sort. I never sustained the like disgrace, by Heaven !
sure I was struck with a planet thence, for I had no
power to touch my weapon.

E. Kn. Ay, like enough ; I have heard of many that
have been beaten under a planet : go, get you to a sur-
geon. [*Exit* BOBADILL.] 'Slid ! an these be your tricks,
your passadas, and your montantos, I'll none of them.
O, manners ! that this age should bring forth such creatures !
that nature should be at leisure to make 'hem ! Come, coz.

Step. Mass, I'll ha' this cloak.

E. Kn. Gods will, 'tis Down-right's.

Step. Nay, it's mine now, another might have ta'en't
up as well as I : I'll wear it, so I will.   [yourself.

E. Kn. How, an he see it ? he'll challenge it, assure

Step. Ay, but he shall not ha' it ; I'll say I bought it.

E. Kn. Take heed, you buy it not too dear, coz. [*Exeunt.*

SCENE VI.[2]—*A Room in* KITELY'S *House.*

Enter KITELY, WELL-BRED, Dame KITELY, *and* BRIDGET.

Kit. Now, trust me, brother, you were much to blame,
T'incense his anger, and disturb the peace
Of my poor house, where there are sentinels,

---

[1] Pickpocket.   [2] Scene viii. in old eds.

That every minute watch, to give alarms
Of civil war, without adjection[1]
Of your assistance, or occasion.

Wel. No harm done, brother, I warrant you, since
there is no harm done. Anger costs a man nothing; and
a tall man is never his own man, till he be angry. To
keep his valour in obscurity, is to keep himself, as it were,
in a cloak-bag. What's a musician, unless he play?
What's a tall man, unless he fight? For indeed, all this,
my wise brother stands upon, absolutely; and that made
me fall in with him, so resolutely.

Dame K. Ay, but what harm might have come of it,
brother?

Wel. Might, sister? so might the good warm clothes your
husband wears, be poisoned, for any thing he knows: or
the wholesome wine he drunk, even now, at the table——

Kit. [*Aside.*] Now, God forbid! O me! now I re-
member,
My wife drunk to me last; and changed the cup;
And bade me wear this cursèd suit to-day.
See, if Heaven suffer murder undiscovered!——
I feel me ill; give me some mithridate,[2]
Some mithridate and oil, good sister, fetch me;
O, I am sick at heart! I burn, I burn.
If you will save my life, go fetch it me.

Wel. O strange humour! my very breath has poisoned
him.

Brid. Good brother, be content, what do you mean?
The strength of these extreme conceits will kill you.

Dame K. Beshrew your heart-blood, brother Well-
bred, now,
For putting such a toy into his head!

Wel. Is a fit simile a toy? will he be poisoned with a
simile?——Brother Kitely, what a strange, and idle imagination is this! For shame, be wiser. O' my soul, there's
no such matter.

---

[1] The casting in, addition.   [2] Supposed general antidote.

Kit. Am I not sick? how am I, then, not poisoned?
Am I not poisoned? how am I, then, so sick?

Dame K. If you be sick, your own thoughts make you
sick.

Wel. His jealousy, is the poison he has taken.

Enter BRAIN-WORM, *in* FORMAL'S *clothes.*

Brai. Master Kitely, my master, Justice Clement,
salutes you; and desires to speak with you, with all
possible speed.

Kit. No time but now? when, I think, I am sick? very
sick! well, I will wait upon his worship.—Thomas? Cob?
[*Aside.*] I must seek them out, and set 'hem sentinels till
I return.—Thomas? Cob? Thomas?   [*Exit.*

Wel. [*Takes him aside.*] This is perfectly rare, Brain-
worm! but how got'st thou this apparel of the justice's
man?

Brai. Marry, sir, my proper fine pen-man would needs
bestow the grist o' me, at the Windmill, to hear some
martial discourse; where so I marshalled him, that I
made him drunk, with admiration! and, because too much
heat was the cause of his distemper, I stripped him stark
naked, as he lay along asleep, and borrowed his suit, to
deliver this counterfeit message in, leaving a rusty armour,
and an old brown bill[1] to watch him, till my return;
which shall be, when I ha' pawned his apparel, and spent
the better part o' the money, perhaps.

Wel. Well, thou art a successful merry knave, Brain-
worm; his absence will be a good subject for more mirth.
I pray thee, return to thy young master, and will him to
meet me, and my sister Bridget, at the Tower instantly;
for, here, tell him, the house is so stored with jealousy,
there is no room for love to stand upright in. We must
get our fortunes committed to some larger prison, say;
and, than the Tower, I know no better air; nor where

---

[1] Between a halbert and a pike.

the liberty of the house may do us more present service.[1]
Away.   [*Exit* BRAIN-WORM.

Re-enter KITELY, CASH *following*.

Kit. Come hither, Thomas.   Now, my secret's ripe,
And thou shalt have it: lay to both thine ears.
Hark, what I say to thee.   I must go forth, Thomas:
Be careful of thy promise, keep good watch,
Note every gallant, and observe him well,
That enters in my absence, to thy mistress:
If she would show him rooms, the jest is stale,
Follow 'hem, Thomas, or else hang on him,
And let him not go after; mark their looks;
Note, if she offer but to see his band,
Or any other amorous toy about him;
But praise his leg; or foot; or if she say,
The day is hot, and bid him feel her hand,
How hot it is; oh, that's a monstrous thing!
Note me all this, good Thomas, mark their sighs,
And, if they do but whisper, break 'hem off:
I'll bear thee out in it.   Wilt thou do this?
Wilt thou be true, my Thomas?
    Cash.   As truth's self, sir.
    Kit. Why, I believe thee:—where is Cob, now? Cob?
                                                          [*Exit.*
    Dame K. He's ever calling for Cob! I wonder how
he employs Cob so!
    Wel. Indeed, sister, to ask how he employs Cob, is a
necessary question for you, that are his wife, and a thing
not very easy for you to be satisfied in: but this, I'll
assure you, Cob's wife is an excellent bawd, sister, and
oftentimes, your husband haunts her house; marry, to
what end?   I cannot altogether accuse him; imagine
you what you think convenient.   But I have known fair
hides have foul hearts ere now, sister.
    Dame K. Never said you truer than that, brother, so

---

[1] They could be immediately married about its precincts.

much I can tell you for your learning.—Thomas, fetch your cloak, and go with me. [*Exit* CASH.] I'll after him presently: I would to fortune, I could take him there, i'faith, I'ld return him his own, I warrant him! [*Exit.*

Wel. So, let 'hem go; this may make sport anon. Now, my fair sister-in-law, that you knew but how happy a thing it were, to be fair and beautiful.

Brid. That touches not me, brother.

Wel. That's true; that's even the fault of it: for indeed, beauty stands a woman in no stead, unless it procure her touching. But sister, whether it touch you or no, it touches your beauties; and I am sure they will abide the touch; an they do not, a plague of all ceruse,[1] say I! and it touches me too in part, though not in the—— Well, there's a dear and respected friend of mine, sister, stands very strongly, and worthily affected toward you, and hath vowed to inflame whole bonfires of zeal at his heart, in honour of your perfections. I have already engaged my promise to bring you, where you shall hear him confirm much more. Ned Kno'well is the man, sister. There's no exception against the party. You are ripe for a husband; and a minute's loss to such an occasion, is a great trespass in a wise beauty. What say you, sister? On my soul, he loves you. Will you give him the meeting?

Brid. Faith, I had very little confidence in mine own constancy, brother, if I durst not meet a man: but this motion of yours savours of an old knight adventurer's servant, a little too much, methinks.

Wel. What's that, sister?

Brid. Marry, of the squire.[2]

Wel. No matter if it did, I would be such an one for my friend. But see, who is returned to hinder us!

Re-enter KITELY.

Kit. What villany is this? called out on a false message?

---

[1] White lead, a cosmetic.
[2] *i.e.* The apple-squire, the attendant and pander.

This was some plot! I was not sent for.—Bridget,
Where's your sister?

   Brid.   I think she be gone forth, sir.

   Kit. How! is my wife gone forth? whither, for God's
sake?

   Brid. She's gone abroad with Thomas.

   Kit. Abroad with Thomas! oh, that villain dors[1] me:
He hath discovered all unto my wife!
Beast that I was, to trust him! whither, I pray you,
Went she?

   Brid.   I know not, sir.

   Wel.   I'll tell you, brother,
Whither I suspect she's gone.[2]

   Kit.   Whither, good brother?

   Wel. To Cob's house, I believe: but, keep my counsel.

   Kit. I will, I will: to Cob's house? doth she haunt
        Cob's?
She's gone a purpose now, to cuckold me,
With that lewd rascal, who, to win her favour,
Hath told her all.   [*Exit.*

   Wel.   Come, he is once more gone,
Sister, let's lose no time; the affair is worth it. [*Exeunt.*

SCENE VII.[3]—*A Street.*

Enter MATTHEW *and* BOBADILL.

   Mat. I wonder, captain, what they will say of my going
away? ha?

   Bob. Why, what should they say? but as of a discreet
gentleman! quick, wary, respectful of nature's fair linea-
ments: and that's all.

---

[1] Fools, deceives as does the dor, or cockchafer.

[2] Ff. give Well-bred's speech as a verse line, but also misplace
"went she," at end of previous line.

[3] Scene ix. in old eds.

Mat. Why, so! but what can they say of your beating?

Bob. A rude part, a touch with soft wood, a kind of gross battery used, laid on strongly, borne most patiently; and that's all.

Mat. Ay, but would any man have offered it in Venice? as you say?

Bob. Tut! I assure you, no: you shall have there your *Nobilis*, your *Gentilezza*,[1] come in bravely upon your "reverse," stand you close, stand you firm, stand you fair, save your "retricato" with his left leg, come to the "assalto" with the right, thrust with brave steel, defy your base wood! But, wherefore do I awake this remembrance? I was fascinated, by Jupiter; fascinated: but I will be unwitched, and revenged, by law.

Mat. Do you hear? is't not best to get a warrant, and have him arrested, and brought before Justice Clement?

Bob. It were not amiss, would we had it!

Enter BRAIN-WORM *still as* FORMAL.

Mat. Why, here comes his man, let's speak to him.

Bob. Agreed, do you speak.

Mat. 'Save you, sir!

Brai. With all my heart, sir.

Mat. Sir, there is one Down-right hath abused this gentleman, and myself, and we determine to make our amends by law; now, if you would do us the favour to procure a warrant, to bring him afore your master, you shall be well considered, I assure you, sir.

Brai. Sir, you know my service is my living; such favours, as these, gotten of my master is his only preferment,[2] and therefore, you must consider me, as I may make benefit of my place.

Mat. How is that, sir?

Brai. Faith sir, the thing is extraordinary, and the gentleman may be of great account; yet, be what he will,

---

[1] Lat. and Ital. meaning the same, " gentry of blood."
[2] The only preferment he gives me.

if you will lay me down a brace of angels, in my hand,
you shall have it, otherwise not.

Mat. How shall we do, captain? he asks a brace
of angels, you have no money?

Bob. Not a cross,[1] by fortune.

Mat. Nor I, as I am a gentleman, but twopence, left of
my two shillings in the morning for wine, and radish:
let's find him some pawn.

Bob. Pawn? we have none to the value of his demand.

Mat. O, yes. I'll pawn this jewel in my ear, and you
may pawn your silk-stockings, and pull up your boots,
they will ne'er be missed: it must be done, now.

Bob. Well, an there be no remedy: I'll step aside and
pull 'hem off.   [*Withdraws.*

Mat. Do you hear, sir? we have no store of money at
this time, but you shall have good pawns; look you, sir,
this jewel, and that gentleman's silk-stockings; because
we would have it dispatched, ere we went to our chambers.

Brai. I am content, sir; I will get you the warrant
presently,[2] what's his name, say you? Down-right?

Mat. Ay, ay, George Down-right.

Brai. What manner of man is he?

Mat. A tall big man, sir; he goes in a cloak most
commonly, of silk-russet, laid about with russet lace.

Brai. 'Tis very good, sir.

Mat. Here, sir, here's my jewel.

Bob. [*Returning.*] And here—are stockings.

Brai. Well, gentlemen, I'll procure you this warrant
presently; but, who will you have to serve it?

Mat. That's true, captain: that must be considered.

Bob. Body o' me, I know not! 'tis service of danger!

Brai. Why, you were best get one o' the varlets o' the
city, a serjeant; I'll appoint you one, if you please.

Mat. Will you, sir? why, we can wish no better.

Bob. We'll leave it to you, sir.

                              [*Exeunt* BOBADILL *and* MATTHEW.

---

[1] The penny and halfpenny were so marked.   [2] Immediately.

Brai. This is rare ! Now will I go pawn this cloak of the justice's man's at the broker's, for a varlet's suit, and be the varlet myself; and get either more pawns, or more money of Down-right, for[1] the arrest.   *[Exit.*

SCENE VIII.[2]—*The Lane before* COB'S *House.*

Enter KNO'WELL.

Kno'. Oh, here it is ; I am glad I have found it now.
Ho ! who is within here ?   *[Knocking.*

Tib. [*Within.*] I am within, sir ; what's your pleasure ?

Kno'. To know, who is within, besides yourself.

Tib. Why, sir, you are no constable, I hope ?

Kno'. O ! fear you the constable ? then I doubt not,
You have some guests within, deserve that fear,
I'll fetch him straight.   *[*TIB *opens.*

Tib.   O' God's name, sir !

Kno'. Go to. Come, tell me, is not young Kno'well here?

Tib. Young Kno'well ? I know none such, sir, o' mine honesty.

Kno'. Your honesty? dame, it flies too lightly from you :
There is no way but, fetch the constable.

Tib. The constable ? the man is mad, I think.
    [Claps to the door.

Enter Dame KITELY *and* CASH.

Cash. Ho ! who keeps house, here ?

Kno'. O, this's the female copesmate[3] of my son:
Now shall I meet him straight.

Dame K.   Knock, Thomas, hard.

Cash. Ho, goodwife?   *[*TIB *slightly re-opens door.*

Tib.   Why, what's the matter with you ?

Dame K. Why, woman, grieves it you to ope your door?
Belike, you get something, to keep it shut.

---

[1] In-tead of.   [2] Scene x. in old eds.   [3] Companion.

Tib. What mean these questions, 'pray ye?

Dame K. So strange you make it! Is not my husband
    here?

Kno'. Her husband!

Dame K.   My tried husband, Master Kitely?

Tib. I hope, he needs not to be tried, here.

Dame K. No, dame; he does it not for need, but
    pleasure.

Tib. Neither for need, nor pleasure, is he here.

Kno'. This is but a device to baulk me withal.

    Enter KITELY, *muffled in his cloak.*

Soft, who is this? 'Tis not my son disguised?

    Dame K. [*Spies her husband, and runs to him.*] O, sir,
        Have I forestalled your honest market?

Found your close walks? you stand amazed now, do you?

I'faith, I'm glad I have smoked you yet at last.

What is your jewel, trow? In: come, let's see her;—

Fetch forth your housewife, dame;—if she be fairer,

In any honest judgment, than myself,

I'll be content with it: but, she is change,

She feeds you fat, she soothes your appetite,

And you are well! your wife, an honest woman,

Is meat twice sod to you, sir! O, you treacher!

    Kno'. She cannot counterfeit thus palpably.

    Kit. Out on thy more than strumpet's [1] impudence!

Steal'st thou thus to thy haunts? and have I taken

Thy bawd, and thee, and thy companion,

This hoary-headed letcher, this old goat,

Close [2] at your villany, and wouldst thou 'scuse it

With this stale harlot's jest, accusing me?——

O, old incontinent, [*To* KNO'WELL.] dost not thou shame,

When all thy powers in chastity is[3] spent,

To have a mind so hot? and to entice,

And feed the enticements of a lustful woman?

---

[1] So Q. F., strumpet F.2. "   [2] Secretly; but a pun.
[3] Singular, through "chastity." Q. Ff.

Dame K. Out, I defy thee, I, dissembling wretch!

Kit. Defy me, strumpet? Ask thy pander here,
Can he deny it? or that wicked elder?

Kno'. Why, hear you, sir.

Kit. Tut, tut, tut; never speak.
Thy guilty conscience will discover thee.

Kno'. What lunacy is this, that haunts this man?

Kit. Well, good wife B A 'D,[1] Cob's wife, and you,
That make your husband such a hoddy-doddy[2];—
And you, young apple-squire,—and old cuckold-maker;
I'll ha' you every one before a justice:
Nay, you shall answer it, I charge you go.

Kno'. Marry, with all my heart, sir: I go willingly;
Though I do taste this as a trick, put on me,
To punish my impertinent search; and justly:
And half forgive my son, for the device.

Kit. Come, will you go?

Dame K. Go? to thy shame believe it.

Enter COB.

Cob. Why, what's the matter here, what's here to do?

Kit. O, Cob, art thou come? I have been abused,
And i' thy house: never was man so wronged!

Cob. 'Slid, in my house? My Master Kitely? Who
wrongs you in my house?

Kit. Marry, young lust in old, and old in young, here:
Thy wife's their bawd, here have I taken 'hem.

Cob. How? bawd? is my house come to that? Am
I preferred thither? [*Beats his wife.*] Did I charge you
to keep your doors shut, Isbel? and do you let 'hem
lie open for all comers?

Kno'. Friend, know some cause, before thou beat'st thy
wife,
This's madness in thee.

---

[1] He spells this word, and, as shown by the 'D, makes a pun or an
attempt at one, as calling Cob's wife " bad " and ." bawd."

[2] Generally a simpleton, but perhaps implying here that he is
horned.

Cob.   Why? is there no cause?

Kit. Yes, I'll show cause before the justice, Cob:
Come, let her go with me.

Cob.   Nay, she shall go.

Tib. Nay, I will go. I'll see an you may be allowed
to make a bundle o' hemp [1] o' your right and lawful wife
thus, at every cuckoldy knave's pleasure. Why do you
not go?

Kit. A bitter quean! Come, we'll ha' you tamed.

[*Exeunt.*

SCENE IX.[2]—*A Street.*

Enter BRAIN-WORM *as a City Serjeant.*

Brai. Well, of all my disguises yet, now am I most
like myself; being in this serjeant's gown. A man, of
my present profession, never counterfeits, till he lays hold
upon a debtor, and says, he 'rests him; for then he
brings him to all manner of unrest. A kind of little
kings we are, bearing the diminutive of a mace, made like
a young artichoke, that always carries pepper and salt, in
itself. Well, I know not what danger I undergo by this
exploit, 'pray Heaven I come well off!

Enter MATTHEW *and* BOBADILL.

Mat. See, I think, yonder is the varlet, by his gown.

Bob. Let's go in quest of him.

Mat. 'Save you, friend! are not you here, by appoint-
ment of Justice Clement's man?

Brai. Yes, an't please you, sir; he told me, two
gentlemen had willed him to procure a warrant from his
master (which I have about me) to be served on one
Down-right.

---

[1] Hemp is prepared by beating.   [2] Scene xi. in old eds.

Mat. It is honestly done of you both ; and see, where the party comes you must arrest ; serve it upon him, quickly, afore he be aware.

Bob. Bear back, Master Matthew.

Enter STEPHEN *in* DOWN-RIGHT'S *cloak.*

Brai. Master Down-right, I arrest you i' the queen's name, and must carry you afore a justice, by virtue of this warrant.

Step. Me, friend? I am no Down-right, I. I am Master Stephen, you do not well to arrest me, I tell you truly : I am in nobody's bonds, nor books, I, would you should know it. A plague on you heartily, for making me thus afraid afore my time !

Brai. Why, now are you deceived, gentlemen !

Bob. He wears such a cloak, and that deceived us : but see, here a' comes indeed ! this is he, officer.

Enter DOWN-RIGHT.

Down. Why, how now, Signior gull ! are you turned filcher of late ? come, deliver my cloak.

Step. Your cloak, sir ? I bought it, even now, in open market.

Brai. Master Down-right, I have a warrant I must serve upon you, procured by these two gentlemen.

Down. These gentlemen ? these rascals !

[*Raises his cudgel.*

Brai. Keep the peace, I charge you, in her majesty's name.

Down. I obey thee. What must I do, officer ?

Brai. Go before Master Justice Clement, to answer what they can object against you, sir, I will use you kindly, sir.

Mat. Come, let's before, and make[1] the justice, captain.

Bob. The varlet's a tall man,[2] afore Heaven !

[*Exeunt* BOBADILL *and* MATTHEW.

Down. Gull, you'll gi' me my cloak.

Step. Sir, I bought it, and I'll keep it.

[1] Prepare or prepossess.   [2] Valiant.

Jon. I.

H

Down. You will.

Step. Ay, that I will.

Down. Officer, there's thy fee, arrest him.

Brai. Master Stephen, I must arrest you.

Step. Arrest me! I scorn it. There take your cloak, I'll none on't.

Down. Nay, that shall not serve your turn now, sir. Officer, I'll go with thee to the justice's: bring him along.

Step. Why, is not here your cloak? what would you have?

Down. I'll ha' you answer it, sir.

Brai. Sir, I'll take your word;[1] and this gentleman's too, for his appearance.

Down. I'll ha' no words taken: bring him along.

Brai. Sir, I may choose to do that: I may take bail.

Down. 'Tis true, you may take bail, and choose, at another time. But you shall not, now, varlet. Bring him along or I'll swindge you. [*Raises cudgel.*]

Brai. Sir, I pity the gentleman's case. Here's your money again.

Down. 'Sdeins, tell not me of my money; bring him away, I say.

Brai. I warrant you he will go with you, of himself, sir.

Down. Yet more ado.

Brai. [*Aside.*] I have made a fair mash on't.

Step. Must I go?

Brai. I know no remedy, Master Stephen.

Down. Come along, afore me, here: I do not love your hanging look behind.

Step. Why, sir: I hope you cannot hang me for it. —Can he, fellow?

Brai. I think not, sir: it is but a whipping matter, sure.

Step. Why, then, let him do his worst, I am resolute. [*Exeunt.*]

---

1 "For your appearance" understood.

ACT THE FIFTH.

SCENE I.—*A Hall in* Justice CLEMENT'S *House.*

Enter CLEMENT, KNO'WELL, KITELY, Dame KITELY, TIB, CASH, COB, *and Servants.*

LEM. Nay, but stay, stay, give me leave:—my chair, sirrah.—You, Master Kno'well, say you went thither to meet your son?

Kno'. Ay, sir.

Clem. But who directed you, thither?

Kno'. That did mine own man, sir.

Clem. Where is he?

Kno'. Nay, I know not, now; I left him with your clerk: and appointed him to stay here for me.[1]

Clem. My clerk? about what time was this?

Kno'. Marry, between one and two, as I take it.

Clem. And what time came my man with the false message to you, Master Kitely?

Kit. After two, sir.

Clem. Very good: but, Mistress Kitely, how chance that you were at Cob's? ha?

Dame K. An please you, sir, I'll tell you: my brother Well-bred told me, that Cob's house, was a suspected place——

Clem. So it appears, methinks; but on.

Dame K. And that my husband used thither, daily.

Clem. No matter, so he used himself well, mistress.

---

[1] Two verse lines in F., but not so in Q. nor in F2.

Dame K. True sir, but you know what grows, by such haunts, oftentimes.

Clem. I see, rank fruits of a jealous brain, Mistress Kitely : but did you find your husband there, in that case, as you suspected ?

Kit. I found her there, sir.

Clem. Did you so ? that alters the case. Who gave you knowledge of your wife's being there ?

Kit. Marry, that did my brother Well-bred.

Clem. How ? Well-bred first tell her ? then tell you, after ? Where is Well-bred ?

Kit. Gone with my sister, sir, I know not whither.

Clem. Why, this is a mere trick, a device ; you are gulled in this most grossly, all !—alas, poor wench, wert thou beaten for this ?

Tib. Yes, most pitifully, an't please you.

Cob. And worthily, I hope : if it shall prove so.

Clem. Ay, that's like, and a piece of a sentence.—

Enter a Servant.

How now, sir ? what's the matter ?

Serv. Sir, there's a gentleman i' the court without, desires to speak with your worship.

Clem. A gentleman ! what's he ?

Serv. A soldier, sir, he says.

Clem. A soldier ? take down my armour, my sword, quickly. A soldier speak with me ! why when,[1] knaves ? come on, come on, hold my cap there, so ; give me my gorget,[2] my sword :——stand by, I will end your matters anon.—Let the soldier enter :   [*Exit* Servant.

[3]Enter BOBADILL and MATTHEW.

now sir, what ha' you to say to me ?

Bob. By your worship's favour——   [*Approaches him.*[4]

Clem. Nay, keep out, sir ; I know not your pretence,

---

[1] How long are you going to be.   [2] Neck armour piece.
[3] Scene ii. in old eds.   [4] Intent.

you send me word, sir, you are a soldier : why, sir, you shall be answered, here, here be them have been amongst soldiers. Sir, your pleasure.

Bob. Faith, sir, so it is, this gentleman, and myself have been most uncivilly wronged, and beaten by one Down-right, a coarse fellow, about the town here, and for mine own part, I protest, being a man, in no sort, given to this filthy humour of quarrelling, he hath assaulted me in the way of my peace ; despoiled me of mine honour ; disarmed me of my weapons ; and rudely laid me along in the open streets : when I not so much as once offered to resist him.

Clem. O, God's precious ! is this the soldier ? here, take my armour off quickly, 'twill make him swoon, I fear; he is not fit to look on't, that will put up a blow.

Mat. An't please your worship, he was bound to the peace.

Clem. Why, an he were, sir, his hands were not bound, were they ?

Re-enter Servant.

Serv. There's one of the varlets of the city, sir, has brought two gentlemen here ; one, upon your worship's warrant.

Clem. My warrant ?

Serv. Yes, sir. The officer says, procured by these two.

Clem. Bid him come in. [*Exit* Servant.] Set by this picture.[1]

Enter DOWN-RIGHT, STEPHEN, *with* BRAIN-WORM *as before.*[2]

What, Master Down-right ! are you brought at Master Freshwater's[3] suit here ? [suit

Down. I'faith, sir. And here's another brought at my

---

[1] This mere picture of a soldier.   [2] Scene iii. in old eds.
[3] A gibing term, because soldiers, who had not crossed the sea, had seen no service. In Greene's *Never too Late*, 1590, Infida says —" Are you such a freshwater soldier, that you faint at the first skirmish ?"

Clem. What are you, sir?

Step. A gentleman, sir.—Oh, uncle!

Clem. Uncle? who? Master Kno'well?

Kno'. Ay, sir! this is a wise kinsman of mine.

Step. God's my witness, uncle, I am wronged here, monstrously, he charges me with stealing of his cloak, and would I might never stir, if I did not find it in the street, by chance.

Down. O, did you "find it," now? You said, "you bought it," ere-while.

Step. And you said, I stole it; nay, now my uncle is here, I'll do well enough with you.

Clem. Well, let this breathe awhile.—You that have cause to complain there, stand forth:—had you my warrant for this gentleman's apprehension?

Bob. Ay, an't please your worship.

Clem. Nay, do not speak in passion[1] so: where had you it?

Bob. Of your clerk, sir.

Clem. That's well! an my clerk can make warrants and my hand not at 'hem! Where is the warrant?—Officer, have you it?

Brai. No sir, your worship's man, Master Formal, bid me do it for these gentlemen, and he would be my discharge.

Clem. Why, Master Down-right, are you such a novice, to be served, and never see the warrant?

Down. Sir.[2] He did not serve it on me.

Clem. No? how then?

Down. Marry, sir, he came to me, and said, he must serve it, and he would use me kindly, and so——

Clem. O, God's pity was it so, sir? "He must serve it!" Give me my long sword there, and help me off: so. Come on, sir varlet, I "must" cut off your legs, sirrah; [BRAIN-WORM *kneels.*] nay, stand up, "I'll use you kindly;"—I "must" cut off your legs, I say.

[*Flourishes over him with his long sword.*

---

[1] Emotion.   [2] Taken aback, he hesitates.

Brai. [*Kneeling again.*] O, good sir, I beseech you; nay, good Master Justice!

Clem. I "must" do it; there is no remedy. I "must" cut off your legs, sirrah—I "must" cut off your ears, you rascal, I must do it—I "must" cut off your nose—I "must" cut off your head.

Brai. O, good your worship!

Clem. Well, rise, how dost thou do now? dost thou feel thyself well? hast thou no harm?

Brai. No, I thank your good worship, sir.

Clem. Why, so! I said "I must cut off thy legs," and, "I must cut off thy arms," and, "I must cut off thy head;" but, I did not do it: so you said, "you must serve this gentleman with my warrant," but, you did not serve him. You knave, you slave, you rogue, do you say you "must?"—Sirrah, away with him to the jail; I'll teach you a trick for your "must," sir.

Brai. Good sir, I beseech you, be good to me.

Clem. Tell him he shall to the jail,—away with him, I say.

Brai. Nay, sir, if you will commit me, it shall be for committing more than this: I will not lose, by my travail, any grain of my fame, certain. [*Takes off his disguises.*]

Clem. How is this!

Kno'. My man Brain-worm!

Step. O yes, uncle: Brain-worm has been with my cousin Edward and I, all this day.

Clem. I told you all, there was some device.

Brai. Nay, excellent justice, since I have laid myself thus open to you; now, stand strong for me: both with your sword, and your balance.

Clem. Body o' me, a merry knave!—give me a bowl of sack:—if he belong to you, Master Kno'well, I bespeak your patience.

Brai. That is it, I have most need of. Sir, if you'll pardon me only,[1] I'll glory in all the rest of my exploits.

---

[1] Then a common form for "Only pardon me."

Kno'. Sir, you know I love not to have my favours come hard from me. You have your pardon; though I suspect you shrewdly, for being of counsel with my son against me.

Brai. Yes, faith, I have, sir, though you retained me doubly this morning for yourself: first, as Brain-worm; after, as Fitz-Sword. I was your reformed[1] soldier, sir. 'Twas I sent you to Cob's, upon the errand without end.

Kno'. Is it possible! or that thou shouldst disguise thy language so, as I should not know thee?

Brai. O, sir, this has been the day of my metamorphosis. It is not that shape alone, that I have run through to-day. I brought this gentleman, Master Kitely, a message too, in the form of Master Justice's man here, to draw him out o' the way, as well as your worship; while Master Well-bred might make a conveyance of Mistress Bridget to my young master.

Kit. How! my sister stolen away?

Kno'. My son is not married, I hope!

Brai. Faith, sir, they are both as sure as love, a priest, and three thousand pound—which is her portion—can make 'hem: and by this time are ready to bespeak their wedding-supper at the Windmill, except some friend here prevent[2] 'hem, and invite 'hem home.

Clem. Marry, that will I (I thank thee for putting me in mind on't).—Sirrah, go you and fetch 'hem hither, "upon my warrant." [*Exit* Servant.] Neither's friends have cause to be sorry, if I know the young couple aright. —Here, I drink to thee for thy good news. But, I pray thee, what hast thou done with my man, Formal?

Brai. Faith, sir, after some ceremony past, as making him drunk, first with story, and then with wine,—but all in kindness—and stripping him to his shirt: I left him in that cool vein, departed, sold "your worship's warrant" to these two, pawned his livery for that varlet's gown, to

---

[1] *i.e.* Reformado, see p. 59.   [2] Anticipate.

serve it in; and thus have brought myself, by my activity, to your worship's consideration.

Clem. And I will consider thee, in another cup of sack. Here's to thee, which having drunk off, this is my sentence:—Pledge me.—Thou hast done, or assisted to nothing, in my judgment, but deserves to be pardoned for the wit o' the offence. If thy master, or any man here, be angry with thee, I shall suspect his ingine[1] while I know him, for't.—How now, what noise is that?

Enter Servant.

Serv. Sir, it is Roger is come home.

Clem. Bring him in, bring him in.

[2]*Enter* FORMAL *in a suit of armour.*

What! drunk in arms, against me? your reason, your reason for this?

Form. I beseech your worship to pardon me; I happened into ill company by chance, that cast me into a sleep, and stript me of all my clothes——

Clem. Well, tell him, I am Justice Clement, and do pardon him:—but what is this to your armour? what may that signify?

Form. An't please you, sir, it hung up i' the room, where I was stript; and I borrowed it of one o' the drawers[3] to come home in, because I was loth to do penance through the street, i' my shirt.

Clem. Well, stand by a while.

[4] *Enter* E. KNO'WELL, WELL-BRED, *and* BRIDGET.

Who be these? O, the young company,—welcome, welcome! Gi' you joy. Nay, Mistress Bridget, blush not; you are not so fresh a bride, but the news of it is come hither afore you. Master bridegroom, I ha' made your

---

[1] Wit, sense.—Lat. *ingenium.* [2] Scene iv. in old eds.
[3] Drawers of liquor. [4] Scene v. in old eds.

peace, give me your hand: so will I for all the rest, ere you forsake my roof.

E. Kn. We are the more bound to your humanity, sir.

Clem. Only these two[1] have so little of man in 'hem, they are no part of my care.

Wel. Yes, sir, let me pray you for this gentleman, he belongs to my sister, the bride.

Clem. In what place, sir?

Wel. Of her delight, sir; below the stairs, and in public: —her poet, sir.

Clem. A poet? I will challenge him myself presently at extempore.

Mount up thy Phlegon,[2] Muse, and testify,
    How Saturn, sitting in an ebon cloud,
    Disrobed his podex, white as ivory,
        And, through the welkin, thundered all aloud.

Wel. He is not for extempore, sir. He is all for the pocket-muse; please you command a sight of it.

Clem, Yes, yes, search him for a taste of his vein.

[*They search* MATTHEW's *pockets.*

Wel. You must not deny the Queen's Justice, sir, under a writ o' rebellion.

Clem. What! all this verse? body o' me, he carries a whole ream,[3] a commonwealth of paper in 's hose; let's see some of his subjects.   [*Reads.*

" Unto the boundless ocean of thy face,
    Runs this poor river, charged with streams of eyes."
How? this is stolen.[4]

E. Kn. A parody! a parody! with a kind of miraculous gift, to make it absurder than it was.

Clem. Is all the rest, of this batch?—Bring me a torch; lay it together, and give fire. Cleanse the air.— Here was enough to have infected the whole city, if it had not been taken in time. See, see, how our poet's glory shines! brighter, and brighter! still it increases!

---

[1] Bobadill and Matthew.   [2] One of the horses of the Sun.
[3] A quibble on realm.   [4] S. Daniel, sonnet to Delia I., ll. 1-2.

Oh, now it's at the highest: and now, it declines as fast.
You may see. *Sic transit gloria mundi !*[1]

Kno'. There's an emblem for you, son, and your studies!

Clem. Nay, no speech, or act of mine be drawn against
such, as profess it worthily. They are not born every
year, as an alderman. There goes more to the making
of a good poet, than a sheriff, Master Kitely. You look
upon me! though I live i' the city here, amongst you, I
will do more reverence to him, when I meet him, than I
will to the mayor—out of his year. But, these paper-
pedlars! these ink-dabblers! they cannot expect reprehension, or reproach.[2] They have it with the fact.

E. Kn. Sir, you have saved me the labour of a
defence.

Clem. It shall be discourse for supper, between your
father and me, if he dare undertake me. But, to dispatch
away these,—you sign o' the soldier, and picture o' the
poet, (but both so false, I will not ha' you hanged out at
my door till midnight,[3]) while we are at supper, you two
shall penitently fast it out in my court, without; and, if
you will, you may pray there, that we may be so merry
within, as to forgive, or forget you, when we come out.
Here's a third,[4] because we tender your safety, shall
watch you, he is provided for the purpose. Look to
your charge, sir.

Step. And what shall I do?

Clem. O! I had lost a sheep, an he had not bleated!
—Why, sir, you shall give Master Down-right his cloak ;
—and I will intreat him to take it. A trencher and a
napkin you shall have, i' the buttery, and keep Cob and
his wife company, here ;—whom I will intreat first to be
reconciled ;—and you to endeavour with your wit to keep
'hem so.

Step. I'll do my best.

---

[1] So passes away the glory of this world.
[2] Merely. They are taken in the fact, *i.e.* the act.
[3] When no one can see you.   [4] *i.e.* Formal.

Cob. Why, now I see thou art honest, Tib, I receive thee as my dear, and mortal wife again.

Tib. And I you, as my loving, and obedient husband.

Clem. Good complement ! It will be their bridal night too. They are married anew. Come, I conjure the rest, to put off all discontent. You, Master Down-right, your anger ; you Master Kno'well, your cares ; Master Kitely and his wife, their jealousy.

> For, I must tell you both, while that is fed,
> Horns i' the mind are worse than o' the head.

Kit. Sir, thus they go from me ;—kiss me, sweetheart.

> "See what a drove of horns fly in the air,
> Winged with my cleansèd, and my cred'lous breath !
> Watch 'hem, suspicious eyes, watch where they fall.
> See, see ! on heads, that think they've none at all !
> O, what a plenteous world, of this will come !
> When air rains horns, all may be sure of some."

I ha' learned so much verse out of a jealous man's part, in a play.

Clem. 'Tis well, 'tis well ! This night we'll dedicate to friendship, love, and laughter. Master bridegroom, take your bride, and lead ;—every one, a fellow. Here is my mistress,—Brain-worm ! to whom all my addresses of courtship shall have their reference. Whose adventures this day, when our grandchildren shall hear to be made a fable, I doubt not, but it shall find both spectators, and applause.   [*Exeunt.*

EVERY MAN OUT OF HIS
HUMOUR.

ONSON'S second play was produced in 1599 by those who had brought out his first unassisted play, namely, by the Globe or Shakespeare's company. On one occasion Queen Elizabeth honoured its performance by her presence, and Jonson took the opportunity to alter the Epilogue to one highly panegyrical, with which her Majesty appears to have been duly pleased, and, in the words of Lord Falkland, "with her judicious favours did infuse courage and strength into his youthful muse." The public, however, resenting the disgrace of Essex after his return from Ireland, did not receive the panegyric so well, as Jonson, in his quarto, thought proper to notice at length. Nor did her Majesty's "favours," after both this play and *Cynthia's Revels*, appear to have resulted in anything of so substantial a character as our author coveted and expected.

With regard to the parts of Clove and Orange, who, as Cordatus says, "are mere strangers to the whole scope of our play," the extravagant diction of John Marston was without a doubt ridiculed in Clove's fustian phrases, while to every appearance Thomas Dekker was ridiculed as Orange.

The play was entered on the Stationers' Registers on 8th April, 1600, and was published, probably on account of its success, about four months before the publication of Jonson's previous play, *Every Man in his Humour*. In it Jonson's learning is amply shown, as it abounds in quotations from the classics and from Erasmus. But it had not in after years the reputation of its predecessor, since there seems to be no evidence of its performance at a later date than 1682.

To the noblest nurseries of humanity, and liberty, in the kingdom,

THE INNS OF COURT.[1]

UNDERSTAND you, Gentlemen, not your houses: and a worthy succession of you, to all time, as being born the judges of these studies. When I wrote this poem, I had friendship with divers in your societies; who, as they were great names in learning, so they were no less examples of living. Of them, and then—that I say no more—it was not despised. Now that the printer, by a doubled charge, thinks it worthy a longer life than commonly the air of such things doth promise, I am careful to put it a servant to their pleasures, who are the inheritors of the first favour borne it. Yet, I command, it lie not in the way of your more noble, and useful studies to the public: for so, I shall suffer for it. But, when the gown and cap is off, and the lord of liberty reigns, then, to take it in your hands, perhaps may make some bencher, tincted with humanity, read—and not repent him.

By your true Honourer,

BEN JONSON.

[1] This dedication is not given in the quarto.

IN THE INDUCTION.

ASPER, the Presenter or Author.
CORDATUS ⎱ his friends.
MITIS ⎰

IN THE PLAY.

MACILENTE (ASPER, *i.e.* B. Jonson " out of his humour.")
Sir PUNTARVOLO.
CARLO BUFFONE, a jester.
FASTIDIUS BRISK, a gallant.
CINEDO, his punk, disguised as his page.
DELIRO, a citizen trader.
FIDO, his servant lad.
SORDIDO, a farmer.
FUNGOSO, his son, FALLACE'S brother, a student of law.
SOGLIARDO, SORDIDO'S younger brother.
SHIFT, a Paul's man, one living more or less basely by his
    wits.
CLOVE ⎱ contemporary playwrights ridiculed by Jonson.
ORANGE ⎰
CORDATUS ⎱ as in Induction, two critical spectators on the
MITIS ⎰   stage.

SAVIOLINA, a Court Lady.
THE LADY OF THE KNIGHT.
HER WAITING-GENTLEWOMAN.
FALLACE, DELIRO'S wife.

Huntsmen, Musicians, two Serving Men with dog and cat,
    Sordido's Hind, five other Rustics, a Notary, Tailor,
    Haberdasher, Shoemaker, Groom, Drawers at the Inn,
    Constable with his Men.

THE CHARACTERS OF THE PERSONS.[1]

SPER.[2] He is of an ingenious and free spirit, eager, and constant in reproof, without fear controlling the world's abuses. One, whom no servile hope of gain, or frosty apprehension of danger, can make to be a parasite, either to time, place, or opinion.

MACILENTE.[3] A man well parted,[4] a sufficient scholar, and travelled ; who, wanting that place in the world's account which he thinks his merit capable of, falls into such an envious apoplexy, with which his judgment is so dazzled, and distasted, that he grows violently impatient of any opposite happiness in another.

PUNTARVOLO.[5] A vain-glorious knight, over-Englishing his travels, and wholly consecrated to singularity ; the very Jacob's staff[6] of compliment ; a Sir that hath lived to see the revolution of time in most of his apparel. Of presence good enough, but so palpably affected to his own praise, that—for want of flatterers—he commends himself, to the floutage of his own family. He deals upon returns,[7] and strange performances, resolving, in despite of public derision, to stick to his own particular fashion, phrase, and gesture.

CARLO BUFFONE.[8] A public, scurrilous, and profane jester, that, more swift than Circe, with absurd similes, will

---

[1] Not in the quarto.
[2] The "rough and rugged one : " Jonson, the presenter.
[3] The "lean (and malevolent) one," Asper transformed, *i.e.* Jonson out of his humour.
[4] Endowed with abilities.   [5] "Affected, self-conceited."
[6] An instrument for measuring altitudes, &c.
[7] Puts out, to receive more on his return from a journey.
[8] Probably some then well-known jester, drawn from life.

Jon. I.   I

transform any person into deformity. A good feast-hound or banquet-beagle, that will scent you out a supper some three miles off, and swear to his patrons, "Damn him! he came in oars," when he was but wafted over in a sculler. A slave that hath an extraordinary gift in pleasing his palate, and will swill up more sack at a sitting, than would make all the guard a posset.[1] His religion is railing, and his discourse ribaldry. They stand highest in his respect, whom he studies most to reproach.

FASTIDIUS BRISK. A neat, spruce, affecting courtier, one that wears clothes well, and in fashion; practiseth by his glass, how to salute; speaks good remnants, notwithstanding the base viol and tobacco; swears tersely, and with variety; cares not what lady's favour he belies, or great man's familiarity: a good property to perfume the boot of a coach. He will borrow another man's horse to praise, and backs him as his own. Or, for a need, on foot can post himself into credit with his merchant, only with the gingle of his spur, and the jerk of his wand.

DELIRO. A good doting citizen, who, it is thought, might be of the common-council for his wealth: a fellow sincerely besotted on his own wife, and so rapt with a conceit of her perfections, that he simply holds himself unworthy of her. And, in that hood-winked humour, lives more like a suitor than a husband; standing in as true dread of her displeasure, as when he first made love to her. He doth sacrifice two-pence in juniper to her, every morning, before she rises, and wakes her with villanous-out-of-tune music, which she out of her contempt (though not out of her judgment) is sure to dislike.

FALLACE.[2] Deliro's wife, and idol; a proud mincing peat,[3] and as perverse, as he is officious. She dotes as perfectly upon the courtier, as her husband doth on her, and only wants the face to be dishonest.

SAVIOLINA.[4] A court-lady, whose weightiest praise is a light wit, admired by herself, and one more, her servant Brisk.

SORDIDO. A wretched hob-nailed chuff,[5] whose recreation is reading of almanacs, and felicity, foul weather. One

---

[1] Wine boiled with milk.   [2] The "deceitful one."
[3] A delicate one.   [4] The "self-conceited one."
[5] Avaricious churl.

that never prayed but for a lean dearth, and ever wept in a fat harvest.

FUNGOSO.[1] The son of Sordido, and a student; one that has revelled in his time, and follows the fashion afar off, like a spy. He makes it the whole bent of his endeavours, to wring sufficient means from his wretched father, to put him in the courtiers' cut; at which he earnestly aims, but so unluckily, that he still lights short a suit.[2]

SOGLIARDO.[3] An essential clown, brother to Sordido, yet so enamoured of the name of a gentlemen, that he will have it, though he buys it. He comes up every term to learn to take tobacco, and see new Motions.[4] He is in his kingdom, when he can get himself into company where he may be well laughed at.

SHIFT. A thread-bare shark. One that never was soldier, yet lives upon lendings. His profession is skel-dring[5] and odling,[6] his bank Paul's, and his warehouse Picthatch.[7] Takes up single testons upon oaths, till doomsday. Falls under executions of three shillings, and enters into five-groat bonds. He way-lays the reports of services, and cons them without book, damning himself he came new from them, when all the while he was taking the diet[8] in a bawdy-house, or lay pawned in his chamber for rent, and victuals. He is of that admirable, and happy memory, that he will salute one for an old acquaintance, that he never saw in his life before. He usurps, upon cheats, quarrels, and robberies, which he never did, only to get him a name. His chief exercises are, taking the whiff, squiring a cockatrice, and making privy searches for imparters.[9]

CLOVE and ORANGE.[10] An inseparable case[11] of cox-combs, city born; the Gemini, or twins of foppery; that like a pair of wooden foils, are fit for nothing but to be practised upon. Being well flattered they'll lend money, and repent when they ha' done. Their glory is to invite

---

[1] The "spongy, mushroom-like one."
[2] Always a fashion behind.   [3] The "lubbard gull."
[4] Puppet-shows.   [5] Cheating.
[6] Doing odds and ends.   [7] A suburb of ill-repute.
[8] *i.e.* Being treated for disease.   [9] Those who will give to him.
[10] Clove is Marston, Orange, Decker, "a couple of mere strangers to the whole play" (III. i.), but brought in to be ridiculed as talkers of fustian.
[11] Pair.

players, and make suppers. And in company of better rank, to avoid the suspect of insufficiency, will inforce their ignorance most desperately, to set upon the understanding of any thing. Orange is the more humorous of the two, (whose small portion of juice being squeezed out) Clove serves to stick him with commendations.

CORDATUS.[1] The author's friend; a man inly acquainted with the scope and drift of his plot: of a discreet and understanding judgment; and has the place of a Moderator.

MITIS. Is a person of no action, and therefore we have reason to afford him no character.

[2] It was not near his thought, that hath published this, either to traduce the author; or to make vulgar and cheap, any the peculiar and sufficient deserts of the actors: but rather—whereas many censures fluttered about it—to give all leave, and leisure, to judge with distinction.

[1] Cordatus and Mitis appear in the Induction, and act as Grex or Chorus in the play itself, being spectators on the stage who criticise, maintain and explain the action of the piece.

[2] The quarto only contains this paragraph, and divided off from the preceding matter.

EVERY MAN OUT OF HIS HUMOUR.

THE INDUCTION.

After the second sounding,[1]

Enter CORDATUS, ASPER, *and* MITIS.

OR. Nay, my dear Asper,

Mit. Stay your mind.

Asp. Away!
Who is so patient of this impious world
That he can check his spirit, or rein his
tongue?
Or who hath such a dead, unfeeling
sense,
That Heaven's horrid thunders cannot wake?
To see the earth, cracked with the weight of sin,
Hell gaping under us, and o'er our heads
Black, ravenous ruin, with her sail-stretched wings,
Ready to sink us down, and cover us.
Who can behold such prodigies as these,
And have his lips sealed up? not I : my soul
Was never ground into such oily colours,
To flatter vice, and daub iniquity :
But, with an armèd and resolvèd hand,
I'll strip the ragged follies of the time,

---

[1] There were three soundings before the play began.

Naked, as at their birth——
   Cor. [*Aside to him.*] Be not too bold.
   Asp. [*Aside.*] You trouble me—and with a whip of steel,
Print wounding lashes in their iron ribs.
I fear no mood stamped in a private brow,
When I am pleased t'unmask a public vice.
I fear no strumpet's drugs, nor ruffian's stab,
Should I detect their hateful luxuries ;
No broker's, usurer's, or lawyer's gripe,
Were I disposed to say, they're all corrupt.
I fear no courtier's frown, should I applaud
The easy flexure of his supple hams.
Tut, these are so innate, and popular,
That drunken custom would not shame to laugh
In scorn, at him, that should but dare to tax 'hem :
And yet, not one of these, but knows his works,
Knows what damnation is, the devil, and hell ;
Yet hourly they persist, grow rank in sin,
Puffing their souls away in perjurous air,
To cherish their extortion, pride, or lusts.
   Mit. Forbear, good Asper, be not like your name.
   Asp. O, but to such, whose faces are all zeal,
And—with the words of Hercules[1]—invade
Such crimes as these ! that will not smell of sin,
But seem as they were made of sanctity !
Religion in their garments, and their hair
Cut shorter than their eye-brows ![2] when the conscience
Is vaster than the ocean, and devours
More wretches than the Counters.[3]
   Mit.   Gentle Asper,
Contain your spirit in more stricter bounds,
And be not thus transported with the violence
Of your strong thoughts.
   Cor.   Unless your breath had power
To melt the world, and mould it new again,
It is in vain to spend it in these moods.
   Asp. [*Turning.*] I not observed this throngèd round till
     now.
Gracious, and kind spectators, you are welcome,

---

[1] Audacious words.   [2] A description of the Puritan.
          [3] The City prisons.

Apollo and the Muses feast your eyes
With graceful objects, and may our Minerva
Answer your hopes, unto their largest strain !
Yet here mistake me not, judicious friends.
I do not this, to beg your patience,
Or servilely to fawn on your applause,
Like some dry brain, despairing in his merit.
Let me be censured by the austerest brow,
Where I want art, or judgment ; tax me freely :
Let envious censors, with their broadest eyes,
Look through, and through me, I pursue no favour.
Only vouchsafe me your attentions,
And I will give you music worth your ears.
O, how I hate the monstrousness of time,
Where every servile imitating spirit,
Plagued with an itching leprosy of wit,
In a mere halting fury, strives to fling
His ulcerous body in the Thespian spring,
And straight leaps forth a poet ! but as lame
As Vulcan, or the founder of Cripplegate.

Mit. In faith, this humour will come ill to some,
You will be thought to be too peremptory.

Asp. " This humour " ? good ! and why " this humour,"
   Mitis ?
Nay, do not turn, but answer.

Mit.   Answer, what ?

Asp. I will not stir your patience, pardon me,
I urged it for some reasons, and the rather
To give these ignorant, well-spoken days
Some taste of their abuse of this word " humour."

Cor. O, do not let your purpose fall, good Asper,
It cannot but arrive most acceptáble,
Chiefly to such, as have the happiness
Daily to see how the poor innocent word
Is racked and tortured.

Mit.   Ay, I pray you proceed.

Asp. Ha ! what ? what is't ?

Cor.   For the abuse of humour.

Asp. O, I crave pardon, I had lost my thoughts.
Why, humour, as 'tis *ens*,[1] we thus define it.

---

[1] A thing existing.

To be a quality of air, or water,
And in itself holds these two properties,
Moisture, and fluxure : as, for demonstration,
Pour water on this floor, 'twill wet, and run :
Likewise the air, forced through a horn, or trumpet,
Flows instantly away, and leaves behind
A kind of dew ; and hence we do conclude,
That whatsoe'er hath fluxure, and humidity,
As wanting power to contain itself,
Is humour.   So in every human body,
The choler, melancholy, phlegm, and blood,
By reason that they flow continually
In some one part, and are not continent,[1]
Receive the name of Humours.   Now thus far
It may, by metaphor, apply itself
Unto the general disposition :
As when some one peculiar quality
Doth so possess a man, that it doth draw
All his affects,[2] his spirits, and his powers,
In their confluctions, all to run one way,
This may be truly said to be a humour.
But that a rook,[3] by wearing a pied feather,
The cable hat-band, or the three-piled[4] ruff,
A yard of shoe-tie, or the Switzer's knot
On his French garters, should affect a " humour " !
O, it is more than most ridiculous.

Cor. He speaks pure truth, now, if an idiot
Have but an apish, or fantastic strain,
It is " his humour."

Asp.   Well, I will scourge those apes
And to these courteous eyes oppose a mirror,
As large as is the stage whereon we act,
Where they shall see the time's deformity
Anatomized in every nerve, and sinew,
With constant courage, and contempt of fear.

Mit. Asper, (I urge it as your friend) take heed,
The days are dangerous, full of exception,
And men are grown impatient of reproof.

Asp.   Ha, ha

---

[1] Staying together in one place.   [2] Affections.
[3] Simpleton-prater.   [4] Three-tiered.

You might as well have told me, yond, is Heaven,
This, earth, these, men, and all had moved alike.
Do not I know the time's condition?
Yes, Mitis, and their souls, and who they be,
That either will, or can, except 'gainst me.
None, but a sort[1] of fools, so sick in taste,
That they contemn all physic of the mind,
And, like galled camels, kick at every touch.
Good men, and virtuous spirits, that loath their vices,
Will cherish my free labours, love my lines,
And, with the fervour of their shining grace,
Make my brain fruitful to bring forth more objects,
Worthy their serious, and intentive eyes.
But why enforce I this? as fainting? No
If any, here, chance to behold himself,
Let him not dare to challenge me of wrong,
For, if he shame to have his follies known,
First, he should shame to act 'hem: my strict hand
Was made to seize on vice, and with a gripe
Squeeze out the humour of such spongy natures
As lick up every idle vanity.

 Cor. Why, this is right *furor poeticus!*[2] [*To audience*
Kind gentlemen, we hope your patience
Will yet conceive the best, or entertain
This supposition, that a madman speaks.

 Asp. [*To those within.*] What! are you ready there?
 ——Mitis, sit down,
And my Cordatus.——Sound ho! and begin.——
I leave you two, as censors, to sit here:
Observe what I present, and liberally
Speak your opinions upon every scene,
As it shall pass the view of these spectators.——
Nay, now y'are tedious, sir, for shame begin.——
And, Mitis, note me, if, in all this front,
You can espy a gallant of this mark,
Who, to be thought one of the judicious,
Sits with his arms thus wreathed, his hat pulled here,
Cries mew,[3] and nods, then shakes his empty head,
Will show more several motions in his face

---

[1] Lot.   [2] Poetic fury.
[3] In token of disapprobation (cat-calls).

Than the new London, Rome, or Niniveh,[1]
And, now and then, breaks a dry biscuit jest,
Which, that it may more easily be chewed,
He steeps in his own laughter.

 Cor.   Why, will that
Make it be sooner swallowed?

 Asp.   O, assure you.
Or if it did not, yet, as Horace sings,
" *Jejunus raro stomachus vulgaria temnit,*"
" Mean cates are welcome still to hungry guests."

 Cor. 'Tis true, but why should we observe 'hem, Asper?

 Asp. O, I would know 'hem, for in such assemblies
They're more infectious than the pestilence:
And therefore I would give them pills to purge,
And make 'hem fit for fair societies.
How monstrous, and detested is't to see
A fellow, that has neither art, nor brain,
Sit like an Aristarchus[2], or—stark-ass,
Taking men's lines, with a tobacco face,
In snuff[3], still spitting, using his wryed looks,
In nature of a vice, to wrest and turn
The good aspect of those that shall sit near him,
From what they do behold! O, 'tis most vile.

 Mit. Nay, Asper.

 Asp.   Peace, Mitis, I do know your thought:
You'll say, your guests, here, will except at this:
Pish! you are too timorous, and full of doubt.
Then he, a patient, shall reject all physic,
'Cause the physician tells him, you are sick:
Or, if I say, " that he is vicious,"
You will not hear of virtue. Come, you're fond.[4]
Shall I be so extravagant, to think,
That happy judgments, and composèd spirits,
Will challenge me for taxing such as these?
I am ashamed.

 Cor.   Nay, but good, pardon us:
We must not bear this peremptory sail,
But use our best endeavours how to please.

 Asp. Why, therein I commend your careful thoughts,

---

[1] The Motions or Puppets in these shows.
[2] A most celebrated critic. [3] In offence, anger. [4] Foolish.

And I will mix with you in industry
To please ; but whom ? attentive auditors,
Such as will join their profit with their pleasure,
And come to feed their understanding parts :
For these, I'll prodigally spend myself,
And speak away my spirit into air ;
For these, I'll melt my brain into invention,
Coin new conceits, and hang my richest words
As polished jewels in their bounteous ears ?[1]
But stay, I lose myself, and wrong their patience ;
If I dwell here, they'll not begin, I see.
Friends, sit you still, and entertain this troop
With some familiar, and by-conference,
I'll haste them sound. [*To audience.*] Now, gentlemen,
    I go
To turn an actor, and a humourist,
Where, ere I do resume my present person,
We hope to make the circles of your eyes
Flow with distillèd laughter : if we fail,
We must impute it to this only chance,
"Art hath an enemy called Ignorance.   [*Exit.*

  Cor. How do you like his spirit, Mitis ?

  Mit. I should like it much better, if he were less confident.

  Cor. Why, do you suspect his merit ?

  Mit. No, but I fear this will procure him much envy.[2]

  Cor. O, that sets the stronger seal on his desert ; if he
had no enemies, I should esteem his fortunes most wretched
at this instant.

  Mit. You have seen his play, Cordatus ? pray you, how
is't ?

  Cor. Faith sir, I must refrain to judge ; only this I can
say of it, 'tis strange, and of a particular kind by itself,
somewhat like *Vetus Comœdia* ;[3] a work that hath boun-
teously pleased me ; how it will answer the general expectation, I know not.

  Mit. Does he observe all the laws of comedy in it ?

  Cor. What laws mean you ?

  Mit. Why, the equal division of it into acts, and scenes,
according to the Terentian manner ; his true number of

---

[1] See p. 92.   [2] Dislike.   [3] The ancient comedy.

actors; the furnishing of the scene with Grex, or Chorus, and that the whole argument fall within compass of a day's business.

Cor. O no, these are too nice observations.

Mit. They are such as must be received, by your favour, or it cannot be authentic.

Cor. Troth, I can discern no such necessity.

Mit. No?

Cor. No, I assure you, signior. If those laws, you speak of, had been delivered us, *ab initio*,[1] and in their present virtue and perfection, there had been some reason of obeying their powers: but 'tis extant, that that which we called *Comœdia*, was at first nothing but a simple and continued song, sung by one only person, till Susario invented a second; after him, Epicharmus a third; Phormus and Chionides devised to have four actors, with a prologue and chorus; to which Cratinus, long after, added a fifth, and sixth; Eupolis, more; Aristophanes, more than they; every man in the dignity of his spirit and judgment supplied something. And, though that in him this kind of poem appeared absolute, and fully perfected, yet how is the face of it changed since, in Menander, Philemon, Cecilius, Plautus, and the rest; who have utterly excluded the chorus, altered the property of the persons, their names, and natures, and augmented it with all liberty, according to the elegancy and disposition of those times, wherein they wrote. I see not then, but we should enjoy the same licence or free power to illustrate and heighten our invention, as they did; and not be tied to those strict and regular forms, which the niceness of a few—who are nothing but form—would thrust upon us.

Mit. Well, we will not dispute of this now; but what's his scene?

Cor. Marry, *Insula Fortunata*, sir.

Mit. O, "the Fortunate Island!"[2] mass, he has bound himself to a strict law there.

Cor. Why so?

Mit. He cannot lightly alter the scene, without crossing the seas.

---

[1] From the beginning.   [2] England.

Cor. He needs not, having a whole island to run through, I think.

Mit. No ? how comes it then, that in some one play we see so many seas, countries, and kingdoms, passed over with such admirable dexterity ?

Cor. O, that but shows how well the authors can travel[1] in their vocation, and outrun the apprehension of their auditory. But, leaving this, I would they would begin once : this protraction is able to sour the best settled patience in the theatre.   [*The third sounding.*

Mit. They have answered your wish, sir ; they sound.

Enter Prologue.

Cor. O, here comes the Prologue :——now, sir, if you had stayed a little longer, I meant to have spoke your prologue for you, i'faith.

Prol. Marry, with all my heart, sir, you shall do it yet, and I thank you.   [*Going.*

Cor. Nay, nay, stay, stay, hear you ?

Prol. You could not have studied to ha' done me a greater benefit at the instant, for I protest to you I am un-perfect, and, had I spoke it, I must of necessity have been out.

Cor. Why, but do you speak this seriously ?

Prol. Seriously ! ay, wit's my help, do I ; and esteem myself indebted to your kindness for it.

Cor. For what ?

Prol. Why, for undertaking the prologue for me.

Cor. How ! did I undertake it for you ?

Prol. Did you ! I appeal to all these gentlemen, whether you did or no ? Come, come, it pleases you to cast a strange look on't now ; but 'twill not serve.

Cor. 'Fore me, but it must serve ; and therefore speak your prologue.

Prol. An I do, let me die poisoned with some venomous hiss, and never live to look as high as the two-penny room[2] again.   [*Exit.*

Mit. He has put you to it, sir.

Cor. 'Sdeath, what a humorous fellow is this !——Gentlemen, good faith I can speak no prologue, howsoever, his weak wit has had the fortune to make this strong use of me, here before you : but I protest——

---

[1] He puns on this and "travail."   [2] The gallery.

Enter CARLO BUFFONE, *and a* Boy *with wine.*

Car. Come, come, leave these fustian protestations;
away, come, I cannot abide these grey-headed ceremonies.
Boy, fetch me a glass quickly, I may bid these gentlemen
welcome; give 'hem a health here: [*Exit* Boy.] I mar'le
whose wit 'twas to put a prologue in yond sackbut's[1] mouth:
they might well think he'd be out of tune, and yet you'ld
play upon him too.

Cor. Hang him, dull block!

Car. O, good words, good words; a well-timbered fellow,
he would ha' made a good column, an he had been thought
on, when the house was a-building—

Re-enter Boy *with a glass.*

O, art thou come? well said;[2] give me, boy; fill, so!
Here's a cup of wine sparkles like a diamond.—Gentlewomen
(I am sworn to put them in first) and gentlemen, a round in
place of a bad prologue, I drink this good draught to your
health here, Canary, the very elixir, and spirit of wine.
This is that our poet calls Castalian liquor, when he comes
abroad, now and then, once in a fortnight, and makes a
good meal among players, where he has *caninum appe-
titum*[3]: marry, at home he keeps a good philosophical diet,
beans and buttermilk: an honest pure rogue, he will take
you off three, four, five of these, one after another, and look
villanously when he has done, like a one-headed Cerberus—
he does not hear me, I hope,—and then, when his belly is
well ballassed, and his brain rigged a little, he sails away
withal, as though he would work wonders when he comes
home. He has made a play here, and he calls it, *Every
Man out of his Humour!* 'sblood an he get me out of the
humour he has put me in, I'll trust none of his tribe again,
while I live. Gentles, all I can say for him is—"you are
welcome." I could wish my bottle here amongst you; but
there's an old rule, *No pledging your own health.* Marry,
if any here be thirsty for it, their best way (that I know) is,
sit still, seal up their lips, and drink so much of the play
in, at their ears.   [*Exit.*

----

[1] A bass trumpet-like instrument.
[2] Then used in sense of 'sayed, tried (and done).
[3] A dog's greedy appetite.

Mit. What may this fellow be, Cordatus ?

Cor. Faith, if the time will suffer his description, I'll give it you. He is one, the author calls him Carlo Buffone, an impudent common jester, a violent railer, and an incomprehensible epicure ; one whose company is desired of all men, but beloved of none : he will sooner lose his soul than a jest, and profane even the most holy things, to excite laughter : no honourable or reverend personage whatsoever can come within the reach of his eye, but is turned into all manner of variety, by his adulterate similes.

Mit. You paint forth a monster.

Cor. He will prefer all countries before his native, and thinks he can never sufficiently, or with admiration enough, deliver his affectionate conceit of foreign atheistical policies : but stay—

Enter MACILENTE *meditating.*

Observe these, he'll appear himself anon.

Mit. O, this is your envious man, Macilente, I think.

Cor. The same, sir.

ACT THE FIRST

SCENE I.—*The Country*

Enter MACILENTE

ACI. *Viri est, fortunæ cæcitatem facilè
     ferre.*[1]
    'Tis true ; but, Stoic, where in the vast
      world,
    Doth that man breathe, than can so
      much command

His blood, and his affection ? well : I see,
I strive in vain to cure my wounded soul ;
For every cordial that my thoughts apply,
Turns to a corr'sive, and doth eat it farther
There is no taste in this philosophy,
'Tis like a potion that a man should drink
But turns his stomach with the sight of it.
I am no such pilled[2] Cynic to believe
That beggary is the only happiness ;
Or, with a number of these patient fools,
To sing : " My mind to me a kingdom is,"
When the lank hungry belly barks for food.
I look into the world, and there I meet
With objects that do strike my blood-shot eyes
Into my brain : where, when I view myself,
Having before observed this man is great,

---

[1] It is the part of one, truly a man, to bear easily the blindness of
Fortune.   [2] Polled.

Mighty, and feared ; that, loved and highly favoured :
A third, thought wise and learnèd ; a fourth, rich,
And therefore honoured ; a fifth, rarely featured ;
A sixth, admired for his nuptial fortunes :
When I see these, I say, and view myself,
I wish the organs of my sight were cracked ;
And that the engine of my grief could cast
Mine eyeballs, like two globes of wildfire, forth,
To melt this unproportioned frame of nature.
Oh, they are thoughts that have transfixed my heart,
And often, i' the strength of apprehension,
Made my cold passion stand upon my face;
Like drops of dew on a stiff cake of ice.

   Cor. This alludes well to that of the poet,
      Invidus suspirat, gemit, incutitque dentes,
      Sudat frigidus, intuens quod odit.[1]
   Mit. O, peace, you break the scene.

   Maci.   Soft, who be these ?
I'll lay me down awhile till they be past.

     Enter SOGLIARDO *and* CARLO BUFFONE.[2]

   Cor. Signior, note this gallant, I pray you.
   Mit. What is he ?
   Cor. A tame rook, you'll take him presently; list.

   Sog. Nay, look you, Carlo ; this is my humour now !
I have land and money, my friends left me well, and I
will be a gentleman, whatsoever it cost me.
   Car. A most gentlemanlike resolution.
   Sog. Tut ! an I take an humour of a thing once, I
am like your tailor's needle, I go through : but for my
name, signior, how think you ? will it not serve for a
gentleman's name, when the signior is put to it, ha ?
   Car. Let me hear ; how is't ?
   Sog. Signior Insulso Sogliardo :[3] methinks it sounds well.

---

[1] Spitefully looking at what he hates, he sighs, groans, gnashes
his teeth, and being cold, sweats.
[2] Scene ii. in old editions.   [3] Senseless lubbard.

Car. O excellent! tut, an all fitted to your name, you might very well stand for a gentleman: I know many Sogliardos gentlemen.

Sog. Why, and for my wealth I might be a Justice of peace.

Car. [*Aside.*] Ay, and a constable for your wit.[1]

Sog. All this is my lordship you see here, and those farms you came by.

Car. Good steps to gentility too, marry: but Sogliardo, if you affect to be a gentleman indeed, you must observe all the rare qualities, humours, and complements[2] of a gentleman.

Sog. I know it, signior, and if you please to instruct, I am not too good to learn, I'll assure you.

Car. Enough, sir. [*Aside.*] I'll make admirable use i' the projection of my medicine upon this lump of copper here.—I'll bethink me for you, sir.

Sog. Signior, I will both pay you, and pray you, and thank you, and think on you.

Cor. Is not this purely good?

Maci. [*Aside.*] S'blood, why should such a prick-eared hind as this
Be rich? ha? a fool? such a transparent gull
That may be seen through? wherefore should he have land,
Houses, and lordships? O, I could eat my entrails,
And sink my soul into the earth with sorrow.

Car. First, to be an accomplished gentleman, that is, a gentleman of the time, you must give o'er housekeeping in the country, and live altogether in the city amongst gallants: where, at your first appearance, 'twere good you turned four or five hundred acres of your best land into two or three trunks of apparel—you may do it without going to a conjurer—and be sure you mix yourself still, with such as flourish in the spring of the fashion, and are least popular;[3] study their carriage and behaviour in

---

[1] As was a Dogberry, &c.   [2] Those things that make up.
[3] Common.

all ; learn to play at primero and passage,[1] and—ever
when you lose—ha' two or three peculiar oaths to swear
by, that no man else swears : but, above all, protest in
your play, and affirm, " Upon your credit "—" As you
are a true gentleman," at every cast ; you may do it with
a safe conscience, I warrant you.

Sog. O admirable rare ! he cannot choose but be a
gentleman, that has these excellent gifts : more, more, I
beseech you.

Car. You must endeavour to feed cleanly at your
Ordinary,[2] sit melancholy, and pick your teeth when you
cannot speak : and when you come to plays, be humorous,
look with a good starched face, and ruffle your brow like
a new boot,[3] laugh at nothing but your own jests, or else
as the noblemen laugh. That's a special grace you must
observe.

Sog. I warrant you, sir.

Car. Ay, and sit o' the stage and flout ;—provided you
have a good suit.

Sog. O, I'll have a suit only for that, sir.

Car. You must talk much of your kindred, and
allies.

Sog. Lies ! no, signior, I shall not need to do so, I
have kindred i' the city to talk of : I have a niece is a
merchant's wife ; and a nephew, my brother Sordido's
son, of the Inns of court.

Car. O, but you must pretend alliance with courtiers
and great persons : and ever when you are to dine or
sup in any strange presence, hire a fellow with a great
chain,[4] (though it be copper, it's no matter) to bring
you letters, feigned from such a nobleman, or such a
knight, or such a lady, " To their worshipful, right rare,
and nobly qualified friend or kinsman, Signior Insulso
Sogliardo :" give yourself style enough. And there,
while you intend [5] circumstances of news, or enquiry of

---

[1] Gambling card games.   [2] Eating house.   [3] See p. 24, note.
[4] Worn by the higher attendants in a large house.   [5] Seek.

their health, or so, one of your familiars, whom you must
carry about you still, breaks it up, as 'twere in a jest, and
reads it publicly at the table: at which, you must seem
to take as unpardonable offence, as if he had torn your
mistress's colours, or breathed upon her picture; and
pursue it with that hot grace, as if you would advance a
challenge upon it presently.[1]

Sog. Stay, I do not like that humour of challenge, it
may be accepted: but I'll tell you what's my humour
now, I will do this; I will take occasion of sending one
of my suits to the tailor's, to have the pocket repaired, or
so; and there such a letter as you talk of—broke open
and all—shall be left: O, the tailor will presently give
out what I am, upon the reading of it, worth twenty of
your gallants.

Car. But then you must put on an extreme face of dis-
contentment at your man's negligence.

Sog. O, so I will, and beat him too: I'll have a man
for the purpose.

Mac. [*Aside.*] You may; you have land and crowns:
O partial fate!

Car. Mass, well remembered, you must keep your men
gallant at the first, fine pied liveries, laid with good gold
lace; there's no loss in it, they may rip't off and pawn it,
when they lack victuals.

Sog. By'r lady, that is chargeable, signior, 'twill bring
a man in debt.

Car. Debt! why that's the more for your credit, sir:
it's an excellent policy to owe much in these days, if you
note it.

Sog. As how, good signior? I would fain be a politician?[2]

Cor. O! look, where you are indebted any great sum,
your creditor observes you with no less regard, than if he
were bound to you for some huge benefit, and will quake
to give you the least cause of offence, lest he lose his

---

[1] At the instant.   [2] *i.e.*, a politic man.

money. I assure you, in these times, no man has his
servant more obsequious and pliant, than gentlemen
their creditors: to whom, if at any time, you pay but a
moiety, or a fourth part, it comes more acceptedly than
if you gave 'hem a new-year's gift.

Sog. I perceive you, sir: I will take up,[1] and bring
myself in credit, sure.

Cor. Marry this, always beware you commerce not
with bankrupts, or poor needy Ludgathians;[2] they are
impudent creatures, turbulent spirits, they care not what
violent tragedies they stir, nor how they play fast and
loose with a poor gentleman's fortunes, to get their own.
Marry, these rich fellows—that ha' the world, or the
better part of it, sleeping in their counting-houses—they
are ten times more placable, they; either fear, hope, or
modesty, restrains them from offering any outrages:
but this is nothing to your followers, you shall not run
a penny more in arrearage for them, an you list, yourself.

Sog. No? how should I keep 'hem then?

Car. Keep 'hem! 'Sblood, let them keep themselves,
they are no sheep, are they? What? you shall come in
houses, where plate, apparel, jewels, and divers other
pretty commodities lie negligently scattered, and I would
ha' those Mercuries follow me, I trow, should remember
they had not their fingers for nothing.

Sog. That's not so good, methinks.

Car. Why, after you have kept 'hem a fortnight, or so,
and showed 'hem enough to the world, you may turn 'hem
away, and keep no more but a boy, it's enough.

Sog. Nay, my humour is not for boys, I'll keep men,
an I keep any; and I'll give coats,[3] that's my humour:
but I lack a cullisen.[4]

Car. Why, now you ride to the city, you may buy
one; I'll bring you where you shall ha' your choice for
money.

---

[1] On credit.   [2] Ludgate Hill tradesmen.   [3] Of arms.
[4] A badge of arms, worn on the arm of the servitor.

Sog. Can you, sir.

Car. O, ay : you shall have one take measure of you, and make you a coat of arms, to fit you, of what fashion you will.

Sog. By word of mouth, I thank you, signior; I'll be once a little prodigal in a humour, i'faith, and have a most prodigious coat.

Mac. [*Aside.*] Torment and death ! break head and
  brain at once,
To be delivered of your fighting issue.
Who can endure to see blind Fortune dote thus ?
To be enamoured on this dusty turf,
This clod ! a whoreson puck-fist [1] ! O God, God, God,
  God, &c.
I could run wild with grief now, to behold
The rankness of her bounties, that doth breed
Such bulrushes; these mushroom gentlemen,
That shoot up in a night to place, and worship.

Car. [*To* SOGLIARDO *who sees* MACILENTE.] Let him alone ; some stray, some stray.

Sog. Nay, I will examine him before I go, sure.

Car. The lord of the soil has all waifs [2] and strays here, has he not ?

Sog. Yes, sir.

Car. [*Aside.*] Faith then I pity the poor fellow, he's fallen into a fool's hands.

Sog. Sirrah, who gave you commission to lie in my

Mac. Your lordship ?   [lordship ?

Sog. How ! " my lordship ?" do you know me, sir ?

Mac. I do know you, sir.

Car. [*Aside.*] He answers him like an echo.

Sog. Why, who am I, sir?

Mac. One of those that fortune favours.

Car. [*Aside.*] The periphrasis of a fool. I'll observe this better.

---

[1] The puff ball fungus.
[2] Q., Ff., " wefts," the more technical form of the same word.

Sog. "That fortune favours?" how mean you that, friend?

Mac. I mean simply: that you are one that lives not by your wits.

Sog. By my wits? No, sir, I scorn to live by my wits, I. I have better means, I tell thee, than to take such base courses, as to live by my wits. 'Sblood, dost thou think I live by my wits?

Mac. Methinks, jester, you should not relish this well.

Car. Ha! does he know me?

Mac. Though yours be the worst use a man can put his wit to, of thousands, to prostitute it at every tavern and ordinary; yet, methinks, you should have turned your broadside at this, and have been ready with an apology,[1] able to sink this hulk of ignorance into the bottom, and depth of his contempt.

Car. 'Sblood, 'tis Macilente! [*To* MACILENTE.] Signior, you are well encountered; how is 't. [*Aside to him.*] O, we must not regard what he says, man, a trout, a shallow fool, he has no more brain than a butterfly, a mere stuft suit; he looks like a musty bottle new wickered, his head's the cork, light, light!—I am glad to see you so well returned, signior.

Mac. You are? gramercy, good Janus!

Sog. Is he one of your acquaintance? I love him the better for that.

Car. God's precious, come away man, what do you mean? an you knew him as I do, you'ld shun him as you'ld do the plague.

Sog. Why, sir?

Car. O, he's a black fellow,[2] take heed on him.

Sog. Is he a scholar, or a soldier?

Car. Both, both; a lean mongrel, he looks as if he were chap-fallen, with barking at other men's good fortunes: 'ware how you offend him; he carries oil and fire in his pen, will scald where it drops: his spirit's like

---

[1] Gr. and Lat. *Apologia*, defence.   [2] Malignant.

powder, quick, violent; he'll blow a man up with a jest:
I fear him worse than a rotten wall does the cannon,
shake an hour after, at the report. Away, come not
near him.

Sog. For God's sake let's be gone; an he be a scholar,
you know I cannot abide him; I had as lief see a cockatrice,[1] specially as Cockatrices go now.

Car. What, you'll stay, signior? this gentleman,
Sogliardo, and I, are to visit the knight Puntarvolo, and
from thence to the city; we shall meet there.

[*Exit with* SOGLIARDO.

Mac. Ay, when I cannot shun you, we will meet.
'Tis strange! Of all the creatures I have seen,
I envy not this Buffoon, for indeed
Neither his fortunes, nor his parts deserve it:
But I do hate him, as I hate the devil,
Or that brass-visaged monster Barbarism.
O, 'tis an open-throated, black-mouthed cur,
That bites at all, but eats on those that feed him.
A slave, that to your face will, serpent-like,
Creep on the ground, as he would eat the dust,
And to your back will turn the tail, and sting
More deadly than a scorpion: stay, who's this?
Now, for my soul, another minion
Of the old lady Chance's! I'll observe him.

[2]*Enter* SORDIDO *with an Almanac.*

Sord. O rare! good, good, good, good, good! I thank
my stars, I thank my stars for it.

Mac. [*Aside.*] Said I not true? doth not his passion
speak
Out of my divination? O my senses,
Why lose you not your powers, and become
Dulled, if not deaded, with this spectacle?

---

[1] The basilisk, a serpent fabled to kill by either sight or breath.
It was then also a fashionable name for a harlot.
[2] Scene iii. in old eds.

I know him, 'tis Sordido, the farmer,
A boor, and brother to that swine was here.

Scor. Excellent, excellent, excellent! as I would wish,
as I would wish.

Mac. See how the strumpet Fortune tickles him,
And makes him swoon with laughter, Oh, oh, oh!

Sord. Ha, ha, ha, I will not sow my grounds this
year. Let me see, what harvest shall we have? [*Turns
over leaves.*] "June—July—August!"

Mac. What is't, a prognostication raps him so?

Sord. "The 20, 21, 22 days, rain and wind." O
good, good! "the 23, and 24, rain and some wind,"
good! "the 25, rain," good still! "26, 27, 28, wind and
some rain;" would it had been rain and some wind!
well, 'tis good, when it can be no better. "29, inclining
to rain:" inclining to rain? that's not so good now:
"30 and 31, wind and no rain," no rain! 'slid, stay;
this is worse and worse. What says he of St. Swithin's?
turn back, look;—"St. Swithin's[1]: no rain?"[2]

Mac. O, here's a precious, dirty, damnèd rogue,
That fats himself with expectation
Of rotten weather, and unseasoned hours;
And he is rich for it, an elder brother!
His barns are full! his ricks and mows[3] well trod!
His garners crack with store! O, 'tis well; ha,
Ha, ha! a plague consume thee, and thy house!

Sord. O here, "St. Swithin's, the 15 day, variable
weather, for the most part rain," good! "for the most
part rain." Why, it should rain forty days after, now,
more or less, it was a rule held, afore I was able to hold
a plough, and yet here are two days no rain; ha! it
makes me muse. We'll see how the next month[4] begins,
if that be better. "September, first, second, third, and

---

[1] 15th July.
[2] Probably in his hurry looks at wrong month, thus allowing of
Macilente's speech.   [3] Stacks.
[4] *i.e.* The next month after August. He has kept his finger there
while for the moment he turned to St. Swithin's Day.

fourth, days, rainy and blustering;" this is well now:
"fifth, sixth, seventh, eighth, and ninth, rainy, with some
thunder;" Ay marry, this is excellent; the other was false
printed sure: "the tenth, and eleventh, great store of
rain;" O good, good, good, good, good! "the twelfth,
thirteenth, and fourteenth days, rain;" good still:
"fifteenth, and sixteenth, rain;" good still: "seventeenth,
and eighteenth, rain;" good still: "nineteenth, and
twentieth," good still, good still, good still, good still,
good still! "one and twentieth, some rain;" some rain!
well, we must be patient, and attend the heavens' pleasure, would it were more though: "the two and twentieth, three and twentieth, great tempests of rain, thunder,
and lightning."
O good again, past expectation good!
I thank my blessed angel; never, never,
Laid [1] I penny better out than this,
To purchase this dear book: not dear for price,
And yet of me as dearly prized as life,
Since in it is contained the very life,
Blood, strength, and sinews,[2] of my happiness.
Blest be the hour, wherein I bought this book;
His studies happy, that composed the book,
And the man fortunate, that sold the book!
Sleep with this charm, and be as true to me,
As I am joyed and confident in thee.

　　　　　　　　　　　　　　　　[Puts it in his girdle.

The Hind *enters and gives a paper.*

　Mac. Ha, ha, ha! I' not this good? Is't not pleasing
Ha, ha, ha![3] God pardon me! ha, ha!　　　　　[this?
Is't possible that such a spacious villain
Should live, and not be plagued? or lies he hid
Within the wrinkled bosom of the world,
Where Heaven cannot see him? 'Sblood! methinks

---

[1] Pronounced as a dissyllable.　　　　[2] Nerves, *i.e.* feeling.
[3] Probably Jonson meant the first or final "ha" to be a prolonged one—Ha-a.

'Tis rare, and strange, that he should breathe, and walk,
Feed with digestion, sleep, enjoy his health,
And, like a boisterous whale, swallowing the poor,
Still swim in wealth, and pleasure ! is't not strange ?
Unless his house, and skin were thunder-proof,
I wonder at it ! Methinks, now, the hectic,
Gout, leprosy, or some such loathed disease,
Might light upon him ; or that fire, from Heaven,
Might fall upon his barns ; or mice, and rats
Eat up his grain ; or else that it might rot
Within the hoary ricks, e'en as it stands :
Methinks this might be well ; and after all
The devil might come and fetch him. Ay, 'tis true !
Meantime he surfeits in prosperity,
And thou, in envy of him, gnaw'st thyself :
Peace, fool, get hence, and tell thy vexèd spirit,
" Wealth in this age will scarcely look on merit.

[*Rises and exit.*

    Sord. Who brought this same, sirrah ?

    Hind. Marry, sir, one of the justices' men, he says
'tis a precept,[1] and all their hands be at it.

    Sord. Ay, and the prints of them stick in my flesh,
Deeper than i' their letters : they have sent me
Pills wrapped in paper here, that, should I take 'hem,
Would poison all the sweetness of my book,
And turn my honey into hemlock-juice.
But I am wiser than to serve[2] their precepts,
Or follow their prescriptions. Here's a device,
To charge me bring my grain unto the markets :
Ay, much[3] ! when I have neither barn nor garner,
Nor earth to hide it in, I'll bring it ; till then,
Each corn I send shall be as big as Paul's.[4]
O, but—say some—the poor are like to starve.
Why, let 'hem starve, what's that to me ? are bees
Bound to keep life in drones, and idle moths ? no :

---

[1] A technical or magisterial order.   [2] Observe.
[3] Much grain I'll bring !   [4] St. Paul's.

Why such are these—that term themselves the poor,
Only because they would be pitièd,
But are indeed a sort of lazy beggars—
Licentious rogues, and sturdy vagabonds,
Bred, by the sloth of a fat plenteous year,
Like snakes in heat of summer, out of dung ;[1]
And this is all that these cheap times are good for.
Whereas a wholesome, and penurious dearth
Purges the soil of such vile excrements,
And kills the vipers up.

    Hind.   O, but master,
Take heed they hear you not.

    Sord.   Why so ?

    Hind. They will exclaim against you.

    Sord.   Ay, their exclaims
Move me as much, as thy breath moves a mountain !
Poor worms, they hiss at me, whilst I at home
Can be contented to applaud myself,
To sit and clap my hands, and laugh, and leap,
Knocking my head against my roof, with joy
To see how plump my bags are, and my barns.—
Sirrah, go hie you home, and bid your fellows
Get all their flails ready 'gain'[2] I come.

    Hind.   I will, sir. [*Exit.*

    Sord. I'll instantly set all my hinds to thrashing
Of a whole rick of corn, which I will hide
Under the ground ; and with the straw thereof
I'll stuff the outsides of my other mows [3] :
That done, I'll have 'hem empty all my garners,
And i' the friendly earth bury my store,
That, when the searchers come, they may suppose
All's spent, and that my fortunes were belied.
And, to lend more opinion to my want,
And stop that many-mouthèd vulgar dog,
Which else would still be baying at my door,

---

[1] A spontaneous generation then believed in.
[2] Q., Ff., "again," but doubtless one vowel was me nt to be elided.   [3] Stacks.

Each market-day, I will be seen to buy
Part of the purest wheat, as for my household;
Where, when it comes, it shall increase my heaps;
'Twill yield me treble gain, at this dear time,
Promised in this dear book : I have cast all,[1]
Till then I will not sell an ear, I'll hang first.
O, I shall make my prices as I list;
My house and I can feed on peas, and barley;
What though a world of wretches starve the while?
He that will thrive, must think no courses vile.   [*Exit.*

Cor. Now, signior, how approve you this? have the humourists expressed themselves truly or no?

Mit. Yes, if it be well prosecuted, 'tis hitherto happy enough : but methinks, Macilente went hence too soon; he might have been made to stay, and speak somewhat in reproof of Sordido's wretchedness, now at the last.

Cor. O, no, that had been extremely improper; besides, he had continued the scene too long with him, as 'twas, being in no more action.

Mit. You may inforce the length, as a necessary reason; but for propriety, the scene would very well have borne it, in my judgment.

Cor. O, worst of both; why, you mistake his humour utterly then.

Mit. How? do I mistake it? Is't not envy?

Cor. Yes, but you must understand, signior, he envies him not as he is a villain, a wolf i' the commonwealth, but as he is rich, and fortunate; for the true condition of envy is, *dolor alienæ felicitatis*,[2] to have our eyes continually fixed upon another man's prosperity, that is, his chief happiness, and to grieve at that. Whereas, if we make his monstrous, and abhorred actions our object, the grief we take then, comes nearer the nature of hate than envy, as being bred out of a kind of contempt and loathing in ourselves.

Mit. So you'll infer it had been hate, not envy in him, to reprehend the humour of Sordido?

Cor. Right, for what a man truly envies in another, he could always love, and cherish in himself : but no man truly reprehends in another, what he loves in himself; therefore reprehension is out of his hate. And this distinction hath he himself made in a speech there, if you marked it, where he says, " I envy not this Buffoon, but I hate him."

[1] Thrown all on the venture.   [2] Grief at another's happiness.

Mit. Stay, sir: "I envy not this Buffoon, but I hate him." Why might he not as well have hated Sordido, as him?

Cor. No, sir, there was subject for his envy in Sordido—his wealth: so was there not in the other. He stood possessed of no one eminent gift, but a most odious, and fiend-like disposition, that would turn charity itself into hate, much more envy, for the present.

Mit. You have satisfied me, sir; O, here comes the fool, and the jester again, methinks.

Cor. 'Twere pity they should be parted, sir.

Mit. What bright-shining gallant's that with them? the knight they went to?

Cor. No, sir, this is one Monsieur Fastidius Brisk, otherwise called the fresh Frenchified courtier.

Mit. A humourist too?

Cor. As humorous as quicksilver, do but observe him; the scene is the country still, remember.

ACT THE SECOND.

SCENE I.—*The Country; before* PUNTARVOLO'S *House.*

Enter FASTIDIUS BRISK, CINEDO, CARLO BUFFONE, *and* SOGLIARDO.

AST. Cinedo, watch when the knight comes, and give us word.

Cin. I will, sir.   [*Exit.*

Fast. How lik'st thou my boy, Carlo?

Car. O, well, well. He looks like a colonel of the Pigmies' horse, or one of these motions[1] in a great antique clock: he would show well upon a haberdasher's stall, at a corner shop, rarely.

Fast. 'Sheart, what a damned witty rogue's this! How he confounds with his similes!

Car. Better with similes, than smiles: and whither were you riding now, signior?

Fast. Who, I? What a silly jest's that! whither should I ride but to the court?

Car. O, pardon me, sir, twenty places more; your hot-house, or your whore-house——

Fast. By the virtue of my soul, this knight dwells in Elysium here.

Car. He's gone now, I thought he would fly out presently. These be our nimble-spirited catsos[2], that ha' their evasions at pleasure, will run over a bog like your wild Irish; no sooner started, but they'll leap from one thing to another, like a squirrel, heigh: dance, and do tricks i' their discourse, from fire to water, from water to

---

[1] Moving figures.   [2] Rogues.

air, from air to earth, as if their tongues did but e'en lick the four elements over, and away.

Fast. Sirrah, Carlo, thou never saw'st my grey hobby yet, didst thou?

Car. No; ha' you such a one?

Fast. The best in Europe, my good villain, thou'lt say when thou seest him.

Car. But when shall I see him?

Fast. There was a nobleman i' the court offered me a hundred pound for him, by this light: a fine little fiery slave, he runs like a—oh, excellent, excellent!—with the very sound of the spur.

Car. How? the sound of the spur?

Fast. O, it's your only humour now extant, sir; a good gingle, a good gingle.

Car. 'Sblood! you shall see him turn morrice-dancer, he has got him bells, a good suit, and a hobby-horse.

Sog. Signior, now you talk of a hobby-horse, I know where one is, will not be given for a brace of angels.

Fast. How is that, sir?

Sog. Marry, sir, I am telling this gentleman of a hobby-horse, it was my father's indeed, and, though "I say it——

Car. That should not say it"—on, on.

Sog. He did dance in it, with as good humour, and as good regard, as any man of his degree whatsoever, being no gentleman: I have danced in it myself too.

Car. Not since the humour of gentility was upon you? did you?

Sog. Yes, once; marry, that was but to show what a gentleman might do, in a humour.

Car. O, very good.

Mit. Why, this fellow's discourse were nothing, but for the word humour.

Cor. O bear with him; an he should lack matter, and words too, 'twere pitiful.

Sog. Nay, look you, sir, there's ne'er a gentleman i' the country has the like humours, for the hobby-horse, as

I have; I have the method for the threading of the needle and all, the——

Car. How, the method?

Sog. Ay, the leigerity for that, and the whigh-hie, and the daggers in the nose, and the travels of the egg from finger to finger, all the humours incident to the quality. The horse hangs at home in my parlour. I'll keep it for a monument as long as I live, sure.

Car. Do so; and when you die, 'twill be an excellent trophy to hang over your tomb.

Sog. Mass, and I'll have a tomb, now I think on't; 'tis but so much charges.

Car. Best build it in your lifetime then, your heirs may hap to forget it else.

Sog. Nay, I mean so, I'll not trust to them.

Car. No, for heirs and executors are grown damnably careless, 'specially since the ghosts of testators left walking:—how like you him, signior?

Fast. 'Fore heavens, his humour arrides me exceedingly.

Car. Arrides you!

Fast. Ay, "pleases me:" a pox on't! I am so hauuted at the court, and at my lodging, with your refined choice spirits, that it makes me clean of another garb,[1] another sheaf, I know not how! I cannot frame me to your harsh vulgar phrase, 'tis against my genius.

Sog. Signior Carlo! [*Takes him aside.*

Cor. This is right to that of Horace, "*Dum vitant stulti vitia, in contraria currunt;*"[2] so this gallant, labouring to avoid popularity,[3] falls into a habit of affectation, ten thousand times hatefuller than the former.

Car. Who, he? a gull, a fool, no salt in him i' the earth, man: he looks like a fresh salmon kept in a tub, he'll be spent shortly. His brain's lighter than his feather already, and his tongue more subject to lie, than that's to wag: he sleeps with a musk-cat every night,

---

[1] Garb (Fr. *Gerbe*) a sheaf.

[2] While fools try to avoid certain vices they run into the opposite ones.   [3] The popular phrasing or habits.

and walks all day hanged in pomander[1] chains for penance; he has his skin tanned in civet, to make his complexion[2] strong, and the sweetness of his youth lasting in the sense of his sweet lady: a good empty puff, he loves you well, signior.

Sog. There shall be no love lost, sir, I'll assure you.

Fast. [*Advancing.*] Nay, Carlo, I am not happy i' thy love, I see: pr'ythee suffer me to enjoy thy company a little, sweet Mischief; by this air, I shall envy this gentleman's place in thy affections, if you be thus private, i' faith. How now! Is the knight arrived?[3]

Enter CINEDO.

Cin. No, sir, but 'tis guessed he will arrive presently, by his fore-runners.[4]

Fast. His hounds! by Minerva, an excellent figure; a good boy.

Car. You should give him a French crown for it; the boy would find two better figures i' that, and a good figure of your bounty beside.

Fast. Tut, the boy wants no crowns.

Car. No crown;[5] speak i' the singular number, and we'll believe you.

Fast. Nay, thou art so capriciously conceited now. Sirrah Damnation, I have heard this knight Puntarvolo reported to be a gentleman of exceeding good humour; thou knowest him; pr'ythee, how is his disposition? I ne'er was so favoured of my stars, as to see him yet. Boy, do you look to the hobby?

Cin. Ay, sir, the groom has set him up.

[*As* CINEDO *is going out,* SOGLIARDO *takes him aside.*

Fast. 'Tis well; I rid out of my way of intent to visit

---

[1] A scent mixture, or paste, contained in perforated beads, etc.
[2] Temperament, constitution.
[3] Some fail to see that their author means persons to be addressed before they enter on the stage.
[4] He puns on fore and four.   [5] Of the head.

him, and take knowledge of his—— Nay, good Wickedness, his humour, his humour.

Car. Why, he loves dogs, and hawks, and his wife, well : he has a good riding face, and he can sit a great-horse ; he will taint[1] a staff well at tilt : when he is mounted, he looks like the sign of the George, that's all I know ; save, that instead of a dragon, he will brandish against a tree, and break his sword as confidently upon the knotty bark, as the other did upon the scales of the beast.

Fast. O, but this is nothing to that's delivered of him. They say he has dialogues and discourses between his horse, himself, and his dog : and that he will court his own lady, as she were a stranger never encountered before.

Car. Ay, that he will, and make fresh love to her every morning : this gentleman has been a spectator of it, Signior Insulso.

Sog. I am resolute to keep a page :—say you, sir ?

> [*Leaps from whispering with the* Boy.

Car. You have seen Signior Puntarvolo accost his

Sog. O, ay, sir.   [lady?

Fast. And how is the manner of it, pr'ythee, good signior ?

Sog. Faith, sir, in very good sort, he has his humours for it, sir : as first (suppose he were now to come from riding, or hunting, or so) he has his trumpet to sound, and then the waiting-gentlewoman she looks out, and then he speaks, and then she speaks,——very pretty, i'faith, gentleman.   [signior ?

Fast. Why, but do you remember no particulars,

Sog. O, yes sir ; first, the gentlewoman, she looks out at the window.

Car. After the trumpet has summoned a parley, not before ?

Sog. No, sir, not before ; and then says he,——ha, ha, ha, ha, ha, etc.[2]

---

[1] Though not break it properly.

[2] *i.e.* He continues to laugh artificially, to hide his ignorance.

Car. What says he? be not rapt so.

Sog. Says he,—ha, ha, ha, etc.

Fast. Nay, speak, speak.

Sog. Ha, ha, ha!—says he; God save you, says he;
—ha, ha, etc.

Car. Was this the ridiculous motive to all this passion?

Sog. Nay, that, that comes after is,—ha, ha, ha, ha, etc.

Car. Doubtless, he apprehends more than he utters,
this fellow; or else——   [*A cry of hounds within.*

Sog. List, list, they are come from hunting; stand by,
close under this terrace, and you shall see it done, better
than I can show it.

Car. So it had need, 'twill scarce poize the observation
else.

Sog. Faith, I remember all, but the manner of it is
quite out of my head.

Fast. O, withdraw, withdraw, it cannot be but a most
pleasing object.

¹ *Enter* PUNTARVOLO, *and his* Huntsman *leading a
greyhound.*

Punt. Forester, give wind to thy horn.   [*He sounds.*]
Enough; by this, the sound hath touched the ears of the
inclosed: depart, leave the dog, and take with thee what
thou hast deserved, the horn, and thanks.

                         [*Exit* Huntsman.

Car. Ay, marry, there's some taste in this.

Fast. Is't not good?

Sog. Ah, peace, now above, now above!

    [*The* Waiting-gentlewoman *appears at the window.*

Punt. Stay: mine eye hath, on the instant, through
the bounty of the window, received the form of a
nymph. I will step forward three paces; of the which,
I will barely retire one; and after some little flexure of
the knee, with an erected grace salute her—one, two,
and three!—Sweet Lady, God save you!

Gent No, forsooth; I am but the waiting gentlewoman.

<hr>

¹ Scene ii. in old eds.

Car. He knew that before.

Punt. Pardon me ; *humanum est errare.*

Car. He learned that of his chaplain.

Punt. To the perfection of complement, (which is the dial of the thought, and guided by the sun of your beauties) are required these three specials ; the gnomon, the puntilios,[1] and the superficies ; the superficies is that we call place ; the puntilios, circumstance ; and the gnomon, ceremony : in either of which, for a stranger to err, 'tis easy and facile—and such am I.

Car. True, not knowing her horizon, he must needs err : which I fear, he knows too well.

Punt. What call you the lord of the castle ? sweet face.

Gent. The lord of the castle is a knight, sir ; signior Puntarvolo.

Punt. Puntarvolo ? O——

Car. Now must he ruminate.

Fast. Does the wench know him all this while, then ?

Car. O, do you know me, man ? why, therein lies the syrup of the jest ; it's a project, a designment of his own, a thing studied, and rehearst as ordinarily at his coming from hawking or hunting, as a jig after a play.

Sog. Ay, e'en like your jig,[2] sir.

Punt. 'Tis a most sumptuous and stately edifice ! of what years is the knight, fair damsel ?

Gent. Faith, much about your years, sir.

Punt. What complexion,[3] or what stature bears he ?

Gent. Of your stature, and very near upon your complexion.

Punt. Mine is melancholy :

Car. So is the dog's, just.

Punt. And doth argue constancy, chiefly in love. What are his endowments ? Is he courteous ?

Gent. O, the most courteous knight in Christian land, sir.

---

[1] The points of the dial (?)

[2] A song—by the clown, who sometimes danced—then followed the play.

[3] Temperament.

Punt. Is he magnanimous?

Gent. As the skin between your brows, sir.

Punt. Is he bountiful?

Car. 'Slud, he takes an inventory of his own good parts.

Gent. Bountiful? ay, sir, I would you should know it; the poor are served at his gate, early, and late, sir.

Punt. Is he learned?

Gent. O, ay, sir, he can speak the French, and Italian.

Punt. Then he is travelled?

Gent. Ay, forsooth, he hath beyond sea, once or twice.

Car. As far as Paris, to fetch over a fashion, and come back again.

Punt. Is he religious?

Gent. Religious? I know not what you call religious, but he goes to church, I am sure.[1]

Fast. 'Slid, methinks these answers should offend him.

Car. Tut, no; he knows they are excellent, and to her capacity that speaks 'hem.

Punt. Would I might see his face!

Car. She should let down a glass from the window at that word, and request him to look in't.

Punt. Doubtless the gentleman is most exact, and absolutely qualified! doth the castle contain him?

Gent. No, sir, he is from home, but his lady is within.

Punt. His lady? what, is she fair? splendidious? and amiable?

Gent. O, Lord, sir.

Punt. Pr'ythee, dear nymph, intreat her beauties to shine on this side of the building.

[*Gentlewoman* leaves the window.

Car. That he may erect a new dial of complement, with his gnomons and his puntilios.

Fast. Nay, thou art such another cynic now, a man had need walk uprightly before thee.

----

[1] By this she meant he was no Puritan.

Car. Heart, can any man walk more upright than he does? Look, look; as if he went in a frame, or had a suit of wainscot on: and the dog watching him, lest he should leap out on't.

Fast. O, villain!

Car. Well, an e'er I meet him in the city, I'll ha' him jointed, I'll pawn him in Eastcheap, among the butchers, else.

Fast. Peace; who be these, Carlo?

[1] *Enter* SORDIDO *and* FUNGOSO.

Sord. Yonder's your godfather; do your duty to him, son.

Sog. This, sir? a poor elder brother of mine, sir, a yeoman, may dispend some seven or eight hundred a year: that's his son, my nephew, there.

Punt. You are not ill-come, neighbour Sordido, though I have not yet said, well-come: what, my godson is grown a great proficient by this?

Sord. I hope he will grow great one day, sir.

Fast. What does he study? the law?

Sog. Ay, sir, he is a gentleman, though his father be but a yeoman.

Car. What call you your nephew, signior?

Sog. Marry, his name is Fungoso.

Car. Fungoso! O, he looked somewhat like a sponge in that pinked yellow doublet, methought; well, make much of him; I see he was never born to ride upon a mule.[2]

Gent. [*At the window.*] My lady will come presently, sir.

Sog. O, now, now!

Punt. Stand by, retire yourselves a space; nay, pray you, forget not the use of your hat: the air is piercing.

[SORDIDO *and* FUNGOSO *withdraw from that part of the stage.*

---

[1] Scene iii. in old eds.
[2] Ridden upon by sergeants at law or judges.

Fast. What? will not their presence prevail against the current of his humour?

Car. O no; it's a mere flood, a torrent carries all afore it.   [Lady PUNTARVOLO *at the window.*

Punt. What more than heavenly pulchritude is this?
What magazine, or treasury of bliss?
Dazzle, you organs to my optic sense,[1]
To view a creature of such eminence:
O, I am planet-struck, and in yond sphere
A brighter star than Venus doth appear!

Fast. How? in verse!

Car. An extasy, an extasy, man.

Lady P. Is your desire to speak with me, sir knight?

Car. He will tell you that anon; neither his brain, nor his body are yet moulded for an answer.

Punt. Most debonair, and luculent lady, I decline me, low as the basis of your altitude.

Car. He makes congies to his wife in geometrical proportions.

Mit. Is't possible there should be any such humourist?

Car. Very easily possible, sir, you see there is.

Punt. I have scarce collected my spirits, but lately scattered in the admiration of your form; to which—if the bounties of your mind be any way responsible—I doubt not, but my desires shall find a smooth and secure passage. I am a poor knight-errant, lady, that hunting in the adjacent forest, was, by adventure, in the pursuit of a hart, brought to this place; which hart, dear madam, escaped by enchantment: the evening approaching, myself, and servant wearied, my suit is, to enter your fair castle and refresh me.

Lady. Sir knight, albeit it be not usual with me, chiefly in the absence of a husband, to admit any entrance to strangers, yet in the true regard of those innated virtues, and fair parts, which so strive to express themselves in you; I am resolved to entertain you to the best of my

---

[1] He makes him imitate Marston.

power ; which I acknowledge to be nothing, valued with what so worthy a person may deserve. Please you but stay, while I descend.

Punt. Most admired lady, you astonish me ! [*Exit* Lady.
　　　　　[*Walks aside with* SORDIDO *and his* Son.

Car. What ! with speaking a speech of your own penning ?

Fast. Nay, look ; pr'ythee, peace.

Car. Pox on't ; I am impatient of such foppery.

Fast. O let's hear the rest.

Car. What a tedious chapter of courtship, after Sir Lancelot and Queen Guenever ? Away ! I mar'le in what dull cold nook he found this lady out ? that, being a woman, she was blest with no more copy [1] of wit but to serve his humour thus. 'Slud, I think he feeds her with porridge, I : she could ne'er have such a thick brain else.

Sog. Why, is porridge so hurtful, signior ?

Car. O, nothing under Heaven more prejudicial to those ascending subtle powers, or doth sooner abate that which we call *acumen ingenii*,[2] than your gross fare : why, I'll make you an instance ; your city-wives, but observe 'hem, you ha' not more perfect true fools i' the world bred, than they are generally ; and yet you see, by the fineness and delicacy of their diet, diving into the fat capons, drinking your rich wines, feeding on larks, spar-rows, potato-pies, and such good unctuous meats, how their wits are refined and rarefied ! and sometimes a very quintessence of conceit flows from 'hem, able to drown a weak apprehension.

Enter Lady PUNTARVOLO *and her* Waiting-woman.

Fast. Peace, here comes the lady.

Lady. God's me, here's company ! turn in again.

Fast. 'Slight, our presence has cut off the convoy of the jest.

---

[1] Plenty, Lat. *copia*.　　　　[2] The point or fineness of wit

Car. All the better, I am glad on't; for the issue was very perspicuous. Come let's discover, and salute the knight. [*They come forward.*

Punt. Stay; who be these that address themselves towards us? What, Carlo? now by the sincerity of my soul, welcome; welcome, gentlemen: and how dost thou, thou "Grand Scourge," or "Second Untruss of the time?"[1]

Car. Faith, spending my metal in this reeling world, here and there, as the sway of my affection carries me, and perhaps stumble upon a yeoman-feuterer,[2] as I do now; or one of fortune's mules, laden with treasure, and an empty cloak-bag, following him, gaping when a bag will untie.

Punt. Peace, you bandog, peace! What brisk Nymphadoro is that in the white virgin boot there?

Car. Marry, sir, one that I must intreat you to take a very particular knowledge of, and with more than ordiary respect :—Monsieur Fastidius.

Punt. Sir, I could wish, that for the time of your vouchsafed abiding here, and more real entertainment, this my house stood on the Muses hill, and these my orchards were those of the Hesperides.

Fast. I possess as much in your wish, sir, as if I were made lord of the Indies; and I pray you believe it.

Car. [*Aside.*] I have a better opinion of his faith, than to think it will be so corrupted.

Sog. Come, brother, I'll bring you acquainted with gentlemen, and good fellows, such as shall do you more grace, than——

Sord. Brother, I hunger not for such acquaintance : Do you take heed, lest—— [CARLO *comes towards them.*

Sog. Husht!—My brother, sir, for want of education, sir, somewhat nodding to the boor, the clown; but I request you in private, sir.

Fung. [*Aside, looking at* BRISK.] By Heaven, it's a very fine suit of clothes!

---

[1] Marston's Satires were "the Scourge of Villany." [2] Dog-keeper.

Cor. Do you observe that, signior? there's another humour has new-cracked the shell.

Mit. What? he is enamoured of the fashion, is he?

Cor. O, you forestall the jest.

Fung. [*Aside.*] I mar'le what it might stand him in.

Sog. Nephew?

Fung. [*Aside.*] 'Fore God, it's an excellent suit, and as neatly becomes him.—What said you, uncle?

Sog. When saw you my niece?

Fung. Marry, yesternight I supped there.—[*Aside.*] That kind of boot does very rare too.

Sog. And what news hear you?

Fung. [*Aide.*] The gilt spur and all! Would I were hanged, but 'tis exceeding good.——Say you, uncle?

Sog. Your mind is carried away with somewhat else: I ask what news you hear?

Fung. Troth, we hear none. [*Aside.*] In good faith, I was never so pleased with a fashion, days of my life. O, an I might have but my wish, I'ld ask no more of God now, but such a suit, such a hat, such a band, such a doublet, such a hose, such a boot, and such a——

Sog. They say, there's a new motion of the city of Nineveh, with Jonas and the whale, to be seen at Fleet-bridge? You can tell, cousin?

Fung. Here's such a world of question with him now!—Yes, I think there be such a thing, I saw the picture: [*Aside.*] would he would once be satisfied! Let me see, the doublet, say fifty shillings the doublet, and between three or four pound the hose; then boots, hat, and band: some ten or eleven pound would do it all, and suit me, fore the Heavens!

Sog. I'll see all those devices an I come to London once.

Fung. [*Aside.*] God's lid, an I could compass it, 'twere rare:—Hark you, uncle.

Sog. What says my nephew?

Fung. Faith, uncle, I 'ld ha' desired you to have made a motion for me to my father, in a thing that——walk aside, and I'll tell you ;—sir, no more but this : there's a parcel of law books (some twenty pounds' worth) that lie in a place for little more than half the money they cost ; and I think, for some twelve pound, or twenty mark, I could go near to redeem 'hem ; there's Plowden, Dyar, Brooke, and Fitz-Herbert, divers such as I must have ere long : and you know, I were as good save five or six pound, as not, uncle. I pray you, move it for me.

Sog. That I will : when would you have me do it? presently ?[1]

Fung. O, ay, I pray you, good uncle : [SOGLIARDO *takes* SORDIDO *aside.*]—God send me good luck, Lord, an't be thy will, prosper it ! O Jesu, now, now, if it take, O Christ, I am made for ever.

Fast. Shall I tell you, sir ? by this air, I am the most beholding to that lord, of any gentleman living ; he does use me the most honourably, and with the greatest respect, more indeed, than can be uttered with any opinion of truth.

Punt. Then, have you the count Gratiato ?

Fast. As true noble a gentleman too, as any breathes ; I am exceedingly endeared to his love : by Jesu I protest to you, signior, I speak it not gloriously,[2] nor out of affectation, but there's he, and the Count Frugale, Signior Illustre, Signior Luculento, and a sort of 'hem that when I am at court, they do share me amongst 'hem. Happy is he can enjoy me most private. I do wish myself sometime an ubiquitary for their love, in good faith.

Car. [*Aside.*] There's ne'er a one of these, but might lie a week on the rack, ere they could bring forth his name ; and yet he pours them out as familiarly, as if he had seen 'hem stand by the fire i' the presence, or ta'en tobacco with them over the stage, i' the lord's room.

Punt. Then you must of necessity know our court-star there ? that planet of wit, Madonna Saviolina ?

Fast. O Lord, sir ! my mistress.

---

[1] At once.   [2] Boastfully.

Punt. Is she your mistress?

Fast. Faith, here be some slight favours of hers, sir, that do speak it, "she is;" as this scarf, sir, or this ribbon in mine ear, or so; this feather grew in her sweet fan sometimes, though now it be my poor fortunes to wear it, as you see, sir: slight, slight, a foolish toy.

Punt. Well, she is the lady of a most exalted, and ingenious spirit.

Fast. Did you ever hear any woman speak like her? or enriched with a more plentiful discourse?

Car. O, villainous! nothing but sound, sound, a mere echo; she speaks as she goes 'tired, in cobweb-lawn, light, thin; good enough to catch flies withal.

Punt. O, manage[1] your affections.

Fast. Well, if thou be'st not plagued for this blasphemy one day——

Punt. Come, regard not a jester: it is in the power of my purse, to make him speak well, or ill, of me.

Fast. Sir, I affirm it to you, upon my credit, and judgment, she has the most harmonious, and musical strain of wit that ever tempted a true ear; and yet to see!—a rude tongue would profane Heaven, if it could.

Punt. I am not ignorant of it, sir.

it flows from her like nectar, and she doth give it tha   uick grace, and exornation[2] in the composure, that, by   ir, as I am an honest man, would I might never stir, sir,   e does observe as pure a phrase, and use as choice figure   er ordinary conferences, as any be i' the "Arcadia."[3]

Car. Or rather in Green's[4] works, whence she may steal with more security.

Sog. Well, if ten pound will fetch 'hem, you shall have it, but I'll part with no more.

Fung. I'll try what that will do, if you please.

---

[1] Control them as in the *manége*.
[2] Adornment.   [3] Of Sir Philip Sidney.
[4] His lately popular works being superseded by the "Arcadia."

Sord. Do so ; and when you have 'hem, study hard.

Fung. Yes, sir. [*Aside.*] An I could "study" to get forty shillings more now ! Well, I will put myself into the fashion, as far as this will go, presently.

Sord. [*Aside.*] I wonder it rains not ! the almanac says, we should have store of rain to-day.

Punt. Why, sir, to-morrow I will associate you to court myself ; and from thence to the city about a business, a project I have, I will expose it to you, sir ;—Carlo, I am sure, has heard of it.

Car. What's that, sir ?

Punt. I do intend, this year of jubilee[1] coming on, to travel : and, because I will not altogether go upon expense, I am determined to put forth some five thousand pound, to be paid me, five for one, upon the return of myself, my wife, and my dog from the Turk's court in Constantinople. If all, or either of us miscarry in the journey, 'tis gone : if we be successful, why, there will be five and twenty thousand pound to entertain time withal. Nay, go not, neighbour Sordido, stay to-night, and help to make our society the fuller. Gentlemen, frolic : Carlo ! what ? dull now ?

Car. I was thinking on your project, sir, an you call it so : is this the dog goes with you ?

Punt. This is the dog, sir.

Car. He do not go barefoot, does he ?

Punt. Away, you traitor, away !

Car. Nay, afore God, I speak simply ; he may prick his foot with a thorn, and be as much as the whole venture is worth. Besides, for a dog that never travelled before, it's a huge journey to Constantinople : I 'll tell you now—an he were mine—I'ld have some present conference with a physician, what antidotes were good to give him, preservatives against poison ; for assure you, if once your money be out, there'll be divers attempts made against the life of the poor animal.

i.e. 1600.

Punt. Thou art still dangerous.

Fast. Is Signior Deliro's wife your kinswoman?

Sog. Ay, sir, she is my niece, my brother's daughter here, and my nephew's sister.

Sord. Do you know her, sir?

Fast. O, God, sir! Signior Deliro, her husband, is my merchant.

Fung. Ay, I have seen this gentleman there, often.

Fast. I cry you mercy, sir [*Salutes elaborately.*] : let me crave your name, pray you.

Fung. Fungoso, sir.

Fast. Good Signior Fungoso, I shall request to know you better, sir.

Fung. I am her brother, sir.

Fast. In fair time, sir.

Punt. Come, gentlemen, I will be your conduct.

Fast. Nay, pray you, sir; we shall meet at Signior Deliro's often.

Sog. You shall ha' me at the herald's office, sir, for some week or so, at my first coming up. Come, Carlo.

[*Exeunt.*

Mit. Methinks, Cordatus, he dwelt somewhat too long on this scene; it hung i'the hand.

Cor. I see not where he could have insisted less, and t' have made the humours perspicuous enough.

Mit. True, as his subject lies; but he might have altered the shape of his argument, and explicated 'hem better in single scenes.

Cor. That had been single[1] indeed: why, be they not the same persons in this, as they would have been in those? and is it not an object of more state, to behold the scene full, and relieved with variety of speakers to the end, than to see a vast empty stage, and the actors come in, one by one, as if they were dropped down with a feather into the eye of the spectators?

Mit. Nay, you are better traded with these things than I, and therefore I'll subscribe to your judgment; marry, you shall give me leave to make objections.

Cor. O, what else? it's the special intent of the author

---

[1] Simple.

you should do so; for thereby others, that are present, may as well be satisfied, who haply would object the same you do.

Mit. So, sir: but when appears Macilente again?

Cor. Marry, he stays but till our silence give him leave: here he comes, and with him, Signior Deliro, a merchant at whose house he is come to sojourn: make your own observation now, only transfer your thoughts to the city, with the scene; where, suppose they speak.

[1] SCENE II.—*A Room in* DELIRO'S *House.*

Enter DELIRO, *to* MACILENTE *and* FIDO.

Deli. I'll tell you by and by, sir.—
Welcome, good Macilente, to my house,
To sojourn at my house[2] for ever: if my best
In cates, and every sort of good entreaty
May move you stay with me.

                       [*He censeth: the* Boy *strews flowers.*

Maci.   I thank you, sir.—
[*Aside.*] And yet the muffled Fates, had it pleased them,
Might have supplied me, from their own full store,
Without this word "I thank you," to a fool.
I see no reason why that dog, called Chance,
Should fawn upon this fellow, more than me;
I am a man, and I have limbs, flesh, blood,
Bones, sinews,[3] and a soul, as well as he:
My parts are every way as good as his,
If I said better? why, I did not lie.
Nath'less, his wealth, but nodding on my wants,
Must make me bow, and cry,—"I thank you, sir."

Deli. Dispatch, take heed your mistress see you not.

Fido. I warrant you, sir, I'll steal by her softly. [*Exit.*

---

[1] Scene iv. in old eds.
[2] In Q., Ff., "even" for "at my house."
[3] Meaning probably, nerves.

Deli. Nay, gentle friend, be merry, raise your looks
Out of your bosom ; I protest, by Heaven,
You are the man most welcome in the world.

Maci. " I thank you, sir."—[*Aside.*] I know my cue, I
think.

Re-enter FIDO, *with more perfumes and flowers.*

Fido. Where will you have 'hem burn, sir ?

Deli. Here, good Fido.
What? she did not see thee ?

Fido. No, sir.

Deli. That's well :
Strew, strew, good Fido, the freshest flowers ; so.

Maci. What means this, Signior Deliro? all this cens-
ing ?

Deli. Cast in more frankincense, yet more, well 'sayed.—
O, Macilente, I have such a wife !
So passing fair ! so passing fair ! unkind,
But of such worth, and right to be unkind,
Since no man can be worthy of her kindness.

Maci. What, can there not ?

Deli. No, that is sure as death.
No man alive ! I do not say, is not,
But cannot possibly be worth her kindness !
Nay, it is certain, let me do her right.
How said I? do her right ? as though I could,
As though this dull, gross tongue of mine could utter
The rare, the true, the pure, the infinite rights,
That sit, as high as I can look, within her !

Maci. This is such dotage, as was never heard.

Deli. Well, this must needs be granted.

Maci. Granted, quoth you ?

Deli. Nay, Macilente do not so discredit
The goodness of your judgment to deny it,
For I do speak the very least of her ;
And I would crave, and beg no more of Heaven.

[1] Farre unkind, in the folios.

For all my fortunes here, but to be able
To utter first, in fit terms, what she is,
And then, the true joys I conceive in her.

   Maci. Is't possible, she should deserve so well,
As you pretend?[1]

   Deli.   Ay, and she knows so well
Her own deserts, that, when I strive t'enjoy them,
She weighs the things I do, with what she merits;
And, seeing my worth out-weighed so in her graces,
She is so solemn, so precise, so froward,
That no observance I can do to her
Can make her kind to me: if she find fault,
I mend that fault; and then she says, I faulted,
That I did mend it. Now, good friend, advise me,
How I may temper this strange spleen in her.

   Maci. You are too amorous, too obsequious,
And make her too assured, she may command you.
When women doubt most of their husbands' loves,
They are most loving. Husbands must take heed
They give no gluts of kindness to their wives,
But use them like their horses; whom they feed
Not with a mangerful of meat together,
But half a peck at once; and keep them so
Still with an appetite to that they give them.
He that desires to have a loving wife,
Must bridle all the show of that desire:
Be kind, not amorous; nor bewraying kindness,
As if love wrought it, but considerate duty.
  Offer no love rites, but let wives still seek them,
  For when they come unsought, they seldom like them.

   Deli. Believe me, Macilente, this is gospel.
O, that a man were his own man so much,
To rule himself thus! I will strive, i'faith,
To be more strange and careless; yet, I hope,
I have now taken such a perfect course,
To make ner kind to me, and live contented.

---

[1] Set forth.

That I shall find my kindness well returned,
And have no need to fight with my affections.
She, late, hath found much fault with every room
Within my house; one was too big, she said,
Another was not furnished to her mind,
And so through all; all which, now, I have altered.
Then here, she hath a place, on my back-side,[1]
Wherein she loves to walk; and that, she said,
Had some ill smells about it. Now, this walk
Have I, before she knows it, thus perfumed
With herbs, and flowers, and laid in divers places—
As 'twere on altars, consecrate to her—
Perfumèd gloves, and delicate chains of amber,
To keep the air in awe of her sweet nostrils:
This have I done, and this I think will please her.
Behold, she comes.

Enter FALLACE.

Fal.   Here's a sweet stink indeed!
What, shall I ever be thus crossed and plagued?
And sick of husband? O, my head doth ache,
As it would cleave asunder, with those savours!
All my rooms altered, and but one poor walk
That I delighted in, and that is made
So fulsome with perfumes, that I am feared,—
My brain doth sweat so—I have caught the plague!

Deli.   Why, gentle wife, is now thy walk too sweet?
Thou said'st of late, it hath sour airs about it,
And found'st much fault that I did not correct it.

Fal.   Why, an I did find fault, sir?
Deli.   Nay, dear wife,
I know thou hast said thou hast loved perfumes,
No woman better.

Fal.   Ay, long since, perhaps;
But now that sence is altered: you would have me,
Like to a puddle, or a standing pool,

----

[2] Back-yard.

To have no motion, nor no spirit within me.
No, I am like a pure, and sprightly river,
That moves for ever, and yet still the same ;
Or fire, that burns much wood, yet still one flame.

Deli. But yesterday, I saw thee at our garden,
Smelling on roses, and on purple flowers,
And since, I hope, the humour of thy sense
Is nothing changed.

Fal. Why, those were growing flowers,
And these, within my walk, are cut and strewed !

Deli. But yet they have one scent.

Fal. Ay ! have they so ?
In your gross judgment. If you make no difference
Betwixt the scent of growing flowers, and cut ones,
You have a sense to taste lamp oil, i'faith.
And with such judgment have you changed the chambers,
Leaving no room, that I can joy to be in,
In all your house : and now my walk, and all,
You smoke me from, as if I were a fox,
And long, belike, to drive me quite away.
Well, walk you there, and I'll walk where I list.

Deli. What shall I do ? Oh, I shall never please her !

Maci. [*Aside.*] Out on thee, dotard ! What star ruled
   his birth,
That brought him such a Star ? Blind Fortune still
Bestows her gifts on such as cannot use them :
How long shall I live, ere I be so happy
To have a wife of this exceeding form ?

Deli. Away with 'hem ! would I had broke a joint
When I devised this, that should so dislike her.
Away, bear all away. [FIDO *bears all away.*

Fal. Ay, do ; for fear
Aught that is there should like[1] her ! O, this man,
How cunningly he can conceal himself !
As though he loved, nay, honoured and adored !—

Deli. Why, my sweet heart ?

---

[1] Please.

Fal. Sweet heart ! Oh, better still !
And, asking, why ? wherefore ? and looking strangely,
As if he were as white as innocence !
Alas, you're simple, you : you cannot change,
Look pale at pleasure, and then red with wonder ;
No, no, not you ! 'tis pity o' your naturals.
I did but cast an amorous eye, e'en now,
Upon a pair of gloves that somewhat liked me,
And straight he noted it, and gave command,
All should be ta'en away.
 Deli. Be they my bane then !
What, sirrah, Fido, bring in those gloves again,
You took from hence.
 Fal. 'Sbody,[1] sir, but do not ;
Bring in no gloves to spite me ; if you do——
 Deli. Ay me, most wretched ; how am I misconstrued ?
 Maci. [*Aside.*] O, how she tempts my heart-strings
  with her eye,
To knit them to her beauties, or to break !
What moved the Heavens, that they could not make
Me such a woman ? but a man, a beast,
That hath no bliss like to others ! Would to Heaven,
In wreak of my misfortunes, I were turned
To some fair water-nymph, that, set upon
The deepest whirl-pit of the ravenous seas,
My adamantine [2] eyes might headlong hale
This iron world to me, and drown it all.

 Cor. Behold, behold, the translated gallant.
 Mit. O, he is welcome.

 [3] *Enter* FUNGOSO, *apparelled as* FASTIDIUS BRISK.

 Fung. 'Save you brother, and sister ; 'save you, sir !
I have commendations for you out i' the country. [*Aside.*]
I wonder they take no knowledge of my suit :——mine

---

[1] 'Sbody, a dissyllable. F 2 omits, but gives nothing in its place,
and therefore an unmetrical line.
[2] Magnetic. [3] Scene v. in old eds.

uncle Sogliardo is in town. Sister, methinks you are melancholy; why are you so sad? I think you took me for Master Fastidius Brisk, sister, did you not?

Fal. Why should I take you for him?

Fung. Nay, nothing—I was lately in Master Fastidius his company, and methinks we are very like.

Deli. You have a fair suit, brother, 'give[1] you joy on't.

Fung. Faith, good enough to ride in, brother; I made it to ride in.

Fal. O, now I see the cause of his idle demand, was his new suit.

Deli. 'Pray you, good brother, try if you can change her mood.

Fung. I warrant you, let me alone. I'll put her out of her dumps. Sister, how like you my suit?

Fal. O, you are a gallant in print[2] now, brother.

Fung. Faith, how like you the fashion? it's the last edition, I assure you.

Fal. I cannot but like it—to the desert.

Fung. Troth, sister, I was fain to borrow these spurs, I ha' left my gown in gage for 'hem, 'pray you lend me an angel.

Fal. Now, beshrew my heart then.

Fung. Good truth, I'll pay you again at my next exhibition.[3] I had but bare ten pound of my father, and it would not reach to put me wholly into the fashion.

Fal. I care not.

Fung. I had spurs of mine own before, but they were not ginglers. Monsieur Fastidius will be here anon, sister.

Fal. You jest!

Fung. Never lend me penny more while you live then; and that I'ld be loth to say, in truth.

Fal. When did you see him?

---

[1] *i.e.*, God give, as Q. [2] Exactly.
[3] Payment of allowance.

Fung. Yesterday, I came acquainted with him at Sir Puntarvolo's : [*Caressingly for money.*] Nay, sweet sister.

Maci. [*Aside.*] I fain would know of Heaven now, why yond fool
Should wear a suit of satin? he? that rook?[1]
That painted jay, with such a deal of outside?
What is his inside, trow? ha, ha, ha, ha, ha!
Good Heaven, give me patience, patience, patience!
A number of these popinjays[2] there are,
Whom, if a man confer, and but examine
Their inward merit, with such men as want;
Lord, Lord, what things they are!

Fal. [*Giving money.*] Come, when will you pay me again, now?

Fung. O God, sister!

Maci. Here comes another.

[3] *Enter* FASTIDIUS BRISK, *in a new suit.*

Fast. 'Save you, Signior Deliro! How dost thou, sweet lady? Let me kiss thee.

Fung. How? a new suit? ay me!

Deli. And how does Master Fastidius Brisk?

Fast. Faith, live in court, Signior Deliro; in grace, I thank God, both of the noble masculine, and feminine. I must speak with you in private, by and by.[4]

Deli. When you please, sir.

Fal. Why look you so pale, brother?

Fung. 'Slid, all this money is cast away, now.

Maci. Ay, there's a newer edition come forth.

Fung. 'Tis but my hard fortune! well, I'll have my suit changed, I'll go fetch my tailor presently, but first I'll devise a letter to my father. Ha' you any pen and ink, sister?

Fal. What would you do withal?

---

[1] Prating gull.
[2] Parrots.
[3] Scene vi. in old eds.
[4] As soon as may be.

Fung. I would use it. 'Slight, an it had come but four days sooner, the fashion.   [*Exit.*

Fast. There was a countess gave me her hand to kiss to-day, i' the presence : did me more good by that light than——and yesternight sent her coach twice to my lodging, to intreat me accompany her, and my sweet mistress, with some two or three nameless ladies more : O, I have been graced by 'hem beyond all aim of affection : this 's her garter my dagger hangs in : and they do so commend, and approve my apparel, with my judicious wearing of it, it's above wonder.

Fal. Indeed, sir, 'tis a most excellent suit, and you do wear it as extraordinary.

Fast. Why, I'll tell you now, in good faith, and by this chair, which, by the grace of God, I intend presently to sit in, I had three suits in one year, made three great ladies in love with me : I had other three, undid three gentlemen in imitation : and other three gat three other gentlemen, widows of three thousand pound a year.

Deli. Is't possible ?

Fast. O, believe it, sir ; your good face is the witch, and your apparel the spells, that bring all the pleasures of the world into their circle.

Fal. Ah, the sweet grace of a courtier !

Maci. Well, would my father had left me but a good face for my portion yet ! though I had shared the unfortunate wit that goes with it, I had not cared : I might have passed for somewhat i' the world then.

Fast. Why, assure you, signior, rich apparel has strange virtues : it makes him that hath it without means, esteemed for an excellent wit : he that enjoys it with means, puts the world in remembrance of his means : it helps the deformities of nature, and gives lustre to her beauties ; makes continual holiday where it shines ; sets the wits of ladies at work, that otherwise would be idle ; furnisheth your two-shilling Ordinary ; takes possession of your stage at your new play ; and enricheth your oars, as scorning to go with your scull.

Maci. 'Pray you, sir, add this ; it gives respect to your fools, makes many thieves, as many strumpets, and no fewer bankrupts.

Fal. Out, out! unworthy to speak, where he breatheth.

Fast. What's he, signior ?

Deli. A friend of mine, sir.

Fast. By Heaven, I wonder at you citizens, what kind of creatures you are !

Deli. Why, sir ?

Fast. That you can consort yourselves with such poor seam-rent fellows.

Fal. He says true.

Deli. Sir, I will assure you, however you esteem of him, he's a man worthy of regard.

Fast. Why, what has he in him of such virtue to be regarded, ha ?

Deli. Marry, he is a scholar, sir.

Fast. Nothing else ?

Deli. And he is well travelled.

Fast. He should get him clothes ; I would cherish those good parts of travel in him, and prefer him to some nobleman of good place.

Deli. Sir, such a benefit should bind me to you for ever, in my friend's right ; and I doubt not, but his desert shall more than answer my praise.

Fast. Why, an he had good clothes, I'ld carry him to court with me to-morrow.

Deli. He shall not want for those, sir, if gold and the whole city will furnish him.

Fast. You say well, sir : faith, Signior Deliro, I am come to have you play the alchemist with me, and change the " species " of my land into that metal you talk of.

Deli. With all my heart, sir ; what sum will serve you ?

Fast. Faith, some three, or four hundred.

Deli. Troth, sir, I have promised to meet a gentleman this morning in Paul's, but upon my return, I'll despatch you.

Fast. I'll accompany you thither.

Deli. As you please, sir; but I go not thither directly.

Fast. 'Tis no matter, I have no other designment in hand, and therefore as good go along.

Deli. [*Aside.*] I were as good have a quartan fever follow me now, for I shall ne'er be rid of him:—bring me a cloak there, one—still, upon his grace at court, am I sure to be visited; I was a beast to give him any hope. Well, would I were in, that I am out with him, once,[1] and —come, Signior Macilente, I must confer with you, as we go.—Nay, dear wife, I beseech thee, forsake these moods: look not like winter thus. Here, take my keys, open my counting-houses, spread all my wealth before thee, choose any object that delights thee: if thou wilt eat the spirit of gold, and drink dissolved pearl in wine, 'tis for thee.

Fal. So, sir.   [*Scornfully and tossing her head.*

Deli. Nay, my sweet wife.

Fal. Good Lord, how you are perfumed! in your terms, and all! pray you leave us.

Deli. Come, gentlemen.

Fast. Adieu, sweet lady.   [*Exeunt all but* FALLACE.

Fal. Ay, ay! Let thy words ever sound in mine ears, and thy graces disperse contentment through all my senses! O, how happy is that lady above other ladies, that enjoys so absolute a gentleman to her servant! "A countess give him her hand to kiss!" ah, foolish countess! he's a man worthy—if a woman may speak of a man's worth—to kiss the lips of an empress.

---

[1] Would I had the money at the rate I've lent it him, and were done with him.

FUNGOSO *returns with his* Tailor.

Fung. What's Master Fastidius gone, sister?

Fal. Ay, brother.—[*Aside.*] He has a face like a cherubin!

Fung. God's me, what luck's this? I have fetched my tailor and all: which way went he, sister? can you tell?

Fal. Not I, in good faith—[*Aside.*] and he has a body like an angel!

Fung. How long is't since he went?

Fal. Why, but e'en now; did you not meet him?—[*Aside.*] and a tongue able to ravish any woman i' the earth!

Fung. O, for God's sake—[*To* Tailor.] I'll please you for your pains.—But e'en now, say you?—Come, good sir:—'Slid, I had forgot it too: sister, if anybody ask for mine uncle Sogliardo, they shall ha' him at the herald's office yonder, by Paul's. [*Exit with his* Tailor.

Fal. Well, I will not altogether despair: I have heard of a citizen's wife has been beloved of a courtier; and why not I? heigh, ho! well, I will into my private chamber, lock the door to me, and think over all his good parts, one after another. [*Exit.*

Mit. Well, I doubt, this last scene will endure some grievous torture.

Cor. How? you fear 'twill be racked, by some hard construction?

Mit. Do not you?

Cor. No, in good faith: unless mine eyes could light me beyond sense. I see no reason, why this should be more liable to the rack, than the rest: you'll say, perhaps, the city will not take it well, that the merchant is made here to dote so perfectly upon his wife; and she again to be so *Fastidiously* affected as she is.

Mit. You have uttered my thought, sir, indeed.

Cor. Why, by that proportion, the court might as well take offence at him we call the courtier, and with much more pretext, by how much the place transcends, and goes before in dignity and virtue: but can you imagine that any noble, or true spirit in court, whose sinewy [1] and altogether unaffected graces, very worthily express him a courtier,

---

[1] Felt (sinew, nerve).

will make any exception at the opening of such an empty trunk, as this Brisk is ? or think his own worth impeached, by beholding his motley inside ?

Mit. No, sir, I do not.

Cor. No more, assure you, will any grave, wise citizen, or modest matron, take the object of this folly in Deliro and his wife ; but rather apply it as the foil to their own virtues. For that were to affirm, that a man writing of Nero, should mean all emperors ; or speaking of Machiavel, comprehend all statesmen ; or in our Sordido, all farmers ; and so of the rest : than which, nothing can be uttered more malicious, or absurd. Indeed there are a sort of these narrow-eyed decypherers, I confess, that will extort strange, and abstruse meanings out of any subject, be it never so conspicuous and innocently delivered. But to such, where'er they sit concealed, let them know, the author defies them, and their writing-tables ; and hopes, no sound or safe judgment will infect itself with their contagious comments, who, indeed, come here only to pervert, and poison the sense of what they hear, and for nought else.

Enter SHIFT, *with two* Si-quisses[1] *in his hand.*

Mit. Stay, what new Mute is this, that walks so suspiciously ?

Cor. O, marry, this is one, for whose better illustration, we must desire you to presuppose the stage, the middle aisle in Paul's, and that, the west end of it.

Mit. So, sir, and what follows ?

Cor. Faith, a whole volume of humour, and worthy the unclasping.

Mit. As how ? what name do you give him first ?

Cor. He hath shift of names, sir : some call him Apple-John,[2] some Signior Whiffe ; marry, his main standing name is Cavalier Shift : the rest are but as clean shirts to his natures.

Mit. And what makes he in Paul's now ?

Cor. Troth, as you see, for the advancement of a *si quis* or two ; wherein he has so varied himself, that if any one of 'hem take, he may hull up and down i' the humorous world a little longer.

Mit. It seems then, he bears a very changing sail ?

Cor. O, as the wind, sir : here comes more.

---

[1] Bills asking "If any person," &c.
[2] *Alias* Apple-squire, *alias* pimp.

ACT THE THIRD.

SCENE I.—*The Middle Aisle of* St. Paul's.

HIFT. [*Coming forward.*] This is rare, I have set up my bills without discovery.

Enter ORANGE.

Orange. What? Signior Whiffe! what fortune has brought you into these west parts?

Shift. Troth, signior, nothing but your rheum; I have been taking an ounce of tobacco hard by here, with a gentleman, and I am come to spit private in Paul's. 'Save you, sir.

Orange. Adieu, good Signior Whiffe.

[*Each passes on his way.*

Enter CLOVE.

Clove. Master Apple-John? you are well met: when shall we sup together, and "laugh, and be fat" with those good wenches, ha?

Shift. Faith, sir, I must now leave you, upon a few humours, and occasions; but when you please, sir. [*Exit.*

Clove. Farewell, sweet Apple-John:—I wonder there are no more store of gallants here.

Mit. What be these two, signior?

Cor. Marry, a couple, sir, that are mere strangers to the whole scope of our play; only come to walk a turn or two i' this scene of Paul's, by chance.

Orange. 'Save you, good Master Clove.

Clove. Sweet Master Orange.

Mit. How? Clove, and Orange?

Cor. Ay, and they are well met, for 'tis as dry an Orange as ever grew: nothing but salutation, and "O God, sir!" and, "It pleases you to say so, sir!" one that can laugh at a jest—for company—with a most plausible and extemporal grace; and some hour after, in private, ask you what it was. The other, Monsieur Clove, is a more spiced youth; he will sit you a whole afternoon sometimes, in a bookseller's shop, reading the Greek, Italian, and Spanish; when he understands not a word of either: if he had the tongues, to his suits, he were an excellent linguist.

Clove. Do you hear this reported for certainty?

Orange. O God, sir!

[2] *Enter* CARLO *and* PUNTARVOLO, *followed by two* Serving-men, *one leading a dog, the other bearing a bag.*

Punt. Sirrah, take my cloak:—and you, sir knave, follow me closer. If thou losest my dog, thou shalt die a dog's death; I will hang thee.

Car. Tut, fear him not, he's a good lean slave, he loves a dog well, I warrant him; I see by his looks, I:—Mass, he's somewhat like him—'Slud [*To the* Servant.] poison him, make him away with a crooked pin, or somewhat man; thou may'st have more security of thy life;—and so, sir: what? you ha' not put out your whole venture yet? ha' you?

Punt. No, I do want yet some fifteen or sixteen hundred pounds; but my lady, my wife, is "out of her Humour," she does not now go.

Car. No? how then?

Punt. Marry, I am now enforced to give it out, upon the return of myself, my dog, and my cat.

Car. Your cat? where is she?

Punt. My squire has her there, in the bag;—sirrah, look to her.—How likest thou my change, Carlo?

Car. Oh, for the better, sir; your cat has nine lives and your wife ha' but one.

Punt. Besides, she will never be sea-sick, which wil

[1] Scene ii. in old eds.

save me so much in conserves : when saw you Signior
Sogliardo ?

Car. I came from him but now, he is at the herald's
office yonder : he requested me to go afore, and take up
a man or two for him in Paul's, against his cognizance
was ready.

Punt. What? has he purchased arms, then?

Car. Ay, and rare ones too ; of as many colours as e'er
you saw any fool's coat in your life. I'll go look among
yond bills, an I can fit him with legs to his arms———

Punt. With legs to his arms ! Good : I will go with
you, sir.   [*They go to look upon the bills.*

[1] *Enter* FASTIDIUS, DELIRO, *and* MACILENTE.

Fast. Come, let's walk in Mediterraneo :[2] I assure you,
sir, I am not the least respected among ladies ; but
let that pass : do you know how to go into the presence, sir.

Maci. Why, on my feet, sir !

Fast. No, on your head, sir ; for 'tis that must bear you
out, I assure you ; as thus, sir. You must first have an
especial care so to wear your hat, that it oppress not confusedly this your predominant, or foretop ;[3] because, when
you come at the presence-door, you may, with once or
twice stroking up your forehead, thus, enter with your
predominant perfect ; that is, standing up stiff.

Maci. As if one were frighted?

Fast. Ay, sir.

Maci. Which, indeed, a true fear of your mistress should
do, rather than gum-water, or whites of eggs : is't not
so, sir ?

Fast. An ingenious observation : give me leave to crave
your name, sir ?

Deli. His name is Macilente, sir.

Fast. Good Signior Macilente ; if this gentleman,

---

[1] Scene iii. in old eds.
[2] He puns, meaning, in the middle aisle.
[3] A front lock of hair worn as upright as might be.

Signior Deliro, furnish you, as he says he will, with clothes, I will bring you, to-morrow by this time, into the presence of the most divine, and acute lady in court; you shall see " sweet silent rhetoric," and " dumb eloquence speaking in her eye;"[1] but when she speaks herself, such an anatomy of wit, so sinewized and arterized, that 'tis the goodliest model of pleasure that ever was to behold. Oh! she strikes the world into admiration of her; Oh, Oh, Oh! I cannot express 'hem, believe me.

Maci. O, your only admiration is your silence, sir.

Punt. 'Fore God, Carlo, this is good; let's read 'hem again. [*Reads.*

" If there be any lady, or gentlewoman of good carriage, that is desirous to entertain to her private uses, a young, straight, and upright gentleman, of the age of five, or six-and-twenty at the most, who can serve in the nature of a gentleman-usher, and hath little legs of purpose, and a black satin suit of his own, to go before her in; which suit, for the more sweetening, now lies in lavender;[2] and can hide his face with her fan, if need require; or sit in the cold at the stair foot for her, as well as another gentleman: let her subscribe her name and place, and diligent respect shall be given."—This is above measure excellent! ha?

Car. No, this, this! here's a fine slave.

Punt. [*Reads.*] " If this city, or the suburbs of the same, do afford any young gentleman of the first, second, or third head,[3] more or less, whose friends are but lately deceased, and whose lands are but new come into his hands, that, to be as exactly qualified as the best of our ordinary gallants are, is affected to entertain the most gentlemanlike use of tobacco: as first, to give it the most exquisite perfume: then, to know all the delicate sweet forms for the assumption of it: as also the rare corollary,

---

[1] An almost quotation from Daniel's "Compl. of Rosamond."
[2] In pawn.
[3] *i.e.* The first, second, or third gentleman of the family. See p. 199.

and practice of the Cuban ebullition, Euripus, and Whiff,[1] which he shall receive, or take in, here at London, and evaporate at Uxbridge, or farther, if it please him. If there be any such generous spirit, that is truly enamoured of these good faculties ; may it please him, but, by a note of his hand, to specify the place, or Ordinary, where he uses to eat and lie ; and most sweet attendance, with tobacco, and pipes of the best sort, shall be ministered. *Stet, quæso, candide Lector.*"[2]—Why, this is without parallel, this.

Car. Well, I'll mark this fellow for Sogliardo's use presently.

Punt. Or rather, Sogliardo, for his use.

Car. Faith, either of 'hem will serve, they are both good properties : I'll design the other a place too, that we may see him.

Punt. No better place than the Mitre, that we may be spectators with you, Carlo. Soft, behold who enters here : —Signior Sogliardo, God save you !

[3]*Enter* SOGLIARDO.

Sog. 'Save you, good Sir Puntarvolo : your dog's in health, sir, I see :—how now, Carlo ?

Car. We have ta'en simple pains, to choose you out followers here !

Punt. Come hither, signior. [*They show him the bills.*

Clove. Monsieur Orange, yond gallants observe us ; pr'ythee let's talk fustian a little, and gull 'hem ; make 'hem believe we are great scholars.

Orange. O Lord, sir !

Clove. Nay, pr'ythee let's, believe me, you have an excellent habit in discourse.

Orange. It pleases you to say so, sir.

Clove. By this church, you ha', la ; nay, come, begin :—

---

[1] The drawing in, and possibly swallowing. The other two are unknown.

[2] " Kind reader, let it stand, I pray thee " [Do not tear it down].

[3] Scene iv. in old eds.

Aristotle, in his Dæmonologia, approves Scaliger for the best navigator in his time; and in his Hypercritics, he reports him to be Heautontimorumenos:—you understand the Greek, sir?

Orange. O God, sir!

Maci. [*Aside.*] For society's sake he does. O, here be a couple of fine tame parrots!

Clove. Now, sir, whereas the ingenuity of the time and the soul's Synderisis are but embrions in nature, added to the paunch of Esquiline, and the inter-vallum of the zodiac, besides the ecliptic line being optic, and not mental, but by the contemplative and theoric part thereof, doth demonstrate to us the vegetable circumference, and the ventosity of the tropics, and whereas our intellectual, or mincing capreal (according to the metaphysics) as you may read in Plato's Histriomastix[1]— You conceive me, sir?

Orange. O Lord, sir!

Clove. Then coming to the pretty animal, as "reason long since is fled to animals," you know, or indeed for the more modelizing, or enamelling, or rather diamondizing of your subject, you shall perceive the hypothesis, or galaxia, (whereof the meteors long since had their initial inceptions and notions,) to be merely Pythagorical, mathematical, and aristocratical——For look you, sir, there is ever a kind of concinnity and species——Let us turn to our former discourse, for they mark us not.

Fast. Mass, yonder's the knight Puntarvolo.

Deli. And my cousin Sogliardo, methinks.

---

[1] Not Plato's but Marston's, whence and from his other writings, many of these fustian phrases are taken or imitated. I give three:—

> "The poor soules better part so feeble is
> So colde and dead is his Synderesis."

> "His very soule, his intellectuall
> Is nothing but a mincing capreall."
>
> *Sc. of Vill.,* Sat. II.

> "More fit to fill the paunch of Esquiline."
>
> *Histrio.,* p. 4.

Maci. Ay, and his familiar that haunts him, the devil with the shining face.

Deli. Let 'hem alone, observe 'hem not.

[SOGLIARDO, PUNTARVOLO, *and* CARLO, *walk together.*

Sog. Nay, I will have him, I am resolute for that. By this parchment, gentlemen, I have been so toiled among the harrots [1] yonder, you will not believe; they do speak i' the strangest language, and give a man the hardest terms for his money, that ever you knew,

Car. But ha' you arms? ha' you arms?

Sog. I'faith, I thank God, I can write myself gentleman now, here's my patent, it cost me thirty pound, by this breath.

Punt. A very fair coat, well charged, and full of armory.

Sog. Nay, it has as much variety of colours in it, as you have seen a coat have; how like you the crest, sir?

Punt. I understand it not well, what is't?

Sog. Marry, sir, it is your boar without a head, rampant.

Punt. A boor without a head, that's very rare!

Car. Ay, and rampant too! [*To* PUNTARVOLO.] troth, I commend the herald's wit, he has decyphered him well: a swine without a head, without brain, wit, anything indeed, ramping to gentility.—You can blazon the rest, signior, can you not?

Sog. O, ay, I have it in writing here o' purpose, it cost me two shillings the tricking. [2]

Car. Let's hear, let's hear.

Punt. [*Aside.*] It is the most vile, foolish, absurd, palpable, and ridiculous escutcheon that ever this eye survised.—'Save you, good Monsieur Fastidius.

[*They salute as they meet in the walk.*

Car. Silence, good knight;—on, on.

Sog. [*Reads.*] "Gyrony of eight pieces; azure and gules, between three plates; a chevron, engrailed

---

[1] Vulgar for heralds.   [2] The drawing out with the pen.

checquy, or, vert, and ermins; on a chief argent, between two ann'lets sables, a boar's head, proper."

Car. How's that? on a chief argent?

Sog. [*Reads.*] "On a chief argent, a boar's head proper, between two ann'lets sables."

Car. [*To* PUNTARVOLO.] 'Slud, it's a hog's cheek and puddings, in a pewter field, this.

> [*Here they shift.* FASTIDIUS *mixes with* PUNTAR-
> VOLO; CARLO *and* SOGLIARDO; DELIRO *and*
> MACILENTE; CLOVE *and* ORANGE; *four couple.*

Sog. How like you 'hem, signior?

Punt. Let the word[1] be, " Not without mustard : " your crest is very rare, sir.

Car. A frying-pan, to the crest, had had no fellow.

Fast. Intreat your poor friend to walk off a little, signior, I will salute the knight.

Car. Come lap't up, lap't up.[2]

Fast. You are right well encountered, sir, how does your fair dog?

Punt. In reasonable state, sir : what citizen is that you were consorted with? A merchant of any worth?

Fast. 'Tis Signior Deliro, sir.

Punt. Is it he?—'Save you, sir!   [*They salute.*

Deli. Good Sir Puntarvolo!

Maci. O what copy[3] of fool would this place minister, to one endued with patience to observe it!

Car. Nay, look you, sir, now you are a gentleman, you must carry a more exalted presence, change your mood, and habit to a more austere form, be exceeding proud, stand upon your gentility, and scorn every man. Speak nothing humbly, never discourse under a nobleman, though you ne'er saw him but riding to the Star-chamber, it's all one. Love no man. Trust no man. Speak ill of no man to his face; nor well of any man behind his back. Salute fairly on the front, and wish 'hem hanged

---

[1] Motto.   [2] Fold it up.   [3] Plenty, Lat. *copia.*

upon the turn. Spread yourself upon his bosom publicly, whose heart you would eat in private. These be principles, think on 'hem ; I'll come to you again presently.

[*Exit.*

Punt. Sirrah, keep close ;—yet not so close : thy breath will thaw my ruff.

Sog. O, good cousin, I am a little busy, how does my niece ? I am to walk with a knight, here.

[1]*Enter* FUNGOSO *with his* Tailor.

Fung. O, he is here,—look you, sir, that's the gentleman.

Tai. What, he i' the blush-coloured satin ?

Fung. Ay, he, sir ; though his suit blush, he blushes not ; look you, that's the suit, sir ; I would have mine such a suit, without difference, such stuff, such a wing,[2] such a sleeve, such a skirt, belly, and all ; therefore, pray you observe it. Have you a pair of tables ?[3]

Fast. Why, do you see, sir ? they say I am fantastical ; why, true, I know it, and I pursue my humour still, in contempt of this censorious age. 'Slight, an a man should do nothing, but what a sort of stale judgments about this town will approve in him, he were a sweet ass : I'ld beg him,[4] i'faith. I ne'er knew any more find fault with a fashion, than they that knew not how to put themselves into't. For mine own part, so I please mine own appetite, I am careless what the fusty world speaks of me. Puh !

Fung. Do you mark, how it hangs at the knee there ?

Tai. I warrant you, sir.

Fung. For God's sake do, note all : do you see the collar, sir ?

Tai. Fear nothing, it shall not differ in a stitch, sir.

Fung. Pray Heaven it do not ! you'll make these lin-

---

[1] Scene v. in old eds.   [2] An upright shoulder-lappet.
[3] Memorandum leaves.
[4] Wealthy lunatics were begged, for their property.

ings serve? and help me to a chapman for the outside, will you?

Tai. I'll do my best, sir: you'll put it off presently?

Fung. Ay, go with me to my chamber, you shall have it——but make haste of it, for the love of a customer, for I'll sit i' my old suit, or else lie a-bed, and read the *Arcadia* till you have done.   [*Exit with* Tailor.

Re-enter CARLO.

Car. O, if ever you were struck with a jest, gallants, now, now. I do usher the most strange piece of military profession that ever was discovered in *Insula Paulina.*[1]

Fast. Where? where?

Punt. What is he, for a creature?

Car. A pimp, a pimp, that I have observed yonder, the rarest superficies of a humour; he comes every morning to empty his lungs in Paul's here; and offers up some five or six hecatombs of faces and sighs, and away again.—Here he comes: nay, walk, walk, be not seen to note him, and we shall have excellent sport.

[2]*Enter* SHIFT; *and walks by.*

Punt. 'Slid, he vented a sigh e'en now, I thought he would have blown up the church.

Car. O, you shall have him give a number of those false fires ere he depart.

Fast. See, now he is expostulating with his rapier! look, look!

Car. Did you ever in your days, observe better passion over a hilt?

Punt. Except it were in the person of a cutler's boy, or that the fellow were nothing but vapour, I should think it impossible.

Car. See again, he claps his sword o' the head, as who should say, well, go to.

---

[1] In the Pauline isle (aisle).   [2] Scene vi. in old eds.

Fast. O violence! I wonder the blade can contain itself, being so provoked.

Car. "With that the moody squire thumpt his breast,
    And reared his eyen to heaven for revenge."

Sog. Troth, an you be good gentlemen, let's make 'hem friends, and take up the matter, between his rapier and him.

Car. Nay, if you intend that, you must lay down the matter,[1] for this rapier it seems, is in the nature of a hanger-on, and the good gentleman would happily[2] be rid of him.

Fast. By my faith, and 'tis to be suspected; I'll ask him.

Mac. [*To* DELIRO.] O, here's rich stuff! for life's sake, let us go.
A man would wish himself a senseless pillar,
Rather than view these monstrous prodigies:
Nil habet infelix paupertas durius in se,
Quam quod ridiculos homines facit——[3]
                                        [*Exit with* DELIRO.

Fast. Signior.

Shift. At your service.

Fast. Will you sell your rapier?

Car. S'blood, he is turned wild upon the question, he looks as he had seen a serjeant.

Shift. Sell my rapier? now God bless me!

Punt. Amen.

Shift. You asked me, if I would sell my rapier, sir?

Fast. I did indeed.

Shift. Now, Lord have mercy upon me!

Punt. Amen, I say still.

Shift. 'Slid, sir, what should you behold in my face, sir, that should move you, as they say, sir, to ask me, sir, if I would sell my rapier?

---

[1] *i.e.* Lay down money.

[2] "Happily" and "haply" were then spelled (and poss¹bly pronounced) alike.

[3] Unhappy poverty has in itself nothing harder, than that it makes men ridiculous.

Fast. Nay, let me pray you, sir, be not moved : I protest, I would rather have been silent, than any way offensive, had I known your nature.

Shift. Sell my rapier? Gods lid!—Nay, sir, for mine own part, as I am a man that has served in causes, or so, so I am not apt to injure any gentleman in the degree of falling foul, but—sell my rapier? I will tell you sir, I have served with this foolish rapier, where some of us dare not appear in haste ! I name no man ; but let that pass. Sell my rapier?—death to my lungs! This rapier, sir, has travelled by my side, sir, the best part of France, and the Low Country : I have seen Flushing, Brill, and the Hague, with this rapier, sir, in my Lord of Leicester's time; and, by God's will, he that should offer to disrapier me now, I would——Look you sir, you presume to be a gentleman of sort, and so likewise your friends here, if you have any disposition to travel for the sight of service, or so, one, two, or all of you, I can lend you letters to divers officers and commanders in the Low Countries, that shall for my cause do you all the good offices, that shall pertain or belong to gentlemen of your——[*Low to* FASTIDIUS.] Please you to shew the bounty of your mind, sir, to impart some ten groats, or half a crown to our use, till our ability be of growth to return it, and we shall think ourself——'Sblood ! sell my rapier?

Sog. I pray you, what said he, signior? he's a proper man.

Fast. Marry, he tells me, if I please to show the bounty of my mind, to impart some ten groats to his use, or so——

Punt. Break his head, and give it him.

Car. I thought he had been playing o' the Jew's trump, I.

Shift. My rapier? no, sir : my rapier is my guard, my defence, my revenue, my honour ;——[*Low as before.*] if you cannot impart, be secret, I beseech you—— and I will maintain it, where there is a grain of dust, or a drop of water. Hard is the choice when the valiant must eat their arms or clem.[1] Sell my rapier? no, my dear, I will not be divorced from thee yet: I have ever found thee true as steel, and——You cannot impart, sir?——'Save you, gentlemen ;——nevertheless, if you have a fancy to it, sir.

Fast. Pr'ythee away :—Is Signior Deliro departed?

Car. Ha' you seen a pimp outface his own wants better?

Sog. I commend him that can dissemble 'em so well.

Punt. True, and having no better a cloak for it, than he has neither.

Fast. God's precious, what mischievous luck is this! adieu, gentlemen.

Punt. Whither in such haste, monsieur Fastidius?

Fast. After my merchant, Signior Deliro, sir.   [*Exit.*

Car. O hinder him not, he may hap lose his tide; a good flounder,[2] i'faith.

Orange. Hark you, Signior Whiffe, a word with you.

[ORANGE *and* CLOVE *call* SHIFT *aside.*

Car. How? Signior Whiffe?

Orange. What was the difference between that gallant that's gone, and you, sir?

Shift. No difference; he would ha' given me five pound for my rapier, and I refused it ; that's all.

Clove. O, was't no otherwise? we thought you had been upon some terms.[3]

Shift. No other than you saw, sir.

Clove. Adieu, good Master Apple-John.

[*Exit with* ORANGE.

Car. How? Whiffe, and Apple-John too? 'Heart, what'll you say if this be the appendix, or label to both yond indentures?

Punt. It may be.

Car. Resolve us of it, Janus, thou that look'st every way ; or thou, Hercules, that hast travelled all countries.

---

[1] Starve.   [2] A grovelling flat-fish.   [3] Ill terms.

Punt. Nay, Carlo, spend not time in invocations now, 'tis late.

Car. Signior, here's a gentleman desirous of your name, sir.

Shift. Sir, my name is Cavalier Shift : I am known sufficiently in this walk, sir.

Car. Shift? I heard your name varied e'en now, as I take it.

Shift. True, sir, it pleases the world, as I am her excellent tobacconist, to give me the style of Signior Whiffe : as I am a poor esquire about the town here, they call me Master Apple-John. Variety of good names does well, sir.

Car. Ay, and good parts, to make those good names : out of which I imagine yond bills to be yours.

Shift. Sir, if I should deny the manuscripts, I were worthy to be banished the middle aisle, for ever.

Car. I take your word, sir : this gentleman has sub-scribed to 'hem, and is most desirous to become your pupil. Marry, you must use expedition.——Signior Insulso Sogliardo, this is the professor.

Sog. In good time, sir ; nay, good sir, house your head :[1] do you profess these sleights in tobacco?

Shift. I do more than profess, sir, and, if you please to be a practitioner, I will undertake in one fortnight to bring you, that you shall take it plausibly in any Ordinary, Theatre, or the Tilt-yard, if need be, i' the most popular[2] assembly that is.

Punt. But you cannot bring him to the whiffe, so soon.

Shift. Yes, as soon, sir ; he shall receive the first, second, and third whiffe, if it please him, and upon the receipt, take his horse, drink his three cups of canary, and expose one at Hounslow, a second at Staines, and a third at Bagshot.

Car. [*Aside.*] Baw-waw !

---

[1] Hats were worn in the aisles.   [2] Peopled.

Sog. You will not serve me, sir, will you? I'll give you more than countenance.

Shift. Pardon me, sir, I do scorn to serve any man.

Car. Who! he serve? 'Sblood, he keeps high men, and low men, he! he has a fair living at Fullam.[1]

Shift. But, in the nature of a fellow, I'll be your follower, if you please.

Sog. Sir, you shall stay, and dine with me, and if we can agree, we'll not part in haste: I am very bountiful to men of quality.——Where shall we go, signior?

Punt. Your Mitre is your best house.

Shift. I can make this dog take as many whiffes as I list, and he shall retain, or effume them, at my pleasure.

Punt. By your patience! follow me, fellows.

Sog. Sir Puntarvolo!

Punt. Pardon me, my dog shall not eat in his company for a million. [*Exit with his* Servants.

Car. Nay, be not you amazed, Signior Whiffe, whate'er that stiff-necked gentleman says.

Sog. No, for you do not know the humour of the dog, as we do:——where shall we dine, Carlo? I would fain go to one of these Ordinaries, now I am a gentleman.

Car. So you may; were you never at any yet?

Sog. No, faith, but they say there resorts your most choice gallants.

Car. True, and the fashion is, when any stranger comes in amongst 'hem, they all stand up and stare at him, as he were some unknown beast, brought out of Afric: but that'll be helped with a good adventurous face. You must be impudent enough, sit down, and use no respect; when anything's propounded above your capacity, smile at it, make two or three faces, and 'tis excellent, they'll think you have travelled; though you argue, a whole day, in silence thus, and discourse in nothing but laughter, 'twill pass. Only, now and then,

---

[1] Three kinds of cheating dice; see *Merry Wives of Windsor,* i. 2, 94.

give fire, discharge a good full oath, and offer a great wager,—'twill be admirable.

Sog. I warrant you, I am resolute;—come, good signior, there's a poor French crown for your Ordinary.

Shift. It comes well, for I had not so much as the least portcullis [1] of coin before.

Mit. I travail with another objection, signior, which I fear will be enforced against the author, ere I can be delivered of it.

Cor. What's that, sir ?

Mit. That the argument of his comedy might have been of some other nature, as of a duke to be in love with a countess, and that countess to be in love with the duke's son, and the son to love the lady's waiting-maid : some such cross wooing, with a clown to their servingman, better than to be thus near, and familiarly allied to the time.

Cor. You say well, but I would fain hear one of these autumn-judgments define once, *Quid sit comœdia ?* [2] if he cannot, let him content himself with Cicero's definition— till he have strength to propose to himself a better—who would have a comedy to be *imitatio vitæ, speculum consuetudinis, imago veritatis;* [3] a thing throughout pleasant, and ridiculous, and accommodated to the correction of manners : if the maker have failed in any particle of this, they may worthily tax him ; but if not, why —— be you, that are for them, silent, as I will be for him ; and give way to the actors.

Enter SORDIDO, *with a halter about his neck, and bearing a stool.*

Sord. Nay, God's precious, if the weather and season be so respectless, that beggars shall live as well as their betters; and that my hunger, and thirst for riches shall not make them hunger and thirst with poverty; that my sleeps shall be broken, and their hearts not broken ; that

---

[1] The penny and ha'fpenny had this on them.
[2] What comedy may be.
[3] The imitation of life, the mirror of manners, the image of truth.
[4] Scene vii. in old eds.

my coffers shall be full, and yet care[1] ; theirs empty, and
yet merry ! 'tis time that a cross should bear flesh and
blood, since flesh and blood cannot bear this cross.

Mit. What, will he hang himself ?

Cor. Faith, ay ; it seems his prognostication has not
kept touch with him, and that makes him despair.

Mit. Beshrew me, he will be " out of his humour " then
indeed.

Sord. Tut, these star-monger knaves, who would trust
'hem ? One says " dark and rainy," when 'tis as clear as
crystal ; another says, " tempestuous blasts and storms,"
and 'twas as calm as a milk-bowl ? here be sweet rascals
for a man to credit his whole fortunes with ! You sky-
staring coxcombs you, you fat-brains, out upon you ; you
are good for nothing but to sweat night-caps, and make
rug-gowns dear![2] You learned men, and have not a
legion of devils " à vostre service ! à vostre service ! "[3] by
Heaven, I think I shall die a better scholar than they :
but soft, how now, sirrah ?

Enter a Hind *with a letter.*

Hind. Here's a letter come from your son, sir.

Sord. From my son, sir ? what would my son, sir ?
some good news, no doubt. [*Reads.*

" Sweet and dear father, desiring you first to send me
your blessing, which is more worth to me than gold or
silver, I desire you likewise to be advertised, that this
Shrove-tide, contrary to custom,[4] we use always to have
revels ; which is indeed dancing, and makes an excellent
show in truth ; especially if we gentlemen be well attired,
which our seniors note, and think the better of our fathers,
the better we are maintained, and that, they shall know if
they come up, and have anything to do in the law : therefore, good father, these are, for your own sake as well as
mine, to re-desire you, that you let me not want that

---

[1] My care be full.   [2] Worn by learned astrologers, &c.
[3] At your service.   [4] Ordinary custom.

which is fit for the setting up of our name, in the honourable volume of gentility, that I may say to our calumniators, with Tully, *Ego sum ortus domus meæ, tu occasus tuæ.*[1] And thus, not doubting of your fatherly benevolence, I humbly ask your blessing, and pray God to bless you."

"Yours, if his own."

How's this! "Yours, if his own!" Is he not my son, except he be his own son? Belike this is some new kind of superscription the gallants use.——Well! wherefore dost thou stay, knave? away; go. [*Exit* Hind.] Here's a letter, indeed! "revels?" and "benevolence?" is this a weather to send benevolence? or is this a season to revel in. 'Slid, the devil and all takes part to vex me, I think! this letter would never have come now else; now, now, when the sun shines, and the air thus clear. 'Soul! if this hold, we shall shortly have an excellent crop of corn spring up out of the high-ways: the streets and houses of the town will be hid with the rankness of the fruits that grow there, in spite of good husbandry. Go to, I'll prevent the sight of it, come as quickly as it can, I will prevent [2] the sight of it. I have this remedy, Heaven. [*Ties his rope to a branch.*] Stay; I'll try the pain thus a little: O, nothing, nothing. Well, now, shall my son gain a benevolence by my death? or anybody be the better for my gold, or so forth? No; alive, I kept it from 'hem, and dead, my ghost shall walk about it, and preserve it, my son and daughter shall starve ere they touch it, I have hid it as deep as hell from the sight of Heaven, and to it I go now. [*Falls off his stool.*

Enter Rustics, *one after another.*

1st Rust. Ay me, what pitiful sight is this! help, help, help! [*Cuts him down.*

2nd Rust. How now, what's the matter?

[1] I am the origin of my house, thou art the death of mine.
[2] Go before, anticipate.

1st Rust. O, here's a man has hanged himself, help to get him again.

2nd Rust. Hanged himself! 'Slid, carry him afore a justice, 'tis chance-medley, o' my word.

3rd Rust. How now, what's here to do?

4th Rust. How comes this?

2nd Rust. One has executed himself, contrary to order of law, and by my consent he shall answer't.

5th Rust. Would he were in case to answer it!

1st Rust. Stand by, he recovers, give him breath.

Sord. Oh!

5th Rust. Mass, 'twas well you went the foot way, neighbour.

1st Rust. Ay, an I had not cut the halter—

Sord. How! cut the halter? ay me, I am undone, I am undone!

2nd Rust. Marry, if you had not been undone, you had been hanged, I can tell you.

Sord. You thread-bare, horse-bread-eating[1] rascals, if if you would needs have been meddling, could you not have untied it, but you must cut it; and in the midst too! ay me!

1st Rust. Out on me, 'tis the caterpillar Sordido! how cursed are the poor, that the viper was blessed with this good fortune!

2nd Rust. Nay, how accurst art thou, that art cause to the curse of the poor!

3rd Rust. Ay, and to save so wretched a caitiff!

4th Rust. Curst be thy fingers that loosed him!

2nd Rust. Some desperate fury possess thee, that thou may'st hang thyself too!

5th Rust. Never may'st thou be saved, that saved so damned a monster!

Sord. What curses breathe these men! how have my deeds
Made my looks differ from another man's,

---

[1] Horses were often fed on rye and other bread.

That they should thus detest, and loath my life!
Out on my wretched humour, it is that
Makes me thus monstrous in true human eyes.
Pardon me, gentle friends, I'll make fair 'mends
For my foul errors past, and twenty-fold
Restore to all men, what with wrong I robbed them:
My barns, and garners shall stand open still
To all the poor that come, and my best grain
Be made alms-bread, to feed half-famished mouths.
Though hitherto amongst you I have lived,
Like an unsavoury muck-hill to myself,
Yet now my gathered heaps being spread abroad,
Shall turn to better, and more fruitful uses.
Bless then this man, curse him no more for saving
My life, and soul, together. [*To himself.*] O, how
          deeply
The bitter curses of the poor do pierce!——
I am by wonder changed; come in with me
And witness my repentance: now, I prove,
"No life is blessed, that is not graced with love. [*Exit.*

2nd Rust. O miracle! see when a man has grace!

3rd Rust. Had 't not been pity so good a man should
have been cast away?

2nd Rust. Well, I'll get our clerk put his conversion
in the "Acts and Monuments." [1]

4th Rust. Do, for I warrant him he's a martyr.

2nd Rust. O God, how he wept, if you marked it!
did you see how the tears trilled?

5th Rust. Yes, believe me, like master vicar's bowls
upon the green, for all the world.

3rd or *4th Rust.* O neighbour, God's blessing o' your
heart, neighbour, 'twas a good grateful deed. [*Exeunt.*

Cor. How now, Mitis? what's that you consider so
seriously?

Mit. Troth, that which doth essentially please me, the
warping condition of this green and soggy [2] multitude; but

---

[1] Fox's "Martyrs."   [2] Muddy

in good faith, signior, your author hath largely outstript my expectation in this scene, I will liberally confess it. For, when I saw Sordido so desperately intended, I thought I had had a hand of him, then.

Cor. What? you supposed he should have hung himself indeed?

Mit. I did, and had framed my objection to it ready which may yet be very fitly urged, and with some necessity: for though his purposed violence lost th' effect, and extended not to death, yet the intent and horror of the object was more than the nature of a comedy will in any sort admit.

Cor. Ay? what think you of Plautus, in his comedy called "Cistellaria"? there, where he brings in Alcesimarchus with a drawn sword ready to kill himself, and as he is e'en fixing his breast upon it, to be restrained from his resolved outrage, by Silenium and the bawd? is not his authority of power to give our scene approbation?

Mit. Sir, I have this only evasion left me, to say, "I think it be so indeed; your memory is happier than mine:" but I wonder, what engine he will use to bring the rest "out of their humours!"

Cor. That will appear anon, never pre-occupy your imagination withal. Let your mind keep company with the scene still, which now removes itself from the country to the court. Here comes Macilente, and Signior Brisk freshly suited; lose not yourself, for now the epitasis,[1] or busy part of our subject, is in act.

[2] SCENE III.—*An Apartment at the Court*

Enter MACILENTE, FASTIDIUS, *and* CINEDO *with tobacco.*

Fast. Well, now, Signior Macilente, you are not only welcome to the court, but also to my mistress's withdrawing chamber:—boy, get me some tobacco—I'll but go in, and show I am here, and come to you presently, sir.

[*Exit.*

---

[1] The old critics gave to a comedy, (1) the Prologue; (2) the Protasis, or setting forth of the subject; (3) the Epitasis, or busy part of it; (4) the Catastrophe.

[2] Scene ix. in old eds.

Jon. I.   O

Maci. What's that he said? by Heaven, I marked him
 not:
My thoughts and I were of another world.
I was admiring mine own outside here,
To think what privilege, and palm it bears
Here, in the court! Be a man ne'er so vile
In wit, in judgment, manners, or what else;
If he can purchase but a silken cover,
He shall not only pass, but pass regarded:
Whereas, let him be poor, and meanly clad,
Though ne'er so richly parted,[1] you shall have
A fellow, that knows nothing but his beef,
Or how to rinse his clammy guts in beer,
Will take him by the shoulders, or the throat,
And kick him down the stairs. Such is the state
Of virtue, in bad clothes!—ha, ha; ha, ha!
That raiment should be in such high request!
How long should I be, ere I should put off [2]
To the lord chancellor's tomb,[3] or the shrives' [4] posts?
By Heaven, I think, a thousand, thousand year.
His gravity, his wisdom, and his faith
To my dread sovereign—graces that survive him—
These I could well endure to reverence,
But not his tomb: no more than I'ld commend
The chapel organ, for the gilt without,
Or this base-viol, for the varnished face.

Re-enter FASTIDIUS.

Fast. I fear I have made you stay somewhat long, sir;
——but is my tobacco ready, boy?

Cin. Ay, sir.

Fast. Give me;——my mistress is upon coming, you
shall see her presently, sir [*Tob.*], you'll say you never
accosted a more piercing wit.—This tobacco is not dried,
boy, or else the pipe's defective.—Oh, your wits of Italy

---

[1] Possessed of parts, mentally endowed.   [2] Put off my hat.
[3] Sir Chr. Hatton, died 1591.   [4] Sheriffs'.

are nothing comparable to her! her brain's a very quiver of jests! and she does dart them abroad with that sweet loose,[1] and judicial aim, that you would——here she comes, sir.   [*She is seen, and goes in again.*

Maci. [*Aside.*] 'Twas time, his invention had been bogged else.

Sav. [*Within.*] Give me my fan there.

Maci. How now, Monsieur Brisk?

Fast. A kind of affectionate reverence strikes me with a cold shivering, methinks.

Maci. [*Aside.*] I like such tempers well, as stand before their mistresses with fear and trembling, and before their Maker, like impudent mountains!

Fast. By this hand, I'ld spend twenty pound my vaulting-horse[2] stood here now, she might see me do but one trick.

Maci. Why, does she love activity?

Cin. Or, if you had but your long stockings on,[3] to be dancing a galliard as she comes by.

Fast. Ay, either. O, these stirring humours make ladies mad with desire;——she comes. My good genius embolden me:——boy, the pipe quickly.

Enter SAVIOLINA.

Maci. What? will he give her music?

Fast. A second good morrow to my fair mistress.

Sav. Fair servant, I'll thank you a day hence, when the date of your salutation comes forth.

Fast. How like you that answer? is't not admirable?

Maci. I were a simple courtier, if I could not admire trifles, sir.

Fast. [*Takes tobacco between the breaks.*] Troth, sweet lady, I shall [*Tob.*]——be prepared to give you thanks for those thanks, and——study more officious, and obse-

---

[1] The letting fly.
[2] A wooden one, for practising vaulting into the saddle.
[3] Dancing stockings reaching above the knee.

quious regards——to your fair beauties.——Mend the pipe, boy.

Maci. [*Aside.*] I ne'er knew tobacco taken as a parenthesis before.

Fast. 'Fore God, sweet lady, believe it, I do honour the meanest rush[1] in this chamber, for your love.

Sav. Ay, you need not tell me that, sir; I do think, you do prize a rush before my love.

Maci. [*Aside.*] Is this the wonder of nations?

Fast. O, by this air, pardon me, I said "*for* your love," by this light: but it is the accustomed sharpness of your ingenuity, sweet mistress, to [*Takes down the viol.*]—— Mass, your viol's new strung, methinks.

Maci. Ingenuity! I see his ignorance will not suffer him to slander her, which he had done most notably, if he had said wit, for ingenuity, as he meant it.

Fast. By the soul of music, lady (*Hum, hum*). [*Strums it.*]

Sav. Would we might hear it once.

Fast. I do more adore, and admire your (*Hum, hum*) predominant perfections, than (*Hum, hum*) ever I shall have power, and faculty to express (*Hum*).

Sav. Upon the viol de gambo,[2] you mean?

Fast. It's miserably out of tune, by this hand.

Sav. Nay, rather by the fingers.

Maci. [*Aside.*] It makes good harmony with her wit.

Fast. Sweet lady, tune it? [*She moves aside to tune it.*] —Boy, some tobacco.

Maci. [*Aside.*] Tobacco again! he does court his mistress with very exceeding good changes.

Fast. Signior Macilente, you take none, sir? [*Tob.*]

Maci. No; unless I had a mistress, signior, it were a great indecorum for me to take tobacco.

Fast. How like you her wit? [*Tob.*]

[*Talks and takes tobacco between again.*]

Maci. Her ingenuity is excellent, sir.

---

[1] Rushes were used instead of carpets.
[2] A violin held between the knees.

Fast. You see the subject of her sweet fingers there——
Oh, she tickles it so, that——she makes it laugh most
divinely;——I'll tell you a good jest now, and yourself
shall say it's a good one: I have wished myself to be
that instrument, I think, a thousand times, and not so
few, by Heaven!——

Maci. Not unlike, sir; but how? to be cased up and
hung by on the wall?

Fast. O no, sir, to be in use, I assure you; as your
judicious eyes may testify.——

Sav. Here, servant, if you will play, come.

Fast. Instantly, sweet lady.——In good faith, here's
most divine tobacco!

Sav. Nay, I cannot stay to dance after your pipe.

Fast. Good! nay, dear lady, stay; by this sweet
smoke, I think your wit be all fire.——

Maci. [*Aside.*] And he's the salamander belongs
to it.[1]

Sav. Is your tobacco perfumed, servant? that you
swear by the sweet smoke?

Fast. Still more excellent! Before Heaven, and these
bright lights, I think——you are made of ingenuity,
I——

Maci. [*Aside.*] True, as your discourse is: oh abominable!

Fast. Will your ladyship take any?

Sav. O, peace, I pray you; I love not the breath of a
woodcock's[2] head.

Fast. Meaning my head, lady?

Sav. Not altogether so, sir; but—as it were fatal to
their follies, that think to grace themselves with taking
tobacco, when they want better entertainment—you see
your pipe bears the true form of a woodcock's head.

Fast. O admirable simile!

Sav. 'Tis best leaving of you in admiration, sir. [*Exit.*

Maci. Are these the admired lady-wits, that having so

---

[1] "That lives in it," in quarto.   [2] Simpleton's.

good a plain-song, can run no better division upon it? All her jests are of the stamp March was, fifteen years ago. Is this the comet, Monsieur Fastidius, that your gallants wonder at so?

Fast. Heart of a gentleman, to neglect me afore presence[1] thus!—Sweet sir, I beseech you be silent in my disgrace. By the Muses, I was never in so vile a humour in my life, and her wit was at the flood too.— Report it not for a million, good sir; let me be so far endeared to your love.   [*Exeunt.*

Mit. What follows next, Signior Cordatus? this gallant's humour is almost spent, methinks it ebbs apace, with this contrary breath of his mistress.

Cor. O, but it will flow again for all this, till there come a general drought of humour among all our actors, and then I fear not, but his will fall as low as any. See, who presents himself here!

Mit. What, i' the old case?

Cor. I'faith, which makes it the more pitiful; you understand where the scene is?

---

[1] So the quarto and folios. **Gifford inserts "the."**

ACT THE FOURTH.

SCENE I.—*A Room in* DELIRO'S *House.*

Enter FUNGOSO, FALLACE *following him.*

AL. Why are you so melancholy, brother?

Fung. I am not melancholy, I thank you, sister.

Fal. Why are you not merry then? there are but two of us in all the world, and if we should not be comforts one to another, God help us!

Fung. Faith, I cannot tell, sister; but if a man had any true melancholy in him, it would make him melancholy, to see his yeomanly father cut his neighbours' throats, to make his son a gentleman; and yet, when he has cut 'hem, he will see his son's throat cut too, ere he make him a true gentleman indeed, before death cut his own throat. I must be the first head [1] of our house, and yet he will not give me the head till I be made so. Is any man termed a gentleman, that is not always i' the fashion? I would know but that.

Fal. If you be melancholy for that, brother, I think I have as much cause to be melancholy as one [2]; for I'll be sworn, I live as little in the fashion, as any woman in

---

[1] As being the first gentleman, see page 176.
[2] So the quarto and folios, "not always in the fashion" being apparently understood. Gifford inserts "any."

London. By the faith of a gentlewoman, beast that I am to say it! I ha' not one friend i' the world besides my husband. When saw you Master Fastidius Brisk, brother?

Fung. But awhile since, sister, I think: I know not well in truth. By this hand, I could fight with all my heart, methinks.

Fal. Nay, good brother, be not resolute.

Fung. [*To himself.*] I sent him a letter,[1] and he writes me no answer neither. [*Walks toward back and busies himself.*

Fal. [*To herself.*] Oh, sweet Fastidius Brisk! Oh, fine courtier! thou art he makest me sigh, and say, how blessed is that woman that hath a courtier to her husband! and how miserable a dame she is, that hath neither husband, nor friend i' the court! O, sweet Fastidius! Oh, fine courtier! How comely he bows him in his curtsy! how full he hits a woman between the lips when he kisses! how upright he sits at the table! how daintily he carves! how sweetly he talks, and tells news of this lord, and of that lady! how cleanly he wipes his spoon at every spoonful of any white-meat[2] he eats, and what a neat case of pick-tooths he carries about him, still! O sweet Fastidius! Oh fine courtier!

[3] *Enter* DELIRO, *with* Musicians.

Deli. See, yonder she is, gentlemen. Now, as ever you'll bear the name of musicians, touch your instruments sweetly, she has a delicate ear, I tell you: play not a false note, I beseech you.

Musi. Fear not, Signior Deliro.

Deli. O, begin, begin, some sprightly thing:—Lord, how my imagination labours with the success of it! [*They strike up a lively tune.*] Well 'sayed, good, i'faith! [*Aside.*] Heaven grant it please her! I'll not be seen, for then she'll be sure to dislike it.

---

[1] His father.   [2] Custard, &c.   [3] Scene ii. in old eds.

Fal. Hey——da! this is excellent! I'll lay my life this is my husband's dotage. [*Looks about.*] I thought so; nay, never play bo-peep with me; I know you do nothing but study how to anger me, sir.

Deli. [*Coming towards her.*] Anger thee, sweet wife? why, didst thou not send for musicians to supper last night thyself?

Fal. To supper, sir? now [*Suiting action to word*], come up to supper, I beseech you: as though there were no difference between supper-time, when folks should be merry, and this time when they would be melancholy. I would never take upon me to take a wife, if I had no more judgment to please her.

Deli. Be pleased, sweet wife, and they shall ha' done: and would to fate, my life were done, if I can never please thee! [*Exeunt* Musicians.

Enter MACILENTE.

Maci. 'Save you, lady; where is Master Deliro?

Deli. Here, Master Macilente: you are welcome from court, sir; no doubt you have been graced exceedingly of Master Brisk's mistress, and the rest of the ladies, for his sake.

Maci. Alas, the poor fantastic! he's scarce known
To any lady there; and those that know him,
Know him the simplest man of all they know:
Deride and play upon his amorous humours,
Though he but apishly doth imitate
The gallant'st courtiers, kissing ladies' pumps,
Holding the cloth[1] for them, praising their wits,
And servilely observing every one,
May do them pleasure: fearful to be seen
With any man, though he be ne'er so worthy,
That's not in grace with some, that are the greatest.
Thus courtiers do, and these he counterfeits,
But sets not such a sightly carriage

---

[1] The hangings at the doors.

Upon their vanities, as they themselves ;
And therefore they despise him : for indeed
He's like the zany to a tumbler,
That tries tricks after him, to make men laugh.

Fal. [*Aside.*] Here's an unthankful spiteful wretch ! the good gentleman vouchsafed to make him his companion, because my husband put him into a few rags, and now see how the unrude[1] rascal backbites him !

Deli. Is he no more graced amongst 'hem then ? say you ?

Maci. Faith, like a pawn at chess : fills up a room, that's all.

Fal. [*Aside.*] O monster of men ! can the earth bear such an envious caitiff ?

Deli. Well, I repent me I e'er credited him so much : but, now I see what he is, and that his masking vizor is off, I'll forbear him no longer. All his lands are mortgaged to me, and forfeited ; besides, I have bonds of his in my hand, for the receipt of now fifty pound, now a hundred, now two hundred ; still, as he has had a fan but wagged at him, he would be in a new suit. Well, I'll salute him by a serjeant, the next time I see him, i'faith, I'll "suit" him.

Maci. Why, you may soon see him, sir, for he is to meet Signior Puntarvolo, at a notary's, by the Exchange, presently ; where he means to take up, upon return——

Fal. Now, out upon thee, Judas ! canst thou not be content to backbite thy friend, but thou must betray him ? wilt thou seek the undoing of any man ? and of such a man too ?——and will you, sir, get your living by the counsel of traitors ?

Deli. Dear wife, have patience.

Fal. The house will fall, the ground will open, and swallow us : I'll not bide here for all the gold and silver in Heaven.   [*Exit.*

---

[1] Rudis is sometimes taken for lybertie from labour. (Th. Cooper, *Thes. L. Latinæ.*) Therefore unrude would be handicraft, mechanical.

Deli. O, good Macilente, let's follow and appease her, or the peace of my life is at an end. [*Exit.*

Maci. Now pease, and not peace, feed that life, whose head hangs so heavily over a woman's manger! [*Exit.*

Re-enter FALLACE *running, and claps to the door.*[1]

Fal. Help me, brother! [*To* DELIRO *within.*] Ods body, an you come here, I'll do myself a mischief.

Deli. [*Within.*] Nay, hear me, sweet wife, unless thou wilt have me go, I will not go.

Fal. Tut, you shall ne'er ha' that vantage of me, to say, you are undone by me: I'll not bid you stay, I.— Brother, sweet brother, here's four angels, I'll give you towards your suit: for the love of gentry, and as ever you came of christen[2] creature, make haste to the water side, (you know where Master Fastidius uses to land,) and give him warning of my husband's malicious intent; and tell him of that lean rascal's treachery: O Heavens, how my flesh rises at him! nay, sweet brother, make haste: you may say, I would have writ to him, but that the necessity of the time would not permit. [*To herself.*] He cannot choose but take it extraordinarily from me;— and commend me to him, good brother; say, I sent you. [*Exit.*

Fung. Let me see, these four angels, and then forty shillings more I can borrow on my gown in Fetter Lane. —Well, I will go presently, 'say on my suit, pay as much money as I have, and swear myself into credit with my tailor for the rest. [*Exit.*

[3] DELIRO *and* MACILENTE *pass over the stage.*

Deli. O, on my soul you wrong her, Macilente. Though she be froward, yet I know she's honest.

Maci. Well, then have I no judgment: would any

---

[1] Gifford, having made Fungoso go out with Fallace, makes here a new scene, viz., Scene ii. [2] Christened.
[3] Gifford makes this Scene iii. Jonson made it a new scene in the quarto, but not in the folio.

woman, but one that were wild in her affections, have broke out into that immodest, and violent passion against her husband? or is't possible——

Deli. If you love me, forbear; all the arguments i' the world shall never wrest my heart to believe it. [*Exeunt.*

Cor. How like you the deciphering of his dotage?
Mit. O, strangely! and of the other's envy, too, that labours so seriously to set debate betwixt a man and his wife. Stay, here comes the knight adventurer.
Cor. Ay, and his scrivener with him.

¹SCENE II.—PUNTARVOLO'S *Lodgings.*

Enter PUNTARVOLO, Notary, *and* Servants *with the dog and cat.*

Punt. I wonder Monsieur Fastidius comes not! but, notary, if thou please to draw the indentures the while, I will give thee thy instructions.

Not. With all my heart, sir; and I'll fall in hand with 'hem presently.

Punt. Well then, first, the sum is to be understood.

Not. [*Writes.*] Good, sir.

Punt. Next, our several appellations, and character of my dog, and cat, must be known:—show him the cat, sirrah.

Not. So, sir.

Punt. Then, that the intended bound is the Turk's court in Constantinople: the time limited for our return, a year: and that if either² of us miscarry, the whole venture is lost. These are general, conceiv'st thou? or if either of us turn Turk.

Not. Ay, sir.

Punt. Now for particulars: that I may make my

---

¹ Scene iii. in old eds.   ² Used for three persons.

travels by sea or land, to my best liking: and that hiring a coach for myself, it shall be lawful for my dog, or cat, or both, to ride with me in the said coach.

Not. Very good, sir.

Punt. That I may choose[1] to give my dog, or cat, fish, for fear of bones; or any other nutriment that, by the judgment of the most authentical physicians where I travel, shall be thought dangerous.

Not. Well, sir.

Punt. That, after the receipt of his money, he shall neither, in his own person, nor any other, either by direct, or indirect means, as magic, witchcraft, or other such exotic[2] arts, attempt, practise, or complot any thing, to the prejudice of me, my dog, or my cat: neither shall I use the help of any such sorceries, or enchantments, as unctions to make our skins impenetrable, or to travel invisible by virtue of a powder, or a ring, or to hang any three-forked charm about my dog's neck, secretly conveyed into his collar: (understand you?) but that all be performed sincerely, without fraud, or imposture.

Not. So, sir.

Punt. That, for testimony of the performance, myself am to bring thence a Turk's mustachio, my dog a Grecian hare's lip, and my cat the train or tail of a Thracian rat.

Not. 'Tis done, sir.

Punt. 'Tis said, sir, not done, sir: but forward. That upon my return, and landing on the Tower-wharf, with the aforesaid testimony, I am to receive five for one, according to the proportion of the sums put forth.

Not. Well, sir.

Punt. Provided, that if before our departure, or setting forth, either myself, or these, be visited with sickness, or any other casual event, so that the whole course of the adventure be hindered thereby; that then, he is to return, and I am to receive, the prenominated proportion upon fair and equal terms.

---

[1] Most would say "choose whether or not."   [2] Outlandish.

Not. Very good, sir, is this all?

Punt. It is all, sir; and dispatch them, good notary.

Not. As fast as is possible, sir. [*Exit.*

Enter CARLO.

Punt. O, Carlo! welcome: saw you Monsieur Brisk?

Car. Not I: did he appoint you, to meet here?

Punt. Ay, and I muse he should be so tardy: he is to take an hundred pounds of me in venture, if he maintain his promise.

Car. Is his hour past?

Punt. Not yet, but it comes on apace.

Car. Tut, be not jealous of him; he will sooner break all the commandments, than his hour; upon my life, in such a case, trust him.

Punt. Methinks, Carlo, you look very smooth! ha?

Car. Why, I come but now from a hot-house, I must needs look smooth.

Punt. From a hot-house!

Car. Ay, do you make a wonder on't? why, it's your only physic. Let a man sweat once a week in a hot-house, and be well rubbed, and froted,[1] with a good plump juicy wench, and sweet linen, he shall ne'er ha' the pox.

Punt. What, the French pox?

Car. The French pox! our pox: 'sblood we have 'hem in as good form as they, man, what?

Punt. Let me perish, but thou art a salt one! was your new-created gallant there with you, Sogliardo?

Car. O porpoise! hang him, no: he's a leiger[2] at Horn's ordinary, yonder: his villanous Ganymede and he ha' been droning a tobacco-pipe there ever sin' yesterday noon.

Punt. Who? Signior Tripartite, that would give my dog the whiffe?

---

[1] More thoroughly and perhaps more quickly rubbed; chafed, without excoriating.   [2] Resident.

Car. Ay, he. They have hired a chamber and all, private, to practise in, for the making of the "patoun," "the receipt reciprocal,"[1] and a number of other mysteries not yet extant. I brought some dozen, or twenty gallants this morning to view 'hem, as you'ld do a piece of perspective,[2] in at a key-hole: and there we might see Sogliardo sit in a chair, holding his snout up like a sow under an apple-tree, while th' other opened his nostrils with a poking-stick,[3] to give the smoke a more free delivery. They had spit some three, or fourscore ounces between 'hem, afore we came away.

Punt. How! spit three or four score ounces?

Car. Ay, and preserved it in porrengers, as a barber does his blood, when he opens a vein.[4]

Punt. Out, pagan! how dost thou open the vein of thy friend?

Car. Friend? is there any such foolish thing i' the world, ha? 'Slid, I ne'er relished it yet.

Punt. Thy humour is the more dangerous.

Car. No, not a whit, signior. Tut, a man must keep time in all: I can oil my tongue when I meet him next, and look with a good sleeck forehead; 'twill take away all soil of suspicion, and that's enough: what Lynceus can see my heart? Pish, the title of a friend! it's a vain, idle thing, only venerable among fools: you shall not have one that has any opinion of wit affect it.

[5] *Enter* DELIRO *and* MACILENTE.

Deli. 'Save you, good Sir Puntarvolo.

Punt. Signior Deliro! welcome.

Deli. Pray you, sir, did you see Master Fastidius Brisk? I heard he was to meet your worship here.

---

[1] Meanings unknown.

[2] Probably in views or motions exhibited.

[3] Small steel rods for plaiting ruffs.

[4] Barbers undertook minor operations in surgery.

[5] Scene iv. in old eds.

Punt. You heard no figment, sir, I do expect him at every pulse of my watch.

Deli. In good time, sir.   [*The two move off a little.*

Car. There's a fellow now, looks like one of the patricians of Sparta, marry, his wit's after ten i' the hundred : a good blood-hound, a close-mouthed dog, he follows the scent well ; marry, he's at a fault now, methinks.

Punt. I should wonder at that creature is free from the danger of thy tongue.

Car. O, I cannot abide these limbs of satin, or rather Satan indeed, that'll walk, like the children of darkness, all day in a melancholy shop, with their pockets full of blanks, ready to swallow up as many poor unthrifts as come within the verge.

Punt. So ! and what hast thou for him that is with him, now ?

Car. O, damn me ! " Immortality ! " I'll not meddle with him, the pure element of fire, all spirit, extraction.

Punt. How, Carlo ? ha, what is he, man ?

Car. A scholar, Macilente, do you not know him ? a lank, raw-boned anatomy, he walks up and down like a charged musket, no man dares encounter him : that's his rest[1] there.

Punt. His rest[2] ! why, has he a forked head ?

Car. Pardon me, that's to be suspended[3] ; you are too quick, too apprehensive.

Deli. Troth, now I think on't, I'll defer it till some other time.

Maci. Not by any means, signior, you shall not lose this opportunity, he will be here presently now.

Deli. Yes faith, Macilente, 'tis best. For look you, sir, I shall so exceedingly offend my wife in't, that——

Maci. Your wife ? now for shame lose these thoughts, and become the master of your own spirits. Should I, if

---

[1] *i.e.,* Deliro, his resting-place and support like a musket-rest.
[2] A musket-rest ψ, which was suspended when not in use.
[3] Held over a while.

I had a wife, suffer myself to be thus passionately carried, to and fro, with the stream of her humour? and neglect my deepest affairs, to serve her affections? 'Slight, I would geld myself first.

Deli. O but signior, had you such a wife as mine is, you would——

Maci. Such a wife! Now God hate me, sir, if ever I discerned any wonder in your wife yet, with all the speculation[1] I have: I have seen some that ha' been thought fairer than she, in my time; and I have seen those, ha' not been altogether so tall, esteemed properer women; and I have seen less noses grow upon sweeter faces, that have done very well too, in my judgment: but, in good faith, signior, for all this, the gentlewoman is a good, pretty, proud, hard-favoured[2] thing, marry, not so peerlessly to be doted upon, I must confess: nay, be not angry.

Deli. Well, sir, however you please to forget yourself, I have not deserved to be thus played upon; but henceforth, pray you forbear my house, for I can but faintly endure the savour of his breath at my table, that shall thus jade me for my courtesies.

Maci. Nay, then, signior, let me tell you, your wife is no proper woman, and by my life, I suspect her honesty, that's more, which you may likewise suspect, if you please: do you see? I'll urge you to nothing, against your appetite, but if you please, you may suspect it.

Deli. Good, sir. [*Exit.*

Maci. "Good sir!" now horn upon horn pursue thee, thou blind, egregious dotard!

Car. O, you shall hear him speak like envy.—Signior Macilente, you saw Monsieur Brisk lately? I heard you were with him at court.

Maci. Ay, Buffone, I was with him.

Car. And how is he respected there? I know you'll

---

[1] Insight.
[2] Not in her countenance, but in her mind.

Jon. I.

P

deal ingenuously with us; is he made of[1] amongst the
sweeter sort of gallants?

Maci. Faith, ay, his civet and his casting-glass[2]
Have helped him to a place amongst the rest:
And there, his seniors give him good slight looks,
After their garb,[3] smile, and salute in French
With some new compliment.

Car. What, is this all?

Maci. Why say, that they should show the frothy fool
Such grace, as they pretend comes from the heart,
He had a mighty windfall out of doubt!
Why, all their graces are, not to do grace
To virtue, or desert, but to ride both;
With their gilt spurs, quite breathless, from themselves.
'Tis now esteemed precisianism in wit,
And a disease in nature, to be kind
Toward desert, to love, or seek good names:
Who feeds with a good name? who thrives with loving?
Who can provide feast for his own desires,
With serving others?—ha, ha, ha?
'Tis folly, by our wisest worldlings proved,
If not to gain by love, to be beloved. [*Turns away.*

Car. How like you him? is't not a good spiteful slave,
ha?

Punt. Shrewd, shrewd.

Car. Damn me! I could eat his flesh now: [*Goes up to*
MACILENTE.] divine sweet villain! [*Embraces him.*

Maci. Nay, pr'ythee leave: what's he there?

Car. Who? this i' the starched beard? it's the dull
stiff knight Puntarvolo, man; he's to travel now presently: he has a good knotty wit, marry, he carries little
o't out of the land with him.

Maci. How then?

Car. He puts it forth in venture, as he does his money;
upon the return of a dog, and cat.

---

[1] *i.e.* Made much of.   [2] Scent-bottle for sprinkling with.
[3] Manner.

Maci. Is this he?

Car. Ay, this is he; a good tough gentleman: he looks like a shield of brawn at Shrove-tide, out of date, and ready to take his leave; or a dry pole of ling upon Easter-eve, that has furnished the table all Lent, as he has done the city this last vacation.

Maci. Come, you'll never leave your stabbing similes: I shall ha' you aiming at me with 'hem by and by; but——

Car. O, renounce me then! pure, honest, good devil, I love thee above the love of women: I could e'en melt in admiration of thee, now! Gods so, look here, man; Sir Dagonet[1] and his squire!

[2] *Enter* SOGLIARDO *and* SHIFT.

Sog. 'Save you, my dear gallantos: nay, come, approach, good cavalier: prithee, sweet knight, know this gentleman, he's one that it pleases me to use as my good friend and companion: and therefore do him good offices: I beseech you, gentles, know him, know him all over.

Punt. Sir, for Signior Sogliardo's sake, let it suffice, I know you.

Sog. Why, as I am true gentleman, I thank you, knight, and it shall suffice. Hark you, Sir Puntarvolo, you'ld little think it; he's as resolute a piece of flesh as any's i' the world.

Punt. Indeed, sir.

Sog. Upon my gentility, sir:——Carlo, a word with you; do you see that same fellow, there?

Car. What? Cavalier Shift?

Sog. O, you know him; cry you mercy: before me, I think him the tallest[3] man living within the walls of Europe.

Car. The walls of Europe! take heed what you say, signior, Europe's a huge thing within the walls.

---

[1] The fool of the "Morte d'Arthur."   [2] Scene v. in old eds.
[3] Bravest.

Sog. Tut, an 'twere as huge again, I'ld justify what I speak. 'Slid, he swaggered e'en now in a place where we were: I never saw a man do it more reso-lute.

Car. Nay, indeed swaggering is a good argument of resolution.—Do you hear this, signior?

Maci. Ay, to my grief. [*Aside.*] O, that such muddy flags,
For every drunken flourish, should achieve
The name of manhood; whilst true perfect valour,
Hating to show itself, goes by despised!
'Heart! I do know now, in a fair just cause,
I dare do more than he, a thousand times:
Why should not they take knowledge of this? ha?
And give my worth allowance, before his?
Because I cannot swagger!—Now the pox
Light on your Pickt-hatch[1] prowess!

Sog. Why, I tell you, sir, he has been the only "Bid-stand" that ever kept New-market, Salisbury-plain, Hockley i' the Hole, Gads-hill; all the high places of any request: he has had his mares and his geldings, he, ha' been worth forty, three-score, a hundred pound a horse, would ha' sprung you over hedge and ditch like your greyhound: he has done five hundred robberies in his time, more or less, I assure you.

Punt. What, and 'scaped?

Sog. "'Scaped!" i' faith, ay: he has broken the gaol when he has been in irons, and irons; and been out, and in again; and out, and in; forty times, and not so few, he.

Maci. [*Aside.*] A fit trumpet, to proclaim such a person.

Car. But can this be possible?

Shift. Why, 'tis nothing, sir, when a man gives his affections to it.

Sog. Good Pylades, discourse a robbery or two, to satisfy these gentlemen of thy worth.

---

[1] A disreputable suburb nigh to the Charter-house.

Shift. Pardon me, my dear Orestes; causes have their quiddits,[1] and 'tis ill jesting with bell-ropes.[2]

Car. How! Pylades and Orestes?

Sog. Ay, he is my Pylades, and I am his Orestes: how like you the conceit?

Car. O, it's an old stale interlude device: no, I'll give you names myself; look you, he shall be your Judas, and you shall be his elder-tree[3] to hang on.

Maci. Nay rather, let him be Captain Pod, and this his motion; for he does nothing but show him.

Car. Excellent: or thus, you shall be Holden, and he your camel.[4]

Shift. You do not mean to ride, gentlemen?

Punt. Faith, let me end it for you, gallants: you shall be his Countenance, and he your Resolution.

Sog. Troth, that's pretty: how say you, cavalier, shall't be so?

Car. Ay, ay, most voices.

Shift. Faith, I am easily yielding to any good impressions.

Sog. Then give hands, good Resolution.

Car. Mass, he cannot say, good Countenance, now— properly—to him again.

Punt. Yes, by an irony.

Maci. O, sir, the countenance of Resolution should, as he is, be altogether grim and unpleasant.

[5] *Enter* FASTIDIUS BRISK.

Fast. Good hours make music with your mirth, gentlemen, and keep time to your humours:—How now, Carlo?

Punt. Monsieur Brisk! many a long look have I extended for you, sir.

Fast. Good faith, I must crave pardon; I was invited this morning, ere I was out of my bed, by a bevy of ladies,

---

[1] Their whys and wherefores. [2] *i.e.* Hanging ropes.
[3] Referring to an European belief of probably late date.
[4] Exhibited by Holden. [5] Scene vi. in old eds.

to a banquet: whence it was almost one of Hercules'
labours for me to come away, but that the respect of my
promise did so prevail with me: I know they'll take it
very ill, especially one, that gave me this bracelet of her
hair but over night, and this pearl another gave me from
her forehead, marry she———what? are the writings ready?

Punt. I will send my man to know.—Sirrah, go you to
the notary's, and learn if he be ready: leave the dog, sir.

[*Exit* Servant.

Fast. And how does my rare qualified friend, Sogliardo?—oh, Signior Macilente! by these eyes, I saw you
not, I had saluted you sooner else, o' my troth: [*To him
apart.*] I hope, sir, I may presume upon you, that you
will not divulge my late check, or disgrace, indeed, sir.

Maci. You may, sir.

Car. 'Sheart, he knows some notorious jest by this gull,
that he hath him so obsequious.

Sog. Monsieur Fastidius, do you see this fellow there?
does he not look like a clown? would you think there
were any thing in him?

Fast. Any thing in him? beshrew me, ay; the fellow
hath a good ingenious face.

Sog. By this element he is as ingenious a tall man as
ever swaggered about London: he, and I, call Countenance, and Resolution; but his name is Cavalier Shift.

Punt. Cavalier, you knew Signior Clog, that was
hanged for the robbery at Harrow o' the hill?

Sog. Knew him, sir! why, 'twas he gave all the directions for the action.

Punt. How? was it your project, sir?

Shift. Pardon me, Countenance, you do me some
wrong to make occasions public, which I imparted to you
in private.

Sog. God's will! here are none but friends, Resolution.

Shift. That's all one; things of consequence must
have their respects, where, how, and to whom.—Yes, sir,
he showed himself a true Clog in the coherence of that

affair, sir; for, if he had managed matters as they were corroborated[1] to him, it had been better for him by a forty or fifty score of pounds, sir; and he himself might ha' lived, in despite of fates, to have fed on woodcocks,[2] with the rest; but it was his heavy fortune to sink, poor Clog, and therefore talk no more of him.

Punt. Why, had he more aiders then?

Sog. O God, sir, ay! there were some present there, that were the Nine Worthies to him, i' faith.

Shift. Ay, sir, I can satisfy you at more convenient conference: but, for mine own part, I have now reconciled myself to other courses, and profess a living out of my other qualities.

Sog. Nay, he has left all now, I assure you, and is able to live like a gentleman, by his qualities. By this dog, he has the most rare gift in tobacco, that ever you knew.

Car. [*To* MACILENTE.] 'Sheart, he keeps more ado with this monster, than ever Banks did with his horse,[3] or the fellow with the elephant.

Maci. [*To* CARLO.] He will hang out his picture shortly, in a cloth, you shall see.[4]

Sog. O, he does manage a quarrel, the best that ever you saw, for terms, and circumstances.

Fast. Good faith, signior, now you speak of a quarrel, I'll acquaint you with a difference, that happened between a gallant, and myself;—Sir Puntarvolo, you know him if I should name him, Signior Luculento.

Punt. Luculento! what inauspicious chance interposed itself to your two loves?

Fast. Faith, sir, the same that sundered Agamemnon, and great Thetis' son;[5] but let the cause escape, sir: he sent me a challenge, mixt with some few braves, which I restored, and in fine we met. Now indeed, sir, I must

---

[1] Query, strongly impressed upon him.
[2] A pun, on noddies and woodcock.
[3] The two were burnt for sorcery (see Jonson's last epigram) at Rome.　　　　[4] As an advertisement or sign.
[5] *i.e.* A woman.

tell you, he did offer at first very desperately, but without judgment: for look you, sir; I cast myself into this figure:[1] now he comes violently on, and withal advancing his rapier to strike, I thought to have took his arm, for he had left his whole body to my election, and I was sure he could not recover his guard. Sir, I missed my purpose in his arm, rashed[2] his doublet sleeve, ran him close by the left cheek, and through his hair. He again, lights me here,—I had on a gold cable hatband, then new come up, which I wore about a murrey French hat I had,—cuts my hatband, and yet it was massy, goldsmith's work, cuts my brims, which by good fortune, being thick embroidered with gold twist, and spangles, disappointed the force of the blow: nevertheless, it grazed on my shoulder, takes me away six purls of an Italian cut-work band I wore, cost me three pound in the Exchange, but three days before.

Punt. This was a strange encounter!

Fast. Nay, you shall hear, sir: with this we both fell out, and breathed. Now, upon the second sign of his assault, I betook me to the former manner of my defence; he, on the other side, abandoned his body to the same danger as before, and follows me still with blows: but I, being loth to take the deadly advantage that lay before me of his left side, made a kind of stramazoun,[3] ran him up to the hilts through the doublet, through the shirt, and yet missed the skin. He, making a reverse blow, falls upon my embossed girdle—I had thrown off the hangers a little before—strikes off a skirt of a thick-laced satin doublet I had, lined with some four taffatas, cuts off two panes, embroidered with pearl, rends through the drawings-out of tissue,[4] enters the linings, and skips the flesh.

Car. I wonder he speaks not of his wrought shirt!

---

[1] Position. [2] Rent.
[3] A downright blow. The rapier was then a cut-and-thrust sword.
[4] Supposed linings of rich material were drawn out through panes or openings in the outer stuff.

Fast. Here—in the opinion of mutual damage—we paused ; but, ere I proceed, I must tell you, signior, that, in this last encounter, not having leisure to put off my silver spurs, one of the rowels catched hold of the ruffle of my boot, and—being Spanish leather, and subject to tear —overthrows me, rends me two pair of silk stockings— that I put on, being somewhat a raw morning, a peach colour and another—and strikes me some half inch deep into the side of the calf ; he, seeing the blood come, presently takes horse, and away. I, having bound up my wound with a piece of my wrought shirt—

Car. O ! comes it in there ?

Fast. Rid after him, and, lighting at the court gate both together, embraced, and marched hand in hand up into the presence. Was not this business well carried ?

Maci. Well ? yes, and by this we can guess what apparel the gentleman wore.

Punt. 'Fore valour, it was a designment begun with much resolution, maintained with as much prowess, and ended with more humanity.——How now, what says the notary ?

Re-enter Servant.

Serv. He says, he is ready, sir,—he stays but your worship's pleasure.

Punt. Come, we will go to him, monsieur.—Gentlemen, shall we entreat you to be witnesses ?

Sog. You shall entreat me, sir.—Come, Resolution.

Shift. I follow you, good Countenance.

Car. Come, signior, come, come.

[*Exeunt all but* MACILENTE.

Maci. O, that there should be fortune
To clothe these men, so naked in desert !
And that the just storm of a wretched life
Beats 'hem not ragged, for their wretched souls,
And, since as fruitless, e'en as black, as coals ! [*Exit.*

Mit. Why, but signior, how comes it, that Fungoso appeared not, with his sister's intelligence, to Brisk ?

Cor. Marry, long of the evil angels that she gave him,

who have indeed tempted the good simple youth to follow the tail of the fashion, and neglect the imposition[1] of his friends. Behold, here he comes, very worshipfully attended, and with good variety.

²SCENE III.—*A Room in* DELIRO'S *House.*

Enter FUNGOSO *in a new suit, with his* Tailor, Shoemaker, *and* Haberdasher.

Fung. Gramercy, good shoemaker, I'll put to strings myself. [*Exit* Shoemaker.]—Now, sir, let me see, what must you have for this hat?

Hab. Here's the bill, sir.

Fung. How does 't become me, well?

Tai. Excellent, sir, as ever you had any hat in your life.

Fung. Nay, you'll say so, all.

Hab. In faith, sir, the hat's as good as any man i' this town can serve you, and will maintain fashion as long; ne'er trust me for a groat else.

Fung. Does it apply well to my suit?

Tai. Exceeding well, sir.

Fung. How lik'st thou my suit, haberdasher?

Hab. By my troth, sir, 'tis very rarely well made, I never saw a suit sit better, I can tell on.

Tai. Nay, we have no art to please our friends, we!

Fung. Here, haberdasher, tell³ this same.

[*Gives money.*

Hab. Good faith, sir, it makes you have an excellent body.

Fung. Nay, believe me, I think I have as good a body in clothes, as another.

Tai. You lack points, to bring your apparel together, sir.

Fung. I'll have points anon:—how now! Is't right?

---

¹ The duty put upon him by. ² Scene vii. in old eds.
³ Count.

Hab. Faith, sir, 'tis too little, but upon farther hopes ——Good morrow to you, sir. [*Exit.*

Fung. Farewell, good haberdasher.—Well, now, master Snip, let me see your bill.

Mit. Methinks he discharges his followers too thick.

Cor. O, therein he saucily imitates some great man. I warrant you, though he turns off them, he keeps this tailor, in place of a page, to follow him still.

Fung. This bill is very reasonable, in faith: hark you, Master Snip. Troth, sir, I am not altogether so well furnished at this present, as I could wish I were, but—— if you'll do me the favour to take part in hand, you shall have all I have, by this hand——

Tai. Sir——

Fung. And but give me credit for the rest, till the beginning of the next term.

Tai. O Lord, sir——

Fung. 'Fore God, and by this light, I'll pay you to the utmost, and acknowledge myself very deeply engaged to you, by the courtesy.

Tai. Why, how much have you there, sir?

Fung. Marry, I have here four angels, and fifteen shillings of white[1] money: it's all I have, as I hope to be blest.

Tai. You will not fail me, at the next term, with the rest?

Fung. No, an I do, pray Heaven I be hanged. Let me never breathe again upon this mortal stage, as the philosopher calls it. By this air, and as I am a gentleman, I'll hold.

Cor. He were an iron-hearted fellow, in my judgment, that would not credit him upon his volley of oaths.

Tai. Well, sir, I'll not stick with any gentleman for a trifle: you know what 'tis remains?

Fung. Ay, sir, and I give you thanks in good faith.—— O fate, how happy I am made in this good fortune!

---

[1] Silver.

Well, now I'll go seek out Monsieur Brisk. 'Ods so, I
have forgot ribbon for my shoes, and points. 'Slid, what
luck's this! how shall I do?—Master Snip, pray let me
reduct some two or three shillings for points, and ribbon: as I am an honest man, I have utterly disfurnished
myself, in the default of memory, pray le'me be beholding to you; it shall come home i' the bill, believe me.

Tai. Faith, sir, I can hardly depart[1] with ready money,
but I'll take up, and send you some by my boy, presently.
What coloured ribbon would you have?

Fung. What you shall think meet i' your judgment,
sir, to my suit.

Tai. Well, I'll send you some presently.

Fung. And points[2] too, sir?

Tai. And points too, sir.   [*Turns to go out.*

Fung. Good Lord, how shall I study to deserve this
kindness of you, sir! Pray, let your youth make haste,
for I should have done a business an hour since, that I
doubt I shall come too late. [*Exit* Tailor.] Now, in
good faith, I am exceeding proud of my suit: [*Exit.*

Cor. Do you observe the plunges, that this poor gallant
is put to, signior, to purchase the fashion?

Mit. Ay, and to be still a fashion behind with the world,
that's the sport.

Cor. Stay: O here they come from "*sealed and delivered.*"

[3] SCENE IV.—PUNTARVOLO'S *Lodgings.*

Enter PUNTARVOLO, FASTIDIUS BRISK *in his new suit,
and* Servants, *with the dog.*

Punt. Well, now my whole venture is forth, I wil
resolve to depart shortly.

---

[1] Part.   [2] Tagged laces for tying, in place of hooks or buttons
[3] Scene viii. in old eds.

Fast. Faith, sir Puntarvolo, go to the court, and take leave of the ladies first.

Punt. I care not, if it be this afternoon's labour. Where is Carlo?

Fast. Here he comes.

Enter CARLO, SOGLIARDO, SHIFT, *and* MACILENTE.

Car. Faith, gallants, I am persuading this gentleman to turn courtier. He is a man of fair revenue, and his estate will bear the charge well. Besides, for his other gifts of the mind, or so, why, they are as nature lent him 'hem, pure, simple, without any artificial drug or mixture of these two threadbare beggarly qualities, learning and knowledge, and therefore the more accommodate,[1] and genuine. Now, for the life itself——

Fast. O, the most celestial, and full of wonder and delight, that can be imagined, signior, beyond all thought, and apprehension of pleasure! A man lives there, in that divine rapture, that he will think himself i' the ninth heaven[2] for the time, and lose all sense of mortality whatsoever, when he shall behold such glorious, and almost immortal beauties, hear such angelical, and harmonious voices, discourse with such flowing and ambrosian spirits, whose wits are as sudden as lightning, and humorous as nectar; oh; it makes a man all quintessence, and flame, and lifts him up, in a moment, to the very crystal crown[3] of the sky, where, hovering in the strength of his imagination, he shall behold all the delights of the Hesperides, the Insulæ Fortunatæ, Adonis' gardens, Tempe, or what else, confined within the amplest verge of poesy, to be mere umbræ,[4] and imperfect figures, conferred[5] with the most essential felicity of your court.

Maci. Well, this encomium was not extemporal, it came too perfectly off.

---

[1] Fit or fitted. It was then a fashionable word used indiscriminately.   [2] Seven were the usual number.
[3] The sixth of the seven heavens.   [4] Shadows.   [5] Compared.

Car. Besides, sir, you shall never need to go to a hot-house, you shall sweat there with courting your mistress, or losing your money at primero,[1] as well as in all the stoves in Sweden. Marry, this, sir, you must ever be sure to carry a good strong perfume about you, that your mistress's dog may smell you out amongst the rest : and, in making love to her, never fear to be out ; for you may have a pipe of tobacco, or a bass viol shall hang o' the wall, of purpose, will put you in presently. The tricks your Resolution has taught you in tobacco, the whiffe, and those sleights, will stand you in very good ornament there.

Fast. Ay, to some, perhaps : but, an he should come to my mistress with tobacco (this gentleman knows) she'ld reply upon him, i'faith. O, by this bright sun, she has the most acute, ready, and facetious wit that——— tut, there's no spirit able to stand her. [*To* MACILENTE.] You can report it, signior, you have seen her.

Punt. Then can he report no less, out of his judgment, I assure him.

Maci. Troth, I like her well enough, but she's too self-conceited, methinks.

Fast. Ay, indeed, she's a little too self-conceited, an 'twere not for that humour, she were the most-to-be-admired lady in the world.

Punt. Indeed, it is a humour that takes from her other excellences.

Maci. Why, it may easily be made to forsake her, in my thought.

Fast. Easily, sir ? then are all impossibilities easy.

Maci. You conclude too quick upon me, signior ; what will you say, if I make it so perspicuously appear now, that yourself shall confess nothing more possible?

Fast. Marry, I will say, I will both applaud, and admire you for it .

Punt. And I will second him, in the admiration.

---

[1] One of the then most fashionable card games.

Maci. Why, I'll show you, gentlemen.—Carlo, come hither. [*All but* SOGLIARDO *and* SHIFT *whisper together.*

Sog. Good faith, I have a great humour to the court: what thinks my Resolution? shall I adventure?

Shift. Troth, Countenance, as you please; the place is a place of good reputation, and capacity.

Sog. O, my tricks in tobacco, as Carlo says, will show excellent there.

Shift. Why, you may go with these gentlemen now, and see fashions: and after, as you shall see correspondence.

Sog. You say true. You will go with me, Resolution?

Shift. I will meet you, Countenance, about three or four of clock; but, to say to go with you, I cannot, for, as I am Apple-John, I am to go before the cockatrice[1] you saw this morning, and therefore, pray, present me excused, good Countenance.

Sog. Farewell, good Resolution, but fail not to meet.

Shift. As I live. [*Exit.*

Punt. Admirably excellent!

Maci. If you can but persuade Sogliardo to court, there's all now.

Car. O let me alone, that's my task. [*Goes to him.*

Fast. Now, by wit, Macilente, it's above measure excellent: 'twill be the only court-exploit that ever proved courtier ingenious.

Punt. Upon my soul, it puts the lady quite "out of her humour," and we shall laugh with judgment.

Car. Come, the gentleman was of himself resolved to go with you, afore I moved it.

Maci. Why then, gallants, you two, and Carlo go afore to prepare the jest; Sogliardo and I will come some while after you.

Car. Pardon me, I am not for the court.

Punt. That's true; Carlo comes not at court, indeed. Well, you shall leave it to the faculty of Monsieur Brisk,

---

[1] Harlot.

and myself; upon our lives, we will manage it happily. Carlo shall bespeak supper at the Mitre, against we come back: where we will meet, and dimple our cheeks with laughter at the success.

Car. Ay, but will you all promise to come?

Punt. Myself shall undertake for them: he that fails, let his reputation lie under the lash of thy tongue.

Car. Gods so, look who comes here!

Enter FUNGOSO.

Sog. What, nephew!

Fung. Uncle, God save you; did you see a gentleman, one Monsieur Brisk, a courtier? he goes in such a suit as I do. [*a suit.*

Sog. Here is the gentleman, nephew, but not in such

Fung. Another suit! [*Swoons.*

Sog. How now, nephew?

Fast. Would you speak to me, sir?

Car. Ay, when he has recovered himself, poor Poll.[1]

Punt. Some rosa-solis.[2]

Maci. How now, signior?

Fung. I am not well, sir.

Maci. Why, this it is to dog the fashion.

Car. Nay, come gentlemen, remember your affairs; his disease is nothing but the flux of apparel.

Punt. Sirs, return to the lodging, keep the cat safe; I'll be the dog's guardian myself. [*Exeunt* Servants.

Sog. Nephew, will you go to court with us? these gentlemen and I are for the court: nay, be not so melancholy.

Fung. By God'slid, I think no man in Christendom has that rascally fortune that I have.

Maci. Faith, your suit is well enough, signior.

Fung. Nay, not for that, I protest; but I had an errand to Monsieur Fastidius, and I have forgot it.

Maci. Why, go along to court with us, and remember it, come. Gentlemen, you three take one boat, and

---

[1] Poor imitator. [2] A spiced spirit.

Sogliardo and I will take another: we shall be there instantly.

Fast. Content: [*To* FUNGOSO.] good sir, vouchsafe us your pleasance.

Punt. Farewell, Carlo; remember.

Car. I warrant you: would I had one of Kemp's[1] shoes to throw after you.

Punt. Good Fortune will close the eyes of our jest, fear not: and we shall frolic. [*Exeunt.*

Mit. This Macilente, signior, begins to be more sociable on a sudden, methinks, than he was before: there's some portent in't, I believe.

Cor. O, he's a fellow of a strange nature. Now does he, in this calm of his humour, plot, and store up a world of malicious thoughts in his brain, till he is so full with 'hem, that you shall see the very torrent of his envy break forth like a land-flood: and, against the course of all their affections, oppose itself so violently, that you will almost have wonder to think, how 'tis possible the current of their dispositions shall receive so quick, and strong an alteration.

Mit. Ay, marry, sir, this is that, on which my expectation has dwelt all this while: for I must tell you, signior, though I was loth to interrupt the scene, yet I made it a question in mine own private discourse, how he should properly call it *Every Man out of his Humour,* when I saw all his actors so strongly pursue, and continue their humours?

Cor. Why, therein his art appears most full of lustre, and approacheth nearest the life; especially when in the flame, and height of their humours, they are laid flat: it fills the eye better, and with more contentment. How tedious a sight were it to behold a proud exalted tree lopt, and cut down by degrees, when it might be felled in a moment? and to set the axe to it before it came to that pride, and fulness, were, as not to have it grow.

Mit. Well, I shall long till I see this fall, you talk of.

Cor. To help your longing, signior, let your imagination be swifter than a pair of oars: and by this, suppose Puntarvolo, Brisk, Fungoso, and the dog, arrived at the court-gate, and going up to the great chamber. Macilente and Sogliardo, we'll leave them on the water, till possibility and natural means may land 'hem. Here come the gallants, now prepare your expectation.

[1] The stage-clown who danced from London to Norwich, and hung up his shoes in the town hall there.

ACT THE FIFTH.

SCENE I.—*The Hall of the Palace.*

Enter PUNTARVOLO, *with his dog,* FASTIDIUS BRISK *and* FUNGOSO.

UNT. Come, gentles.—Signior, you are sufficiently instructed.

Fast. Who, I, sir?

Punt. No, this gentleman. But stay, I take thought how to bestow my dog, he is no competent attendant for the presence.

Fast. Mass, that's true, indeed, knight, you must not carry him into the presence.

Punt. I know it, and I, like a dull beast, forgot to bring one of my cormorants[1] to attend me. [lodge.

Fast. Why, you were best leave him at the porter's

Punt. Not so; his worth is too well known amongst them, to be forth-coming.

Fast. 'Slight, how'll you do then?

Punt. I must leave him with one, that is ignorant of his quality, if I will have him to be safe. And see! Here comes one that will carry coals, ergo, will hold my dog.[2]

Enter a Groom, *with a charcoal basket.*

My honest friend, may I commit the tuition[3] of this dog to thy prudent care?

---

[1] Gormandizing servants.

[2] Coal carriers and minders of dogs were alike despised. See p. 228.

[3] Safe keeping.

Groom. You may, if you please, sir.

Punt. Pray thee, let me find thee here at my return: it shall not be long, till I will ease thee of thy employment, and please thee.—Forth, gentles.

Fast. Why, but will you leave him with so slight a command, and infuse no more charge upon the fellow?

Punt. Charge? no; there were no policy in that: that were to let him know the value of the gem he holds, and so, to tempt frail nature against her disposition. No, [*Aloud to* Groom.] pray thee let thy honesty be sweet, as it shall be short.[1]

Groom. Yes, sir.

Punt. But hark you, gallants, and chiefly Monsieur Brisk. When we come in eye-shot, or presence of this lady, let not other matters carry us from our project; but, if we can, single her forth to some place——

Fast. I warrant you.

Punt. And be not too sudden, but let the device induce itself with good circumstance. On.

Fung. Is this the way? good truth, here be fine hangings. [*Exeunt* PUNTARVOLO, FASTIDIUS, *and* FUNGOSO.

Groom. "Honesty!" "sweet, and short!" Marry, it shall, sir, doubt you not; for even at this instant if one would give me twenty pounds, I would not deliver him; there's for the "sweet": but now, if any man come offer me but two-pence, he shall have him; there's for the "short" now. 'Slid, what a mad humorous gentleman is this to leave his dog with me! I could run away with him now, an he were worth anything.[2]

Enter MACILENTE *and* SOGLIARDO.

Maci. Come on, signior, now prepare to court this all-witted lady, most naturally, and like yourself.

---

[1] In the quarto, "short and sweet," a proverbial saying.
[2] In the quarto there is added, "Well, I pray God send him quickly again."

Sog. Faith, an you say the word, I'll begin to her in tobacco.

Maci. O, fie on't! no; you shall begin with, "How does my sweet lady?" or, "Why are you so melancholy, madam?" though she be very merry, it's all one. Be sure to kiss your hand often enough; pray for her health, and tell her, how "more than most fair" she is. Screw your face o' t'one side thus, and protest; let her fleer, and look askance, and hide her teeth with her fan, when she laughs a fit, to bring her into more matter, that's nothing: you must talk forward, (though it be without sense, so it be without blushing) 'tis most court-like and well.

Sog. But shall I not use tobacco at all?

Maci. O, by no means, 'twill but make your breath suspected, and that you use it only to confound the rankness of that.

Sog. Nay, I'll be advised, sir, by my friends.

Maci. God's my life, see where Sir Puntar's dog is.

Groom. I would the gentleman would return for his follower here, I'll leave him to his fortunes else.

Maci. [*Aside.*] S'heart, 'twere the only true jest in the world to poison him now: ha! by this hand I'll do it, if I could but get him of the fellow.—Signior Sogliardo, walk aside, and think upon some device to entertain the lady with.

Sog. So I do, sir.   [*Walks off meditating.*

Maci. How now, mine honest friend? whose dog-keeper art thou?

Groom. Dog-keeper, sir? I hope I scorn that, i'faith.

Maci. Why? dost thou not keep a dog?

Groom. Sir, now I do, and now—I do not: [*Throws off the dog.*] I think this be "sweet" and "short." Make me his dog-keeper!   [*Exit.*

Maci. This is excellent, above expectation, nay, stay, sir; you'ld be travelling; but I'll give you a dram shall shorten your voyage: here. So, sir, I'll be bold to take my leave of you. Now to the Turk's court in the devil's name, for you shall never go o' God's name.—Sogliardo, come.

Sog. I ha't i'faith, now, will sting it.

Maci. Take heed you leese[1] it not, signior, ere you come there: preserve it. [*Exeunt.*

Cor. How like you this first exploit of his?

Mit. O, a piece of true envy; but I expect the issue of the other device.

Cor. Here they come, will make it appear.

SCENE II.—*An Apartment in the Palace.*

Enter SAVIOLINA, PUNTARVOLO, FASTIDIUS BRISK, *and* FUNGOSO.

Sav. Why, I thought, Sir Puntarvolo, you had been gone your voyage?

Punt. Dear, and most amiable lady, your divine beauties do bind me to those offices, that I cannot depart when I would.

Sav. 'Tis most court-like spoken, sir: but how might we do to have a sight of your dog, and cat?

Fast. His dog is in the court, lady.

Sav. And not your cat? how dare you trust her behind you, sir.

Punt. Troth, madam, she hath sore eyes, and she doth keep her chamber: marry, I have left her under sufficient guard, there are two of my followers to attend her.

Sav. I'll give you some water for her eyes: when do you go, sir?

Punt. Certes, sweet lady, I know not.

Fast. He doth stay the rather, madam, to present your acute judgment with so courtly, and well parted[2] a gentleman as yet your ladyship hath never seen.

---

[1] Lose. [2] Mentally endowed.

Sav. What's he, gentle Monsieur Brisk? not that gentleman? [*Points to* FUNGOSO.

Fast. No, lady, this is a kinsman to Justice Silence.[1]

Punt. Pray', sir, give me leave to report him:—He's a gentleman, lady, of that rare and admirable faculty, as I protest, I know not his like in Europe: he is exceedingly valiant, an excellent scholar, and so exactly travelled, that he is able, in discourse, to deliver you a model of any prince's court in the world: speaks the languages with that purity of phrase, and facility of accent, that it breeds astonishment: his wit, the most exuberant, and, above wonder, pleasant, of all that ever entered the concave of this ear.

Fast. 'Tis most true, lady; marry, he is no such excellent proper man.

Punt. His travels have changed his complexion,[2] madam.

Sav. O, Sir Puntarvolo, you must think, every man was not born to have my servant Brisk's feature.[3]

Punt. But that which transcends all, lady; he doth so peerlessly imitate any manner of person for gesture, action, passion, or whatever——

Fast. Ay, especially a rustic, or a clown, madam, that it is not possible for the sharpest-sighted wit in the world to discern any sparks of the gentleman in him, when he does it.

Sav. O, Monsieur Brisk, be not so tyrannous to confine all wits within the compass of your own: not find the sparks of a gentleman in him, if he be a gentleman?

Fung. No, in truth, sweet lady, I believe you cannot.

Sav. Do you believe so? [*To* FUNGOSO.] Why, I can find sparks of a gentleman in you, sir.

Punt. Ay, he is a gentleman, madam, and a reveller.

Fung. Indeed, I think I have seen your ladyship at our revels.

---

[1] Shakespeare's; possibly, therefore, a Shallow.
[2] Constitution.   [3] Make.

Sav. Like enough, sir; but would I might see this wonder you talk of: may one have a sight of him, for any reasonable sum?

Punt. Yes, madam, he will arrive presently.

Sav. What, and shall we see him clown it?

Fast. I'faith, sweet lady, that you shall: see, here he comes.

Enter MACILENTE *with* SOGLIARDO.

Punt. This is he! pray observe him, lady.

Sav. Beshrew me, he clowns it properly indeed.

Punt. Nay, mark his courtship.

Sog. How does my sweet lady? "hot and moist? beautiful and lusty?" ha?

Sav. Beautiful, an it please you, sir, but not lusty.

Sog. O ho, lady, it pleases you to say so, in truth: and "how does my sweet lady?" in health? "*Bona roba, quæso, que novelles? que novelles?*"[1] sweet creature!

Sav. O excellent! why gallants, is this he that cannot be deciphered? they were very blear-witted, i'faith, that could not discern the gentleman in him.

Punt. But do you, in earnest, lady?

Sav. Do I, sir? why, if you had any true court-judgment in the carriage of his eye, and that inward power that forms his countenance, you might perceive his counterfeiting, as clear as the noon-day: alas—Nay, if you would have tried my wit, indeed, you should never have told me he was a gentleman, but presented him for a true clown indeed; and then have seen if I could have deciphered him.

Fast. 'Fore God, her ladyship says true, knight:— but does he not affect the clown most naturally, mistress?

Punt. O, she cannot but affirm that, out of the bounty of her judgment.

Sav. Nay, out of doubt he does well, for a gentleman,

---

[1] A jumble of Italian, Latin, and French signifying "Handsomely dressed lady, I ask you, what news, what news?" "Bona roba" was equivocal, being also used in the sense of harlot.

to imitate; but I warrant you, he becomes his natural carriage of the gentleman, much better than his clownery.

Fast. 'Tis strange, in truth, her ladyship should see so far into him!

Punt. Ay, is't not?

Sav. Faith, as easily as may be; not decipher him, quoth you?

Fung. Good sadness,[1] I wonder at it!

Maci. Why, has she deciphered him, gentlemen?

Punt. O most miraculously, and beyond admiration!

Maci. Is't possible?

Fast. She hath gathered most infallible signs of the gentleman in him, that's certain.

Sav. Why, gallants, let me laugh at you, a little: was this your device, to try my judgment in a gentleman?

Maci. Nay, lady, do not scorn us, though you have this gift of perspicacy above others —What if he should be no gentleman now, but a clown indeed, lady?

Punt. How think you of that? would not your ladyship be " out of your humour? "

Fast. O, but she knows it is not so.

Sav. What if he were not a man, ye may as well say? nay, if your worships could gull me so, indeed, you were wiser than you are taken for.

Maci. In good faith, lady, he is a very perfect clown, both by father, and mother: that I'll assure you.

Sav. O, sir, you are very pleasurable.

Maci. Nay, do but look on his hand, and that shall resolve you: look you, lady, what a palm here is.

Sog. Tut, that was with holding the plough.

Maci. The plough! did you discern any such thing in him, madam?

Fast. Faith no, she saw the gentleman as bright, as at noon-day, she: she deciphered him at first.

---

[1] Soberness.

Maci. Troth, I am sorry your ladyship's sight should be so suddenly struck.

Sav. O, you're goodly beagles!   [*Turns away.*

Fast. What, is she gone?

Sog. Nay, stay, sweet lady! "*que novelles? que novelles?*"

Sav. Out, you fool, you!   [*Exit.*

Fung. She's "out of her humour," i'faith.

Fast. Nay, let's follow it while 'tis hot, gentlemen.

Punt. Come, on mine honour we shall make her blush in the presence: my spleen is great with laughter.

Maci. [*aside.*] Your laughter will be a child of a feeble life, I believe, sir.——Come, signior, your looks are too dejected, methinks; why mix you not mirth with the rest?

Fung. By God's will, this suit frets me at the soul. I'll have it altered to-morrow, sure.   [*Exeunt.*

SCENE III.—*The Palace Hall.*

Enter SHIFT.

Shift. I am come to the court to meet with my Countenance, Sogliardo: poor men must be glad of such countenance, when they can get no better. Well. Need may insult upon a man, but it shall never make him despair of consequence. The world will say, 'tis base: tush, base! 'tis base to live under the earth, not base to live above it, by any means.

Enter FASTIDIUS, PUNTARVOLO, SOGLIARDO, FUNGOSO, *and* MACILENTE.

Fast. The poor lady is most miserably "out of her humour," i'faith.

Punt. There was never so witty a jest broken, at the tilt of all the court wits christened.[1]

---

[1] Called by that title

Maci. [*Aside.*] O, this applause taints it, foully.

Sog. I think I did my part in courting.—O! Resolution!

Punt. Ay me, my dog!

Maci. Where is he?

Fast. God's precious, go seek for the fellow, good signior. [*Exit* FUNGOSO.

Punt. Here, here I left him.

Maci. Why, none was here when we came in now, but Cavalier Shift, enquire of him.

Fast. Did you see Sir Puntarvolo's dog here, cavalier, since you came?

Shift. His dog, sir? he may look his dog, sir! I saw none of his dog, sir.[1]

Maci. [*Aside to* PUNTARVOLO.] Upon my life, he hath stolen your dog, sir, and been hired to it by some that have ventured with you; you may guess by his peremptory answers.

Punt. Not unlike; for he hath been a notorious thief by his own confession.—Sirrah, where is my dog?

Shift. Charge me with your dog, sir? I ha' none of your dog, sir.

Punt. Villain, thou liest.

Shift. Lie, sir? 'Sblood,—y'are but a man, sir!

Punt. Rogue and thief, restore him.

Sog. Take heed, Sir Puntarvolo, what you do: he'll bear no coals, I can tell you, o' my word.

Maci. [*Aside.*] This is rare.

Sog. It's mar'le he stabs you not: By this light he hath stabbed forty, for forty times less matter, I can tell you, of my knowledge.

Punt. I will make thee stoop, thou abject.

Sog. Make him stoop, sir!—Gentlemen, pacify him, or he'll be killed.

Maci. Is he so tall a man?

Sog. Tall a man? if you love his life, stand betwixt them: make him stoop!

---

[1] One gathers from this play in what low esteem the dog (though much used) and his keepers were held in England.

Punt. My dog, villain, or I will hang thee : thou hast confest robberies, and other felonious acts, to this gentleman, thy Countenance—

Sog. I'll bear no witness.

Punt. And without my dog, I will hang thee, for them.   [SHIFT *kneels.*

Sog. What ? kneel to thine enemies ?

Shift. Pardon me, good sir ; God is my witness, I never did robbery in all my life.

Re-enter FUNGOSO.

Fung. O, Sir Puntarvolo, your dog lies giving up the ghost in the woodyard.

Maci. [*Aside.*] Heart ! is he not dead yet ?

Punt. O, my dog, born to disastrous fortune !—'Pray you conduct me, sir.   [*Exit with* FUNGOSO.

Sog. How ? did you never do any robbery, "in your life ?"

Maci. [*Aside.*] O, this is good !—so he swore, sir.

Sog. Ay, I heard him.—And did you swear true, sir ?

Shift. Ay, as I hope to be forgiven, sir, I ne'er robbed any man ; I never stood by the highway-side, sir, but only said so, because I would get myself a name, and be counted a tall man.

Sog. Now out, base viliaco !¹ thou my Resolution ? I thy Countenance ? By this light, gentlemen, he hath confessed to me the most inexorable² company of robberies, and damned himself that he did 'hem ; you never heard the like : out, scoundrel, out ! follow me no more, I command thee : out of my sight, go, hence, speak not : I will not hear thee : away, camouccio !³   [*Exit* SHIFT.

Maci. [*Aside.*] O, how I do feed upon this now, and fat myself ! here were a couple unexpectedly dishumoured :

---

¹ Ital. *vigliacco,* a coward or scoundrel.

² Relentless (?) or not to be spoken of (?).

³ (?) Ital. *camoccio* and *camoscio,* the male chamois, signifying also "flat-nosed," characteristic of the Moors, and thence used as a term of reproach.

well, by this time, I hope, Sir Puntarvolo and his dog are both "out of humour" to travel.—Nay, gentlemen, why do you not seek out the knight, and comfort him? our supper at the Mitre must of necessity hold to-night, if you love your reputations.

Fast. 'Fore God, I am so melancholy for his dog's disaster, but I'll go.

Sog. Faith, and I may go too, but I know, I shall be so melancholy.

Maci. Tush, melancholy! you must forget that now, and remember you lie at the mercy of a fury: Carlo will rack your sinews asunder, and rail you to dust, if you come not.   [*Exeunt.*

Mit. O, then, their fear of Carlo, belike, makes them hold their meeting.

Cor. Ay, here he comes: conceive him but to be entered the Mitre, and 'tis enough.

SCENE IV.—*A Room at the Mitre.*

Enter CARLO.

Car. Holla! where be these shot-sharks?[1]

Enter Drawer.

Draw. By and by—you're welcome, good Master Buffone.

Car. Where's George? call me George hither, quickly.

Draw. What wine please you have, sir? I'll draw you that's neat, Master Buffone.

Car. Away, neophite, do as I bid thee, bring my dear George to me:—Mass, here he comes.

Enter GEORGE.

George. Welcome, Master Carlo.

---

[1] The drawers, the seekers of the shot or reckoning.

Car. What ! is supper ready, George ?

George. Ay, sir, almost : will you have the cloth laid, Master Carlo ?

Car. O, what else ? Are none of the gallants come yet ?

George. None yet, sir.

Car. Stay, take me with you,[1] George ; let me have a good fat loin of pork laid to the fire, presently.

George. It shall, sir.

Car. And withal, hear you ? draw me the biggest shaft you have, out of the butt you wot of : away, you know my meaning, George, quick.

George. Done, sir.   [*Exit.*

Car. I never hungered so much for thing in my life, as I do to know our gallants' success[2] at court ; now is that lean bald-rib, Macilente, that salt villain, plotting some mischievous device, and lies a soaking in their frothy humours like a dry crust, till he has drunk 'hem all up : could the pumice[3] but hold up his eyes at other men's happiness, in any reasonable proportion : 'Slid, the slave were to be loved next Heaven, above honour, wealth, rich fare, apparel, wenches, all the delights of the belly, and the groin, whatever.

Re-enter GEORGE *with a large jug of wine.*

George. Here, Master Carlo.

Car. Is't right, boy ?

George. Ay, sir, I assure you 'tis right.

Car. Well said, my dear George, depart :—Come, my small gimlet, you in the false scabbard,[4] away, [*Puts forth the* Drawers, *and shuts the door.*] so—. Now to you, Sir Burgomaster,[5] let's taste of your bounty.

Mit. What, will he deal upon such quantities of wine, alone ?

Cor. You will perceive that, sir.

---

[1] Take my intentions with you, understand me.
[2] Results, good or bad.   [3] The absorbent.   [4] Dress of a drawer.
[5] The big-bellied jug, sometimes with a similar figure on it.

Car. [*Drinks.*] Ay, marry, sir, here's purity; O, George —I could bite off his nose for this now; sweet rogue, he has drawn nectar, the very soul of the grape! I'll wash my temples with some on't presently, and drink some half a score draughts; 'twill heat the brain, kindle my imagination, I shall talk nothing but crackers and firework to-night. So, sir! please you to be here, sir, and I here: so.

> [*Sets the two cups asunder, drinks with the one, and pledges with the other.*

Cor. This is worth the observation, signior.

Car. at 1st Cup. Now, sir, here's to you; and I present you with so much of my love.

Car. at 2nd Cup. I take it kindly from you, sir, [*Drinks.*] and will return you the like proportion; but withal, sir, remembering the merry night we had at the countess's, you know where, sir.

1st Cup. By Heaven, you put me in mind now of a very necessary office, which I will propose in your pledge, sir: the health of that honourable countess, and the sweet lady that sat by her, sir.

2nd Cup. I do vail[1] to it with reverence. [*Drinks.*] And now, signior, with these ladies, I'll be bold to mix the health of your divine mistress.

1st Cup. Do you know her, sir?

2nd Cup. O Lord, sir, ay; and in the respectful memory and mention of her, I could wish this wine were the most precious drug in the world.

1st Cup. Good faith, sir, you do honour me in't exceedingly. [*Drinks.*]

Mit. Whom should he personate in this, signior?
Cor. Faith, I know not, sir; observe, observe him.

2nd Cup. If it were the basest filth, or mud that runs in the channel, I am bound to pledge it, respectively,[2] sir.

---

[1] Lower to it, bend my knee.   [2] Respectfully.

[*Drinks.*] And now, sir, here is a replenished bowl, which I will reciprocally turn upon you, to the health of the Count Frugale.

1st Cup. The Count Frugale's health, sir? I'll pledge it on my knees, by this light.

2nd Cup. Will you, sir? I'll drink it on my knee, then, by the light.

Mit. Why, this is strange.

Cor. Ha' you heard a better drunken dialogue?

2nd Cup. Nay, do me right, sir.

1st Cup. So I do, in good faith.

2nd Cup. Good faith you do not; mine was fuller.

1st Cup. Why, by Jesu,[1] it was not.

2nd Cup. By Jesu, it was: and you do lie.

1st Cup. Lie, sir?

2nd Cup. Ay, sir.

1st Cup. 'Swounds!

2nd Cup. O, come, stab, if you have a mind to it.

1st Cup. Stab! dost thou think I dare not?

Car. [*Speaking in his own person.*] Nay, I beseech you, gentlemen, what means this? nay, look, for shame respect your reputations.

[*Overturns wine, pot, cups, and all.*]

[2] *Enter* MACILENTE.

Maci. Why, how now, Carlo! what humour's this?

Car. O, my good Mischief! art thou come? where are the rest, where are the rest?

Maci. Faith, three of our ordnance are burst.

Car. Burst? how comes that?

Maci. Faith, overcharged, overcharged.

Car. But did not the train hold?

Maci O, yes, and the poor lady is irrecoverably blown up.

Car. Why, but which of the munition is miscarried, ha?

Maci. *Imprimis*, Sir Puntarvolo: next, the Countenance, and Resolution.

---

[1] " Believe me " in the folios, on account of the Act 7 James I.

[2] Scene v. in old eds.

Car. How? how, for the love of wit?

Maci. Troth, the Resolution is proved recreant: the Countenance hath changed his copy:[1] and the passionate knight is shedding funeral tears over his departed dog.

Car. What's his dog dead?

Maci. Poisoned, 'tis thought; marry, how, or by whom, that's left for some cunning woman here o' the Bank-side to resolve. For my part, I know nothing, more than that we are like to have an exceeding melancholy supper of it.

Car. 'Slife, and I had purposed to be extraordinarily merry, I had drunk off a good preparative of old sack here:[2] but will they come, will they come?

Maci. They will assuredly come: marry, Carlo, as thou lov'st me, run over 'hem all freely to-night, and especially the knight; spare no sulphurous jest that may come out of that sweaty forge of thine; but ply 'hem with all manner of shot, minion, saker, culverin,[3] or anything, what thou wilt.

Car. I warrant thee, my dear case of petronels:[4] so I stand not in dread of thee, but that thou'lt second me.

Maci. Why, my good German tapster, I will.

Car. What George! " Lomtero, Lomtero, &c."

[*Sings and dances.*

Re-enter GEORGE.

George. Did you call, Master Carlo?

Car. More nectar, George: " Lomtero, &c."

George. Your meat's ready, sir, an your company were come.

Car. Is the loin of pork enough?[5]

George. Ay, sir, it is enough. [*Exit.*

Maci. Pork? heart, what dost thou with such a greasy dish? I think thou dost varnish thy face with the fat on't, it looks so like a glue-pot.

---

[1] Turned him away.   [2] Probably drinks again.
[3] Two, five-and-a-half, and eighteen pounders.
[4] A couple of short carbines.   [5] Done enough.

Car. True, my raw-boned-rogue, and if thou wouldst farce[1] thy lean ribs with it too, they would not, like ragged laths, rub out so many doublets as they do: but thou know'st not a good dish, thou. O, it's the only nourishing meat in the world. No marvel, though that saucy, stubborn generation, the Jews, were forbidden it; for what would they ha' done, well pampered with fat pork, that durst murmur at their Maker, out of garlic and onions? 'Slight! fed with it, the whoreson strummel, patched,[2] goggle-eyed Grumbledories,[3] would have Gigantomachized—[4]

Re-enter GEORGE *with wine.*

Well said, my sweet George, fill, fill.

Mit. This savours too much of profanation.
Cor. Oh ———————— *Servetur ad imum,*
Qualis ab incœpto processerit, et sibi constet.[5]
The necessity of his vein compels a toleration, for, bar this, and dash him out of humour before his time!

Car. 'Tis an axiom in natural philosophy, "What comes nearest the nature of that it feeds, converts quicker to nourishment, and doth sooner essentiate." Now nothing in flesh, and entrails assimilates or resembles man more than a hog or swine. [*Drinks.*

Maci. True; and he, to requite their courtesy, oftentimes doffeth his own nature, and puts on theirs; as when he becomes as churlish as a hog, or as drunk as a sow: but to your conclusion. [*Drinks.*

Car. Marry, I say, nothing resembling man more than a swine, it follows, nothing can be more nourishing: for indeed (but that it abhors from our nice nature) if we fed upon one another, we should shoot up a great deal

---

[1] Stuff.   [2] Long dishevelled haired.
[3] Possibly compounded of grumble and dor (beetle), meaning cheat or fool.
[4] Made a giants' battle of it; gormandised excessively.
[5] As it has proceeded from the beginning, so let it be preserved to the last, that it may be consistent.

faster, and thrive much better: I refer me to your usurous cannibals,[1] or such like; but since it is so contrary, pork, pork is your only feed.

Maci. I take it, your devil be of the same diet; he would ne'er ha' desired to been incorporated into swine else.—O, here comes the melancholy mess; upon 'hem Carlo, charge, charge!

[2] *Enter* PUNTARVOLO, FASTIDIUS BRISK, SOGLIARDO, *and* FUNGOSO.

Car. 'Fore God, Sir Puntarvolo, I am sorry for your heaviness: body a me, a shrewd mischance! why, had you no unicorn's horn, nor bezoar's stone[3] about you, ha?

Punt. Sir, I would request you be silent.

Maci. Nay, to him again.

Car. Take comfort, good knight, if your cat ha' recovered her catarrh, fear nothing; your dog's mischance may be holpen.

Fast. Say how, sweet Cario, for, so God mend me, the poor knight's moans draw me into fellowship of his misfortunes. But be not discouraged, good Sir Puntarvolo, I am content your adventure shall be performed upon your cat.

Maci. [*Aside to* CARLO.] I believe you, musk-cod, I believe you, for rather than thou would'st make present repayment, thou would'st take it upon his own bare return from Calais.

Car. [*Aside to him.*] Nay, udslife, he'ld be content, so he were well rid out of his company, to pay him five for one; at his next meeting him in Paul's.—But for your dog, Sir Puntar, if he be not out-right dead, there is a friend of mine, a quack-salver, shall put life in him again, that's certain.

Fung. O, no, that comes too late.

Maci. [*Aside.*] God's precious! knight, will you suffer this?

Punt. Drawer, get me a candle, and hard wax presently.[1] [*Exit* Drawer.

Sog. Ay, and bring up supper; for I am so melancholy.

Car. O, signior, where's your Resolution?

Sog. Resolution! hang him, rascal: O, Carlo, if you love me, do not mention him.

Car. Why, how so? how so?

Sog. O, the arrant'st crocodile that ever Christian was acquainted with. By my gentry, I shall think the worse of tobacco while I live, for his sake: I did think him to be as tall a man——

Maci. [*aside to* CARLO.] Nay, Buffone, the knight, the knight.

Car. 'Slud, he looks like an image carved out of box, full of knots: his face is, for all the world, like a Dutch purse, with the mouth downward, his beard the tassels: and he walks—let me see—as melancholy as one o' the master's side[2] in the Counter.—Do you hear, Sir Puntar?

Punt. Sir, I do entreat you no more, but enjoin you to silence, as you affect your peace.

Car. Nay, but dear knight, understand—here are none but friends, and such as wish you well—I would ha' you do this now; flay me your dog presently, (but in any case keep the head) and stuff his skin well with straw, as you see these dead monsters at Bartholomew fair——

Punt. I shall be sudden, I tell you.

Car. Or, if you like not that, sir, get me somewhat a less dog, and clap into the skin; here's a slave about the town here, a Jew, one Yohan;[3] or a fellow that makes perukes will glue it on artificially, it shall ne'er be discerned; besides, 'twill be so much the warmer for the hound to travel in, you know.

Maci. [*Aside to him.*] Sir Puntarvolo, 'death, can you be so patient!

---

[1] At once.

[2] The master's side ranked between the knights' ward (occupied by those who could pay the best) and the hole in which the poorest prisoners were confined.

[3] Not improbably the publican Yaughan alluded to in *Hamlet*, v. i.

Car. Or thus, sir : you may have—as you come through Germany—a familiar for little or nothing, shall turn itself into the shape of your dog, or any thing, what you will, for certain hours——[PUNTARVOLO *beats him.*]—— 'Ods my life, knight, what do you mean ? you'll offer no violence, will you ? hold, hold !

[1]*Re-enter* Drawer, *with wax, and a lighted candle.*

Punt. 'Sdeath, you slave, you ban-dog, you !

Car. As you love wit, stay the enraged knight, gentlemen.

Punt. By my knighthood, he that stirs in his rescue, dies.—Drawer, begone ! [*Exit* Drawer.

Car. Murder, murder, murder !

Punt. Ay, are you howling, you wolf ?—Gentlemen, as you tender your lives, suffer no man to enter, till my revenge be perfect. Sirrah, Buffone, lie down ; make no exclamations, but down : down, you cur, or I will make thy blood flow on my rapier hilts.

Car. Sweet knight, hold in thy fury, and 'fore Heaven, I'll honour thee more, than the Turk does Mahomet.

Punt. Down, I say ! [CARLO *lies down — knocking within*]—Who's there ?

Cons. [*Within.*] Here's the constable, open the doors.

Car. Good Macilente——

Punt. Open no door, if the Adelantado of Spain [2] were here he should not enter : one help me with the light, gentlemen ;—you knock in vain, sir officer.

Car. Et tu, Brute ! [3]

Punt. Sirrah, close your lips, or I will drop it in thine eyes, by Heaven. [*Seals up his lips.*

Car. O ! O !

Cons. [*Within.*] Open the door, or I will break it open.

---

[1] Not George. See onward, "George was not here."
[2] The king's deputy.
[3] Wrongly attributed to Cæsar as his last words, "And thou, O Brutus." He addresses Macilente.

Maci. Nay, good constable, have patience a little; you shall come in presently; we have almost done.

Punt. So, now, are you "out of your humour," sir? —Shift, gentlemen.   *[They all draw, and disperse.*

[1]*Enter* Constable *and Officers.*

Cons. Lay hold upon this gallant, and pursue the rest.

Fast. Lay hold on me, sir! for what?

Cons. Marry, for your riot here, sir, with the rest of your companions.

Fast. My riot! master constable, take heed what you do. Carlo, did I offer any violence?

Cons. O, sir, you see he is not in case to answer you, and that makes you so paramptory.[2]

Re-enter GEORGE *and* Drawer.

Fast. Peremptory! 'Slife, I appeal to the drawers, if I did him any hard measure.

George. They are all gone, there's none of them will be laid any hold on.

Cons. Well, sir, you are like to answer till the rest can be found out.

Fast. 'Slid, I appeal to George here.

Cons. Tut, George was not here: away with him to the Counter, sirs.—Come, sir, you were best get yourself dressed somewhere.   *[Exeunt all but the two* Drawers.

George. Good Lord, that Master Carlo could not take heed, and knowing what a gentleman the knight is, if he be angry.

Drawer. A pox on 'hem, they have left all the meat on our hands,—would they were choked with it for me!

Re-enter MACILENTE.

Maci. What, are they gone, sirs?

---

[1] Scene vii. in old eds.
[2] A constable's pronunciation of a strange word.

George. O, here's Master Macilente.

Maci. Sirrah, George, do you see that concealment there? that napkin under the table?

George. God's so, Signior Fungoso!

Maci. He's good pawn for the reckoning; be sure you keep him here, and let him not go away till I come again, though he offer to discharge all: I'll return presently. [*Exit.*

George. Sirrah, we have a pawn for the reckoning.

Draw. What? of Macilente?

George. No, look under the table.

Fung. [*looking out.*] I hope all be quiet now: if I can get but forth of this street, I care not; masters, I pray you tell me, is the constable gone?

George. What? Master Fungoso!

Fung. Was't not a good device this same of me, sirs?

George. Yes, faith; ha' you been here all this while?

Fung. O God, ay; good sir, look an the coast be clear, I'ld fain be going.

George. All's clear, sir, but the reckoning! and that you must clear, and pay before you go, I assure you.

Fung. I pay? 'Slight, I eat not a bit since I came into the house, yet.

Draw. Why, you may when you please, 'tis all ready below, that was bespoken.

Fung. Bespoken? not by me, I hope?

George. By you, sir? I know not that; but 'twas for you, and your company, I am sure.

Fung. My company? 'Slid, I was an invited guest, so I was.

Draw. Faith we have nothing to do with that, sir, they're all gone but you, and we must be answered; that's the short and the long on't.

Fung. Nay, if you will grow to extremities, my masters, then would this pot, cup, and all were in my belly, if I have a cross[1] about me.

---

[1] A penny or other coin.

George. What, and have such apparel? do not say so, signior, that mightily discredits your clothes.

Fung. As I am an honest man, my tailor had all my money this morning, and yet I must be fain to alter my suit too: good sirs, let me go, 'tis Friday night, and in good truth I have no stomach in the world to eat anything.

Draw. That's no matter, so you pay, sir.

Fung. Pay? God's light, with what conscience can you ask me to pay that I never drank for?

George. Yes, sir, I did see you drink once.

Fung. By this cup, which is silver, but you did not, you do me infinite wrong, I looked in the pot once, indeed, but I did not drink.

Draw. Well, sir, if you can satisfy our master, it shall be all one to us.

One within. George!

George. By and by.[1]   [*Exeunt.*

Cor. Lose not yourself now, signior.

[2] SCENE V.—*A Room in* DELIRO'S *House.*

Enter MACILENTE *and* DELIRO.

Maci. Tut, sir, you did bear too hard a conceit of me in that, but I will now make my love to you most transparent, in spite of any dust of suspicion, that may be raised to cloud it: and henceforth, since I see it is so against your humour, I will never labour to persuade you.

Deli. Why, I thank you, signior; but what's that you tell me, may concern my peace so much?

Maci. Faith, sir, 'tis thus. Your wife's brother, Signior Fungoso, being at supper to-night at a tavern, with a sort[3] of gallants, there happened some division amongst

---

[1] Immediately.   [2] Scene viii. in old eds.   [3] Lot, number.

'hem, and he is left in pawn for the reckoning : now, if ever you look that time shall present you with an happy occasion to do your wife some gracious and acceptable service, take hold of this opportunity, and presently go, and redeem him ; for, being her brother, and his credit so amply engaged as now it is, when she shall hear, (as he cannot himself, but he must out of extremity report it) that you came, and offered yourself so kindly, and with that respect of his reputation, why, the benefit cannot but make her dote, and grow mad of your affections.

Deli. Now, by Heaven, Macilente, I acknowledge myself exceedingly indebted to you, by this kind tender of your love ; and I am sorry to remember that I was ever so rude, to neglect a friend of your importance :— bring me shoes and a cloak, there.—I was going to bed, if you had not come ; what tavern is it ?

Maci. The Mitre, sir.

Deli. O, why Fido, my shoes.—Good faith, it cannot but please her exceedingly.

Enter FALLACE.

Fal. Come, I mar'le what piece of night-work you have in hand now, that you call for your cloak and your shoes ! what, is this your pander ?

Deli. O, sweet wife, speak lower, I would not he should hear thee for a world——

Fal. Hang him, rascal, I cannot abide him for his treachery, with his wild quick-set beard there.—Whither go you now with him ?

Deli. No " whither, with him," dear wife ; I go alone to a place, from whence I will return instantly.— Good Macilente, acquaint not her with it by any means, it may come so much the more accepted, frame some other answer.—I'll come back immediately.   [*Exit.*

Fal. Nay, an I be not worthy to know whither you go, stay, till I take knowledge of your coming back.

Maci. Hear you, Mistress Deliro.

Fal. So sir, and what say you?

Maci. Faith lady, my intents will not deserve this slight respect, when you shall know 'hem.

Fal. Your intents? why, what may your 'intents' be, for God's sake?

Maci. Troth, the time allows no circumstance, lady, therefore know, this was but a device to remove your husband hence, and bestow him securely, whilst, with more conveniency, I might report to you a misfortune that hath happened to Monsieur Brisk——nay, comfort, sweet lady. This night being at supper, a sort of young gallants committed a riot, for which he only is apprehended, and carried to the Counter, where, if your husband, and other creditors, should have but knowledge of him, the poor gentleman were undone forever.

Fal. Ay me! that he were.

Maci. Now therefore, if you can think upon any present means for his delivery, do not foreslow [1] it. A bribe, to the officer that committed him, will do it.

Fal. O God, sir! he shall not want for a bribe: 'pray you, will you commend me to him, and say I'll visit him presently.

Maci. No, lady, I shall do you better service, in protracting your husband's return, that you may go with more safety.

Fal. Good truth, so you may: farewell, good sir. [*Exit* MACILENTE.]—Lord, how a woman may be mistaken in a man! I would have sworn upon all the Testaments in the world he had not loved Master Brisk.—Bring me my keys there, maid.—Alas, good gentleman, if all I have i' this earthly world will pleasure him, it shall be at his service.   [*Exit.*

Mit. How Macilente sweats i' this business, if you mark him.

Cor. Ay, you shall see the true picture of spite, anon: here comes the pawn, and his redeemer.

---

[1] Over-slow.

[1] SCENE VI.—*In the Mitre.*

Enter DELIRO, FUNGOSO, *and* GEORGE.

Deli. Come, brother, be not discouraged for this, man; what!

Fung. No, truly, I am not discouraged, but I protest to you, brother, I have done imitating any more gallants either in purse or apparel, but as shall become a gentleman, for good carriage, or so.

Deli. You say well.—This is all i' the bill here, is't not?

George. Ay, sir.

Deli. There's your money, tell it:—and, brother, I am glad I met with so good occasion to show my love to you.

Fung. I will study to deserve it in good truth, an I live.

Deli. What, is't right?

George. Ay, sir, and I thank you.

Fung. Let me have a capon's leg saved, now the reckoning is paid.

George. You shall, sir. [*Exit.*

Enter MACILENTE.

Maci. Where's Signior Deliro?

Deli. Here, Macilente.

Maci. Hark you, sir, ha' you dispatched this same?

Deli. Ay, marry have I.

Maci. Well then, I can tell you news, Brisk is i' the Counter.

Deli. I' the Counter!

Maci. 'Tis true, sir, committed for the stir here to-night. Now would I have you send your brother home afore, with the report of this your kindness done him, to his sister, which will so pleasingly possess her, and out of his mouth too, that i' the meantime you may clap your action on Brisk, and your wife, being in so happy a mood, cannot entertain it ill, by any means.

---

[1] Scene ix. in old eds.

Deli. 'Tis very true, she cannot indeed, I think.

Maci. Think? why 'tis past thought, you shall never meet the like opportunity, I assure you.

Deli. I will do it.—Brother, pray you go home afore—this gentleman and I have some private business—and tell my sweet wife, I'll come presently.

Fung. I will, brother.

Maci. And, signior, acquaint your sister, how liberally, and out of his bounty, your brother has used you. Do you see? made you a man of good reckoning; redeemed that you never were possessed of, credit; gave you as gentlemanlike terms as might be; found no fault with your coming behind the fashion; nor nothing.

Fung. Nay, I am out of those humours now.

Maci. Well, if you be out, keep your distance, and be not made a shot-clog[1] any more.—Come, signior, let's make haste.   *[Exeunt.*

[2]SCENE VII.—*The Counter.*

Enter FALLACE *and* BRISK.

Fal. O Master Fastidius, what pity is't to see so sweet a man as you are, in so sour a place! *[Kisses him.*

Cor. As upon her lips, does she mean?

Mit. O, this is to be imagined the Counter, belike.

Fast. Troth, fair lady, 'tis first the pleasure of the fates, and next of the constable, to have it so: but I am patient, and indeed comforted the more, in your kind visit.

Fal. Nay, you shall be comforted in me, more than this, if you please, sir. I sent you word by my brother, sir, that my husband laid to 'rest you this morning, I know not whether you received it or no.

Fast. No, believe it, sweet creature, your brother gave me no such intelligence.

---

[1] Payer of his comrades' reckonings.   [2] Scene x. in old eds.

Fal. O, the Lord.

Fast. But has your husband any such purpose?

Fal. O, sweet Master Brisk, yes: and therefore be presently discharged, for if he come with his actions upon you, Lord deliver you! you are in for one half-a-score year; he kept a poor man in Ludgate once twelve year, for sixteen shillings. Where's your keeper? for love's sake call him, let him take a bribe, and despatch you. Lord, how my heart trembles! here are no spies? are there?

Fast. No, sweet mistress, why are you in this passion?

Fal. O Lord, Master Fastidius, if you knew how I took up my husband to-day, when he said he would arrest you; and how I railed at him that persuaded him to't, the scholar there, (who, on my conscience, loves you now) and what care I took to send you intelligence by my brother; and how I gave him four sovereigns[1] for his pains; and now, how I came running out hither without man or boy with me, so soon as I heard on't; you'ld say I were in a passion indeed: your keeper, for God's sake! O, Master Brisk, as 'tis in Euphues,[2] "Hard is the choice, when one is compelled either by silence to die with grief, or by speaking to live with shame."

Fast. Fair lady, I conceive you, and may this kiss assure you, that where adversity hath, as it were, contracted, prosperity shall not——God's me! your husband.

Fal. O me!

Enter DELIRO, MACILENTE *following.*

Deli. Ay! Is't thus?

Maci. Why, how now, Signior Deliro? has the wolf seen you,[3] ha? Hath Gorgon's head made marble of you?

Deli. Some planet strike me dead!

Maci. Why, look you, sir, I told you, you might have

---

[1] Angels.   [2] Lilly's book lately most fashionable.
[3] and made you speechless!

suspected this long afore, had you pleased, and ha' saved this labour of admiration now, and passion, and such extremities as this frail lump of flesh is subject unto. Nay, why do you not doat now, signior? methinks you should say it were some enchantment, *deceptio visus*,[1] or so, ha? if you could persuade yourself it were a dream now, 'twere excellent: faith, try what you can do, signior; it may be your imagination will be brought to it in time, there's nothing impossible.

Fal. Sweet husband!

Deli. Out, lascivious strumpet!   [*Exit.*

Maci. What? did you see how ill that stale vein became him afore, of "sweet wife," and "dear heart;" and are you fallen just into the same now, with "sweet husband!" Away, follow him, go, keep state; what! remember you are a woman, turn impudent: gi' him not the head, though you gi' him the horns. Away. And yet, methinks, you should take your leave of *Enfans-perdus* here, your "forlorn hope." [*Exit* FALLACE.]—How now, Monsieur Brisk? what! Friday night, and in affliction too, and yet your *pulpamenta?*[2] your delicate morsels? I perceive the affection of ladies and gentlewomen pursues you, wheresoever you go, monsieur.

Fast. Now, in good faith, and as I am gentle, there could not have come a thing i' this world to have distracted me more, than the wrinkled fortunes of this poor spinster.[3]

Maci. O yes, sir; I can tell you a thing will distract you much better, believe it. Signior Deliro has entered three actions against you, three actions, monsieur! marry, one of them (I'll put you in comfort) is but three thousand, and the other two, some five thousand apiece; trifles, trifles.

Fast. O, I am undone.

---

[1] Deception of the sight.   [2] Nicely seasoned delicacies.

[3] Spinster as now used commonly for an unmarried woman was then a common law term for such.

Maci. Nay, not altogether so, sir; the knight must have his hundred pound repaid, that'll help too; and then six score pound for a diamond, you know where. These be things will weigh, monsieur, they will weigh.

Fast. O, Heaven.

Maci. What! do you **sigh**? this it is to "kiss the hand of a countess," to "have her coach sent for you," to "hang poniards in ladies' garters," to "wear bracelets of their hair," and for every one of these great favours to "give some slight jewel of five hundred crowns, or so;" why, 'tis nothing. Now, monsieur, you see the plague that treads o' the heels of your foppery: well, go your ways in, remove yourself to the two-penny ward quickly, to save charges, and there set up your rest[1] to spend Sir Puntar's hundred pound for him. Away, good pomander,[2] go! [*Exit* FASTIDIUS.[3]
Why, here's a change! Now is my soul at peace.
I am as empty of all envy now,
As they of merit to be envied at.
My humour, like a flame, no longer lasts
Than it hath stuff to feed it; and their folly
Being now raked up in their repentant ashes,
Affords no ampler subject to my spleen.
I am so far from malicing their states,
That I begin to pity 'hem. It grieves me
To think they have a being. I could wish
They might turn wise upon it, and be saved now,
So Heaven were pleased: but let them vanish, vapours!
And now with Asper's tongue (though not his shape)
Kind patrons of our sports—you that can judge,
And with discerning thoughts measure the space
Of our strange Muse in this her maze of humour,
You, whose true notions do confine the forms
And nature of sweet poesy—to you

---

[1] Gambling term, meaning stakes; a pun is intended.
[2] Scent box, pomander being then a fashionable scent.
[3] See note at the end of the play.

I tender solemn and most durious[1] thanks,
For your stretch[ed] patience and attentive grace.
We know—and we are pleased to know so much—
The cates[2] that you have tasted were not seasoned
For every vulgar palate, but prepared
To banquet pure, and apprehensive ears :
Let then their voices speak for our desert ;
Be their applause the trumpet to proclaim
Defiance to rebelling Ignorance,
And the green spirits of some tainted few,
That, spite of pity [do] betray themselves
To scorn and laughter ; and like guilty children,
Publish their infancy before their time
By their own fond[3] exception : such as these
We pawn 'hem to your censure, till Time, Wit,
Or Observation, set some stronger seal
Of Judgment on their judgments ; and entreat
The happier spirits in this fair-filled Globe[4]
(So many as have sweet minds in their breasts,
And are too wise to think themselves are taxed
In any general figure, or too virtuous
To need that wisdom's imputation :)
That with their bounteous hands, they would confirm
This, as their pleasure's patent : which not so signed,
Our lean and spent endeavours shall renew
Their beauties with the spring to smile on you.

---

[1] Lasting. [2] Any victuals except bread.—*Minshen.*
[3] Foolish. [4] The name of the theatre.

THE EPILOGUE,

AT THE

PRESENTATION BEFORE QUEEN ELIZABETH.

BY MACILENTE.

Blest, divine, unblemished, sacred, pure,
Glorious, immortal, and indeed immense ;
O that I had a world of attributes,[1]
Never till now did object greet mine eyes
With any light content : but in her graces,
All my malicious powers have lost their stings.
Envy is fled my soul, at sight of her,
And she hath chased all black thoughts from my bosom,
Like as the sun doth darkness from the world.
My stream of humour is run out of me,
And as our city's torrent, bent t'infect
The hallowed bowels of the silver Thames,
Is checked by strength, and clearness of the river,
Till it hath spent itself e'en at the shore ;
So in the ample, and unmeasured flood
Of her perfections, are my passions drowned ;
And I have now a spirit as sweet, and clear
As the most rarefied and subtle air.
With which, and with a heart as pure as fire,
Yet humble as the earth, do I implore,—— 　　[*Kneels.*
O Heaven, that She, whose presence hath effected
This change in me, may suffer most late change
In her admired and happy government :
May still this Island be called Fortunate,
And rugged Treason tremble at the sound,
When Fame shall speak it with an emphasis.
Let foreign Polity be dull as lead,
And pale Invasion come with half a heart,
When he but looks upon her blessèd soil.

---

[1] These three lines are only given in the quarto.

The throat of War be stopped within her land,
And turtle-footed Peace dance fairy rings
About her court : where, never may there come
Suspect, or danger, but all trust, and safety :
Let Flattery be dumb, and Envy blind
In her dread presence : Death himself admire her :
And may her virtues make him to forget
The use of his inevitable hand.
Fly from her, Age, sleep, Time, before her throne —
Our strongest wall falls down, when she is gone.

[*Here the trumpets sound a flourish, in which time*
MACILENTE *converts* [1] *himself to them that supply the place
of* Grex *and speaks.*]

How, now, sirs? how like you it? has't not been
tedious?

Cor. Nay, we ha' done censuring now.
Mit. Yes, faith.

Maci. How so?

Cor. Marry, because we'll imitate your actors, and be
"out of our humours." Besides, here are those, round
about you, of more ability in censure than we, whose judgments can give it a more satisfying allowance : we'll refer
you to them.

Maci. Ay, is't even so?—[*To audience.*] Well, gentlemen, I should have gone in, and returned to you as I
was Asper at the first : but by reason the shift would
have been somewhat long, and we are loth to draw your
patience farther, we'll entreat you to imagine it. And
now, that you may see I will be "out of humour" for
company, I stand wholly to your kind approbation, and
indeed am nothing so peremptory as I was in the beginning : marry, I will not do as Plautus in his "*Amphytrio,*"
for all this, *Summi Jovis causâ plaudite ;* [2] "beg a plaudite
for God's sake ;" but if you, out of the bounty of your

---

[1] Turns.
[2] "Your applause for the sake of high Jove."

good-liking, will bestow it, why, you may, in time, make
lean Macilente as fat,—as Sir John Falstaff. *Non ego
ventosæ plebis suffragia venor.*[1]   [*Exeunt.*

In the quarto edition of the play Jonson has inserted
the following note. No doubt the disapproval of his
eulogy, to which he refers, was intended by the Londoners
to express their dissatisfaction of the Queen's treatment of
their favourite, the Earl of Essex.

It had another catastrophe or conclusion, at the first
playing which, δια το την Βασιλισσαν προσωποεσθαι,[2] many
seemed not to relish it; and therefore 'twas since altered:
yet that a right eyed and solid reader may perceive it was
not so great a part of the Heaven awry, as they would
make it; we request him but to look down upon these
following reasons.

1. There hath been precedent of the like presentation
in divers plays: and is yearly in our city pageants or
shows of triumph.

2. It is to be conceived, that Macilente being so
strongly possessed with envy, as the poet here makes
him, it must be no slight or common object, that should
effect so sudden and strange a cure upon him, as the
putting him clean "out of his humour."

3. If his imagination had discoursed the whole world
over for an object, it could not have met with a more
proper, eminent, or worthy figure, than that of her Majesty's: which his election (though boldly, yet respectively [*i.e.* respectfully]) used to a moral and mysterious
end.

4. His greediness to catch at any occasion, that might

---

[1] "I hunt not for the suffrages of the windy multitude." Jonson
evidently hoped to be substantially noticed by the Queen. The
lines only occur in the quarto.

express his affection to his sovereign, may worthily plead for him.

5. There was nothing, in his examined opinion, that could more near or truly exemplify the power and strength of her invaluable virtues, than the working of so perfect a miracle on so opposed a spirit ; who not only persisted in his humour, but was now come to the court, with a purposed resolution—his soul as it were now dressed in envy—to malign at any thing that should front him : when suddenly, against expectation, and all steel of his malice, the very wonder of her presence strikes him to the earth dumb, and astonished. From whence rising and recovering heart, his passion thus utters itself :

" Blest, divine, unblemished, sacred, pure,' &c

THE POETASTER;

OR,

HIS ARRAIGNMENT.

ONSON, provoked, as he tells us, for three years on every stage—though it is questionable whether his arrogance and ill-temper were not the true beginners of the fray—retaliated in this play. It appears from *The Return from Parnassus*, IV. iii., that, amongst the rest, the gentle Shakespeare, taking up the cause of his fellow dramatists, and perhaps also the interests of himself and his fellow actors, ridiculed him in some piece that has not come down to us, and, in the purge that he administered, gave Jonson the precedent for Horace's pills. How greatly Jonson was provoked appears most plainly from the fact that his play was produced, not after his usual incubation of a year, but after one of fifteen weeks, and this his haste is evidenced by his bringing in Ovid's *Amorum*, l. i. Elegia 15—Marlowe's translation but slightly varied. In the midst of his haste and anger there was, however, method, as is shown by his not ridiculing Shakespeare; and it is, perhaps, one of the best evidences of his sense of that dramatist's supremacy that he did not retaliate on him, but only on the smaller fry of his poetasters.

In this play his poetasters in chief are John Marston as Crispinus, and Thomas Dekker as Demetrius, whom he had previously brought on the stage as persons to be laughed at in an otherwise unnecessary episode (III. i.) of his *Every Man out of his Humour*. It was produced at the Blackfriars in 1601, by the children of Queen Elizabeth's Chapel, Jonson having ceased to write for the Globe after his *Every Man out of his Humour*, and having written for these children his *Cynthia's Revels* in 1600.

Entered on the Stationers' registers, the 21st December, 1601, the play was published by M[atthew] L[owndes] in 1602; and Dekker, known by Jonson to be meditating an onslaught on him (see *Poetaster*, III. i. Histrio) and whom he thus anticipated, responded with the *Satiro-Mastix, or the Untrussing of the Humorous Poet*. Perhaps the *Satiro-Mastix* was not the play in which Dekker originally intended to bring in Horace-Jonson; but, obliged at once to produce his counterbuff, he added his untrussing to the plot of the play he was then writing; and this view seems supported by the above reference to Dekker's intentions. It need only be added that, as Scene ii. Act III. is not in the quarto, and is taken bodily from Horace, so it seems to have been written at some time between the production of the quarto in 1602 and that of the folio in 1616; and thus evidences that Jonson's anger was not that of a day.

To the Virtuous, and my Worthy Friend,

MR. RICHARD MARTIN.[1]

Sir,-

A thankful man owes a courtesy ever; the unthankful, but when he needs it. To make mine own mark appear, and show by which of these seals I am known, I send you this piece of what may live of mine; for whose innocence, as for the author's, you were once a noble and timely undertaker, to the greatest justice of this kingdom. Enjoy now the delight of your goodness: which is, to see that prosper, you preserved, and posterity to owe the reading of that, without offence, to your name; which so much ignorance and malice of the times then conspired to have supprest.

Your true lover,

BEN JONSON.

[1] This dedication is not in the quarto.

DRAMATIS PERSONÆ.

AUGUSTUS CÆSAR.

MECÆNAS.

MARC. OVIDIUS, Father of the Poet.

COR. GALLUS.

SEX. PROPERTIUS.

FUS. ARISTIUS.

PUB. OVIDIUS, the Poet [Ben Jonson].

VIRGIL.

HORACE.

TREBATIUS.

ASINIUS LUPUS.

PANTILIUS TUCCA [Posing as a man of war].

LUSCUS.

RUF. LAB. CRISPINUS [John Marston].

HERMOGENES TIGELLIUS.

DEMETRIUS FANNIUS [Thomas Dekker].

ALBIUS.

MINOS.

HISTRIO [*i.e.* a player].

ÆSOP.

TWO PYRGI.

Lictors, Equites, &c.

JULIA.

CYTHERIS.

PLAUTIA.

CHLOE.

Maids.

SCENE,—ROME.

¹ Etymologically, engines used in sieges; hence applied to pages used by Tucca to carry out his designs.

THE POETASTER.

After the second sounding,
ENVY *arises in the midst of the stage.*

LIGHT, I salute thee, but with wounded
        nerves ;
    Wishing thy golden splendour, pitchy
        darkness.
    What's here ? "TH' ARRAIGNMENT ?"
    ay : this, this is it.
    That our sunk eyes have waked for,
all this while :
Here will be subject for my snakes and me.
Cling to my neck and wrists, my loving worms,
And cast you round, in soft and amorous folds,
Till I do bid uncurl : then, break your knots,
Shoot out yourselves at length, as[1] your forced stings
Would hide themselves within his maliced sides,
To whom I shall apply you.   Stay ! the shine
Of this assembly here offends my sight,—
I'll darken that first, and outface their grace.
Wonder not, if I stare : these fifteen weeks—[2]
So long as since the plot was but an embrion—
Have I, with burning lights mixed vigilant thoughts,
In expectation of this hated play :
To which, at last, I am arrived as Prologue.
Nor would I you should look for other looks,
Gesture, or compliment from me, than what
Th' infected bulk of Envy can afford :
For I am risse[3] here with a covetous hope,

---

[1] As [though].   [2] Hit at in *Satiro-Mastix.*
[3] Old variant of "risen."

To blast your pleasures and destroy your sports,
With wrestings, comments, applications,
Spy-like suggestions, privy whisperings,
And thousand such promoting[1] sleights as these.
Mark, how I will begin: The scene is, ha!—
"Rome? Rome? and Rome?" Crack, eye-strings, and
      your balls
Drop into earth; let me be ever blind.
I am prevented; all my hopes are crossed,
Checked and abated! fie, a freezing sweat
Flows forth at all my pores, my entrails burn:
What should I do? "Rome? Rome?" O my vexed soul,
How might I force this to the present state?
Are there no players here? no poet-apes,
That come with basilisk's eyes, whose forkèd tongues
Are steeped in venom, as their hearts in gall?
Either of these would help me! they could wrest,
Pervert, and poison all they hear, or see,
With senseless glosses, and allusions.
Now, if you be good devils, fly me not.
You know what dear, and ample faculties
I have endowed you with: I'll lend you more.
Here, take my snakes among you, come, and eat,
And while the squeezed juice flows in your black jaws,
Help me to damn the author. Spit it forth
Upon his lines, and show your rusty teeth
At every word, or accent: or else choose
Out of my longest vipers, to stick down
In your deep throats; and let the heads come forth
At your rank mouths; that he may see you armed
With triple malice, to hiss, sting, and tear
His work, and him: to forge, and then declaim,
Traduce, corrupt, apply, inform, suggest:
O, these are gifts wherein your souls are blest.
What? do you hide yourselves? will none appear?
None answer? what, doth this calm troop affright you?

---

[1] Informer's sleights.

Nay, then I do despair : down, sink again :
This travail is all lost with my dead hopes.
If, in such bosoms, spite have left to dwell,
Envy is not on earth, nor scarce in hell. [*Descends slowly.*

The third sounding.
Enter PROLOGUE *hastily.*

Stay, monster, ere thou sink—thus on thy head
Set we our bolder foot; with which we tread
Thy malice into earth : so Spite should die,
Despised and scorned by noble Industry.
If any muse why I salute the stage,
An armed Prologue ; know, tis a dangerous age :
Wherein who writes, had need present his scenes
Forty-fold-proof against the conjuring means
Of base detractors, and illiterate apes,
That fill up rooms in fair and formal shapes.
'Gainst these, have we put on this forced defence :
Whereof the allegory and hid sense
Is, that a well erected confidence
Can fright their pride, and laugh their folly hence.
Here now, put case, our author should, once more,
Swear that his play were good ;[1] he doth implore,
You would not argue him of arrogance :
Howe'er that common spawn of ignorance,
Our fry of writers, may beslime his fame,
And give his action that adulterate name.
Such full-blown vanity he more doth loth,
Than base dejection : there's a mean 'twixt both.
Which, with a constant firmness, he pursues,
As one, that knows the strength of his own muse.
And this he hopes all free souls will allow ;
Others, that take it with a rugged brow,
Their moods he rather pities, than enviés :
His mind it is above their injuries.

[1] Jonson's Epilogue to *Cynthia's Revels* had :—
    " By God 'tis good, and if you like't, you may ".—
and he had been much laughed at for it.

ACT THE FIRST.

SCENE I.—OVID *discovered in his study.*

OVID. "Then, when this body falls in funeral fire,
My name shall live, and my best part aspire."
It shall go so.

Enter LUSCUS.

Lusc. Young master! master Ovid! do you hear? Gods a'me! away with your songs and sonnets, and on with your gown and cap quickly; here, here, your father will be a man of this room presently. Come, nay, nay, nay, nay, be brief. These verses too, a poison on 'hem! I cannot abide 'hem, they make me ready to cast,[1] by the banks of Helicon! Nay, look, what a rascally untoward thing this poetry is; I could tear 'hem now.

Ovid. Give me; how near's my father?

Lusc. Heart a'man: get a law book in your hand, I will not answer you else. Why, so! now there's some formality in you. By Jove, and three or four of the gods more, I am right of mine old master's humour for that; this villainous poetry will undo you, by the welkin.

Ovid. What, hast thou buskins on, Luscus, that thou swear'st so tragically and high?

Lusc. No, but I have boots on, sir, and so has your father too by this time; for he called for 'hem ere I came from the lodging.

Ovid. Why? was he no readier?

---

[1] Vomit.

Lusc. O no : and there was the mad skeld'ring[1] captain, with the velvet arms, ready to lay hold on him as he comes down : he that presses every man he meets, with an oath, to lend him money, and cries, " Thou must do't, old boy, as thou art a man, a man of worship."

Ovid. Who, Pantilius Tucca ?

Lus. Ay, he : and I met little master Lupus, the tribune, going thither too.

Ovid. Nay, an he be under their arrest, I may, with safety enough, read over my elegy before he come.

Lus. Gods a'me ! what'll you do ? why, young master, you are not Castalian mad,[2] lunatic, frantic, desperate, ha !

Ovid. What ailest thou, Luscus ?

Lus. God be with you, sir, I'll leave you to your poetical fancies, and furies. I'll not be guilty, I.   [*Exit.*

Ovid. Be not, good ignorance : I'm glad th'art gone :
For thus alone, our ear shall better judge
The hasty errors of our morning muse.
" Envy, why twitt'st thou me, ' my time's spent ill,'[3]
And call'st my verse, 'fruits of an idle quill?'
Or that, 'unlike the line from whence I sprung,
War's dusty honours I pursue not young?'
Or 'that I study not the tedious laws,
And prostitute my voice in every cause?'
Thy scope is mortal ; mine, eternal fame :
Which, through the world, shall ever chaunt my name.
Homer will live whilst Tenedois stands, and Ide,
Or, to the sea, fleet Simoïs doth slide :
And so shall Hesiod too, while vines do bear,
Or crooked sickles crop the ripened ear.
Callimachus, though in invention low,
Shall still be sung, since he in art doth flow.
No loss shall come to Sophocles' proud vein.
With sun and moon, Aratus shall remain.

---

[1] Swindling.   [2] Poetry-mad.
[3] This is Jonson's improved variant of Marlowe's vision of Ovid's First Book of *Loves*, Elegy 15, and a variant not improbably first made for this play.

Whilst slaves be false, fathers hard, and bawds be whorish,
Whilst harlots flatter, shall Menander flourish.
Ennius, though rude, and Accius' high-reared strain,
A fresh applause in every age shall gain.
Of Varro's name, what ear shall not be told ?
Of Jason's Argo and the fleece of gold ?
Then shall Lucretius' lofty numbers die,
When earth and seas, in fire and flame, shall fry.
Tityrus, Tillage, Ænee shall be read,
Whilst Rome of all the conquered world is head.
Till Cupid's fires be out, and his bow broken,
Thy verses, neat Tibullus, shall be spoken.
Our Gallus shall be known from east to west :
So shall Lycóris, whom he now loves best.
The suffering plough-share or the flint may wear,
But heavenly Poësy no death can fear.
Kings shall give place to it, and kingly shows,
The banks o'er which gold-bearing Tagus flows.
Kneel hinds to trash : me let bright Phœbus swell
With cups full flowing from the Muses' well.
Frost-fearing myrtle shall impale my head,
And of sad lovers I'll be often read.
Envy the living, not the dead, doth bite ;
For after death all men receive their right.
Then, when this body falls in funeral fire,
My name shalt live, and my best part aspire."

[1]*Enter* OVID *senior, followed by* LUSCUS, TUCCA, *and*
LUPUS.

Ovid sen. "Your name shall live" indeed, sir ! you say
true : but how infamously, how scorned and contemned
in the eyes and ears of the best and gravest Romans, that,
you think not on ; you never so much as dream of that.
Are these the fruits of all my travail and expenses ? is this
the scope and aim of thy studies ! are these the hopeful
courses, wherewith I have so long flattered my expecta-

[1] Scene ii. in old eds.

tion from thee? Verses? Poetry? Ovid, whom I thought
to see the pleader, become Ovid the play-maker?

Ovid jun. No, sir.

Ovid sen. Yes, sir: I hear of a tragedy of yours coming
forth for the common players there, called "Medea."
By my household gods, if I come to the acting of it,
I'll add one tragic part, more than is yet expected, to it:
believe me when I promise it. What? shall I have my
son a stager now? an ingle[1] for players? a gull, a rook,
a shot-clog,[3] to make suppers, and be laughed at? Publius, I will set thee on the funeral pile first.

Ovid jun. Sir, I beseech you to have patience.

Lus. Nay, this 'tis to have your ears dammed up to
good counsel.—I did augur all this to him beforehand,
without poring into an ox's paunch for the matter, and
yet he would not be scrupulous.[4]

Tuc. How now, goodman slave? what, rowly-powly?[5]
all rivals, rascal? Why, my master of worship, dost hear?
are these thy best projects? is this thy designs and thy
discipline, to suffer knaves to be competitors with commanders and gentlemen? Are we parallels, rascal? are we
parallels?

Ovid sen. Sirrah, go get my horses ready. You'll still
be prating.

Tuc. Do, you perpetual stinkard, do, go; talk to tap-
sters and ostlers, you slave; they are i' your element, go;
here be the emperor's captains, you ragamuffin rascal;
and not your comrades.　　　　　　　　[*Exit* LUSCUS.

Lup. Indeed, Marcus Ovid, these players are an idle
generation, and do much harm in a state, corrupt young
gentry very much, I know it: I have not been a tribune
thus long, and observed nothing:[6] besides, they will rob

---

[1] The minion or parasite.　　　　　　[2] A ninni-hammer.
[3] A payer of the reckoning.　　　　　[4] Careful.
[5] Query—crop-headed and vulgar, or of no more shape than a roll-
pudding?
[6] A reference to the dislike that the London authorities had to the
players.

us, us, that are magistrates, of our respect bring us
upon their stages, and make us ridiculous to the ple-
beians; they will play you, or me, the wisest men they can
come by still, only to bring us in contempt with the vulgar, and make us cheap.

Tuc. Th'art in the right, my venerable cropshin,[1] they
will indeed: the tongue of the oracle never twanged truer.
Your courtier cannot kiss his mistress's slippers in quiet
for 'hem; nor your white innocent gallant pawn his
revelling suit, to make his punk a supper. An honest
decayed commander cannot skelder,[2] cheat, nor be seen
in a bawdy-house, but he shall be straight in one of their
wormwood comedies. They are grown licentious, the
rogues; libertines, flat libertines. They forget they are
i' the statute,[3] the rascals; they are blazoned there; there
they are tricked, they and their pedigrees; they need no
other heralds, I wiss.

Ovid sen. Methinks, if nothing else, yet this alone, the
very reading of the public edicts, should fright thee from
commerce with them, and give thee distaste enough of
their actions. But this betrays what a student you are;
this argues your proficiency in the law!

Ovid jun. They wrong me, sir, and do abuse you
        more,
That blow your ears with these untrue reports.
I am not known unto the open stage,
Nor do I traffic in their theatres.
Indeed, I do acknowledge, at request
Of some near friends, and honourable Romans,
I have begun a poem of that nature.

Ovid sen. You have, sir, a poem? and where is it?
that's the law you study.

Ovid jun. Cornelius Gallus borrowed it to read.

Ovid sen. Cornelius Gallus! There's another gallant
too hath drunk of the same poison; and Tibullus and

---

¹ Hobbler.   ² Swindle.
³ By XXXIX. Elizabeth, players were vagabonds, unless (nomi-
nally retained by some great one.

Propertius.   But these are gentlemen of means, and reve-
nues now.   Thou art a younger brother, and hast nothing
but thy bare exhibition ;[1] which I protest shall be bare
indeed, if thou forsake not these unprofitable by-courses,
and that timely too.   Name me a profest poet, that his
poetry did ever afford him so much as a competency,
Ay, your god of poets there, whom all of you admire and
reverence so much, Homer, he whose worm-eaten statue
must not be spewed against, but[2] hallowed lips and grovelling adoration, what was he ? what was he ?

Tuc. Marry, I'll tell thee, old swaggerer ? he was a poor,
blind, rhyming rascal, that lived obscurely up and down
in booths,[3] and tap-houses, and scarce ever made a good
meal in his sleep, the whoreson hungry beggar.

Ovid sen. He says well : nay, I know this nettles you
now, but answer me ; is't not true ? You'll tell me
his name shall live ; and that, now being dead, his works
have eternized him, and made him divine.   But could
this divinity feed him, while he lived ? could his name
feast him ?

[*Tuc.* Or purchase him a senator's revenue ? could it ?

Ovid sen. Ay, or give him place in the commonwealth ?
worship, or attendants ? make him be carried in his
litter ?]

Tuc. Thou speakest sentences, old Bias.[4]

[*Lup.* All this the law will do, young sir, if you'll follow
it.

Ovid sen. If he be mine, he shall follow and observe
what I will apt him to, or I profess here openly, and
utterly to disclaim him.

Ovid jun. Sir, let me crave, you will forego these
         moods ;
I will be anything, or study anything :
I'll prove the unfashioned body of the law

---

[1] Allowance.
[2] Approached, or worshipped, being understood.   [3] Ale-booths.
[4] One of four or seven sages of Greece, known by his practical
apothegms.   [5] Fit.

Pure elegance, and make her rugged'st strains
Run smoothly as Propertius' elegies.

Ovid sen. Propertius' elegies? good!

Lup. Nay, you take him too quickly, Marcus.

Ovid sen. Why, he cannot speak, he cannot think out
of poetry; he is bewitched with it.

Lup. Come, do not misprize him.

Ovid sen. "Misprise!" ay, marry, I would have him
use some such words now: they have some touch, some
taste of the law. He should make himself a style out of
these, and let his Propertius' elegies go by.

Lup. Indeed, young Publius, he that will now hit the
mark, must shoot through the law; we have no other
planet reigns, and in that sphere, you may sit, and sing
with angels. Why, the law makes a man happy, without
respecting any other merit: a simple scholar, or none at
all, may be a lawyer.

Tuc. He tells thee true, my noble neophyte; my little
grammaticaster, he does: it shall never put thee to thy
mathematics, metaphysics, philosophy, and I know not
what supposed sufficiencies; if thou canst but have the
patience to plod enough, talk, and make noise enough,
be impudent enough, and 'tis enough.[1]

Lup. Three books will furnish you.

Tuc. And the less art, the better: besides, when it
shall be in the power of thy chevril[2] conscience, to do
right or wrong, at thy pleasure, my pretty Alcibiades.

Lup. Ay, and to have better men than himself, by
many thousand degrees, to observe him, and stand bare.

Tuc. True, and he to carry himself proud, and stately,
and have the law on his side for't, old boy.

Ovid sen. Well, the day grows old, gentlemen, and I
must leave you. Publius, if thou wilt hold my favour,
abandon these idle, fruitless studies, that so bewitch thee.
Send Janus[3] home his back face again, and look only

[1] These passages gave offence to the lawyers.
[2] Of kid leather, able to be stretched.
[3] The two-faced god (not improbably of time).

forward to the law: intend that. I will allow thee, what shall suit thee in the rank of gentlemen, and maintain thy society with the best: and under these conditions I leave thee. My blessings light upon thee, if thou respect them: if not, mine eyes may drop for thee, but thine own heart will ache for itself; and so farewell!——What, are my horses come?

Lus. [*Re-entering.*] Yes, sir, they are at the gate without.

Ovid sen. That's well.——Asinius Lupus, a word.—— Captain, I shall take my leave of you? [*walks aside with* LUPUS.]

Tuc. No, my little old boy, dispatch with Cothurnus there: I'll attend thee, I——

Lus. [*Aside.*] To borrow some ten drachmes,[2] I know his project.

Ovid sen. [*To* LUPUS.] Sir, you shall make me beholding to you.—Now, captain Tucca? what say you?

Tuc. Why, what should I say? or what can I say, my flower o' the order? Should I say, thou art rich? or that thou art honourable, or wise? or valiant, or learned, or liberal? Why, thou art all these, and thou knowest it, my noble Lucullus, thou knowest it: come, be not ashamed of thy virtues, old stump. Honour's a good brooch to wear in a man's hat at all times.[3] Thou art the man of war's Mecænas,[4] old boy. Why shouldst not thou be graced then by them, as well as he is by his poets?——

Enter PYRGUS.

How now, my carrier, what news?

Lus. [*Aside.*] The boy has stayed within for his cue his half-hour.

Tuc. Come, do not whisper to me, but speak it out: what? it is no treason against the state I hope, is't?

---

[1] Stretch towards.			[2] The drachma $= 9\frac{3}{4}$d.
[3] To wear a brooch in the hat was then the fashion.
[4] His patron, as Mecænas was, to learned men in the time of Augustus.

Lus. [*Aside.*] Yes, against the state of my master's purse.

Pyr. Sir, Agrippa desires you to forbear him till the next week : his mules are not yet come up.

Tuc. His mules ! now the bots, the spavin, and the glanders, and some dozen diseases more, light on him and his mules ! what, ha' they the yellows, his mules, that they come no faster ? or are they foundered, ha ? his mules ha, the staggers belike, ha' they ?

Pyr. O no, sir :—[*Aside.*] Then your tongue might be suspected for one of his mules.[1]

Tuc. He owes me almost a talent, and he thinks to bear it away with his mules, does he ? Sirrah, you nut cracker, go your ways to him again, and tell him I must ha' money, I : I cannot eat stones and turfs, say. What will he clem[2] me and my followers ? ask him, an he will clem me ; do go. He would have me fry my jerkin, would he ? Away, setter, away. Yet, stay, my little tumbler this old boy shall supply now. I will not trouble him, cannot be importunate, I ; I cannot be impudent.

Pyr. [*Aside.*] Alas, sir, no ; you are the most maid enly blushing creature upon the earth.

Tuc. Dost thou hear, my little six and fifty, or there abouts ? thou art not to learn the humours and tricks of that old bald cheater, Time : thou hast not this chain for nothing. Men of worth have their chimeras, as well as other creatures : and they do see monsters sometimes they do, they do, brave boy.

Pyr. [*Aside.*] Better cheap[4] than he shall see you, warrant, him.

Tuc. Thou must let me have six—six drachmes, mean, old boy ; thou shalt do it : I tell thee, old boy thou shalt, and in private too, dost thou see ?—[*to th* Boy] Go, walk off :—There, there. Six is the sum. Thy son's a gallant spark, and must not be put out of a sudden

---

[1] Tucca is a stammerer.   [2] Make my guts stick together, starve

[3] Another kind of hunting dog.   [4] *I.e.*, cheaper.

ome hither, Callimachus;[1] thy father tells me thou art
oo poetical, boy; thou must not be so, thou must
eave them, young novice, thou must; they are a sort of
oor starved rascals, that are ever wrapt up in foul linen;
nd can boast of nothing but a lean visage, peering out
f a seam-rent suit; the very emblems of beggary. No,
lost hear? turn lawyer, thou shalt be my solicitor.—'Tis
ight, old boy, is't?

Ovid sen. You were best tell[2] it, captain.

Tuc. No: fare thou well mine honest horseman; and
thou, old beaver.[3] [*to* LUPUS]—Pray thee, Roman, when
thou comest to town, see me at my lodging, visit me
sometimes? thou shalt be welcome, old boy. Do not
baulk me, good swaggerer. Jove keep thy chain from
pawning, go thy ways, if thou lack money, I'll lend thee
some; I'll leave thee to thy horse, now. Adieu.

Ovid sen. Farewell, good captain.

Tuc. [*Aside.*] Boy, you can have but half a share now,
boy.   [*Exit, followed by* PYRGUS.

Ovid sen. 'Tis a strange boldness that accompanies
this fellow.—Come.

Ovid jun. I'll give attendance on you, to your horse,
sir, please you.

Ovid sen. No; keep your chamber, and fall to your
studies; do so: The gods of Rome bless thee!
                              [*Exit with* LUPUS.

Ovid jun. "And give me stomach to digest this law."
That should have followed sure, had I been he.
O, sacred Poësy, thou spirit of arts,
The soul of science, and the queen of souls;
What profane violence, almost sacrilege,
Hath here been offered by divinities![4]
That thine own guiltless poverty should arm
Prodigious ignorance to wound thee thus!
For thence, is all their force of argument

---

[1] Calls him by the name of a celebrated Alexandrine poet and
writer.   [2] Count.
[3] Because he looked after himself.   [4] *I.e.*, the Muses.

Drawn forth against thee ; or, from the abuse
Of thy great powers in adulterate brains :
When, would men learn but to distinguish spirits,
And set true difference 'twixt those jaded wits
That run a broken pace for common hire,
And the high raptures of a happy Muse,
Borne on the wings of her immortal thought,
That kicks at earth with a disdainful heel,
And beats at heaven gates with her bright hoofs ;
They would not then, with such distorted faces,
And desperate censures, stab at Poësy.[1]
They would admire bright knowledge, and their minds
Should ne'er descend on so unworthy objects
As gold, or titles : they would dread far more
To be thought ignorant, than be known poor.
" The time was once, when wit drowned wealth ; but now,
" Your only barbarism is t'have wit, and want.
" No matter now in virtue who excels,
" He that hath coin, hath all perfection else.

 Tib. [*within.*] Ovid.
 Ovid.   Who's there ? Come in.

     Enter TIBULLUS.

 Tib.   Good
  morrow, lawyer.
 Ovid. Good morrow, dear Tibullus ; welcome : sit
  down.
 Tib. Not I. What, so hard at it ? Let's see, what's
  here ?
[2]Nay, I will see it——
 Ovid. Prithee away——
 Tib. " If thrice in field, a man vanquish his foe,
   'Tis after in his choice to serve or no."
How now, Ovid ! Law cases in verse ?

  [1] As referred to in *Satiro-Mastix,* in the form given in quarto.
  [2] Q., with some variation in the rest, makes *Tib.* repeat the head-
ing—" *Numa in decimo nono ?*—Numa in this nineteenth [chapter
of his laws]."

Ovid. In troth, I know not; they run from my pen
unwittingly, if they be verse. What's the news abroad?

Tib. Off with this gown, I come to have thee walk.

Ovid. No, good Tibullus, I'm not now in case.
Pray let me alone.

Tib. How, not in case?
'Slight, thou'rt in too much case,[1] by all this law.

Ovid. Troth, if I live, I will new dress the law
In sprightly Poësy's habiliments.

Tib. The hell thou wilt! What! turn law into verse?
Thy father hath schooled thee, I see. Here, read that
      same.
There's subject for you; and, if I mistake not,
A *supersedeas*[2] to your melancholy.

Ovid. How! subscribed *Julia!* O, my life, my heaven!

Tib. Is the mood changed?

Ovid. Music of wit! note for th' harmonious spheres!
Celestial accents, how you ravish me!

Tib. What is it, Ovid?

Ovid. That I must meet my Julia, the princess Julia.

Tib. Where?

Ovid. Why, at ——
Heart, I've forgot; my passion so transports me.

Tib. I'll save your pains: it is at Albius' house,
The jeweller's, where the fair Lycóris lies.

Ovid. Who? Cytheris, Cornelius Gallus' love?

Tib. Ay, he'll be there too, and my Plautia.

Ovid. And why not your Delila?

Tib. Yes, and your Corinna.

Ovid. True, but my sweet Tibullus, keep that secret;
I would not, for all Rome, it should be thought,
I veil bright Julia underneath that name:
Julia, the gem and jewel of my soul,
That takes her honours from the golden sky,

---

[1] " Too much immersed in cases, and cased too in thy gown."

[2] A writ commanding one to forbear what seemingly ought to be
done.

As beauty doth all lustre from her eye.
The air respires the pure Elysian sweets
In which she breathes; and from her looks descend
The glories of the summer.   Heaven she is,
Praised in herself above all praise; and he
Which hears her speak, would swear the tuneful orbs
Turned in his zenith only.

 Tib. Publius, thou'lt lose thyself.

 Ovid. O, in no lab'rinth can I safelier err,
Than when I lose myself in praising her.
Hence, law, and welcome, Muses; though not rich,
Yet are you pleasing: let's be reconciled,
And now[1] made one.   Henceforth I promise faith
And all my serious hours to spend with you:
With you, whose music striketh on my heart,
And with bewitching tones steals forth my spirit,
In Julia's name; fair Julia: Julia's love
Shall be a law, and that sweet law I'll study,
The law, and art of sacred Julia's love:
All other objects will but abjects prove.

 Tib. Come, we shall have thee as passionate as Propertius, anon.

 Ovid. O, how does my Sextus?

 Tib. Faith, full of sorrow for his Cynthia's death.

 Ovid. What, still?

 Tib. Still, and still more, his griefs do grow upon him,
As do his hours.[2]   Never did I know
An understanding spirit so take to heart
The common work of Fate.

 Ovid.   O, my Tibullus,
Let us not blame him; for against such chances
The heartiest strife of virtue is not proof.
We may read constancy, and fortitude
To other souls; but had ourselves been struck
With the like planet, had our loves, like his,
Been ravished from us by injurious death.

---

 [1] " New " in quarto.   [2] A di-syllable.

And in the height and heat of our best days,
It would have cracked our sinews,[1] shrunk our veins,
And made our very heart-strings jar, like his.
Come, let's go take him forth, and prove, if mirth
Or company will but abate his passion.

　　Tib. Content, and I implore the gods it may.

　　　　　　　　　　　　　　　　　　[*Exeunt.*

---

[1] " Sinew " was at that time the more usual word for our "nerve."

Come, let's go take him forth, and prove, if mirth
Or company will but abate his passion.
Tib. Content, and I implore the gods it may. [Exeunt.
... sing ... ...

ACT THE SECOND.

SCENE I.—*A Room in* ALBIUS'S *House.*

Enter ALBIUS *and* CRISPINUS.

LB. Master Crispinus, you are welcome :
pray use a stool, sir. Your cousin Cy-
theris will come down presently. We
are so busy for the receiving of these
courtiers here, that I can scarce be a
minute with myself, for thinking of them :
Pray you sit, sir. Pray you sit, sir.

Crisp. I am very well, sir. Ne'er trust me, but you
are most delicately seated here, full of sweet delight and
blandishment ! an excellent air, an excellent air !

Alb. Ay, sir, 'tis a pretty air. [*Aside.*] These courtiers
run in my mind still ; I must look out.—For Jupiter's
sake, sit, sir. Or please you walk into the garden ?
There's a garden on the back-side.[1]

Crisp. I am most strenuously[2] well, I thank you, sir.

Alb. Much good do you, sir. [*Exit.*

Enter CHLOE, *with two* Maids.

Chloe. Come, bring those perfumes forward a little,
and strew some roses, and violets here : Fie ! here be
rooms savour the most pitifully rank that ever I felt : I
cry the gods mercy, [*sees* ALBIUS.] my husband's in the
wind of us !

Alb. [*Re-entering.*] Why, this is good, excellent, excel-

---

[1] Of the house.
[2] One of his parodical imitations of Marston's forced phraseology.

lent! well said, my sweet Chloe. Trim up your house most obsequiously.

Chloe. For Vulcan's sake, breathe somewhere else: in troth, you overcome our perfumes exceedingly, you are too predominant.

Alb. Hear but my opinion, sweet wife.

Chloe. A pin for your pinion! In sincerity, if you be thus fulsome to me in every thing, I'll be divorced. Gods my body! you know what you were, before I married you; I was a gentlewoman born, I; I lost all my friends to be a citizen's wife; because I heard, indeed, they kept their wives as fine as ladies; and that we might rule our husbands, like ladies, and do what we listed: do you think I would have married you else.

Alb. I acknowledge, sweet wife: [*to* CRISPINUS] she speaks the best of any woman in Italy, and moves as mightily; which makes me, I had rather she should make bumps on my head, as big as my two fingers, than I would offend her.—But sweet wife——

Chloe. Yet again! Is't not grace enough for you, that I call you husband, and you call me wife; but you must still be poking me, against my will, to things?

Alb. But you know, wife; here are the greatest ladies, and gallantest gentlemen of Rome, to be entertained in our house now: and I would fain advise thee, to[2] entertain them in the best sort, i' faith, wife.

Chloe. In sincerity, did you ever hear a man talk so idly? You would seem to be master? you would have your spoke in my cart? you would advise me to entertain ladies and gentlemen? Because you can marshal your pack-needles, horse-combs, hobby-horses, and wall-candlesticks in your warehouse better than I, therefore you can tell how to entertain ladies, and gentlefolks better than I?

---

[1] I suspect a pun, and that the doting Albius would embrace his wife, but that she pushes away his arm, and hits him on the head. Otherwise, the "bumps on the head" are dragged in apropos of nothing.   [2] *I.e.* So as to entertain them.

Alb. O my sweet wife, upbraid me not with that: gain savours sweetly from any thing; he that respects to get, must relish all commodities alike, and admit no difference betwixt woad and frankincense; or the most precious balsamum and a tar-barrel.

Chloe. Marry, foh! You sell snuffers[1] too, if you be remembered; but I pray you let me buy them out of your hand; for I tell you true, I take it highly in snuff,[2] to learn how to entertain gentlefolks of you, at these years, i'faith. Alas, man, there was not a gentleman come to your house i' your t'other wife's time, I hope! nor lady, nor music, nor masque! Nor you nor your house were so much as spoken of, before I disbased myself, from my hood and my farthingal,[3] to these bum-rowls[4] and your whale-bone bodice.

Alb. Look here, my sweet wife; I am mum, my dear mummia,[5] my balsamum, my spermaceti, and my very city of——She has the most best, true, feminine wit in Rome.

Cris. I have heard so, sir; and do most vehemently desire to participate the knowledge of her fair features.[6]

Alb. Ah, peace; you shall hear more anon: be not seen yet, I pray you; not yet; observe.   [*Exit.*

Chloe. 'Sbody! give husbands the head a little more, and they'll be nothing but head shortly;—What's he there?

1st Maid. I know not, forsooth.

2nd Maid. Who would you speak with?

Cris. I would speak with my cousin Cytheris.

2nd Maid. He is one, forsooth, would speak with his cousin Cytheris.

Chloe. Is she your cousin, sir?

---

[1] Maybe small dishes for holding snuff.   [2] In dudgeon.
[3] Half hoops.   [4] Bustles.
[5] Mummy, then accounted a valuable medicine.
[6] Makings, *i.e.*, the proportions of her shape, the word not being, as now, restricted to the features of the face.

Cris. Yes in truth,[1] forsooth, for fault of a better.

Chloe. She is a gentlewoman.

Cris. Or else she should not be my cousin, I assure you.

Chloe. Are you a gentleman born ?

Cris. That I am, lady; you shall see mine arms, if't please you.

Chloe. No, your legs do sufficiently show you are a gentleman born, sir; for a man borne upon little legs, is always a gentleman born.

Cris. Yet, I pray you, vouchsafe the sight of my arms, mistress; for I bear them about me, to have 'hem seen : my name is Crispinus, or " Cri-spinas " indeed ; which is well expressed in my arms, a face crying *in chief;* and beneath it a bloody toe, between three thorns *pungent.*

Chloe. Then you are welcome, sir ; now you are a gentleman born, I can find in my heart to welcome you : for I am a gentlewoman born too, and will bear my head high enough, though 'twere my fortune to marry a trades-man.

Cris. No doubt of that, sweet feature,[2] your carriage shows it in any man's eyes, that is carried upon you with judgment.

ALBIUS *still going out and in.*

Alb. Dear wife, be not angry.

Chloe. Gods my passion !

Alb. Hear me but one thing; let not your maids set cushions in the parlour windows ; nor in the dining-chamber windows ; nor upon stools, in either of them, in any case ; for 'tis tavern-like ; but lay them one upon another, in some out-room, or corner of the dining-chamber.

Chloe. Go, go, meddle with your bed-chamber only, or rather with your bed in your chamber only ; or rather with your wife in your bed only ; or, on my faith, I'll not be pleased with you only.

---

[1] I am her cousin, being understood.   [2] *I.e.* Make.

Alb. Look here, my dear wife, entertain that gentleman kindly, I prithee——mum.   [*Exit.*

Chloe. Go, I need your instructions indeed! anger me
no more, I advise you. Citi-sin, quotha! she's a wise
gentlewoman, i'faith, will marry herself to the sin of the
city.

Alb. [*Re-entering.*] But this time, and no more, by
Heaven, wife: hang no pictures in the hall, nor in the
dining-chamber, in any case, but in the gallery only, for
'tis not courtly else, o' my word, wife.

Chloe. 'Sprecious,[1] never have done!

Alb. Wife[2]——   [*Exit.*

Chloe. Do I bear a reasonable corrigible hand over
him, Crispinus?

Cris. By this hand, lady, you hold a most sweet hand
over him.

Alb. [*Re-entering.*] And then for the great gilt andirons?——

Chloe. Again! Would the andirons were in your great
guts for me!

Alb. I do vanish, wife.   [*Exit.*

Chloe. How shal I do, Master Crispinus? here will be
all the bravest ladies in court presently, to see your
cousin Cytheris: O the gods! how might I behave myself now, as to entertain them most courtly?

Cris. Marry, lady, if you will entertain them most
courtly, you must do thus: as soon as ever your maid,
or your man brings you word they are come, you must
say, "A pox on 'em! what do they here?" And yet,
when they come, speak them as fair, and give them the
kindest welcome in words, that can be.

Chloe. Is that the fashion of courtiers, Crispinus?

Cris. I assure you it is, lady, I have observed it.

Chloe. For your pox, sir, it is easily hit on; but 'tis
not so easy to speak fair after, methinks.

---

[1] God's precious.
[2] She makes some sudden sign of anger.

Alb. [*Re-entering.*] O, wife, the coaches are come, on my word, a number of coaches and courtiers.

Chloe. "A pox on them! what do they here?"

Alb. How now wife! would'st thou not have them come?

Chloe. Come? come, you are a fool, you. [*To* CRISPINUS.] He knows not the trick on't.——Call Cytheris, I pray you:——and good Master Crispinus, you can observe, you say; let me entreat you for all the ladies' behaviours, jewels, jests, and attires, that you marking, as well as I, we may put both our marks together, when they are gone, and confer of them.

Cris. I warrant you, sweet lady! let me alone to observe, till I turn myself to nothing but observation.

Enter CYTHERIS.

Good morrow, cousin Cytheris.

Cyth. Welcome, kind cousin. What? are they come?

Alb. Ay, your friend Cornelius Gallus, Ovid, Tibullus, Propertius, with Julia, the emperor's daughter, and the lady Plautia, are 'lighted at the door; and with them Hermogenes Tigellius, the excellent musician.

Cyth. Come, let us go meet them, Chloe.

Chloe. Observe, Crispinus.

Cris. At a hair's breadth, lady, I warrant you.

[1]*Enter* GALLUS, OVID, TIBULLUS, PROPERTIUS, HERMOGENES, JULIA, *and* PLAUTIA.

Gal. Health to the lovely Chloe! you must pardon me, mistress, that I prefer this fair gentlewoman.

Cyth. I pardon, and praise you for it, sir; [*To* JULIA.] and beseech your Excellence, receive her beauties into your knowledge and favour.

Jul. Cytheris, she hath favour, and behaviour, that commands as much of me:——and, sweet Chloe, know I do exceedingly love you, and that I will approve, in

---

[1] Scene ii. in old eds.

any grace my father the emperor may show you. Is this your husband?

Alb. For fault of a better, if it please your highness.

Chloe. [*Aside to* CYTHERIS.] Gods my life, how he shames me!

Cyth. Not a whit, Chloe, they all think you politic and witty;[1] wise women choose not husbands for the eye, merit, or birth, but wealth, and sovereignty.

Ovid. Sir, we all come to gratulate, for the good report of you.

Tib. And would be glad to deserve your love, sir.

Alb. My wife will answer you all, gentlemen; I'll come to you again, presently.   [*Exit.*

Plau. You have chosen you a most fair companion here, Cytheris, and a very fair house.

Cyth. To both which, you and all my friends are very welcome, Plautia.

Chloe. With all my heart, I assure your ladyship.

Plau. Thanks, sweet mistress Chloe.

Jul. You must needs come to court, lady, i'faith, and there be sure your welcome shall be as great to us.

Ovid. She will well deserve it, madam. I see, even in her looks, gentry, and general worthiness.

Tib. I have not seen a more certain character of an excellent disposition.

Alb. [*Re-entering.*] Wife!

Chloe. O, they do so commend me here, the courtiers! what's the matter now?

Alb. For the banquet, sweet wife.

Chloe. Yes; and I must needs come to court, and be welcome, the princess says.   [*Exit with* ALBIUS.

Gal. Ovid and Tibullus, you may be bold to welcome your mistresses here.

Ovid. We find it so, sir.

Tib. And thank Cornelius Gallus.

---

[1] *I.e.* Wise.

Ovid. Nay, my sweet Sextus, in faith thou art not
sociable.

Prop. In faith I am not, Publius ; nor I cannot.
Sick minds are like sick men that burn with fevers,
Who when they drink, please but a present taste,
And after bear a more impatient fit,
Pray, let me leave you ; I offend you all,
And my self most.

   Gal.   Stay, sweet Propertius.

Tib. You yield too much unto your griefs, and fate.
Which never hurts, but when we say it hurts us.

Prop. O peace, Tibullus ; your philosophy
Lends you too rough a hand to search my wounds.
Speak they of griefs, that know to sigh, and grieve :
The free and unconstrainèd spirit feels
No weight of my oppression.   [*Exit*

   Ovid.   Worthy Roman !
Methinks I taste his misery ; and could
Sit down, and chide at his malignant stars.

Jul. Methinks I love him, that he loves so truly.

Cyth. This is the perfect'st love, lives after death.

Gal. Such is the constant ground of virtue still.

Plau. It puts on an inseparable face.

Re-enter CHLOE.

Chloe. Have you marked every thing, Crispinus ?

Cris. Every thing, I warrant you.

Chloe. What gentlemen are these ? do you know them ?

Cris. Ay, they are poets, lady.

Chloe. Poets ? they did not talk of me since I went,
did they ?

Cris. O yes, and extolled your perfections to the
heavens.

Chloe. Now in sincerity, they be the finest kind of men
that ever I knew : Poets ! Could not one get the emperor to make my husband a 'poet,' think you ?

Cris. No, lady, 'tis love, and beauty make poets : and

since you like poets so well, your love and beauties shall
make me a poet.

Chloe. What! shall they? and such a one as these?

Cris. Ay, and a better than these: I would be sorry
else.

Chloe. And shall your looks change, and your hair
change,[1] and all, like these?

Cris. Why, a man may be a poet, and yet not change
his hair, lady.

Chloe. Well, we shall see your cunning:[2] yet if you
can change your hair, I pray do.

Re-enter ALBIUS.

Alb. Ladies and lordings, there's a slight banquet stays
within for you; please you draw near, and accost[3] it.

Jul. We thank you, good Albius: but when shall we
see those excellent jewels you are commended to have?

Alb. "At your ladyship's service." [*Aside.*] I got that
speech by seeing a play last day, and it did me some
grace now: I see, 'tis good to collect sometimes; I'll frequent these plays more than I have done, now I come to
be familiar with courtiers.

Gal. Why, how now, Hermogenes? what ailest thou,
trow?

Her. A little melancholy, let me alone, prithee.

Gal. Melancholy! how so?

Her. With riding: a plague on all coaches for me.

Chloe. Is that hard-favoured gentleman a poet too,
Cytheris?

Cyth. No, this is Hermogenes, as humourous as a poet,
though: he s a musician.

Chloe. A musician? then he can sing.

Cyth. That he can, excellently; did you never hear
him?

---

[1] His hair was red, but, besides the sting of this, there seems to be
some other allusion; possibly to the long locks of other gallants.
[2] Skill.
[3] Fr., *accoster*, draw near to; then in English a fashionable cant
word.

Chloe. O no : will he be entreated, think you ?

Cyth. I know not.—Friend, mistress Chloe would fain hear Hermogenes sing : are you interested in him ?

Gal. No doubt, his own humanity will command him so far, to the satisfaction of so fair a beauty ; but rather than fail, we'll all be suitors to him.[1]

Her. 'Cannot sing.

Gal. Prithee, Hermogenes.

Her. 'Cannot sing.

Gal. For honour of this gentlewoman, to whose house I know thou mayest be ever welcome.

Chloe. That he shall, in truth, sir, if he can sing.

Ovid. What's that ?

Gal. This gentlewoman is wooing Hermogenes for a song.

Ovid. A song ? come, he shall not deny her. Hermogenes ?

Her. 'Cannot sing.

Gal. No, the ladies must do it, he stays but to have their thanks acknowledged as a debt to his cunning.

Jul. That shall not want : ourself will be the first shall promise to pay him more than thanks, upon a favour so worthily vouchsafed.

Her. Thank you, madam, but 'will not sing.

Tib. [*In a low voice.*] Tut, the only way to win him, is to abstain from entreating him.

Cris. Do you love singing, lady ?

Chloe. O, passingly.[2]

Cris. Entreat the ladies, to entreat me to sing then, I beseech you.

Chloe. I beseech your Grace, entreat this gentleman to sing.

Jul. That we will, Chloe ; can he sing excellently ?

Chloe. I think so, madam ; for he entreated me, to entreat you, to entreat him to sing.

---

[1] Spoken at him in the third person.
[2] Greatly. beyond measure.

Cris. Heaven and earth! would you tell that?

Jul. Good sir, let's entreat you to use your voice.

Cris. Alas, madam, I cannot, in truth.

Pla. The gentleman is modest: I warrant you, he sings excellently.

Ovid. Hermogenes, clear your throat: I see by him, here's a gentleman will worthily challenge you.

Cris. Not I, sir, I'll challenge no man.

Tib. That's your modesty, sir: but we, out of an assurance of your excellency, challenge him in your behalf.

Cris. I thank you, gentlemen, I'll do my best.

Her. Let that best be good, sir, you were bet.

Gal. O this contention is excellent! What is t you sing, sir?

Cris. "If I freely may discover," &c., sir; I'll sing that.

Ovid. One of your own compositions, Hermogenes. He offers you vantage enough.

Cris. Nay truly, gentlemen, I'll challenge no man :— I can sing but one stave of the ditty neither.

Gal. The better: Hermogenes himself will be entreated to sing the other.

CRISPINUS, *accompanied, sings.*

    If I freely may discover
    What would please me in my lover:
    I would have her fair, and witty,
    Savouring more of court, than city;
    A little proud, but full of pity:
    Light, and humourous in her toying,
    Oft building hopes, and soon destroying,
    Long, but sweet in the enjoying;
    Neither too easy, nor too hard:
    All extremes I would have barred.

Gal. Believe me, sir, you sing most excellently.

Ovid. If there were a praise above excellence, the gentleman highly deserves it.

Her. Sir, all this doth not make me envy you? for I know I sing better than you.

Tib. Attend Hermogenes, now.

HERMOGENES, *accompanied, sings.*

She should be allowed her passions,
So they were but used as fashions ;
Sometimes froward, and then frowning,
Sometimes sickish, and then swowning,
Every fit with change still crowning.
Purely jealuos I would have her,
Then only constant when I crave her :
'Tis a virtue should not save her.
Thus, nor her delicates would cloy me,
Neither her peevishness annoy me.

Jul. Nay, Hermogenes, your merit hath long since been both known, and admired of us.

Her. You shall hear me sing another : now will I begin.

Gal. We shall do this gentleman's banquet too much wrong, that stays for us, ladies.

Jul. 'Tis true ; and well thought on, Cornelius Gallus.

Her. Why 'tis but a short air, 'twill be done presently, pray stay ; strike music.

Ovid. No, good Hermogenes ; we'll end this difference within.

Jul. 'Tis the common disease of all your musicians, that they know no mean, to be entreated either to begin, or end.

Alb. Please you lead the way, gentles?

All. Thanks, good Albius.   [*Exeunt all but* ALBIUS.

Alb. O, what a charm[1] of thanks was here put upon me !   O Jove, what a setting forth it is to a man, to have many courtiers come to his house !   Sweetly was it said of a good old housekeeper, " I had rather want meat, than want guests ;" specially, if they be courtly guests.   For,

---

[1] Musical concert of birds.

never trust me, if one of their good legs[1] made in a house,
be not worth all the good cheer a man can make them.
He that would have fine guests, let him have a fine wife ;
he that would have a fine wife, let him come to me.

Re-enter CRISPINUS.

Cris. By your kind leave, Master Albius.

Alb. What, you are not gone, Master Crispinus ?

Cris. Yes, faith, I have a design draws me hence :
pray sir, fashion me an excuse to the ladies.

Alb. Will you not stay ? and see the jewels, sir ? I
pray you stay.

Cris. Not for a million, sir, now : let it suffice, I must
relinquish ; and so in a word, please you to expiate[2] this
compliment.

Alb. Mum.   [*Exit.*

Cris. I'll presently go and ingle[3] some broker for a
poet's gown, and bespeak a garland : and then jeweller,
look to your best jewel, i'faith.   [*Exit.*

---

[1] Knee-bends.   [2] Clear me with, be satisfied with.   [3] Cajole.

ACT THE THIRD.

SCENE I.—*The Via Sacra (or Holy Street).*

HORACE *meditating.*

OR. Hmh? yes, I will begin an ode so: and it shall be to Mecænas.

Enter CRISPINUS.

Cris. 'Slid, yonder's Horace! they say he's an excellent poet: Mecænas loves him. I'll fall into his acquaintance, if I can; I think he be composing as he goes i' the street! ha? 'tis a good humour, if he be: I'll compose too.

Hor. "Swell me a bowl with lusty wine,
Till I may see the plump Lyæus swim
  Above the brim:
I drink, as I would write,
In flowing measure, filled with flame and sprite."[1]

Cris. Sweet Horace, Minerva, and the Muses stand auspicious to thy designs! How farest thou, sweet man? frolic? rich? gallant? ha?

Hor. Not greatly gallant, sir; like my fortunes, well. I'm bold to take my leave, sir; you'ld nought else, sir, would you?

Cris. Troth, no, but I could wish thou didst know us, Horace; we are scholars, I assure thee.

---

[1] Quoted, *Satiro-Mastix,* I. ii.

Hor. A scholar, sir? I shall be covetous of your fair knowledge.

Cris. Gramercy, good Horace. Nay, we are new turned poet too, which is more; and a satirist too, which is more than that : I write just in thy vein, I. I am for your "Odes," or your "Sermones,"[1] or any thing indeed; we are a gentleman besides : our name is Rufus Laberius Crispinus, we are a pretty Stoic too.

Hor. To the proportion of your beard,[2] I think it, sir.

Cris. By Phœbus, here's a most neat, fine street, is't not? I protest to thee, I am enamoured of this street now, more than of half the streets of Rome again; 'tis so polite and terse! There's the front of a building now! I study architecture too : if ever I should build, I'd have a house just of that prospective.

Hor. [*Aside.*] Doubtless, this gallant's tongue has a good turn, when he sleeps.

Cris. I do make verses, when I come in such a street as this : O your city ladies, you shall ha' 'hem sit in every shop like the Muses—offering you the Castalian dews, and the Thespian liquors, to as many as have but the sweet grace and audacity to——sip of their lips. Did you never hear any of my verses?

Hor. No, sir;—[*Aside.*] but I'm in some fear I must now.

Cris. I'll tell thee some, if I can but recover 'hem, I composed e'en now of a dressing I saw a jeweller's wife wear, who indeed was a jewel herself : I prefer that kind of tire now [*Describing it with his hands.*]; what's thy opinion, Horace?

Hor. With your silver bodkin, it does well, sir.

Cris. I cannot tell, but it stirs me more than all your court-curls, or your spangles, or your tricks; I affect not these high gable-ends, these Tuscan tops, nor your coro-

---

[1] So Horace cal'ed his Satires.

[2] Being rufus or red, it was the reverse of a stoic's temperament.

nets, nor your arches,[1] nor your pyramids ; give me a
fine, sweet——little delicate dressing, with a bodkin, as
you say ; and a mushroom for all your other ornatures !

Hor. [*Aside.*] Is't not possible to make an escape from
him ?

Cris. I have remitted my verses all this while ; I think
I ha' forgot 'hem.

Hor. [*Aside.*] Here's he could wish you had else.

Cris. Pray Jove I can entreat 'hem of my memory !

Hor. You put your memory to too much trouble, sir.

Cris. No, sweet Horace, we must not ha' thee think so.

Hor. I cry you mercy ; [*Aside.*] then they are my ears
That must be tortured : well, you must have patience,
ears.

Cris. Pray thee, Horace, observe.

Hor. Yes, sir : your satin sleeve begins to fret at the
rug that is underneath it, I do observe : and your ample
velvet bases[2] are not without evident stains of a hot disposition naturally.

Cris. O——I'll dye them into another colour, at pleasure : how many yards of velvet dost thou think they
contain ?

Hor. [*Aside.*] 'Heart ! I have put him now in a fresh
way
To vex me more :—faith, sir, your mercer's book
Will tell you with more patience than I can :   [*Aside.*]
For I am crost, and so's not that, I think.

Cris. 'Slight, these verses have lost me again,—I shall
not invite them to mind, now !

Hor. Rack not your thoughts, good sir ; rather defer it
To a new time ; I'll meet you at your lodging,
Or where you please : 'till then, Jove keep you, sir !

Cris. Nay, gentle Horace, stay ; I have it, now.

Hor. Yes, sir.   [*Aside.*] Apollo, Hermes, Jupiter, look
down upon me.

---

[1] Some of the many forms of dressing the hair then adopted.
[2] Kilt-like skirts.

Cris.

"Rich was thy hap, sweet dainty cap,
      There to be placed ;
Where thy smooth black, sleek white may smack,
      And both be graced."

'White' is there usurped for her brow; her forehead :
and then 'sleek,' as the parallel to 'smooth,' that went
before. A kind of paranomasie, or agnomination : do
you conceive, sir ?

Hor. Excellent. Troth, sir, I must be abrupt, and
leave you.

Cris. Why, what haste hast thou ? prithee, stay a little ;
thou shalt not go yet, by Phœbus.

Hor. [*Aside.*] I shall not ! what remedy ? fie, how I
sweat with suffering !

Cris. And then ——

Hor. Pray, sir, give me leave to wipe my face a little.

Cris. Yes, do, good Horace.

Hor. Thank you, sir.—[*Aside.*]

Death ! I must crave his leave to piss anon ;
Or that I may go hence with half my teeth :
I am in some such fear. This tyranny
Is strange, to take mine ears up by commission,
(Whether I will or no) and make them stalls
To his lewd solecisms, and worded trash.
Happy thou, bold Bolanus, now I say ;[1]
Whose freedom, and impatience of this fellow,
Would, long ere this, have called him fool, and fool,
And rank, and tedious fool ! and have slung[2] jests
As hard as stones, till thou hadst pelted him
Out of the place : whilst my tame modesty
Suffers my wit be made a solemn ass
To bear his fopperies—

Cris. Horace, thou art miserably affected to be gone, I

---

[1] The quarto has " Happy the," &c. ; then the line, " Rome's
common buffoon : his free impudence would," &c.

[2] So the quarto and folios ; Gifford has " flung."

see. But—prithee let's prove[1] to enjoy thee a while.
Thou hast no business, I assure me. Whither is thy
journey directed, ha?

Hor. Sir, I am going to visit a friend, that's sick.

Cris. A friend! what's he; do not I know him?

Hor. No, sir, you do not know him; [*Aside.*] and 'tis
not the worse for him.

Cris. What's his name? where's he lodged?

Hor. Where I shall be fearful to draw you out of your
way, sir; a great way hence; pray, sir, let's part.

Cris. Nay, but where is't? I pray thee[2] say.

Hor. On the far side of all Tyber yonder, by Cæsar's
gardens.

Cris. O, that's my course directly; I am for you.
Come, go; why stand'st thou?

Hor. Yes, sir: marry, the plague is in that part of the
city; I had almost forgot to tell you, sir.

Cris. Foh! it's no matter, I fear no pestilence; I ha'
not offended Phœbus.

Hor. [*Aside.*] I have, it seems, or else this heavy
　　　　scourge
Could ne'er have lighted on me.

Cris. Come along.

Hor. I am to go down some half mile, this way, sir,
first, to speak with his physician: and from thence to his
apothecary, where I shall stay the mixing of divers drugs.

Cris. Why, it's all one, I have nothing to do, and I
love not to be idle; I'll bear thee company. How call'st
thou the apothecary?

Hor. [*Aside.*] O that I knew a name would fright
　　　　him now!—

Sir, Rhadamanthus, Rhadamanthus, sir.
There's one so called, is a just judge in hell,
And doth inflict strange vengeance on all those
That, here on earth, torment poor patient spirits.

---

[1] Try.
[2] The quarto and folio always has "pray thee."

Cris. He dwells at the Three Furies, by Janus' temple.

Hor. Your 'pothecary does, sir.

Cris. Heart, I owe him money for sweetmeats, and he has laid to arrest me, I hear : but——

Hor. Sir, I have made a most solemn vow : I will never bail any man.

Cris. Well then, I'll swear, and speak him fair, if the worst come. But his name is Minos, not Rhadamanthus, Horace.

Hor. That may be : sir, I but guessed at his name by his sign. But your Minos is a judge too, sir.

Cris. I protest to thee, Horace, (do but taste[1] me once) if I do know myself, and mine own virtues truly, thou wilt not make that esteem of Varius, or Virgil, or Tibullus, or any of 'hem indeed, as now in thy ignorance thou dost ; which I am content to forgive : I would fain see which of these could pen more verses in a day, or with more facility, than I ; or that could court his mistress, kiss her hand, make better sport with her fan, or her dog——

Hor. I cannot bail you yet, sir.

Cris. Or that could move his body more gracefully, or dance better ; you should see me, were it not i' the street——

Hor. Nor yet.

Cris. Why, I have been a reveller, and at my cloth of silver suit, and my long stocking, in my time, and will be again——

Hor. [*Aside.*] If you may be trusted,[2] sir.

Cris. And then for my singing, Hermogenes himself envies me, that is your only master of music you have in Rome.

Hor. Is your mother living, sir ?[3]

Cris. Au ! convert thy thoughts to somewhat else, I pray thee.

---

[1] This is still noticeable in Devonshire and was perhaps brought thence (with others) by Raleigh and became a fashionable word.

[2] *I.e.* By his tailor.

[3] Have you not a mother to praise you, since you praise yourself.

Hor. You have much of the mother in you, sir: your
father is dead?

Cris. Ay, I thank Jove, and my grandfather too, and
all my kinsfolks, and well composed in their urns.

Hor. The more their happiness, that rest in peace,—
Aside.] Free from th' abundant torture of thy tongue:
Would I were with them too !

Cris.   What's that, Horace?

Hor. I now remember me, sir, of a sad fate
A cunning woman, one Sabella, sung,
When in her urn she cast my destiny,
I being but a child.

Cris.   What was't, I pray thee?

Hor. She told me, I should surely never perish
By famine, poison, or the enemy's sword ;
The hectic fever, cough, or pleurisy,
Should never hurt me, nor the tardy gout :
But in my time, I should be once surprised
By a strong tedious talker, that should vex
And almost bring me to consumption.
Therefore, if I were wise, she warned me shun
All such long-winded monsters, as my bane ;
For if I could but 'scape that one discourser,
I might no doubt prove an old agèd man.—
By your leave, sir.   [*Going.*

Cris. Tut, tut ; abandon this idle humour, 'tis nothing
but melancholy. 'Fore Jove, now I think on't, I am to
appear in Court here, to answer to one that has me in
suit ; sweet Horace, go with me, this is my hour: if I
neglect it, the law proceeds against me.   Thou art familiar with these things ; prithee, if thou lov'st me, go.

Hor. Now, let me die, sir, if I know your laws ;
Or have the power to stand still half so long
In their loud[1] courts, as while a case is argued.
Besides, you know, sir, where I am to go,
And the necessity.——

---

[1] Instead of "loud" the quarto has a "significant."

Cris. 'Tis true :——   [*He meditates.*

Hor. I hope the hour of my release be come : he will,
upon this consideration, discharge me, sure.

Cris. Troth, I am doubtful, what I may best do,
whether to leave thee, or my affairs, Horace.

Hor. O Jupiter! me, sir, me, by any means; I beseech you, me, sir.

Cris. No, faith, I'll venture those now; thou shalt see
I love thee—come, Horace.

Hor. [*Aside.*] Nay, then, I am desperate :——I follow
you, sir.——[*Aside.*] 'Tis hard contending with a man
that overcomes thus.

Cris. And how deals Mecænas with thee? liberally,
ha? is he open-handed? bountiful?

Hor. He's still himself, sir.

Cris. Troth, Horace, thou art exceeding happy in thy
friends and acquaintance; they are all most choice
spirits, and of the first rank of Romans : I do not know
that poet, I protest, has used his fortune more prosperously
than thou hast. If thou wouldst bring me known to
Mecænas, I should second thy desert well; thou shouldst
find a good sure assistant of me : one that would speak
all good of thee in thy absence, and be content with the
next place, not envying thy reputation with thy patron.
Let me not live, but I think thou and I, in a small time,
should lift them all out of favour, both Virgil, Varius,
and the best of them; and enjoy him wholly to ourselves.

Hor. [*Aside.*] Gods, you do know it I can hold no
longer;——sweet Horace, go with me, this is my
This brize [1] has pricked my patience :——Sir, your silk-
enness
Clearly mistakes Mecænas and his house,
To think, there breathes a spirit beneath his roof,
Subject unto those poor affections
Of undermining envy and detraction,
Moods only proper to base grovelling minds.

———
[1] Gad-fly.

That place is not in Rome, I dare affirm,
More pure, or free from such low common evils.
There's no man grieved, that this is thought more rich,
Or this, more learned; each man hath his place,
And to his merit, his reward of grace,
Which, with a mutual love, they all embrace.

Cris. You report a wonder! 'tis scarce credible, this.

Hor. I am no torturer, to enforce you to believe it,
but it is so.

Cris. Why this inflames me with a more ardent desire
to be his, than before : but I doubt I shall find the entrance to his familiarity somewhat more than difficult,
Horace.

Hor. Tut, you'll conquer him as you have done me ;
there's no standing out against you, sir, I see that: either
your importunity, or the intimation of your good parts,
or—

Cris. Nay, I'll bribe his porter, and the grooms of his
chamber ; make his doors open to me that way first :
and then, I'll observe my times. Say he should extrude
me his house to-day ; shall I therefore desist, or let fall
my suit to-morrow ? No ; I'll attend him, follow him,
meet him i' the street, the highways, run by his coach,
never leave him. What? man hath nothing given him
in this life without much labour.

Hor. [*Aside.*] And impudence.
Archer of heaven, Phœbus, take thy bow,
And with a full-drawn shaft nail to the earth
This Python, that I may yet run hence, and live
Or, brawny Hercules, do thou come down,
And—tho' thou mak'st it up thy thirteenth labour
Rescue me from this hydra of discourse here.

[1]*Enter* FUSCUS ARISTIUS. CRISPINUS *not knowing him
stands apart.*

Ari. Horace, well met.

---

[1] Scene ii. in old eds.

Hor.   O welcome, my reliever ;
Aristius, as thou lov'st me, ransom me.

Ari. What ail'st thou, man ?

Hor.   'Death, I am seized on here
By a land remora ;[1] I cannot stir ;
Not move, but as he pleases.

Cris.   Wilt thou go, Horace ?

Hor. 'Heart! he cleaves to me like Alcides' shirt,
Tearing my flesh and sinews :[2] O, I ha' been vexed
And tortured with him, beyond forty fevers.
For Jove's sake, find some means to take me from him.

Ari. Yes, I will ; but I'll go first and tell Mecænas.

Cris. Come, shall we go ?

Ari. The jest will make his eyes run, i'faith.

Hor. Nay, Aristius !

Ari. Farewell, Horace.

Hor. 'Death ! will a leave me ? Fuscus Aristius, do
you hear ? Gods of Rome ! you said you had somewhat
to say to me, in private.

Ari. Ay, but I see you are now employed with that
gentleman : 'twere offence to trouble you ; I'll take some
fitter opportunity, farewell.   [*Exit.*

Hor. Mischief and torment ! O, my soul and heart,
How are you cramped with anguish ! Death itself
Brings not the like convulsions. O, this day,
That ever I should view thy tedious face——

Cris. Horace, what passion? what humour is this ?

Hor. Away, good prodigy, afflict me not.
A friend, and mock me thus ! Never was man
So left under the axe.——

Enter MINOS *with two* Lictors.

How now ?

Min. That's he in the embroidered hat, there, with the
ash-coloured feather : his name is Laberius Crispinus.

---

[1] The sucking-fish, about six inches in length, was in classical
times supposed to stay a ship even against storms.

[2] Probably=nerves.

Lict. Laberius Crispinus, I arrest you in the emperor's name.

Cris. Me, sir? do you arrest me?

Lict. Ay, sir, at the suit of master Minos the 'pothecary.

Hor. Thanks, great Apollo, I will not slip thy favour offered me in my escape, for my fortunes.   [*Exit hastily.*

Cris. Master Minos? I know no master Minos. Where's Horace? Horace? Horace?

Min. Sir, do not you know me?

Cris. O yes, I know you, master Minos; 'cry you mercy. But Horace? God's me, is he gone?

Min. Ay, and so would you too, if you knew how.— Officer, look to him.

Cris. Do you hear, master Minos? pray' let's be used like a man of our own fashion. By Janus, and Jupiter, I meant to have paid you next week, every drachmé. Seek not to eclipse my reputation thus vulgarly.

Min. Sir, your oaths cannot serve you, you know I have forborne you long.

Cris. I am conscious of it, sir.—Nay, I beseech you, gentlemen, do not exhale[1] me thus; remember 'tis but for sweatmeats——

Lict. Sweatmeats must have sour sauce, sir. Come along.

Cris. Sweet master Minos, I am forfeited to eternal disgrace, if you do not commiserate. Good officer, be not so officious.

[2]*Enter* TUCCA *and two* Pyrgi.

Tuc. Why, how now, my good brace of bloodhounds? whither do you drag the gentleman? you mongrels, you curs, you ban-dogs! we are captain Tucca that talk to you, you inhuman pilchers.[3]

Min. Sir, he is their prisoner.

---

[1] Drag me out.   [2] Scene iv. in old eds.
[3] Bailiffs then wore buff jerkins or pilchers, and possibly, as pilgers are fish spears, *i.e.* grains, Tucca may have punned.

Tuc. Their pestilence! What are you, sir?

Min. A citizen of Rome, sir.

Tuc. Then you are not far distant from a fool, sir.

Min. A 'pothecary, sir.

Tuc. I knew thou wast not a physician; foh! out of my nostrils, thou stink'st of lotium [1] and the syringe: away, quack-salver!—Follower, my sword.

1 *Pyr.* Here, noble leader; [*Aside.*] you'll do no harm with it, I'll trust you.

Tuc. Do you hear, you, goodman slave? Hook, ram, rogue, catchpole, loose the gentleman, or by my velvet arms——

Lict. What will you do, sir?

[*Strikes up his heels, and seizes his sword.*

Tuc. Kiss thy hand, my honourable active varlet, and embrace thee, thus.

Pyr. [*Aside to the other.*] O patient metamorphosis!

Tuc. My sword, my tall [2] rascal.

Lict. Nay, soft, sir; some wiser than some.

Tuc. What? and a wit too! By Pluto, thou must be cherished, slave; here's three drachmes for thee; hold.

Pyr. [*Aside.*] There's half his lendings gone.

Tuc. Give me.

Lict. No, sir, your first word shall stand; I'll hold all.

Tuc. Nay, but rogue :——

Lict. You would make a rescue of our prisoner, sir, you.

Tuc. I a rescue? away, inhuman varlet! Come, come, I never relish above one jest at most; do not disgust me sirrah; do not: rogue, I tell thee, rogue, do not.

Lict. How, sir! rogue?

Tuc. Ay; why, thou art not angry, rascal, art thou?

Lict. I cannot tell, sir; I am little better upon these terms.

Tuc. Ha! gods and fiends! why, dost hear? rogue, thou give me thy hand; I say unto thee, thy hand, rogue

---

[1] Latin for lotion. The syringe = enema-syringe.
[2] *I.e.* valiant.

What, dost not thou know me? not me, rogue? not captain Tucca, rogue?

Min. Come, pra' surrender the gentleman his sword, officer; we'll have no fighting here.

Tuc. What's thy name?

Min. Minos, an't please you.

Tuc. Minos? come hither, Minos; thou art a wise fellow, it seems: let me talk with thee.

Cris. Was ever wretch so wretched, as unfortunate I!

Tuc. Thou art one of the centumviri,[1] old boy, art not?

Min. No, indeed, Master captain.

Tuc. Go to, thou shalt be then: I'll ha' thee one, Minos. Take my sword from those rascals, dost thou see! go, do it; I cannot attempt with patience. What does this gentleman owe thee, little Minos?

Min. Fourscore sesterces,[2] sir.

Tuc. What? no more? Come, thou shalt release him, Minos: what, I'll be his bail, thou shalt take my word, old boy, and cashier these furies: thou shalt do't, I say, thou shalt, little Minos, thou shalt.

Cris. Yes, and as I am a gentleman and a reveller, I'll make a piece of poetry, and absolve all, within these five days.

Tuc. Come, Minos is not to learn how to use a gentleman of quality, I know:—my sword:—If he pay thee not, I will, and I must, old boy. Thou shalt be my 'pothecary too, hast good eringos,[3] Minos?

Min. The best in Rome, sir.

Tuc. Go to, then——Vermin, know the house.

Pyr. I warrant you, colonel.

Tuc. For this gentleman, Minos——

Min. I'll take your word, captain.

Tuc. Thou hast it. My sword——

---

[1] One of the minor magistrates.
[2] About thirteen shillings.
[3] Species of sea-holly held to be provocative.

Min. Yes, sir ;——But you must discharge the arrest, master Crispinus.[1]

Tuc. How, Minos? look in the gentleman's face, and but read his silence. Pay, pay ; 'tis honour, Minos.

Cris. By Jove, sweet captain, you do most infinitely endear, and oblige me to you.

Tuc. Tut, I cannot compliment, by Mars ; but Jupiter love me, as I love good words, and good clothes, and there's an end. Thou shalt give my boy that girdle and hangers,[2] when thou hast worn them a little more.

Cris. O Jupiter! captain, he shall have them now, presently :—Please you to be acceptive, young gentleman.

1st Pyr. Yes, sir, fear not ; I shall accept ; [*Aside.*] I have a pretty foolish humour of taking, if you knew all.

Tuc. Not now, you shall not take, boy.

Cris. By my truth, and earnest, but he shall, captain, by your leave.

Tuc. Nay, an a swear by his truth, and earnest, take it, boy : do not make a gent'man forsworn.

Lict. Well, sir, there is your sword ; but thank master Minos : you had not carried it as you do else.

Tuc. Minos is just, and you are knaves, and——

Lict. What say you, sir?

Tuc. Pass on, my good scoundrel, pass on, I honour thee : [*Lictors move off.*] But that I hate to have action with such base rogues as these, you should ha' seen me unrip their noses now, and have sent 'hem to the next barber's to stitching : for, do you see [*Overhearing in part, they return.*] I am a man of humour, and I do love the varlets, the honest varlets, they have wit and valour, and are indeed good profitable, [*Exeunt* Lictors.] errant rogues, as any live in an empire. [*To* CRISPINUS.] Dost thou hear, poetaster? second me.—Stand up, Minos, close, gather, yet, so ! Sir—[*Aside to 1st* PYRGUS.] thou shalt have a quarter-share, be resolute—you shall, at my

---

[1] Pay the bailiffs' fees.
[2] The straps suspendi g the swo:d and dagger.

request, take Minos by the hand here,—little Minos, I
will have it so; all friends and a health; be not inexor-
able. And thou shalt impart the wine, old boy, thou
shalt do't, little Minos, thou shalt: make us pay it in our
physic. What? we must live, and honour the gods sometimes; now Bacchus, now Comus, now Priapus; every
god a little. [HISTRIO *passes by.*] What's he that stalks
by there? boy, Pyrgus, you were best let him pass, sirrah;
do, ferret, let him pass, do.

Pyr. 'Tis a player, sir.

Tuc. A player? call him, call the lousy slave hither:
what, will he sail by, and not once strike, or vail[1] to a
man of war? ha!—Do you hear? you player, rogue,
stalker, come back here!—

Re-enter HISTRIO.

no respect to men of worship, you slave? What, you are
proud, you rascal, are you proud, ha? you grow rich, do
you? and purchase, you twopenny tear-mouth?[2] you
have FORTUNE,[3] and the good year on your side, you
stinkard? you have, you have?[4]

Hist. Nay, sweet captain, be confined to some reason;
I protest I saw you not, sir.

Tuc. You did not? where was your sight, Œdipus?
you walk with hare's eyes,[5] do you? I'll ha' 'hem glazed,
rogue; an you say the word, they shall be glazed for you:
come, we must have you turn fiddler again, slave, get a
base violin at your back, and march in a tawny coat, with
one sleeve, to Goose-fair; and then you'll know us, you'll
see us then, you will, gulch,[6] you will. Then—"Will't
please your worship to have any music, captain?"

Hist. Nay, good captain.

---

[1] Salute by lowering or doffing.   [2] The gallery price.
[3] The play-house so called. A pun.
[4] He queries it, as though his good fortune were the cause of his
(assumed) insolence.
[5] Who when awake were said to shut them.
[6] Fat glutton, probably connected with gulch filth, sediment.

Tuc. What? do you laugh, Howleglas?[1] death, you perstemptuous[2] varlet, I am none of your fellows; I have commanded a hundred and fifty[3] such rogues, I.

2nd Pyr. [*Aside.*] Ay, and most of that hundred and fifty have been leaders of a legion.[4]

Hist. If I have exhibited wrong, I'll tender satisfaction, captain.

Tuc. Say'st thou so, honest vermin! Give me thy hand, thou shalt make us a supper one of these nights.

Hist. When you please, by Jove, captain, most willingly.

Tuc. Dost thou swear? to-morrow then; say, and hold, slave. There are some of you players honest, gent'man-like scoundrels; *and suspected to ha' some wit, as well as your poets, both at drinking, and breaking of jests; and are companions for gallants.* [5] A man may skelder ye, now and then, of half a dozen shillings, or so. Dost thou not know that Pantalabus there?

Hist. No, I assure you, captain.

Tuc. Go, and be acquainted with him then; he is a gent'man, parcel-poet,[6] you slave: his father was a man of worship, I tell thee. Go, he pens high, lofty, in a new stalking strain; bigger than half the rhymers i' the town again: he was born to fill thy mouth, Minotaurus, he was; he will teach thee to tear and rand.[7] Rascal, to him, cherish his muse, go; thou hast forty—forty shillings, I mean, stinkard; give him in earnest, do, he shall write for thee, slave! If he pen for thee once, thou shalt not need to travel with thy pumps full of gravel any more, after a blind jade and a hamper, *and stalk upon boards and barrel heads to an old cracked trumpet.*

---

[1] The Saxon jester, hero of a German tale.

[2] In this use of a corruption of "presumptuous" Jonson would, it is to be supposed, set forth the ignorance and presumption of Tucca.

[3] The then number of a company.   [4] *I.e.* of lice.

[5] From "*and suspected" not in the quarto.

[6] A poet, as a parcel-gilt goblet is gold. A poet on the surface, but inwardly and truly of base metal.

[7] Query the verbal form of randy = to be noisy or obstreperous = rant.

Hist. Troth, I think I ha' not so much about me, captain.

Tuc. It's no matter; give him what thou hast, Stiff-toe; I'll give my word for the rest: though it lack a shilling or two it skills not: go, thou art an honest shifter; I'll ha' the statute repealed for thee.—Minos, I must tell thee, Minos, thou hast dejected yon gent'man's spirit exceedingly: dost observe? dost note, little Minos?

Min. Yes, sir.

Tuc. Go to then, raise, recover, do. Suffer him not to droop in prospect of a player, a rogue, a stager: put twenty into his hand—twenty sesterces I mean,—and let nobody see; go, do it—the work shall commend itself; be Minos,[1] I'll pay.

Min. Yes, forsooth, captain.

2nd Pyr. [*To 1st.*] Do not we serve a notable shark?

Tuc. And what new matters have we now afoot, sirrah, ha? I would fain come with my cockatrice[2] one day, and see a play; if I knew when there were a good bawdy one; but they say you ha' nothing but 'HUMOURS,' 'REVELS,' and 'SATIRES,'[3] that gird and fart at the time, you slave.

Hist. No, I assure you, captain, not we. They are on the other side of Tyber: we have as much ribaldry in our plays, as can be, as you would wish, captain: all the sinners i' the suburbs come and applaud our action daily.

Tuc. I hear you'll bring me o' the stage there; you'll play me, they say; I shall be presented by a sort of copper-laced scoundrels of you: life of Pluto, an you stage me, stinkard, your mansions shall sweat for't, your tabernacles, varlets, your Globes, and your Triumphs.

Hist. Not we, by Phœbus, captain: do not do us imputation without desert.

Tuc. I wu' not, my good twopenny rascal; reach me thy neuf.[4] Dost hear? what wilt thou give me a week,

---

[1] Be the just judge.
[2] Then cant for harlot.   [3] Jonson's own plays.   [4] Fist.

for my brace of beagles here, my little point-trussers ?[1]
you shall ha' them act among ye.—Sirrah, you, pronounce.—Thou shalt hear him speak in King Darius'
doleful strain.

1st Pyr. "O doleful days!   O direful deadly dump!
O wicked world, and worldly wickedness!
How can I hold my fist from crying thump,
In rue of this right rascal wretchedness!"

Tuc. In an amorous vein now, sirrah : peace!

1st Pyr. "O, she is wilder, and more hard, withal,
Than beast, or bird, or tree, or stony wall.
Yet might she love me, to uprear her state :
Ay, but perhaps, she hopes some nobler mate.
Yet might she love me to content her sire :
Ay, but her reason masters her desire.
Yet might she love me as her beauty's thrall :
Ay, but I fear, she cannot love at all."[2]

> [DEMETRIUS *enters during this or during the*
> Darius' *bit.*

Tuc. Now, the horrible, fierce soldier, you, sirrah.

2nd Pyr. "What! will I brave thee? ay, and beard
thee too ;
A Roman spirit scorns to bear a brain
So full of base pusillanimity."

Hist. Excellent!

Tuc. Nay, thou shalt see that, shall ravish thee anon :
prick up thine ears, stinkard.—The ghost, boys!

1st Pyr. *Vindicta.*

2nd Pyr. *Timoria.*

1st Pyr. *Vindicta.*

2nd Pyr. *Timoria.*

1st Pyr. *Veni.*

2nd Pyr. *Veni.*

Tuc. Now thunder, sirrah, you, the rumbling player.

---

[1] Tiers of his tags (used instead of buttons).
[2] This is culled from the beginning of Act ii. of *Hieronimo is
mad again.*   The sources of those unnoticed are unknown.

2nd Pyr. Ay, but somebody must cry 'Murder!' then, in a small voice.

Tuc. Your fellow-sharer there, shall do't; cry, sirrah, cry.

1st Pyr. "Murder, murder!

2nd Pyr. Who calls out murder? lady, was it you?"[1]

Dem. and Hist. O, admirable good, I protest.

Tuc. Sirrah, boy, brace your drum a little straiter, and do the t'other fellow there, he in the——what sha' call him——and 'yet, stay' too.[2]

2nd Pyr. "Nay, an thou dalliest, then I am thy foe,
And fear shall force, what friendship cannot win;
Thy death shall bury what thy life conceals.
Villain! thou diest, for more respecting her——

1st Pyr. O stay, my lord.

2nd Pyr. Than me:
Yet speak the truth, and I will guerdon thee;
But if thou dally once again, thou diest."

Tuc. Enough of this, boy.

2nd Pyr. Why, then lament therefore:[3] damned be
    thy guts
Unto king Pluto's Hell, and princely Erebus;
For sparrows must have food——

Hist. Pray, sweet captain, let one of them do a little of a lady.

Tuc. O! he will make thee eternally enamoured of him, there:—do, sirrah, do: 'twill allay your fellow's fury a little.

1st Pyr. "Master, mock on: the scorn thou givest me,
'Pray Jove some lady may return on thee."

2nd Pyr. No: you shall see me do the Moor: Master, lend me your scarf a little.

---

[1] From Chapman's *Blind Beggar of Alexandria*, near the end. —*Daniel.*

[2] This "yet stay" appears to me to be his attempt to remember the passage. We have in it "*O stay*," and close to it, "*Yet* speak."

[3] Pistol quotes these words, but this speech seems to be from the play whence that "Ancient" drew some of his phrases.

Tuc. Here, 'tis at thy service, boy.

2nd Pyr. You, Master Minos, hark hither a little.

[*Exit with* MINOS.

Tuc. How dost like him? art not rapt, art not tickled now? dost not applaud, rascal? dost not applaud?

Hist. Yes: what will you ask for 'hem a week, captain.

Tuc. No, you mangonizing[1] slave, I will not part from 'hem; you'll sell them for ingles, you: let's ha' good cheer to-morrow night at supper, stalker, and then we'll talk; good capon, and plover, do you hear, sirrah? and do not bring your eating player with you there; I cannot away with him: he will eat a leg of mutton while I am in my porridge, the lean Poluphagus, his belly is like Barathrum; he looks like a midwife in man's apparel, the slave: nor the villanous-out-of-tune fiddler, Ænobarbus, bring not him. What hast thou there? six and thirty, ha?

Hist. No, here's all I have, captain, some five and twenty: pray, sir, will you present, and accommodate[2] it unto the gentleman? for mine own part, I am a mere stranger to his humour: besides, I have some business invites me hence, with master Asinius Lupus, the tribune.

Tuc. Well, go thy ways; pursue thy projects, let me alone with this design; my Poetaster shall make thee a play, and thou shalt be a man of good parts in it. But stay, let me see: do not bring your Æsop, your politician; unless you can ram up his mouth with cloves: the slave smells ranker than some sixteen dunghills, and is seventeen times more rotten. Marry, you may bring Frisker, my zany: he's a good skipping swaggerer; and your fat fool there, my mango:[3] bring him too: but let him not beg rapiers nor scarfs, in his over-familiar play-ing face, nor roar out his barren bold jests with a tor-

---

[1] *I.e.*, slave dealing.

[2] Then a cant fashionable word, applied in any way the speaker thought fit.

[3] Pander. These actors of the rival house or houses were then, of course, known to all. "Frisker, the good skipping" is not improbably Kemp, who in 1600 skipped his morris to Norwich.

menting laughter, between drunk and dry. Do you hear, Stiff-toe? give him warning, admonition, to forsake his saucy glavering grace, and his goggle eye; it does not become him, sirrah; tell him so. I have stood up and defended you, I, to gent'men, when you have been said to prey upon puisnes,[1] and honest citizens, for socks or buskins; or when they ha' called you usurers or brokers, or said you were able to help to a piece of flesh——I have sworn, I did not think so. Nor that you were the common retreats for punks decayed i' their practice. I cannot believe it of you.

Hist. 'Thank you, captain: Jupiter and the rest of the gods confine your modern delights, without disgust.

Tuc. Stay, thou shalt see the Moor, ere thou goest.—— What's he, with the arms there, that salutes us out of his cloak, like a motion,[2] ha?

Hist. O, sir, his doublet's a little decayed; he is otherways a very simple honest fellow, sir, one Demetrius, a dresser of plays about the town, here; we have hired him to abuse Horace, and bring him in, in a play, with all his gallants: as Tibullus, Mecænas, Cornelius Gallus, and the rest.

Tuc. And why so, stinkard?

Hist. O, it will get us a huge deal of money, captain, and we have need on't; for this winter has made us all poorer than so many starved snakes: nobody comes at us; not a gentleman, nor a——

Tuc. But you know nothing by him, do you, to make a play of?

Hist. Faith, not much, captain; but our author will devise that, that shall serve in some sort.

Tuc. Why, my Parnassus here shall help him, if thou wilt: can thy author do it impudently enough?

Hist. O, I warrant you, captain, and spitefully enough too; he has one of the most overflowing rank wits in

---

[1] Freshmen, novices.
[2] Puppet.

Rome. He will slander any man that breathes, if he disgust him.

Tuc. I'll know the poor, egregious, nitty rascal; an he have these commendable qualities, I'll cherish him— stay, here comes the Tartar—I'll make a gathering for him, I, a purse, and put the poor slave in fresh rags. Tell him so to comfort him.—

[DEMETRIUS *comes forward.*

Re-enter MINOS, *with* 2nd *Pyrgus on his shoulders, and stalks as the boy acts.*

Well said, boy.

2nd Pyr. " Where art thou, boy ? Where is Calipolis ? Fight earthquakes in the entrails of the earth, And eastern whirlwinds in hellish shades ; Some foul contagion of the infected heavens Blast all the trees, and in their cursèd tops The dismal night-raven and tragic owl Breed and become forerunners of my fall !"[2]

Tuc. Well, now fare thee well, my honest pennybiter : commend me to seven-shares and a half,[3] and remember to-morrow.—If you lack a service, you shall play in my name, rascals; but you shall buy your own cloth, and I'll ha' two shares for my countenance. Let thy author stay with me.   [*Exit* HISTRIO.

Dem. Yes, sir.

Tuc. 'Twas well done, little Minos, thou didst stalk well; forgive me that I said thou stunk'st, Minos ; 'twas the savour of a poet, I met sweating in the street, hangs yet in my nostrils.

Cris. Who, Horace ?

Tuc. Ay, he; dost thou know him ?

Cris. O, he forsook me most barbarously, I protest.

Tuc. Hang him, fusty satyr, he smells all goat ; he

---

[1] Assayed, done.   [2] Peele's *Alcazar*, ii., 3.
[3] The principal or manager. See preface to Crashaw's " Poems," 1670.

carries a ram, under his arm-holes, the slave : I am the worse when I see him.—[*Aside to* CRISPINUS.] Did not Minos impart ?

Cris. Yes, here are twenty drachmes he did convey.

Tuc. Well said, keep 'hem, we'll share anon ; come, little Minos.

Cris. Faith, captain, I'll be bold to show you a mistress of mine, a jeweller's wife, a gallant, as we go along.

Tuc. There spoke my Genius. Minos, some of thy eringos, little Minos ; send—come hither, Parnassus, I must ha' thee familiar with my little locust here, 'tis a good vermin, they say.[1]—[HORACE *and* TREBATIUS *pass over the stage.*]—See, here's Horace, and old Trebatius, the great lawyer, in his company · let's avoid him now, he is too well seconded.   [*Exeunt.*

SCENE II.[2]

Hor., Sat. 1. *Lib.* 2.

Hor. There are, to whom I seem excessive sour,
And past a satire's law t' extend my power :
Others that think whatever I have writ
Wants pith, and matter to eternise it ;
And that they could, in one day's light, disclose
A thousand verses, such as I compose.
What shall I do, Trebatius ? say.

Treb.   Surcease.

Hor. And shall my Muse admit no more increase ?

Treb. So I advise.

Hor.   An ill death let me die,
If 'twere not best ; but sleep avoids mine eye,
And I use these, lest nights should tedious seem.

Treb. Rather contend to sleep, and live like them,

---

[1] From this to the end of the act is not in quarto.
[2] Scene v. in old eds.

That, holding golden sleep in special price,
Rubbed with sweet oils, swim silver Tyber thrice,
And ev'ry even with neat wine steepèd be :
Or, if such love of writing ravish thee,
Then dare to sing unconquered Cæsar's deeds ;
Who cheers such actions, with abundant meeds.

Hor. That, father, I desire ; but when I try,
I feel defects in ev'ry faculty :
Nor is't a labour fit for ev'ry pen,
To paint the horrid troops of armèd men,
The lances burst,[1] in Gallia's slaughtered forces ;
Or wounded Parthians, tumbled from their horses :
Great Cæsar's wars cannot be fought with words.

Treb. Yet, what his virtue in his peace affords,
His fortitude, and justice thou canst show ;
As wise Lucilius honoured Scipio.

Hor. Of that, my powers shall suffer no neglect,
When such slight labours may aspire respect :
But, if I watch not a most chosen time,
The humble words of Flaccus cannot climb
Th' attentive ear of Cæsar ; nor must I
With less observance shun gross flattery :
For he, reposèd safe in his own merit,
Spurns back the gloses of a fawning spirit.

Treb. But, how much better would such accents sound,
Than with a sad and serious verse to wound
Pantolabus, railing in his saucy jests ?
Or Nomentanus spent in riotous feasts ?
" In satires, each man, though untouched, complains
As he were hurt ; and hates such biting strains."

Hor. What shall I do ?   Milonius shakes his heels
In ceaseless dances, when his brain once feels
The stirring fervour of the wine ascend ;
And that his eyes false numbers apprehend.
Castor his horse, Pollux loves handy-fights ;
A thousand heads, a thousand choice delights.

[1] Used instead of " broke," as in Spenser, *F. Q.*, iv., 4, 41.

My pleasure is, in feet my words to close,
As—both our better—old Lucilius does:
He, as his trusty friends, his books did trust
With all his secrets; nor, in things unjust,
Or actions lawful, ran to other men:
So, that the old man's life described, was seen,
As in a votive table, in his lines:
And to his steps my genius inclines,
Lucanian, or Apulian, I[1] not whether,
For the Venusian colony ploughs either;
Sent thither, when the Sabines were forced thence—
As old fame sings—to give the place defence
'Gainst such as, seeing it empty, might make road
Upon the empire; or there fix abode:
Whether th' Apulian borderer it were,
Or the Lucanian violence they fear.—
But this my style no living man shall touch,
If first I be not forced by base reproach;
But, like a sheathèd sword, it shall defend
My innocent life; for why should I contend[2]
To draw it out, when no malicious thief
Robs my good name, the treasure of my life?[3]
O Jupiter, let it with rust be eaten,
Before it touch, or insolently threaten
The life of any with the least disease;
So much I love, and woo a gen'ral peace.
But, he that wrongs me, better, I proclaim,
He never had assayed to touch my fame.
For he shall weep, and walk, with ev'ry tongue
Throughout the city, infamously sung.
Servius, the prætor, threats the laws, and urn,
If any at his deeds repine or spurn;
The witch, Canidia, that Albutius got,
Denounceth witchcraft, where she loveth not:

---

[1] Gifford, unnecessarily making an alexandrine, inserts "know," a word understood by the tone and gesture of the speaker.
[2] Latinate, as just before; strain or strive.
[3] Compare *Othello* iii., 3, 156, &c.

Thurius, the judge, doth thunder worlds of ill,
To such as strive with his judicial will.
" All men affright their foes in what they may,
Nature commands it, and men must obey."
    Observe with me : " The wolf his tooth doth use,
The bull his horn.   And who doth this infuse,
But nature?"   There's luxurious Scæva ; trust
His long-lived mother with him ; his so just
And scrupulous right-hand no mischief will ;
No more than with his heel a wolf will kill,
Or ox with jaw : marry, let him alone
With tempered poison to remove the crone.
But briefly, if to age I destined be,
Or that quick death's black wings environ me ;
If rich or poor ; at Rome ; or fate command
I shall be banished to some other land ;
What hue soever my whole state shall bear,
I will write satires still, in spite of fear.
    Treb. Horace, I fear thou draw'st no lasting breath ;
And that some great man's friend will be thy death.
    Hor. What? when the man that first did satirize
Durst pull the skin over the ears of vice,
And make, who stood in outward fashion clear,
Give place, as foul within ; shall I forbear ?
Did Lælius, or the man so great with fame,
That from sacked Carthage fetched his worthy name,
Storm, that Lucilius did Metellus pierce?
Or bury Lupus quick[1] in famous verse ?
Rulers, and subjects, by whole tribes he checkt,
But virtue, and her friends did still protect :
And when from sight, or from the judgment-seat,
The virtuous Scipio and wise Lælius met,
Unbraced, with him in all light sports they shared,
Till their most frugal suppers were prepared.
Whate'er I am, though both for wealth, and wit
Beneath Lucilius I am pleased to sit ;

               [1] **Alive.**

Yet Envy, spite of her empoisoned breast,
Shall say, I live in grace here with the best :
And seeking in weak trash to make her wound,
Shall find me solid, and her teeth unsound :
'Less learned Trebatius' censure disagree.

   Treb. No, Horace ; I of force must yield to thee;
Only take heed, as being advised by me,
Lest thou incur some danger : better pause,
Than rue thy ign'rance of the sacred laws ;
There's justice, and great action may be sued
'Gainst such, as wrong men's fame with verses lewd.

   Hor. Ay, with lewd verses, such as libels be,
And aimed at persons of good quality.
I rev'rence and adore that just decree :
But if they shall be sharp, yet modest rhymes,
That spare men's persons, and but tax their crimes,
Such, shall in open court find current pass,
Were Cæsar judge, and with the maker's grace.

   Treb. Nay, I'll add more; if thou thyself being clear,
Shalt tax in person, a man fit to bear
Shame and reproach, his suit shall quickly be
Dissolved in laughter, and thou thence sit free.

ACT THE FOURTH.

SCENE I.—*A Room in* ALBIUS'S *House.*

Enter CHLOE, CYTHERIS, *and* Attendants.

HLOE. But, sweet lady, say : am I well enough attired for the court, in sadness?[1]

Cyth. Well enough? excellent well, sweet Mistress Chloe ; this strait-bodied city attire, I can tell you, will stir a courtier's blood, more than the finest loose sacks the ladies used to be put in ; and then you are as well jewelled as any of them ; your ruff and linen about you is much more pure than theirs : and for your beauty, I can tell you, there's many of them would defy the painter, if they could change with you. Marry, the worst is, you must look to be envied, and endure a few court-frumps for it.

Chloe. O, God, madam, I shall buy them too cheap !—Give me my muff, and my dog there.—And will the ladies be any thing familiar with me, think you?

Cyth. O Juno ! why you shall see 'hem flock about you with their puff wings,[2] and ask you where you bought your lawn? and what you paid for it? who starches you? and entreat you to help 'hem to some pure laundress, out of the city.

Chloe. O Cupid !—Give me my fan, and my mask too : —and will the lords, and the poets there, use one well too, lady?

---

[1] Soberness.
[2] Shoulder-wings, worn, with a difference, by both sexes.

Cyth. Doubt not of that : you shall have kisses from
them, go pit-pat, pit-pat, pit-pat upon your lips, as thick as
stones out of slings at the assault of a city.   And then
your ears will be so furred with the breath of their com-
pliments, that you cannot catch cold of your head, if
you would, in three winters after.

Chloe. Thank you, sweet lady.   O heaven ! and how
must one behave herself amongst 'hem ?   You know all.

Cyth. Faith, impudently enough, Mistress Chloe, and
well enough.   Carry not too much under thought betwixt yourself and them ; nor your city-mannerly word,
'forsooth,' use it not too often in any case ; but plain,
'Ay, madam,' and 'no, madam :' nor never say, 'your
lordship,' nor 'your honour :' but, 'you,' and 'you, my
lord,' and 'my lady :' the other they count too simple
and too mincitive.[1]   And though they desire to kiss
heaven with their titles, yet they will count them fools
that give them too humbly.

Chloe. O intolerable, Jupiter ! by my troth, lady, I
would not for a world but you had lain in my house ;
and, i' faith, you shall not pay a farthing for your board,
nor your chambers.

Cyth. O, sweet Mistress Chloe.

Chloe. I'faith you shall not, lady, nay, good lady, do
not offer it.

Enter GALLUS *and* TIBULLUS.[2]

Gal. Come, where be these ladies ?—By your leave,
bright stars, this gentleman and I are come to man you
to court ; where your late kind entertainment is now to
be requited with a heavenly banquet.

Cyth. A heavenly banquet, Gallus ?

Gal. No less, my dear Cytheris.

Tib. That were not strange, lady, if the epithet were
only given for the company invited thither ; your self
and this fair gentlewoman.

---

[1] Here apparently = making the users of such too small.
[2] Scene ii. in old eds.

Chloe. Are we invited to court, sir?

Tib. You are, lady, by the great princess Julia; who longs to greet you with any favours, that may worthily make you an often courtier.

Chloe. In sincerity, I thank her, sir. You have a coach, ha' you not?

Tib. The princess hath sent her own, lady.

Chloe. O Venus! that's well: I do long to ride in a coach most vehemently.

Cyth. But, sweet Gallus, pray you resolve me why you give that heavenly praise, to this earthly banquet?

Gal. Because, Cytheris, it must be celebrated by the heavenly powers: all the Gods and Goddesses will be there; to two of which, you two must be exalted.

Chloe. A pretty fiction, in truth.

Cyth. A fiction indeed, Chloe, and fit for the fit of a poet.

Gal. Why, Cytheris, may not poets (from whose divine spirits all the honours of the Gods have been deduced) entreat so much honour of the Gods, to have their divine presence at a poetical banquet?

Cyth. Suppose that no fiction; yet, where are your habilities to make us two, Goddesses at your feast?

Gal. Who knows not, Cytheris, that the sacred breath of a true poet can blow any virtuous humanity, up to deity?

Tib. To tell you the female truth—which is the simple truth—ladies; and to show that poets, in spite of the world, are able to deify themselves: at this banquet, to which you are invited, we intend to assume the figures of the Gods; and to give our several loves the forms of Goddesses. Ovid will be Jupiter; the princess Julia, Juno; Gallus here, Apollo; you Cytheris, Pallas; I will be Bacchus; and my love Plautia, Ceres: and to install you, and your husband, fair Chloe, in honours equal with ours, you shall be a Goddess, and your husband a God.

Chloe. A God?—O my Gods!

Tib. A God, but a lame God, lady; for he shall be
Vulcan, and you Venus: and this will make our banquet
no less than heavenly.

Chloe. In sincerity, it will be sugared.   Good Jove,
what a pretty foolish thing it is to be a poet! but hark
you, sweet Cytheris;   could they not possibly leave out
my husband? methinks a body's husband does not so
well at court; a body's friend, or so—but, husband! 'tis
like your clog to your marmoset, for all the world, and
the heavens.

Cyth. Tut, never fear, Chloe: your husband will be
left without in the lobby, or the great chamber, when you
shall be put in, i' the closet, by this lord, and by that lady.

Chloe. Nay, then I am certified; he shall go.

                    Enter HORACE.[1]

Gal. Horace! welcome.

Hor. Gentlemen, hear you the news?

Tib. What news, my Quintus!

Hor. Our melancholic friend, Propertius,
Hath closed himself, up in his Cynthia's tomb;
And will by no entreaties be drawn thence.

Enter ALBIUS, *introducing* CRISPINUS *and* DEMETRIUS,
              followed by TUCCA.

Alb. Nay, good Master Crispinus, 'pray you bring near
the gentleman.

Hor. Crispinus?   Hide me, good Gallus: Tibullus,
shelter me.

Cris. Make your approach, sweet captain.

Tib. What means this, Horace?

Hor. I am surprised again, farewell.

Gal. Stay, Horace.

Hor. What, and be tired on[2] by yond' vulture! No:
Phœbus defend me!   [*Exit hastily.*

---

    [1] Scene iii. in old eds.   [2] Eagerly seized on.

Tib.   'Slight, I hold my life
This same is he, met him in Holy-street.

Gal. Troth, 'tis like enough.—This act of Propertius
relisheth very strange with me.

Tuc. By thy leave, my neat scoundrel : what, is this
the mad boy you talked on ?

Cris. Ay, this is master Albius, captain.

Tuc. Give me thy hand, Agamemnon ; we hear abroad
thou art the Hector of citizens : what sayest thou ? are
we welcome to thee, noble Neoptolemus ?

Alb. Welcome, captain ? by Jove, and all the Gods i'
the Capitol——

Tuc. No more, we conceive thee. Which of these is
thy wedlock,[1] Menelaus ? thy Helen ? thy Lucrece ? that
we may do her honour, mad boy.

Cris. She i' the little fine dressing, sir, is my mistress.

Alb. For fault of a better, sir.

Tuc. A better ? profane rascal ! I cry thee mercy, my
good scroyle,[2] was't thou ?

Alb. No harm, captain.

Tuc. She is a Venus, a Vesta, a Melpomene :—come
hither, Penelope ; what's thy name, Iris ?

Chloe. My name is Chloe, sir ; I am a gentlewoman.

Tuc. Thou art in merit to be an empress, Chloe, for
an eye, and a lip ; thou hast an emperor's nose : kiss me
again : 'tis a virtuous punk ; so. Before Jove, the Gods
were a sort of goslings, when they suffered so sweet a
breath to perfume the bed of a stinkard : thou hadst ill
fortune, Thisbe ; the Fates were infatuate, they were,
punk ; they were.

Chloe. That's sure, sir : let me crave your name, I pray
you, sir.

Tuc. I am known by the name of captain Tucca, punk ;
the noble Roman, punk : a gentleman, and a commander,
punk.

---

[1] A Latinism then in use for " wife."
[2] Scab.

Chloe. In good time : a gentleman, and a commander?
that's as good as a poet, methinks.

Cris. A pretty instrument! It's my cousin Cytheris'
viol this, is't not?

Cyth. Nay, play cousin; it wants but such a voice,
and hand to grace it, as yours is.

Cris. Alas, cousin, you are merrily inspired.

Cyth. 'Pray you play, if you love me.

Cris. Yes, cousin; you know, I do not hate you.

Tib. A most subtile wench! how she hath baited him
with a viol yonder, for a song!

Cris. Cousin, 'pray you call Mistress Chloe; she shall
hear an essay of my poetry.

Tuc. I'll call her.—Come hither, cockatrice : here's
one, will set thee up, my sweet punk; set thee up.

Chloe. Are you a puet[1] so soon, sir?

Alb. Wife, mum.

SONG.

Love is blind, and a wanton;
  In the whole world, there is scant-[2]
    One such another :
      No, not his mother.
He hath plucked her doves and sparrows,
  To feather his sharp arrows,
    And alone prevaileth,
      Whilst sick Venus waileth.
But if Cypris once recover
  The wag; it shall behove her
    To look better to him :
      Or she will undo him.

Alb. O, most odoriferous music

Tuc. A, ha! stinkard. Another Orpheus, you slave,

---

[1] So in quarto and folios ; a peewit, Jonson's sneering pun.

[2] To make rhyme Gifford prints "scant one," but the metres,
as also the quarto and folios show that Jonson meant to make his
adversary thus err as no true poet.

another Orpheus ! an Arion, riding on the back of a dolphin, rascal !

Gal. Have you a copy of this ditty, sir ?

Cris. Master Albius has.

Alb. Ay, but in truth they are my wife's verses ; I must not show 'hem.

Tuc. Show 'hem, bankrupt, show 'hem ; they have salt in 'hem, and will brook the air, stinkard.

Gal. How ? " To his bright mistress Canidia ? "

Cris. Ay, sir, that's but a borrowed name ; as Ovid's Corinna, or Propertius his Cynthia, or your Nemesis, or Delia, Tibullus.

Gal. It's the name of Horace his witch, as I remember.

Tib. Why, the ditty's all borrowed ! 'tis Horace's : hang him, plagiary !

Tuc. How ? he borrowed of Horace ? he shall pawn himself to ten brokers[1] first.   Do you hear, Poetasters ? I know you to be men of worship——He shall write with Horace, for a talent : and let Mecænas, and his whole college of critics take his part : thou shalt do't, young Phœbus ; thou shalt, Phaeton ; thou shalt.

Dem. Alas, sir, Horace ! he is a mere sponge ; nothing but Humours, and observation ; he goes up and down sucking from every society, and when he comes home, squeezes himself dry again.   I know him, I.

Tuc. Thou say'st true, my poor poetical Fury, he will pen all he knows. A sharp thorny-toothed satirical rascal, fly him ; he carries hay in his horn :[2] he will sooner lose his best friend, than his least jest.   What he once drops upon paper, against a man, lives eternally to upbraid him in the mouth of every slave, tankard-bearer, or waterman ; not a bawd, or a boy that comes from the bake-house, but shall point at him : 'tis all dog, and scorpion ; he carries poison in his teeth, and a sting in his tail.   Fough ! body of Jove ! I'll have the slave whipt one of these days

---

[1] Shows that brokers were also pawnbrokers.
[2] As did dangerous cattle.

for his Satires, and his Humours, by one cashiered clerk or another.

Cris. We'll undertake him, captain.

Dem. Ay, and tickle him i'faith, for his arrogancy, and his impudence, in commending his own things; and for his translating: I can trace him, i'faith. O, he is the most open fellow living; I had as lieve as a new suit I were at it.

Tuc. Say no more then, but do it; 'tis the only way to get thee a new suit; sting him, my little newts; I'll give you instructions: I'll be your intelligencer; we'll all join, and hang upon him like so many horse-leeches, the players and all. We shall sup together, soon; and then we'll conspire, i'faith.

Gal. O, that Horace had stayed still here!

Tib. So would not I; for both these would have turned Pythagoreans then.

Gal. What, mute?

Tib. Ay, as fishes, i'faith :—come, ladies, shall we go?

Cyth. We await you, sir. But mistress Chloe asks, if you have not a God to spare, for this gentleman.

Gal. Who, captain Tucca?

Cyth. Ay, he.

Gal. Yes, if we can invite him along, he shall be Mars.

Chloe. Has Mars any thing to do with Venus?

Tib. O, most of all, lady.

Chloe. Nay, then I pray' let him be invited: and what shall Crispinus be?

Tib. Mercury, mistress Chloe.

Chloe. Mercury? that's a poet, is't?

Gal. No, lady, but somewhat inclining that way; he is a Herald at arms.[1]

Chloe. A herald at arms? good; and Mercury? pretty: he has to do with Venus too?

Tib. A little with her face, lady; or so.[2]

---

[1] A hit at their invention of pedigrees.
[2] Quicksilver in cosmetics.

Chloe. 'Tis very well ; pray, let us go, I long to be at it.

Cyth. Gentlemen, shall we pray your companies along?

Cris. You shall not only pray, but prevail, lady.—
Come, sweet captain.

Tuc. Yes, I follow :—but thou must not talk of this
now, my little bankrupt.

Alb. Captain, look here ; mum.

Dem. I'll go write, sir.

Tuc. Do, do, stay : there's a drachme to purchase
ginger-bread for thy muse.   [*Exeunt.*

SCENE II.[1]—*A Room in* LUPUS'S *House.*

Enter LUPUS, HISTRIO, *and* LICTORS.

Lup. Come, let us talk here ; here we may be private :
—shut the door, lictor.—You are a player, you say

Hist. Ay, an't please your worship.

Lup. Good ; and how are you able to give this intelligence.

Hist. Marry, sir, they directed a letter to me, and my
fellow-sharers.

Lup. Speak lower, you are not now i' your theatre,
stager :—my sword, knave.—They directed a letter to you,
and your fellow-sharers : forward.

Hist. Yes, sir ; to hire some of our properties ; as a
sceptre and a crown for Jove ; and a caduceus for Mercury ; and a petasus————

Lup. Caduceus ? and petasus ? let me see your letter.
This is a conjuration ; a conspiracy, this. Quickly, on
with my buskins ;—I'll act a tragedy, i'faith. Will nothing
but our Gods serve these poets to profane—dispatch !—
Player, I thank thee. The emperor shall take knowledge
of thy good service. [*A knocking within.*] Who's there

———
[1] Scene iv. in old eds.

now? Look, knave. [*Exit* Lictor.] "A crown and a sceptre!" this is good rebellion, now.

Re-enter Lictor.

Lic. 'Tis your 'pothecary, sir, master Minos.

Lup. What tell'st thou me of 'pothecaries, knave? Tell him, I have affairs of state in hand; I can talk to no 'pothecaries now. [*Muses for a moment or two.*] Heart of me! Stay the 'pothecary there. [*Muses for a little while.*] You shall see, I have finished out a cunning piece of plot now: they have had some intelligence, that their project is discovered, and now have they dealt with my 'pothecary, to poison me; 'tis so; knowing that I meant to take physic to-day: as sure as death, 'tis there. Jupiter, I thank thee, that thou hast yet made me so much of a politician.

Enter MINOS.

You are welcome, sir; take the potion from him there; I have an antidote more than you wot of, sir; throw it on the ground there: so! Now fetch in the dog; and yet we cannot tarry to try experiments now: arrest him; —you shall go with me, sir; I'll tickle you, 'pothecary; I'll give you a glister, i'faith.—Have I the letter? ay, 'tis here.—Come, your fasces, lictors: the half pikes and the halberds, take them down from the Lares[1] there. Player, assist me.

Enter MECÆNAS *and* HORACE.

Mec. Whither now, Asinius Lupus, with this armory?

Lup. I cannot talk now; I charge you assist me: treason! treason!

Hor. How! treason?

Lup. Ay: if you love the emperor, and the state, follow me. [*Exeunt.*

---

[1] Images of the tutelary ancestors of the family.

SCENE III.[1]—*An Apartment in the Palace.*

Enter OVID, JULIA, GALLUS, CYTHERIS, TIBULLUS,
PLAUTIA, ALBIUS, CHLOE, TUCCA, CRISPINUS, HER-
MOGENES, Pyrgus, *characteristically habited, as gods and
goddesses.*

Ovid. Gods and goddesses, take your several seats.
Now, Mercury, move your caduceus, and in Jupiter's
name, command silence.

Cris. In the name of Jupiter ; silence.

Her. The crier of the court hath too clarified[2] a voice.

Gal. Peace, Momus.

Ovid. Oh, he is the god of reprehension ; let him alone.
'Tis his office.   Mercury, go forward, and proclaim, after
Phœbus, our high pleasure, to all the deities that shall
partake this high banquet.

Cris. Yes, sir.

Gal. The great god, Jupiter,——[*Here, and at every
break, Crispinus repeats aloud the words of Gallus.*]——Of
his licentious goodness,——Willing to make this feast no
fast——From any manner of pleasure ;——Nor to bind
any god or goddess——To be any thing the more god
or goddess, for their names :——He gives them all free
licence——To speak no wiser than persons of baser titles ;
——And to be nothing better, than common men, or
women.——And therefore no god——Shall need to keep
himself more strictly to his goddess——Than any man
does to his wife :——Nor any goddess——Shall need to
keep herself more strictly to her god——Than any woman
does to her husband.——But, since it is no part of wisdom,
——In these days, to come into bonds ;——It shall be
lawful for every lover——to break loving oaths,——To
change their lovers, and make love to others,——As the
heat of every one's blood,——And the spirit of our nectar, shall inspire.——And Jupiter save Jupiter !

Tib. So ; now we may play the fools, by authority.

---

[1] Scene v. in old eds.   [2] He insinuates "too thin."

Her. To play the fool by authority, is wisdom.

Jul. Away with your mattery sentences, Momus; they are too grave and wise for this meeting.

Ovid. Mercury, give our jester a stool, let him sit by; and reach him one of our cates.

Tuc. Dost hear, mad Jupiter? we'll have it enacted, ' he that speaks the first wise word, shall be made cuckold.' What say'st thou? I'st not a good motion?

Ovid. Deities, are you all agreed?

All. Agreed, great Jupiter.

Alb. I have read in a book, that to play the fool wisely, is high wisdom.

Gal. How now, Vulcan! will you be the first wizard?[1]

Ovid. Take his wife, Mars, and make him cuckold quickly.

Tuc. Come, cockatrice.

Chloe. No, let me alone with him, Jupiter:—I'll make you take heed, sir, while you live again; if there be twelve in a company, that you be not the wisest of 'hem.

Alb. No more; I will not indeed, wife, hereafter; I'll be here;—mum.[2]

Ovid. Fill us a bowl of nectar, Ganymede: we will drink to our daughter Venus.

Gal. Look to your wife, Vulcan: Jupiter begins to court her.

Tib. Nay, let Mars look to it: Vulcan must do, as Venus does, bear.

Tuc. Sirrah, boy; catamite: Look you play Ganymede well now, you slave. Do not spill your nectar; carry your cup even: so! You should have rubbed your face with whites of eggs, you rascal; till your brows had shone like our sooty brother's here, as sleek as a horn-book:[3] or ha' steeped your lips in wine, till you made

---

[1] *I.e.*, wise man.

[2] After an expressive pause, he says "Mum," placing his finger on his lips.

[3] A primer-sheet covered with horn.

them so plump, that Juno might have been jealous of
'hem.—Punk, kiss me, punk.

Ovid. Here, daughter Venus, I drink to thee.

Chloe. Thank you, good father Jupiter.

Tuc. Why, Mother Juno! Gods and fiends! what,
wilt thou suffer this ocular temptation?

Tib. Mars is enraged, he looks big, and begins to stut
for anger.

Her. Well played, Captain Mars.

Tuc. Well said, minstrel Momus: I must put you in,
must I? when will you be in good fooling of yourself,
fidler? never?

Her. O, 'tis our fashion to be silent, when there is a
better fool in place, ever.

Tuc. Thank you, rascal.

Ovid. Fill to our daughter Venus, Ganymede, who
fills her father with affection.

Jul. Wilt thou be ranging, Jupiter, before my face?

Ovid. Why not, Juno? why should Jupiter stand in
awe of thy face, Juno?

Jul. Because it is thy wife's face, Jupiter.

Ovid. What, shall a husband be afraid of his wife's
face? will she paint it so horribly? We are a king, cotquean,[1] and we will reign in our pleasures; and we will
cudgel thee to death, if thou find fault with us.

Jul. I will find fault with thee, king cuckold-maker:
what, shall the king of gods turn the king of good-fellows,
and have no fellow in wickedness? This makes our
poets, that knows our profaneness, live as profane as we:
By my godhead, Jupiter, I will join with all the other
Gods here; bind thee hand and foot, throw thee down
into[2] earth and make a poor poet of thee if thou abuse
me thus.

Gal. A good smart-tongued goddess, a right Juno!

Ovid. Juno, we will cudgel thee, Juno:[3] we told

---

[1] Masculine hussy. [2] The second folio has, "the" earth.
[3] Jupiter did so serve Juno (Hera) when she conspired against him.

thee so yesterday, when thou wert jealous of us for Thetis.

Pyr. Nay, to-day she had me in inquisition too.

Tuc. Well said, my fine Phrygian fry; inform, inform. Give me some wine, king of heralds, I may drink to my cockatrice.

Ovid. No more, Ganymede,—we will cudgel thee, Juno: by Styx we will.

Jul. Ay, 'tis well; Gods may grow impudent in iniquity, and they must not be told of it——

Ovid. Yea, we will knock our chin against our breast, and shake thee out of Olympus, into an oyster-boat, fo thy scolding.

Jul. Your nose is not long enough to do it, Jupiter, if all thy strumpets thou hast among the stars took thy part. And there is never a star in thy forehead but shall be a horn, if thou persist to abuse me.

Cris. A good jest, i'faith.

Ovid. We tell thee, thou angerest us, cotquean; and we will thunder thee in pieces, for thy cotqueanity.

Cris. Another good jest.

Alb. O, my hammers, and my Cyclops! This boy fills not wine enough to make us kind enough to one another.

Tuc. Nor thou hast not collied[1] thy face enough, stinkard.

Alb. I'll ply the table with nectar, and make them friends.

Her. Heaven is like to have but a lame skinker,[2] then.

Alb. "Wine and good livers[3] make true lovers:" I'll sentence them together. Here, father, here, mother, for shame, drink yourselves drunk, and forget this dissension; you two should cling together before our faces, and give us example of unity.

Gal. O, excellently spoken, Vulcan, on the sudden!

---

[1] Blackened.   [2] A drawer of liquor.
[3] The liver was then thought to be the seat of love.

Tib. Jupiter may do well to prefer his tongue to some office, for his eloquence.

Tuc. His tongue shall be gent'emen-usher to his wit, and still go before it.

Alb. An excellent fit office!

Cris. Ay, and an excellent good jest besides.

Her. What, have you hired Mercury to cry your jests you make?

Ovid. Momus, you are envious.

Tuc. Why, you whoreson blockhead, 'tis your only block of wit in fashion, now-a-days, to applaud other folks' jests.

Her. True; with those that are not artificers themselves. Vulcan, you nod, and the mirth of the jest droops.

Pyr. He has filled nectar so long, till his brain swims in it.

Gal. What, do we nod, fellow-Gods! sound music, and let us startle our spirits with a song.

Tuc. Do, Apollo, thou art a good musician.

Gal. What says Jupiter?

Ovid. Ha? ha?

Gal. A song.

Ovid. Why, do, do, sing.

Pla. Bacchus, what say you?

Tib. Ceres?

Pla. But, to this song?

Tib. Sing, for my part.

Jul. Your belly weighs down your head, Bacchus; here's a song toward.

Tib. Begin, Vulcan.

Tib. What else, what else?

Tuc. Say, Jupiter——

Ovid. Mercury——

Cris. Ay, say, say.   [*Music*

SONG.

Alb. Wake! our mirth begins to die;
      Quicken it with tunes and wine:

Raise your notes; you're out; fie, fie!
This drowsiness is an ill sign.
We banish him the quire of gods,
That droops agen:
Then all are men,
For here's not one, but nods.

Ovid. I like not this sudden and general heaviness
amongst our godheads: 'tis somewhat ominous. Apollo,
command us louder music, and let Mercury and Momus
contend to please and revive our senses.   [*Music.*

Herm. Then, in a free and lofty strain.
Our broken tunes we thus repair;
Cris. And we answer them again,
Running division on the panting air:
Both. To celebrate this feast of sense,
As free from scandal as offence.
Herm. Here is beauty for the eye;
Cris. For the ear sweet melody.
Herm. Ambrosiac odours, for the smell!
Cris. Delicious nectar for the taste;
Both. For the touch, a lady's waist;
Which doth all the rest excel.

Ovid. Ay; this has waked us. Mercury, our herald;
go from ourself, the great god Jupiter, to the great emperor Augustus Cæsar, and command him from us, of
whose bounty he hath received his surname Augustus,
that for a thank-offering to our beneficence, he presently
sacrifice, as a dish to this banquet, his beautiful and
wanton daughter Julia: she's a curst quean, tell him;
and plays the scold behind his back; therefore let her
be sacrificed. Command him this, Mercury, in our high
name of Jupiter Altitonans.

Jul. Stay, feather-footed Mercury, and tell Augustus,
from us, the great Juno Saturnia; if he think it hard to
do, as Jupiter hath commanded him, and sacrifie his
daughter, that he had better to do so ten times, than
suffer her to love the well-nosed poet, Ovid; whom he

shall do well to whip, or cause to be whipped, about the capitol, for soothing her in her follies.

Enter Cæsar, Mecænas, Horace, Lupus, Histrio, Minos, *and* Lictors.[1]

Cæs. What sight is this? Mecænas! Horace! say? Have we our senses? do we hear? and see? Or are these but imaginary objects Drawn by our phantasy? Why speak you not? Let us do sacrifice! Are they the Gods? Reverence, amaze, and fury fight in me.

[Ovid *and the rest kneel.*

What? do they kneel? Nay, then I see 'tis true I thought impossible: Oh, impious sight! Let me divert mine eyes; the very thought Everts my soul with passion: look not, man.[2] There is a panther, whose unnatural eyes[3] Will strike thee dead: turn then, and die on her With her own death. [*Offers to kill his daughter.*

Mec. Hor. What means imperial Cæsar?

Cæs. What, would you have me let the strumpet live That, for this pageant, earns so many deaths?

Tuc. Boy, slink, boy.

Pyr. Pray Jupiter we be not followed by the scent, master. [*Exeunt* Tucca *and* Pyrgus.

Cæs. Say, sir, what are you?

Alb. I play Vulcan, sir.

Cæs. But, what are you, sir?

Alb. Your citizen and jeweller, sir.

Cæs. And what are you, dame?

Chloe. I play Venus, forsooth.

Cæs. I ask not, what you play, but what you are.

Chloe. Your citizen and jeweller's wife, sir.

---

[1] Scene vi. in old eds.
[2] He addresses himself.
[3] "His hideous looks made him hide his head when he would entice his prey with his sweet savour."—Pliny.

Cæs. And you, good sir ?

Cris. Your gentleman, parcel-poet, sir.   [*Exit.*

Cæs. O, that profaned name !—

And are these seemly company for thee,   [*To* JULIA.

Degen'rate monster ?   All the rest I know,

And hate all knowledge, for their hateful sakes.

Are you, that first the deities inspired

With skill of their high natures and their powers,

The first abusers of their useful light ;

Profaning thus their dignities, in their forms,

And making them, like you, but counterfeits ?

O, who shall follow Virtue, and embrace her,

When her false bosom is found nought but air

And yet, of those embraces centaurs spring,[1]

That war with human peace, and poison men.

Who shall, with greater comfort comprehend

Her unseen being, and her excellence ;

When you, that teach, and should eternize her,

Live, as she were no law unto your lives,

Nor lived herself, but with your idle breaths ?

If you think Gods but feigned, and virtue painted,

Know we sustain an actual residence ;

And, with the title of an emperor,

Retain his spirit, and imperial power ;

By which—in imposition too remiss,

Licentious Naso, for thy violent wrong,

In soothing the declined affections

Of our base daughter—we exile thy feet

From all approach to our imperial court,

On pain of death ; and thy misgotten love

Commit to patronage of iron doors ;

Since her soft-hearted sire cannot contain her.

Mec. O, good my lord, forgive ; be like the gods

Hor. Let royal bounty, Cæsar, mediate.

---

[1] Ixion embraced a cloud in the shape of Hera (Juno) and begot
a centaur.

Cæs. There is no bounty to be shewed to such,
As have no real goodness : bounty is
A spice of virtue ; and what virtuous act
Can take effect on them, that have no power
Of equal habitude to apprehend it,
But live in worship of that idol, vice,
As if there were no virtue, but in shade
Of strong imagination, merely enforced ?
This shews, their knowledge is mere ignorance,
Their far-fetched dignity of soul, a fancy ;
And all their square pretext of gravity,
A mere vain-glory ; hence, away with 'hem !
I will prefer for knowledge, none but such
As rule their lives by it, and can becalm
All sea of humour with the marble trident
Of their strong spirits : others fight below
With gnats, and shadows ; others nothing know.

                            [*Exeunt.*

SCENE IV.—*A Street before the Palace.*

Enter TUCCA, CRISPINUS, *and* PYRGUS.

Tuc. What's become of my little punk, Venus, and the poult-foot[2] stinkard, her husband, ha ?

Cris. O, they are rid home i' the coach, as fast as the wheels can run.

Tuc. God Jupiter is banished, I hear, and his cockatrice Juno locked up. 'Heart, an all the poetry in Parnassus get me to be a player again, I'll sell 'hem my share for a sesterce. But this is Humours,[4] Horace, that goat-footed envious slave ; he's turned fawn[1] now, an informer, the rogue ! 'tis he has betrayed us all. Did you not see him, with the emperor, crouching ?

---

[1] Scene vii. in old eds.   [2] Club-foot.
[3] "Humorous Horace," F. 2.   [4] A parasitical spy.

Cris. Yes.

Tuc. Well, follow me. Thou shalt libel, and I'll cudgel
the rascal. Boy, provide me a truncheon. Revenge shall
gratulate him, *tam Marti, quam Mercurio.*[1]

Pyr. Ay, but master, take heed how you give this out ;
Horace is a man of the sword.

Cris. 'Tis true, in troth ; they say he's valiant.[2]

Tuc. Valiant ? so is mine arse. Gods and fiends ! I'll
blow him into air, when I meet him next : he dares not
fight with a puck-fist.[3]

[*Horace passes over the stage.*

Pyr. Master, here he comes !

Tuc. Where ? Jupiter save thee, my good poet, my
noble prophet, my little fat Horace.—I scorn to beat the
rogue i' the court ; and I saluted him thus fair, because
he should suspect nothing, the rascal :—come, we'll go
see how forward our journeyman is toward the untrussing
of him.

Cris. Do you hear, captain ? I'll write nothing in it
but innocence, because I may swear I am innocent.

[*Exeunt.*

SCENE V.[4]

Enter HORACE, MECÆNAS, LUPUS, HISTRIO, *and* Lictors.

Hor. Nay, why pursue you not the emperor for your
reward now, Lupus ?

Mec. Stay, Asinius ;
You, and your stager, and your band of lictors :
I hope your service merits more respect,
Than thus, without a thanks, to be sent hence.

---

[1] By Mars [cudgel], as well as by Mercury [libel].
[2] These two speeches quoted in *Satiromastix.*
[3] *i.e.* even with a " puff-ball."
[4] Jonson has a new scene here in the folios, against his own
rule. There is no new scene marked in the quarto.

His. Well, well, jest on, jest on.

Hor. Thou base, unworthy groom !

Lup.　　　　　　Ay, ay, 'tis good.

Hor. Was this the treason ? this the dangerous plot,
Thy clam'rous tongue so bellowed through the court?
Hadst though no other project to encrease
Thy grace with Cæsar, but this wolfish train,[1]
To prey upon the life of innocent mirth
And harmless pleasures, bred of noble wit ?
Away ! I loath thy presence ; such as thou,
They are the moths and scarabs[2] of a state,
The bane of empires, and the dregs of courts ;
Who, to endear themselves to any employment,
Care not whose fame they blast, whose life they endanger ;
And, under a disguised and cobweb mask,
Of love unto their sovereign, vomit forth
Their own prodigious malice ; and pretending
To be the props, and columns of their safety,
The guards unto his person, and his peace,
Disturb it most, with their false, lapwing-cries.[3]

Lup. Good ! Cæsar shall know of this, believe it.

Mec. Cæsar doth know it, wolf, and to his knowledge,
He will, I hope, reward your base endeavours.
" Princes that will but hear, or give access
" To such officious spies, can ne'er be safe :
" They take in poison, with an open ear,
" And, free from danger, become slaves to fear.

　　　　　　　　　　　　　　　　[*Exeunt.*

SCENE VI.[4]—*An open Space before the Palace.*

Enter OVID.

Banished the court ! Let me be banished life ;
Since the chief end of life is there concluded :[5]

---

[1] Lure, stratagem. *Lupus* is Latin for a wolf.　　[2] Beetles.
[3] The lapwing flutters and cries to divert attention from its nest.
[4] Scene viii. in old eds.　　[5] Shut up, included—a Latinism.

Within the court, is all the kingdom bounded,
And as her sacred sphere doth comprehend
Ten thousand times so much, as so much place
In any part of all the empire else ;
So every body, moving in her sphere,
Contains ten thousand times as much in him,
As any other, her choice orb excludes,
As in a circle, a magician, then
Is safe, against the spirit he excites ;
But out of it, is subject to his rage,
And loseth all the virtue of his art :
So I, exiled the circle of the court,
Lose all the good gifts that in it I 'joyed.
" No virtue current is, but with her stamp,
" And no vice vicious, blanched with her white hand.
The court's the abstract of all Rome's desert,
And my dear Julia th' abstract of the court.
Methinks, now I come near her, I respire
Some air of that late comfort I received ;
And while the evening, with her modest veil,
Gives leave to such poor shadows as myself
To steal abroad, I, like a heartless ghost,
Without the living body of my love,
Will here walk, and attend her.   For I know
Not far from hence she is imprisonéd,
And hopes, of her strict guardian, to bribe
So much admittance,[1] as to speak to me,
And cheer my fainting spirits with her breath.

 Julia. [*At her chamber window.*][2]   Ovid? my love ?
 Ovid.   Here, heavenly Julia.
 Jul. Here ! and not here ! O, how that world doth play
With both our fortunes, differing, like ourselves,
Both one ; and yet divided, as opposed !
I high, thou low : Oh, this our plight of place
Doubly presents the two lets[3] of our love,

---

[1] Permission given.   [2] Scene ix. in old eds.
[3] Hindrances.

Local, and ceremonial height, and lowness:
Both ways, I am too high, and thou too low.
Our minds are even, yet; Oh, why should our bodies,
That are their slaves, be so without their rule?
I'll cast myself down to thee; if I die,
I'll ever live with thee: no height of birth,
Of place, of duty, or of cruel power,
Shall keep me from thee; should my father lock
This body up within a tomb of brass,
Yet I'll be with thee.   If the forms, I hold
Now in my soul, be made one substance with it;
That soul immortal, and the same 'tis now;
Death cannot raze th' affects,[1] she now retaineth:
And then, may she be anywhere she will.
The souls of parents rule not children's souls,
When death sets both in their dissolved estates;
Then is no child, nor father: then eternity
Frees all from any temporal respect.
I come, my Ovid, take me in thine arms;
And let me breathe my soul into thy breast.

Ovid. O stay, my love; the hopes thou dost conceive
Of thy quick[2] death, and of thy future life,
Are not authentical.   Thou chooseth death,
So thou might'st 'joy thy love in th' other life:
But know, my princely love, when thou art dead,
Thou only must survive in perfect soul;
And in the soul, are no affections.
We pour out our affections with our blood;
And, with our blood's affections, fade our loves.
" No life hath love in such sweet state, as this;
" No essence is so dear to moody sense,
" As flesh and blood, whose quintessence is sense.
" Beauty, composed of blood and flesh, moves more,
" And is more plausible to[3] blood and flesh,
" Than spiritual beauty can be to the spirit.
Such apprehension as we have in dreams,

---

[1] Affections.   [2] A punning use = both quick and living.
[3] Approved by.

When sleep, the bond of senses, locks them up,
Such shall we have, when death destroys them quite.
If love be then thy object, change not life ;
Live high, and happy still : I still below,
Close[1] with my fortunes, in thy height shall joy.

Jul. Ay me, that virtue, whose brave eagle's wings
With every stroke blow stars in burning heaven,
Should, like a swallow, preying toward storms,[2]
Fly close to earth, and with an eager plume,
Pursue those objects which none else can see,
But seem, to all the world, the empty air !
Thus thou, poor Ovid, and all virtuous men
Must prey, like swallows, on invis'ble food,
Pursuing flies, or nothing : and thus love,
And every worldly fancy, is transposed
By worldly tyranny to what plight it list.
O, father, since thou gav'st me not my mind,
Strive not to rule it ; take but what thou gav'st
To thy disposure : thy affections
Rule not in me ; I must bear all my griefs ;
Let me use all my pleasures ; virtuous love
Was never scandal to a Goddess' state.
But he's inflexible ! and, my dear love,
Thy life may chance be shortened, by the length
Of my unwilling speeches to depart.
Farewell, sweet life ; though thou be yet exiled
Th' officious court, enjoy me amply, still :
My soul, in this my breath, enters thine ears,
And on this turret's floor will I lie dead,
Till we may meet again.   In this proud height,
I kneel beneath thee, in my prostrate love,
And kiss the happy sands that kiss thy feet.
" Great Jove submits a sceptre to a cell ;
" And lovers, ere they part, will meet in hell.

Ovid. Farewell all company, and, if I could,
All light with thee ! hell's shade should hide my brows,

---

[1] Secretly.
[2] Seemingly his way of saying that they (alone) prey flying.

Till thy dear beauty's beams redeemed my vows. [*Going.*

Jul. Ovid, my love; alas! may we not stay
A little longer, think'st thou, undiscerned?

Ovid. For thine own good, fair Goddess, do not stay.
Who would engage[1] a firmament of fires
Shining in thee, for me, a falling star?
Be gone, sweet life-blood; if I should discern
Thyself but touched for my sake, I should die.

Jul. I will begone, then; and not heaven itself
Shall draw me back.   [*Going.*

Ovid.   Yet, Julia, if thou wilt,
A little longer stay.

Jul.   I am content.

Ovid. O, mighty Ovid! what the sway of heaven
Could not retire,[2] my breath hath turnèd back.

Jul. Who shall go first, my love? my passionate eyes
Will not endure to see thee turn from me.

Ovid. If thou go first, my soul will follow thee.

Jul. Then we must stay.

Ovid.   Ay me, there is no stay
In amorous pleasures; if both stay, both die.
I hear thy father; hence, my deity.   [*Exit* JULIA.
Fear forgeth sounds in my deluded ears;
There is no spirit under heaven, that works
With such illusion; yet[3] such witchcraft kill me,
I did not hear him: I am mad with love.
Ere a sound mind, without it, save my life!
Here, on my knees, I worship the blesst place
That held my Goddess; and the loving air,
That closed her body in his silken arms:
Vain Ovid! kneel not to the place, nor air;
She's in thy heart; rise then, and worship there.
" The truest wisdom silly men can have,
" Is dotage on the follies of their flesh.[4]   [*Exit.*

---

[1] Put in gage or peril.
[2] Draw back, cause to retire.
[3] " May " is understood.
[4] Gifford rightly calls this " a ridiculous love scene," and " not
much in the manner of Ovid." I should say, not at all.

ACT THE FIFTH.

SCENE I.—*An Apartment in the Palace.*

CÆSAR, MECÆNAS, GALLUS, TIBULLUS, HORACE,
Attendants *and* Guards *of the equestrian order.*

ÆS. We, that have conquered still, to save
    the conquered,
    And loved to make inflictions feared,
      not felt;
    Grieved to reprove, and joyful to reward,
    More proud of reconcilement, than re-
      venge;
Resume into the late state of our love,
Worthy Cornelius Gallus, and Tibullus:
You both are gentlemen; and, you, Cornelius,
A soldier of renown, and the first provost
That ever let our Roman eagles fly
On swarthy Egypt, quarried[1] with her spoils.
Yet (not to bear cold forms, nor men's out-terms,
Without the inward fires, and lives of men)
You both have virtues, shining through your shapes;
To show, your titles are not writ on posts,
Or hollow statues, which the best men are
Without Promethean stuffings reached from heaven!
Sweet poesy's sacred garlands crown your gentry:[2]
Which is, of all the faculties on earth,
The most abstract, and perfect; if she be
True-born, and nursed with all the sciences.
She can so mould Rome, and her monuments,

---

[1] Made a prey of.   [2] Gentle birth, gentility.

Within the liquid marble of her lines,
That they shall stand fresh and miraculous,
Even when they mix with innovating dust;
In her sweet streams shall our brave Roman spirits
Chase, and swim after death, with their choice deeds
Shining on their white shoulders; and therein
Shall Tiber, and our famous rivers fall
With such attraction, that th' ambitious line
Of the round world shall to her centre shrink,
To hear her music: and, for these high parts,
Cæsar shall reverence the Pierian arts.

Mec. Your majesty's high grace to poesy,
Shall stand 'gainst all the dull detractions
Of leaden souls; who, for the vain assumings
Of some, quite worthless of her sovereign wreaths,
Contain[1] her worthiest prophets in contempt.

Gal. Happy is Rome of all earth's other states,
To have so true and great a president,
For her inferior spirits to imitate,
As Cæsar is; who addeth to the sun
Influence, and lustre; in increasing thus
His inspirations, kindling fire in us.

Hor. Phœbus himself shall kneel at Cæsar's shrine,
And deck it with bay garlands dewed with wine,
To quite the worship Cæsar does to him:
Where other princes, hoisted to their thrones
By Fortune's passionate and disordered power,
Sit in their height, like clouds before the sun,
Hind'ring his comforts; and, by their excess
Of cold in virtue, and cross heat in vice,
Thunder, and tempest[2] on those learned heads,
Whom Cæsar with such honour doth advance.

Tib. All human business Fortune doth command
Without all order; and with her blind hand,
She, blind, bestows blind gifts, that still have nurst,
They see not who, nor how, but still, the worst.

---

[1] Hold.   [2] A verb, as in Milton, *Paradise Lost.* vii. 412.

Cæs. Caesar, for his rule, and for so much stuff
As Fortune puts in his hand, shall dispose it,
As if his hand had eyes and soul in it,
With worth and judgment. " Hands, that part with gifts,
" Or will restrain their use, without desert,
" Or with a mis'ry, numbed to virtue's right,
" Work, as they had no soul to govern them,
" And quite reject her ; sev'ring their estates
" From human order.   Whosoever can,
" And will not cherish virtue, is no man.

Enter an Eques.

Eques. Virgil is now at hand, imperial Caesar.
Cæs. Rome's honour is at hand then.   Fetch a chair,
And set it on our right hand ; where 'tis fit
Rome's honour, and our own should ever sit.
Now he is come out of Campania,
I doubt not he hath finished all his Æneids.
Which, like another soul, I long t' enjoy.
What think you three,[1] of Virgil, gentlemen,
That are of his profession, though ranked higher ;
Or Horace, what say'st thou, that art the poorest,
And likeliest to envy, or to detract ?
Hor. Caesar speaks after common men in this,
To make a diff'rence of me, for my poorness;
As if the filth of pov'rty sunk as deep
Into a knowing spirit, as the bane
Of riches doth into an ign'rant soul.
No, Caesar, they be pathless, moorish minds,
That being once made rotten with the dung
Of damnèd riches, ever after sink
Beneath the steps of any villainy.
But knowledge is the nectar that keeps sweet
A perfect soul, even in this grave of sin ;
And for my soul, it is as free, as Caesar's,
For what I know is due, I'll give to all.

[1] Mecænas, Gallus, Tibullus.

" He that detracts, or envies virtuous merit,
" Is still the cov'tous and the ign'rant spirit.

   Cæs. Thanks, Horace, for thy free, and wholesome
                  sharpness,
Which pleaseth Cæsar more than servile fawns.
" A flattered prince soon turns the prince of fools.
And for thy sake, we'll put no difference more
Between the great, and good, for being poor.
Say then, loved Horace, thy true thought of Virgil.

   Hor. I judge him of a rectified spirit,
By many revolutions of discourse[1]
(In his bright reason's influence) refined
From all the tartarous moods of common men :
Bearing the nature, and similitude
Of a right heav'nly body ; most severe
In fashion[2] and collection of himself ;
And, then, as clear, and confident as Jove.

   Gal. And yet so chaste and tender is his ear,
In suffering any syllable to pass,
That he thinks may become the honoured name
Of issue to his so examined self ;
That all the lasting fruits of his full merit,
In his own poems, he doth still distaste ;
As if his mind's peace, which he strove to paint,
Could not with fleshly pencils have her right.

   Tib. But, to approve his works of sov'reign worth,
This observation, me thinks, more than serves,
And is not vulgar.   That, which he hath writ,
Is with such judgment laboured, and distilled[3]
Through all the needful uses of our lives,
That could a man remember but his lines,
He should not touch at any serious point,
But he might breathe his spirit out of him.

   Cæs. You mean, he might repeat part of his works,

---

  [1] Divers runnings about. Thus badly would he express, "By much revolving of his thoughts."
  [2] The fashioning.   [3] Dropped down diversely.

As fit for any conference he can use ?

Tib. True, royal Cæsar.

Cæs.   Worthily observed ;
And a most worthy virtue in his works.
What thinks material[1] Horace of his learning ?

Hor. His learning savours not the school-like gloss,
That most consists in echoing words and terms,
And soonest wins a man an empty name ;
Nor any long, or far-fetched, circumstance
Wrapped in the curious gen'ralities of arts ;
But a direct, and analytic sum
Of all the worth and first effects of arts.
And for his poesy, 'tis so rammed with life,
That it shall gather strength of life, with being,
And live hereafter, more admired, than now.

Cæs. This one consent, in all your dooms of him,
And mutual loves of all your sev'ral merits,
Argues a truth of merit in you all.

Enter VIRGIL.[2]

See, here comes Virgil ; we will rise and greet him :
Welcome to Cæsar, Virgil.   Cæsar and Virgil
Shall differ but in sound : to Cæsar, Virgil,
Of his expressèd greatness, shall be made
A second sirname, and to Virgil, Cæsar.
Where are thy famous Æneids ? do us grace
To let us see, and surfeit on their sight.

Virg. Worthless they are of Cæsar's gracious eyes,
If they were perfect ; much more with their wants,
Which yet are more than my time could supply.
And, could great Cæsar's expectation
Be satisfied with any other service,
I would not shew them.

Cæs.   Virgil is too modest ;
Or seeks, in vain, to make our longings more.
Shew them, sweet Virgil.

---

¹ Matter-ful.   ² Scene ii. in old eds.

Virg.　　　　　　　　Then, in such due fear
As fits presenters of great works to Cæsar,
I humbly shew them.
　　Cæs.　　　　　　Let us now behold
A human soul made visible in life ;
And more refulgent in a senseless paper,
Than in the sensual compliment of kings.
Read, read, thyself, dear Virgil ; let not me
Profane one accent with an untuned tongue :
" Best matter, badly shown, shews worse than bad.
See then, this chair, of purpose set for thee
To read thy poem in :[1] refuse it not.
" Virtue, without presumption, place may take
"Above best kings, whom only she should make.
　　Virg. It will be thought a thing ridiculous
To present eyes, and to all future times
A gross untruth, that any poet, void
Of birth, or wealth, or temporal dignity,
Should, with decorum, transcend Cæsar's chair.
Poor virtue raised, high birth and wealth set under,
Crosseth heaven's courses, and makes worldlings wonder.
　　Cæs. The course of heaven, and fate itself, in this,
Will Cæsar cross ; much more all worldly custom.
　　Hor. Custom, in course of honour, ever errs ;
And they are best whom Fortune least prefers.
　　Cæs. Horace hath but more strictly spoke our
　　　　　　thoughts.
The vast rude swing of general confluence
Is, in particular ends, exempt from sense :
And therefore reason (which in right should be
The special rector of all harmony)
Shall shew we are a man distinct by it,
From those, whom custom rapteth in her press.
Ascend then, Virgil ; and where first by chance
We here have turned thy book, do thou first read.
　　Virg. Great Cæsar hath his will ; I will ascend.

---

[1] By action **Virgil** declines it.

'Twere simple injury to his free hand,
That sweeps the cobwebs from unusèd virtue,
And makes her shine proportioned to her worth,
To be more nice to entertain his grace,
Than he is choice, and lib'ral to afford it.

    Cæs. Gentlemen of our chamber, guard the doors,
And let none enter; [*Exeunt some of the* Equites.] peace.
      Begin, good Virgil.

    Virg. " Meanwhile, the skies 'gan thunder, and in tail
Of that, fell pouring storms of sleet and hail :
The Tyrian lords, and Trojan youth, each here,
With Venus' Dardane nephew, now, in fear,
Seek out for sev'ral shelter through the plain,
Whilst floods come rolling from the hills amain.
Dido a cave, the Trojan prince the same
Lighted upon.   There earth and heav'n's great dame,
That had the charge of marriage, first gave sign
Unto this contract; fire and air did shine,
As guilty of the match; and from the hill
The nymphs with shriekings do the region fill.
Here first began their bane; this day was ground
Of all their ills; for now, nor rumour's sound,
Nor nice respect of state, moves Dido ought;
Her love, no longer now by stealth, is sought;
She calls this wedlock, and with that fair name
Covers her fault.   Forthwith the bruit and fame,
Through all the greatest Lybian towns, is gone;
Fame, a fleet evil, than which is swifter none :
That moving grows, and flying gathers strength;
Little at first, and fearful; but at length
She dares attempt the skies, and stalking proud
With feet on ground, her head doth pierce a cloud !
This child, our parent earth, stirrèd up with spite
Of all the gods, brought forth; and, as some write,
She was last sister of that giant race,
That thought to scale Jove's court; right swift of
    pace,

   Jon. I.   A A

And swifter far of wing; a monster vast,
And dreadful.   Look, how many plumes are placed
On her huge corps, so many waking eyes
Stick underneath; and, which may stranger rise
In the report, as many tongues she bears,
As many mouths, as many list'ning ears.
Nightly, in midst of all the heav'n, she flies,
And through the earth's dark shadow shrieking cries!
Nor do her eyes once bend to taste sweet sleep:
By day, on tops of houses she doth keep,
Or on high towers; and doth thence affright
Cities and towns of most conspicuous site:
As covetous she is of tales, and lies,
As prodigal of truth: this monster,——"

    Lup.[1] [*Within.*] Come, follow me, assist me, second
    me:
Where's the emp'ror?[2]
    1st Eques. [*Within.*] Sir, you must pardon us.
    2nd Eques. [*Within.*] Cæsar is private now; you may
    not enter.
    Tuc. [*Within.*] Not enter! Charge 'hem upon their
    allegiance, cropshin.[3]
    1st Eques. [*Within.*] We have a charge to the con-
    trary, sir.
    Lup. [*Within.*] I pronounce you all traitors, horrible
    traitors:
What! do you know my affairs?   I have matter
Of danger and state to impart to Cæsar.[4]
    Cæs. What noise is there? who's that names Cæsar?
    Lup. [*Within.*] A friend to Cæsar.
One that, for Cæsar's good, would speak with Cæsar.

---

    [1] Scene iii. in the old eds.
    [2] The stage was then at times divided, either crossways or per-
pendicularly by curtains into two scenes. Here the division was
perpendicular.   There are no written stage directions in either the
quarto or the folios.   [3] Nobbler.
    [4] Here we have verse almost rythmic prose, so as to descend
more gradually from Virgil's verse. These three lines are, in F 2,
printed as verse, but have been wrongly divided.

Cæs. Who is't? look, Cornelius.

1st Eques. [*Within.*]   Asinius Lupus.

Cæs. O, bid the turbulent informer hence;
We have no vacant ear now, to receive
Th' unseasoned fruits of his officious tongue.

Mec. You must avoid[1] him there.

Lup. [*Within.*] I conjure thee, as thou art Cæsar, or
respect'st thine own safety, or the safety of the state,
Cæsar, hear me, speak with me, Cæsar; 'tis no common
business I come about, but such, as being neglected, may
concern the life of Cæsar.

Cæs. The life of Cæsar!   Let him enter.—Virgil, keep
thy seat.

Equites. [*Within.*] Bear back, there: whither will you?
keep back!

Enter LUPUS, TUCCA, *and* Lictors.

Tuc. By thy leave, goodman usher: mend thy pe-
ruke; so.

Lup. Lay hold on Horace there; and on Mecænas,
lictors.—Romans, offer no rescue, upon your allegiance:
—read, royal Cæsar.   I'll tickle you, Satyr.

Tuc. He will, Humours, he will: he will squeeze you,
poet puck-fist.[2]

Lup. I'll lop you off for an unprofitable branch, you
satirical varlet.

Tuc. Ay, and Epaminondas your patron here, with his
flagon chain;[3] come, resign: [*Takes off* MECÆNAS' *chain,*]
though 'twere your great grandfather's, the law has made
it mine now, sir.   Look to him, my party-coloured rascals; look to him.

Cæs. What is this, Asinius Lupus?   I understand it
not.

Lup. Not understand it?   A libel, Cæsar; a dangerous, seditious libel.   A libel in picture.

---

[1] Make him clear out.   [2] Puff-ball fingers.
[3] A massive gold chain.

Cæs. A libel!

Lup. Ay, I found it in this Horace his study, in Mecænas his house, here; I challenge the penalty of the laws against 'hem.

Tuc. Ay, and remember to beg their land betimes; before some of these hungry court-hounds scent it out.

Cæs. Shew it to Horace: ask him, if he know it.

Lup. Know it? his hand is at it, Cæsar.

Cæs. Then 'tis no libel.[1]

Hor. It is the imperfect body of an emblem, Cæsar, I began for Mecænas.

Lup. An emblem! right: that's Greek for a libel. Do you mark how confident he is.

Hor. A just man cannot fear, thou foolish tribune;
Not, though the malice of traducing tongues,
The open vastness of a tyrant's ear,
The senseless rigour of the wrested laws,
Or the red eyes of strained authority,
Should, in a point, meet all to take his life:
His innocence is armour 'gainst all these.

Luc. Innocence! Oh impudence! let me see, let me see. Is not here an eagle? and is not that eagle meant by Cæsar, ah? Does not Cæsar give the eagle? answer me: what sayest thou?

Tup. Hast thou any evasion, stinkard?

Lup. Now he's turned dumb. I'll tickle you, Satyr.

Hor. Pish: ha, ha!

Lup. Dost thou pish me? Give me my long sword.

Hor. With reverence to great Cæsar, worthy Romans,
Observe but this ridiculous commenter;
The soul to my device was in this distich:

"Thus, oft, the base and ravenous multitude
Survives,[2] to share the spoils of fortitude."

---

[1] These two speeches are repeated in *Satiromastix.*

[2] This singular plural in the folios is the more remarkable as the previous quarto has "survive."

Which, in this body, I have figured here,
A vulture——

Luc. A vulture? [*Looks at it.*] Ay, now, 'tis a vulture![1]
O abominable! monstrous! monstrous! has not your
'vulture' a beak? has it not legs? and talons? and
wings? and feathers?

Tuc. Touch him, old buskins.

Hor. And therefore must it be an eagle?

Mec. Respect him not, good Horace: say your device.

Hor. A vulture and a wolf——

Lup. A wolf? [*Looks again*] good: that's I; I am the
wolf: my name's Lupus; I am meant by the wolf. On,
on; a vulture and a wolf——

Hor. Preying upon the carcass of an ass——

Lup. An ass? [*Looks*] good still; that's I too: I am
the ass. You mean me by the ass——

Mec. Prithee, leave prying then.

Hor. If you will needs take it, I cannot with modesty
give it from you.

Mec. But, by that beast, the old Egyptians
Were wont to figure, in their hieroglyphics,
Patience, frugality, and fortitude;
For none of which, we can suspect you, tribune.

Cæs. Who was it, Lupus, that informed you first,
This should be meant by us?[2] Or was't your comment?

Lup. No, Cæsar; a player gave me the first light of
it indeed.

Tuc. Ay, an honest sycophant-like slave, and a politician besides.

Cæs. Where is that player?

Tuc. He is without here.

Cæs. Call him in.

Tuc. Call in the player there: master Æsop, call him.

Equites. [*Within.*] Player? where is the player? bear
back: none but the player enter.

---

[1] Spoken scoffingly.
[2] " By " is here used in the sense of " of."

Tuc. Yes, this gentleman, and his Achate must.

[*Enter* Æsop, *followed by* Crispinus *and* Demetrius.

Cris. Pray you, master usher:—we'll stand close, here.

Tuc. 'Tis a gentleman of quality, this [1]; though he be somewhat out of clothes, I tell ye.—Come, Æsop, hast a bay-leaf i' thy mouth? Well said,—be not out, stinkard. Thou shalt have a monopoly of playing, confirmed to thee and thy covey, under the emperor's broad seal, for this service.

Cæs. Is this he?

Lup. Ay, Cæsar, this is he.

Cæs. Let him be whipped. Lictors, go take him
    hence.
And, Lupus, for your fierce credulity,—
One fit him with a pair of larger ears:
'Tis Cæsar's doom, and must not be revoked.
We hate to have our court and peace disturbed
With these quotidian clamours. See it done.

Lup. Cæsar!

        [*Exeunt some, with* Lupus *and* Æsop.

Cæs.   Gag him, we may have his silence.

Virg. Cæsar hath done like Cæsar. Fair, and just
Is his award, against these brainless creatures.
'Tis not the wholesome sharp morality,
Or modest anger of a satiric spirit,
That hurt, or wounds the body of state:
But the sinister application
Of the malicious, ignorant, and base
Interpreter: who will distort, and strain
The general scope and purpose of an author
To his particular and private spleen.

Cæs. We know it, our dear Virgil, and esteem it
A most dishonest practice in that man,
Will seem too witty in another's work.—
What would Cornelius Gallus, and Tibullus?

        [*They whisper* Cæsar.

---

[1] Marston seems to have prided himself on being of gentle birth.

Tuc. [*to* MECÆNAS.] Nay, but as thou art a man, dost hear? a man of worship, and honourable : hold, here, take thy chain again. Resume, mad Mecænas. What? dost thou think I meant t' have kept it, bold boy? no : I did it but to fright thee, I, to try how thou would'st take it. What? will I turn shark upon my friends? or my friends' friends? I scorn it with my three souls.[1] Come, I love bully Horace, as well as thou dost, I : 'tis an honest hieroglyphic. Give me thy wrist, Helicon. Dost thou think I'll second e'er a rhinoceros of them all, against thee, ha! or thy noble Hippocrene,[2] here? I'll turn stager first, and be whipt[3] too : dost thou see, bully?

Cæs. You have your will of Cæsar : use it, Romans.
Virgil shall be your prætor ; and ourself
Will here sit by, spectator of your sports ;
And think it no impeach of royalty.
Our ear is now too much profaned, grave Maro,
With these distastes, to take thy sacred lines :
Put up thy book, till both the time and we
Be fitted with more hallowed circumstance
For the receiving so divine a work.—
Proceed with your design.

Mec., Gal., Tib. Thanks, to great Cæsar.

Gal. Tibullus, draw you the indictment then, whilst Horace arrests them on the statute of Calumny : Mecænas and I will take our places here. Lictors, assist him.

Hor. I am the worst accuser under heaven.

Gal. Tut, you must do 't ; 'twill be noble mirth.

Hor. I take no knowledge that they do malign me.

Tib. Ay, but the world takes knowledge.

Hor.   Would the world knew
How heartily I wish a fool should hate me !

---

[1] Vegetal, sensitive, and rational.
[2] A fountain sacred to the Muses.
[3] As a stager and vagrant could be in Jonson's time.

Tuc. Body of Jupiter; what? will they arraign my
brisk Poetaster, and his poor journeyman, ha? Would
I were abroad skeldering for a drachme, so I were out of
this labyrinth again! I do feel myself turn stinkard
already. But I must set the best face I have upon't
now: [*Aside.*]—Well said, my divine, deft Horace, bring
the whoreson detracting slaves to the bar, do. Make
them hold up their spread golls:[1] I'll give in evidence
for thee, if thou wilt. [*Aside to him,*] Take courage,
Crispinus; would thy man had a clean hand!

Cris. What must we do, captain?

Tuc. Thou shalt see anon: do not make division with
thy legs on.

Cæs. What's he, Horace?

Hor. I only know him for a motion,[2] Cæsar.

Tuc. I am one of thy commanders, Cæsar; a man of
service, and action: my name is Pantilius Tucca: I have
served i' thy wars against Mark Antony, I.

Cæs. Do you know him, Cornelius?

Gal. He's one that hath had the mustering, or convoy
of a company now and then: I never noted him by any
other employment.

Cæs. We will observe him better.

Tib. Lictor, proclaim silence in the court.

Lict. In the name of Cæsar, silence!

Tib. Let the parties, the accuser and the accused, present themselves.

Lict. The accuser, and the accused: present yourselves
in court.

Cris., Dem. Here.

Virg. Read the indictment.

Tib. (*Reads.*) "Rufus Laberius Crispinus, and Demetrius Fannius, hold up your hands. You are, before
this time, jointly and severally indicted, and here presently to be arraigned upon the statute of calumny, or

---

[1] Hands.   [2] A puppet.

Lex Remmia, the one by the name of Rufus Laberius Crispinus, alias Crispinas,[1] poetaster, and plagiary; the other by the name of Demetrius Fannius, play-dresser,[1] and plagiary. That you (not having the fear of Phœbus, or his shafts, before your eyes) contrary to the peace of our liege lord, Augustus Cæsar, his crown and dignity, and against the form of a statute, in that case made and provided, have most ignorantly, foolishly, and—more like yourselves—maliciously, gone about to deprave, and calumniate the person and writings of Quintus Horatius Flaccus, here present, poet, and priest to the Muses : and to that end have mutually conspired, and plotted, at sundry times, as by several means, and in sundry places, for the better accomplishing your base and envious purpose ; taxing him, falsely, of self-love, arrogancy, impudence, railing, filching by translation, &c. Of all which calumnies, and every of them, in manner and form aforesaid ; what answer you ? Are you guilty, or not guilty ?"

Tuc. [*Aside.*] Not guilty, say.

Cris.. Dem. Not guilty.

Tib. How will you be tried ?

Tuc. [*Aside.*] By the Roman gods, and the noblest Romans.

Cris. and Dem. By the Roman gods, and the noblest Romans.

Virg. Here sits Mecænas, and Cornelius Gallus. Are you contented to be tried by these ?

Tuc. [*Aside.*] Ay, so the noble captain may be joined with them in commission, say.

Cris. and Dem. Ay, so the noble captain may be joined with them in commission.

Virg. What says the plaintiff ?

Hor. I am content.

Virg. Captain, then take your place.

Tuc. Alas, my worshipful prætor ! 'tis more of thy

---

[1] Repeated in *Satiromastix.*

gentleness, than of my deserving, I wusse.[1] But since it
hath pleased the court to make choice of my wisdom and
gravity, come, my calumnious varlets ; let's hear you talk
for yourselves, now, an hour or two. What can you say ?
Make a noise.   Act, act !

Virg. Stay, turn, and take an oath first. " You shall
    swear,
By thunder-darting Jove, the king of gods ;
And by the genius of Augustus Cæsar ;
By your own white and uncorrupted souls,
And the deep reverence of our Roman justice ;
To judge this case, with truth and equity :
As bound, by your religion, and your laws."
Now read the evidence : but first demand
Of either prisoner, if that writ be theirs.

Tib. Show this unto Crispinus.   Is it yours?

Tuc. [*Aside.*] Say, ay.—What ! dost thou stand upon
it, pimp? Do not deny thine own Minerva, thy Pallas,
the issue of thy brain.

Cris. Yes, it is mine.

Tib. Show that unto Demetrius.   Is it yours?

Dem. It is.

Tuc. There's a father will not deny his own bastard
now, I warrant thee.

Virg. Read them aloud.

Tib. " Ramp up my genius ; be not retrograde :
But boldly nominate a spade, a spade.
What, shall thy lubrical and glibbery Muse
Live, as she were defunct, like punk in stews ? "

Tuc. [*Aside.*] Excellent.

" Alas ! that were no modern consequence,
To have cothurnal buskins frighted hence.
No, teach thy Incubus to poetize ;
And throw abroad thy spurious smotteries,
Upon that puft-up lump of barmy froth,

    Tuc. Ah, ha !

---

[1] I know

Or clumsy chilblained judgment;[1] that, with oath,
Magnificates his merit ; and besprawls
The conscious time, with humourous foam, and brawls,
As if his organons of sense would crack
The sinews of my patience.[2]   Break his back,
O poets all and some ! for now we list
Of strenuous vengeance to clutch the fist."

Subscri. CRIS.

Tuc. Ay, marry, this was written like a Hercules in
poetry, now.

Cæs. Excellently well threatened !

Virg. Ay, and as strangely worded, Cæsar.

Cæs. We observe it.

Virg. The other now.

Tuc.   This 's a fellow of a good prodigal tongue too,
this 'll do well.

Tib. " Our Muse is in mind for th' untrussing a poet ;
I slip by his name, for most men do know it :
A critic, that all the world bescumbers
With satirical humours, and lyrical numbers : "

Tuc. [*Aside.*] Art thou there, boy?

" And for the most part, himself doth advance
With much self-love, and more arrogance."

Tuc. [*Aside.*] Good again !

" And, but that I would not be thought a prater,
I could tell you he were a translator.
I know the authors from whence he has stole,
And could trace him too, but that I understand 'hem not
   full and whole."

Tuc. [*Aside.*] That line is broke loose from all his
fellows : chain him up shorter, do.

---

[1] These phrases of Crispinus, like those cast up by him, are
gathered from John Marston, who, therefore, is satirised under
that name. As showing also that *Jack Drum's Entertainment* was,
in part at least, by him, I give these from it :

   " Let clumsie judgments, chilblain'd gowtie wits."
   " Cracke not the sinews of my patience."

[2] Demetrius is Thomas Dekker, who wrote the play *Satiromastix.*

" The best note I can give you to know him by,
Is, that he keeps gallants' company ;
Whom I could wish, in time should him fear,
Lest after they buy repentance too dear."

Subscri. DEME. FAN.[1]

Tuc. Well said ! This carries palm[2] with it.

Hor. And why, thou motley gull ? why should they
    fear ?
When hast thou known us wrong, or tax a friend ?
I dare thy malice to betray it. Speak.
Now thou curl'st up, thou poor, and nasty snake,
And shrink'st thy pois'nous head into thy bosom :
Out, viper ! thou that eat'st thy parents,[3] hence !
Rather, such speckled creatures, as thyself,
Should be eschewed, and shunned ; such as will bite
And gnaw their absent friends, not cure their fame :
Catch at the loosest laughters, and affect
To be thought jesters ; such, as can devise
Things never seen, or heard, t'impair men's names,
And gratify their cred'lous adversaries;
Will carry tales, do basest offices,
Cherish divided fires, and still encrease
New flames, out of old embers ; will reveal
Each secret that's committed to their trust ;
These be black slaves : Romans, take heed of these.

Tuc. Thou twang'st right, little Horace : they be
    indeed
A couple of chap-fall'n curs. Come, we of the bench,
Let's rise to the urn, and condemn 'hem quickly.

Virg. Before you go together, worthy Romans,
We are to tender our opinion ;
And give you those instructions, that may add
Unto your even judgment in the cause :
Which thus we do commence. First, you must know,

---

[1] The first line shows this to be Dekker.
[2] Is worthy of praise.
[3] Vipers were supposed to eat their way out at birth.

That where there is a true and perfect merit,
There can be no dejection ; and the scorn
Of humble baseness, oftentimes, so works
In a high soul, upon the grosser spirit,
That to his blearèd and offended sense,
There seems a hideous fault blazed in the object ;
When only the disease is in his eyes.
Here hence it comes, our Horace now stands taxed
Of impudence, self-love, and arrogance,
By these, who share no merit in themselves ;
And therefore think his portion is as small.
For they, from their own guilt, assure their souls,
If they should confidently praise their works,
In them it would appear inflation :
Which, in a full, and well digested man,
Cannot receive that foul abusive name,
But the fair title of erection.[1]
And, for his true use of translating men,
It still hath been a work of as much palm,
In clearest judgments, as t' invent or make.
His sharpness,—that is most excusable ;
As being forced out of a suff'ring virtue,
Oppressèd with the license of the time ;
And howsoever fools, or jerking pedants,
Players, or such like buffoon-barking [2] wits,
May with their baggarly and barren trash
Tickle base vulgar ears, in their despite ;
This, like Jove' thunder, shall their pride controul,
The honest satire hath the happiest soul.
Now, Romans, you have heard our thoughts ; withdraw
    when you please.
    Tib. Remove the accused from the bar.
    Tuc. Who holds the urn to us, ah ? [*Aside.*] Fear
nothing, I'll quit you, mine honest pitiful stinkards ; I'll do't.

---

[1] Lifting himself up to his true height or place.
[2] Buffonary in the quarto ; buffon barking in the first folio ;
buffons, barking, in the second.

Cris. Captain, you shall eternally girt me to you, as I a generous.[1]

Tuc. Go to.

Cæs. Tibellus, let there be a case[2] of vizards privately provided; we have found a subject to bestow them on.

Tib. It shall be done, Cæsar.

Cæs. [CRISPINUS' *verses in his hand.*] Here be words, Horace, able to bastinado a man's ears.

Hor. Ay, please it, great Cæsar, I have pills about me,
Mixt with the whitest kind of hellebore,
Would give a light vomit; that should pure
His brain and stomach of those tumorous heats:
Might I have leave to minister unto him.

Cæs. O! be his Æsculapius, gentle Horace;
You shall have leave, and he shall be your patient.
Virgil, use your authority, command him forth.

Virg. Cæsar is careful of your health, Crispinus;
And hath himself chose a physician
To minister unto you: take his pills.

Hor. They're somewhat bitter, sir, but very wholesome.
Take yet another; so: stand by, they'll work anon.

Tib. Romans, return to your several seats: lictors,
bring forward the urn; and set the accused to the bar.

Tuc. Quickly, you whoreson egregious varlets; come
forward. What? shall we sit all day upon you? You
make no more haste now, than a beggar upon pattens;
or a physician to a patient that has no money, you
pilchers.[3]

Tib. " Rufus Laberius Crispinus, and Demetrius Fannius, hold up your hands. You have, according to the
Roman custom, put yourselves upon trial to the urn, for
divers and sundry calumnies, whereof you have, before
this time, been indicted, and are now presently arraigned:

---

[1] *Generosus, i.e.*, a gentleman.   [2] A couple.
[3] May mean carman or the like, or scabbards or coverings with
nothing within them.

prepare yourselves to hearken to the verdict of your
tryers. Caius Cilnius Mecænas pronounceth you, by
this hand-writing, guilty. Cornelius Gallus, guilty. Pan-
tillus Tucca——"

Tuc. Parcel-guilty, I.

Dem. He means himself: for it was he indeed
Suborned us to the calumny.

Tuc. I, you whoreson cantharides![1] wasn't it?

Dem. I appeal to your conscience, captain.

Tib. Then, you confess it, now?

Dem. I do, and crave the mercy of the court.

Tib. What saith Crispinus?

Cris. O, the captain, the captain——

Hor. My physic begins to work with my patient, I see.

Virg. Captain, stand forth and answer.

Tuc. Hold thy peace, poet prætor: I appeal from thee
to Cæsar, I. Do me right, royal Cæsar.

Cæs. Marry, and I will, sir.—Lictors, gag him;
And put a case of vizards o'er his head,
That he may look bi-fronted, as he speaks.

Tuc. Gods, and fiends! Cæsar! thou wilt not, Cæsar,
wilt thou? Away, you whoreson vultures; away. You
think I am a dead corpse now, because Cæsar is disposed
to jest with a man of mark, or so. Hold your hooked
talons out of my flesh, you inhuman harpies. Go to,
do't. What? will the royal Augustus cast away a gentleman of worship, a captain and a commander, for a couple
of condemned caitiff calumnious cargos?[2]

Cæs. Dispatch, lictors. [*The vizards are put upon him.*

Tuc. Cæsar!

Cæs. Forward, Tibullus.

Virg. Demand what cause they had to malign Horace.

Dem. In troth, no great cause, not I, I must confess;

---

[1] *I.e.*, blisterer of my reputation.

[2] *Cargo*, sp. c. burden = the soldier's month's booty. Hence
possibly, in English, the bearers of these, and either porters or
bravos.

but that he kept better company, for the most part, than
I ; and that better men loved him, than love me ; and
that his writings thrived better than mine, and were better
liked and graced : nothing else.

Virg. Thus envious souls repine at others' good.

Hor. If this be all ; faith, I forgive thee freely.
Envy me still, so long as Virgil loves me,
Gallus, Tibullus, and the best-best Cæsar,
My dear Mecænas : while these, with many more,
Whose names I wisely slip, shall think me worthy
Their honoured and adored society,
And read and love, prove and applaud my poems ;
I would not wish but such as you should spite them.

   Cris. O——————!

   Tib. How now, Crispinus ?

   Cris. O, I am sick——— !

   Hor. A bason, a bason, quickly ; our physic works.
Faint not, man.

   Cris. O——" retrograde "——" reciprocal "——" in-
     cubus."

   Cæs. What's that, Horace ?

   Hor. Retrograde, reciprocal, and incubus, are come
     up.

   Gal. Thanks be to Jupiter !

   Cris. O——" glibbery "—" lubrical "—" defunct "—
     O—— !

   Hor. Well said ; here's some store.

   Virg. What are they ?

   Hor. " Glibbery," " lubrical," and " defunct."

   Gal. O, they come up.   O————Oh—— !

   Tib. What's that ?

   Hor. Nothing yet.

   Cris. " Magnificate."

   Mec. Magnificate !   That came up somewhat hard.

   Hor. Ay.   What cheer, Crispinus ?

   Cris. O, I shall cast up my " spurious —snotteries "——

   Hor. Good.   Again.

Cris. " Chilblained " —— Oh —— Oh —— " clumsie "——

Hor. That " clumsie " stuck terribly.

Mec. What's all that, Horace ?

Hor. " Spurious snotteries," " chilblained," " clumsie."

Tib. O dupter !

Gal. Who would have thought, there should ha' been
such a deal of filth in a poet ?

Cris. O——" ba—my froth "——

Cæs. What's that ?

Cris. —" Puffie "—" inflate "—" turgidous "—" ventosity."

Hor. Barmy froth, puffie, inflate, turgidous, and ventosity are come up.

Tib. O terrible windy words.

Gal. A sign of a windy brain.

Cris. O——" oblatrant " [1]——" furibund "——" fatuate "——" strenuous "——

Hor. Here's a deal ; oblatrant, furibund, fatuate,
strenuous.

Cæs. Now all's come up, I trow. What a tumble he
had in his belly !

Hor. No, there's the often " conscious damp " behind
still.

Cris. O——" conscious "——" damp."

Hor. It is come up, thanks to Apollo and Æsculapius :
—yet there's another ; you were best take a pill more.

Cris. O, no ; Oh——Oh——Oh——Oh—

Hor. Force yourself then a little with your finger.

Cris. O——Oh——" prorumped."

Tib. Prorumped ! What a noise it made ! as if his
spirit would have prorumpt with it.

Cris. Oh——Oh——Oh !

Virg. Help him ; it sticks strangely, whatever it is.

Cris. O——" clutcht."

---

[1] The quarto here adds " Obcæcate," and leaves out " damp " in
the " conscious " passage.

Hor. Now it's come; " clutcht."

Cæs. " Clutcht!" it's well that's come up ; it had but a narrow passage.

Cris. O———— !

Virg. Again, hold him ; hold his head there.

Cris. " Snarling gusts "—ᵧ—" quaking custard." [1]

Hor. How now, Crispinus ?

Cris. O————" obstupefact."

Tib. Nay ; that are all we, I assure vou.

Hor. How do you feel yourself ?

Cris. Pretty and well, I thank you.

Virg. These pills can but restore him for a time.
Not cure him quite of such a madady,
Caught by so many surfeits, which have filled
His blood and brain thus full of crudities :
'Tis necessary, therefore, he observe
A strict and wholesome diet.   Look you take,
Each morning, of old Cato's principles
A good draught, next your heart ; that walk upon,
Till it be well digested : then come home,
And taste a piece of Terence, suck his phrase
Instead of liquorice ; and at any hand,
Shun Plautus, and Ennius : they are meats
Too harsh for a weak stomach.   Use to read
(But not with a tutor) the best Greeks,
As Orpheus, Musæus, Pindarus,
Hesiod, Callimachus, and Theocrite,
High Homer ; but beware of Lycophron,
He is too dark, and dangerous a dish.
You must hunt for wild, outlandish terms,
To stuff out a peculiar dialect,
But let your matter run before your words :
And if, at any time, you chance to meet
Some Gallo-Belgic phrase, you shall not straight
Rack your poor verse to give it entertainment ;

---

[1] The quarto has " Tropological "—" Anagogical "—" Loqua-
city "—" Pinosity."

But let it pass: and do not think yourself
Much damnified, if you do leave it out,
When, nor your understanding, nor the sense
Could well receive it. This fair abstinence,
In time, will render you more sound, and clear:
And this have I described to you, in place
Of a strict sentence ;—which till he perform,
Attire him in that robe.—And henceforth, learn
To bear yourself more humbly; not to swell,
Or breathe your insolent and idle spite
On him whose laughter can your worst affright.

   Tib. Take him away.

   Cris. Jupiter guard Cæsar

   Virg. And for a week, or two, see him locked up
In some dark place, removed from company ;
He will talk idly else after his physic.
Now, to you, sir, [*to* DEMETRIUS.] Th' extremity of law
Awards you to be branded in the front,[1]
For this your calumny : but, since it pleaseth
Horace, the party wrong'd, t' entreat of Cæsar
A mitigation of that juster doom,
With Cæsar's tongue thus we pronounce your sentence.
Demetrius Fannius, thou shalt here put on
That coat and cap ;[2] and henceforth think thyself
No other than they make thee ; vow to wear them
In every fair, and generous assembly,
Till the best sort of minds shall take to knowledge
As well thy satisfaction, as thy wrongs.

   Hor. Only, grave prætor, here, in open court,
I crave the oath for good behaviour
May be administered unto them both.

   Virg. Horace, it shall :—Tibellus, give it them.

   Tib. Rufus Laberius Crispinus, and Demetrius Fannius,
lay your hands on your hearts.—" You shall here solemnly
attest and swear ; that never, after this instant, either at

---

[1] According to Lex Remnia.
[2] Those of a fool. Referred to in *Satiromastix.*

booksellers' stalls, in taverns, two-penny rooms,[1] tyring-houses, noblemen's butteries, puisnés' chambers,[2] (the best and farthest places where you are admitted to come,) you shall once offer, or dare (thereby to endear yourself the more to any player, ingle, or guilty gull, in your company) to malign, traduce, or detract the person, or writings of Quintus Horatius Flaccus, or any other eminent man, transcending you in merit, whom your envy shall find cause to work upon, either, for that, or for keeping himself in better acquaintance, or enjoying better friends; or if, transported by any sudden and desperate resolution, you do; that then, you shall not under the batton,[3] or in the next presence, being an honourable assembly of his favourers, be brought as voluntary gentlemen to undertake the forswearing of it. Neither shall you, at any time, ambitiously affecting the title of the Untrussers or Whippers of the age, suffer the itch of writing to over-run your performance in libel, upon pain of being taken up for lepers in wit, and, losing both your time, and your prayers, be irrecoverably forfeited to the hospital for fools. So help you our Roman Gods, and the Genius of great Cæsar."

Virg. So! now dissolve the court.

Hor., Tib., Gal., Mec., Virg.　　　And thanks to Cæsar, That thus he hath exercised his patience.

Cæs. We have, indeed, you worthiest friends of Cæsar.
It is the bane and torment of our ears,
To hear the discords of those jangling rhymers,
That, with their bad and scandalous practices,
Bring all true arts and learning in contempt.
But let not your high thoughts descend so low
As these despisèd objects; let them fall,
With their flat grovelling souls: be you, yourselves.
And as with our best favours your stand crowned,
So let your mutual loves be still renowned.

---

[1] Our gallery in a theatre.　　　[2] Young law-students, &c.
[3] Cudgel.

Envy will dwell where there is want of spirit,
Though the deserving man should crack his spirit.

SONG.

Blush, folly, blush ; here's none that fears
The wagging of an ass's ears,
Although a wolfish case he wears.
Detraction is but baseness' varlet :
And apes are apes, though clothed in scarlet,
                                                    [*Exeunt.*

"Rumpatur, quisquis rumpitur invidiâ."

TO THE READER.[1]

 F, by looking on what is past, thou hast deserved that name, I am willing thou should'st yet know more, by that which follows, an APOLOGETICAL DIALOGUE; which was only once spoken upon the stage, and all the answer I ever gave to sundry impotent libels—then cast out (and some yet remaining)—against me, and this play. Wherein I take no pleasure to revive the times; but that posterity may make a difference between their manners that provoked me then, and mine that neglected them ever. For, in these strifes, and on such persons, were as wretched to affect a victory, as it is unhappy to be committed with them.

"Non annorum canities est laudana, sed morum."[2]

---

[1] In the quarto of 1602 he has—"Here, reader, in place of the Epilogue was meant to thee an Apology from the Author, with his reasons for the publishing of this book: but—since he is no less restrained, than more deprived of it, by Authority—he prays thee to think charitably of what thou hast read, till thou mayest hear him speak what he hath written."

[2] "Not the greyness of years, but that of manners, is to be praised."

Scene.—*The* Author's *Lodgings.*

Enter Nasutus *and* Polyposus.

Nas. I pray you, let's go see him, how he looks
After these libels.

Pol.   O vexed, vexed, I warrant you.

Nas. Do you think so?   I should be sorry for him,
If I found that.

Pol.   O, they are such bitter things,
He cannot choose.

Nas.   But, is he guilty of 'hem?

Pol. Fuh! that's no matter.

Nas.   No?

Pol.   No.   Here's his
      lodging.
We'll steal upon him : or let' listen, stay.
He has a humour oft to talk t' himself.

Nas. They are your manners lead me, not mine own.

They draw near.   The second scene opens.

Aut. The Fates have not spun him the coarsest thread,
That (free from knots of perturbation)
Doth yet so live, although but to himself,
As he can safely scorn the tongues of slaves,
And neglect Fortune, more than she can him.
It is the happiest thing, this not to be
Within the reach of malice; it provides
A man so well, to laugh off injuries;
And never sends him farther for his vengeance,
Than the vexed bosom of his enemy.
I, now, but think, how poor their spite sets off,
Who, after all their waste of sulphurous terms,
And burnt-out thunder of their chargèd mouths,
Have nothing left but the unsav'ry smoke
Of their black vomit, to upbraid themselves :

Whilst I, at whom they shot, sit here shot-free,
And as unhurt of envy, as unhit.

[POL. *and* NAS. *enter.*

Pol. Ay, but the multitude think not so, sir,
They think you hit, and hurt : and dare give out.
Your silence argues it, in not rejoining
To this, or that, late libel.

Aut.   'Las, good rout !
I can afford them leave, to err so still ;
And, like the barking students of Bears-college,
To swallow up the garbage of the time
With greedy gullets, whilst myself sit by,
Pleased, and yet tortured, with their beastly feeding.
'Tis a secret madness runs along with them,
To think, all that are aimed at, still are struck :
Then, where the shaft still lights, make that the mark ;
And so each fear or fever-shaken fool
May challenge Teucer's hand in archery.
Good troth, if I knew any man so vile,
To act the crimes these Whippers [1] reprehend,
Or what their servile apes gesticulate,
I should not then much muse their shreds were liked :
Since all men have a lust t' hear others' sins,
And good men have a zeal to hear sin shamed.
But when it is all excrement they vent,
Base filth, and offal : or thefts, notable
As ocean-piracies, or highway-stands ;
And not a crime there taxed, but is their own,
Or what their own foul thoughts suggested to them ;
And, that in all their heat of taxing others,
Not one of them but lives himself, if known,
Improbior satiram scribente cinœdo. [2]
What should I say more, than turn stone with wonder !

Nas. I never say this play bred all this tumult :

[1] The word being in the plural, may refer not only to the
Untrusser Dekker (though report associated Marston with him), but
to *Whipping of the Satyre,*" by W. J.

[2] More wicked than a catamite who writes a satire.—*Juvena*

What was there in it could so deeply offend?
And stir so many hornets?

    Aut.   Shall I tell you?

    Nas. Yes, and ingenuously.

    Aut.   Then, by the hope
Which I prefer unto all other objects,
I can profess, I never writ that piece
More innocent, or empty of offence.
Some salt it had, but neither tooth nor gall,
Nor was there in it any circumstance
Which, in the setting down, I could suspect
Might be perverted by an enemy's tongue.
Only, it had the fault to be called mine;
That was the crime.

    Pol.   No! why, they say you taxed
The law, and lawyers; captains, and the players,
By their particular names.

    Aut.   It is not so.
I used no name. My books have still been taught
To spare the persons, and to speak the vices.
These are mere slanders, and enforced by such
As have no safer ways to men's disgraces,
But their own lies, and loss of honesty:
Fellows of practised and most laxative tongues,
Whose empty and eager bellies, i' the year,
Compel their brains to many desp'rate shifts,
(I spare to name 'hem; for their wretchedness,
Fury itself would pardon.) These, or such,
Whether of malice, or of ignorance,
Or itch t' have me their adversary, I know not,
Or all these mixt; but sure I am, three years
They did provoke me with their petulant styles
On every stage: and I at last unwilling,
But weary, I confess, of so much trouble,
Thought I would try, if shame could win upon 'hem;
And therefore chose Augustus Cæsar's times,
When wit, and arts were at their height in Rome,

To shew that Virgil, Horace, and the rest
Of those great master-spirits, did not want
Detractors then, or practicers against them:
And by this line, although no parallel,
I hoped at last they would sit down, and blush.
But nothing could I find more contrary.
And though the impudence of flies be great,
Yet this has so provoked the angry wasps,
Or, as you said, of the next nest, the hornets,
That they fly buzzing, mad, about my nostrils,
And, like so many screaming grasshoppers,
Held by the wings, fill every ear with noise.
First, of the law. Indeed I brought in Ovid
Chid, by his angry father, for neglecting
The study of their laws for poetry:
And I am warranted by his own words:

> " *Sæpe pater dixii, studium quid inutile tentas?*
> *Mæonides nullas ipse reliquit opes.*"[1]

And in far harsher terms elsewhere, as these:

> " *Non me verbosas leges ediscere, non me*
> *Ingrato voces prostituisse foro.*"[2]

But how this should relate unto our laws,
Or their just ministers, with least abuse,
I reverence both too much to understand!
  Then, for the captain, I will only speak
An epigram I here have made: it is
" Unto true soldiers." *That's the lemma:*[3] *mark it.*
Strength of my country, whilst I bring to view
Such as are mis-call'd captains, and wrong you,
And your high names; I do desire, that thence,

---

[1] " Renounce this thriftless trade, my father cried:
  Mæonides himself—a beggar died."—*Trist*, l. iv., el. 10.

[2] " To learn the wrangling law was ne'er my choice,
  Nor, at the hateful bar, to sell my voice."—*Amor*, l. i., ei. 15.

[3] Subject.

Be nor put on you, nor you take offence :
I swear by your true friend, my Muse, I love
Your great profession, which I once did prove ;
And did not shame it with my actions, then,
No more than I dare, now, do with my pen.
He that not trusts me, having vowed thus much,
But's angry for the captain, still : is such.[2]

Now for the players, it is true, I taxed 'hem,
And yet, but some ; and those so sparingly,
As all the rest might have sat still, unquestioned,
Had they but had the wit, or conscience
To think well of themselves.   But impotent, they
Thought each man's vice belonged to their whole tribe ;
And much good do't 'hem ! What they've done 'gainst me,
I am not moved with.   If it gave 'hem meat,
Or got 'hem clothes.   'Tis well : that was their end.
Only amongst them, I am sorry for
Some better natures, by the rest so drawn,
To run in that vile line.[3]

 Pol.   And is this all !
Will you not answer then the libels ?

 Aut.   No.

 Pol. Nor the Untrussers ?

 Aut.   Neither.

 Pol.   Y'are undone then.

 Aut. With whom ?

 Pol.   The world.

 Aut.   The bawd !

 Pol.   It will be
  taken
To be stupidity or tameness in you.

 Aut. But they that have incensed me, can in soul
Acquit me of that guilt.   They know, I dare

---

[1] Try.   [2] *I.e.* as this 'captain' is.
[3] Shakespeare included, " but our fellow Shakespeare hath given
him [B. J.] a purge that made him bewray his credit."—*Return
from Parnassus,* iv. iii.

To spurn, or baffle 'hem, or squirt their eyes
With ink or urine: or I could do worse,
Armed with Archilochus' fury, write Iambics,
Should make the desperate lashers hang themselves:
Rhime 'hem to death, as they do Irish rats
In drumming tunes. Or, living, I could stamp
Their foreheads with those deep, and public brands,
That the whole company of barber-surgeons
Should not take off, with all their art and plasters.
And these my prints should last, still to be read
In their pale fronts; when, what they write 'gainst
        me
Shall, like a figure drawn in water, fleet.
And the poor wretched papers be employed
To clothe tobacco, or some cheaper drug.
This I could do, and make them infamous.
But, to what end? when their own deeds have mark'd
        'hem,
And that I know, within his guilty breast
Each slanderer bears a whip, that shall torment him
Worse than a million of these temporal plagues:
Which to pursue, were but a feminine humour,
And far beneath the dignity of man.

  Nas. 'Tis true; for to revenge their injuries,
Were to confess you felt 'hem. Let 'hem go,
And use the treasure of the fool, their tongues,
Who makes his gain, by speaking worst of best.

  Pol. O, but they lay particular imputations——

  Aut. As what?

  Pol.   That all your writing is mere railing.

  Aut. Ha!
        If all the salt in the old comedy
Should be so censured, or the sharper wit
Of the bold satire termèd scolding rage,
What age could then compare with those, for buffoons?
What should be said of Aristophanes,
Persius, or Juvenal? whose names we now

So glorify in schools, at least pretend it.
Ha' they no other?
   Pal.   Yes ; they say you're slow,
And scarce bring forth a play a year.
    Aut.   'Tis true
I would they could not say, that I did that!
There's all the joy that I take i' their trade,
Unless such scribes as they might be proscribed
Th' absurd theatres.   They would think it strange, now,
A man should take but colt's-foot, for one day,
And, between whiles, spit out a better poem
Than e'er the master of art, or giver of wit,
Their belly, made.   Yet, this is possible,
If a free mind had but the patience,
To think so much, together, and so vile.
But, that these base and beggarly conceits
Should carry it, by the multitude of voices,
Against the most abstracted work, opposed
To the stuffed nostrils of the drunken rout !
O, this would make a learned, and liberal soul
To rive his stained quill, up to the back,
And damn his long-watch'd labours to the fire ;
Things that were born, when none but the still night
And his dumb candle saw his pinching throes ;
Were not his own free merit more a crown
Unto his travails than their reeling claps.
This 'tis, that strikes me silent, seals my lips
And apts me rather to sleep out my time,
Than I would waste it in contemnèd strifes
With these vile Ibides,[1] these unclean birds,
That make their mouths their clysters, and still purge
From their hot entrails.   But, I leave the monsters
To their own fate.   And, since the Comic Muse
Hath proved so ominous to me, I will try
If Tragedy[2] have a more kind aspect;

---

[1] Pliny says this of the ibis, l. 8, c. 41.
[2] His Sejanus.

Her favours in my next I will pursue,
Where, if I prove the pleasure but of one,
So he judicious be, he shall b' alone
A theatre unto me ; Once I'll say
To strike the ear of time in those fresh strains,
    As shall, beside the cunning of their ground,
Give cause to some of wonder, some despite,
    And unto more despair, to imitate their sound.[1]
I, that spend half my nights, and all my days,
    Here in a cell, to get a dark, pale face,
To come forth worth the ivy or the bays,
    And in this age can hope no other grace—
Leave me ! There's something come into my thought !
That must, and shall be sung, high, and aloof,
Safe from the wolf's black jaw, and the dull ass's hoof.

Nas. I reverence these raptures, and obey 'hem.

                          [The scene closes.

---

[1] Gifford struck out "unto," but the last line but one is also an Alexandrine.

The Gresham Press,
UNWIN BROTHERS, LIMITED,
WOKING AND LONDON